# INDUSTRIAL ORGANIZATION, TRADE, AND SOCIAL INTERACTION

Essays in Honour of B. Curtis Eaton

# Industrial Organization, Trade, and Social Interaction

Essays in Honour of B. Curtis Eaton

*Edited by Gregory K. Dow, Andrew Eckert, and Douglas S. West*

UNIVERSITY OF TORONTO PRESS
Toronto Buffalo London

© University of Toronto Press Incorporated 2010
Toronto Buffalo London
www.utppublishing.com
Printed in Canada

ISBN 978-0-8020-9702-6

Printed on acid-free, 100% post-consumer recycled paper with vegetable-based inks.

**Library and Archives Canada Cataloguing in Publication**

Industrial organization, trade, and social interaction: essays in honour of B. Curtis Eaton/edited by Gregory K. Dow, Andrew Eckert, and Douglas S. West.

Includes bibliographical references.
ISBN 978-0-8020-9702-6

1. Eaton, B. Curtis, 1943–.   2. Microeconomics.   I. Dow, Gregory K., 1954–.
II. Eckert, Andrew, 1972–   III. West, Douglas Scott, 1953–

HB172.I53 2010      338.5      C2010-900547-3

University of Toronto Press acknowledges the financial assistance to its publishing program of the Canada Council for the Arts and the Ontario Arts Council.

University of Toronto Press acknowledges the financial support for its publishing activities of the Government of Canada through the Book Publishing Industry Development Program (BPIDP).

*To Curt Eaton, and his students, co-authors, colleagues, and friends*

# Contents

# PART I

## B. Curtis Eaton: His Impact on Economics and Economists

# 1 Introduction

GREGORY K. DOW, ANDREW ECKERT,
AND DOUGLAS S. WEST

On 4 and 5 June 2008, a conference in honour of B. Curtis Eaton, one of Canada's leading microeconomists, was held at Simon Fraser University's downtown Vancouver campus. Economists from across Canada and beyond came together to recognize Curt's contributions to teaching, learning, and the economics profession over a career that so far has spanned some 40 years. For the conference, 12 original works were solicited from among those who were present at the conference or who are colleagues, co-authors, or students of Curt's.

B. Curtis Eaton received his BA and PhD degrees from the University of Colorado in 1965 and 1969, respectively. His first appointment, as an assistant professor at the University of British Columbia, came in 1969, and in 1979 he was promoted to the rank of professor. Curt left Vancouver in 1981 to join the economics department at the University of Toronto. In 1987, Curt became a member of the economics department at Simon Fraser University, where he stayed until 1999, when he moved to the University of Calgary. He became a University Professor there in 2002.

Curt has been a visiting professor at a number of institutions, including the University of Colorado, Yale University, Stanford University, the University of Tasmania, and Canterbury University. He has served the economics profession as president of the Canadian Economics Association and editor of the *Canadian Journal of Economics*, and was chair of the Board of Directors of the British Columbia Ferry Corporation. He is currently a member of the Advisory Committee of the Social Interactions, Identity and Well-Being program at the Canadian Institute for Advanced Research and a member of the Board of Directors of the Van Horne Institute for Transportation and Regulatory Affairs.

Over the years, Curt has published papers in fields as diverse as spatial competition and urban/regional economics, industrial organization, labour economics, microeconomic theory, and game theory. His contributions also extend to the economics of information and social interaction. Two volumes of a selection of his papers have been published, and his *Microeconomics* text, co-authored with Diane Eaton and Douglas Allen, is in its seventh edition (see Eaton and Lipsey 1997; Eaton 2002; and Eaton, Eaton, and Allen 2009). Curt's work clearly influences all of the papers in his honour in this volume. Together, they advance our knowledge and approach to important theoretical and empirical problems.

## The Economics of Information

In Chapter 2 of this volume, Richard Lipsey discusses Curt Eaton's contributions to the field of the economics of information. As Lipsey documents, Eaton's research with various co-authors on the economics of information spans a range of specific topics, including efficiency wage theory, price discrimination, law and economics, advertising, and migration. Lipsey argues that, in several of these areas, Curt's papers were among the earliest contributions. He notes that articles by Eaton and White (1982, 1983) on wages in excess of opportunity cost 'were both published prior to any other modern paper on efficiency wage theory' and that '[t]o the best of my knowledge, no one had before studied the case in which it was optimal to pay a wage that is not only higher than the agent's opportunity cost, but also higher than the agent's direct marginal product to the firm.' Likewise, Lipsey observes that Donaldson and Eaton's (1981) work on price discrimination represents an early contribution to the sorting literature. Finally, Lipsey notes two key features of Curt's work on information economics: the motivation of the research by important policy questions, and the use of models that are as simple as possible while still allowing the authors to address questions of interest.

## Spatial Competition and Industrial Organization

Curt's first contribution in the field of spatial competition was in 1972, with the publication of 'Spatial Competition Revisited' in the *Canadian Journal of Economics*. From 1974 to 1975, Curt worked with Richard Lipsey at the University of Colorado. During this time, they mapped out a research program and presented a number of papers that are discussed in 'The Introduction of Space into the Neo-Classical Model of Value Theory'

(Eaton and Lipsey 1977). They had already published two journal articles (Eaton and Lipsey 1975, 1976) by the time the 1977 overview appeared, and soon afterward published a number of other papers (Eaton and Lipsey 1978, 1979a, 1979b, 1982). Their work not only helped to reinvigorate applied microeconomics; it also laid the foundation for future empirical work involving spatial location data.

Eaton and Lipsey (1979b) were the first to construct a model of market pre-emption. This paper was one of the earliest on strategic entry deterrence, a subject that has since become part of the core of industrial organization. They also wrote seminal papers (1979a, 1982) showing how consumer behaviour and demand externalities along with profit-maximizing locational choice could explain both the clustering of retail firms selling similar products and the clustering of firms selling different products. These papers helped us understand both urban spatial structure and competition among shopping centres, the latter topic one that has received little attention from economists.

Eaton and Lipsey developed a more general approach to spatial analysis in two papers dealing with address models (Archibald, Eaton, and Lipsey 1986; Eaton and Lipsey 1989). At the time this work was published, Curt was constructing other models of entry and entry deterrence, some with Lipsey and some with others. For example, Eaton and Lipsey (1980, 1981) consider the use of capital for purposes of entry deterrence when capital is not infinitely durable; Eaton and Wooders (1985) examine entry in a spatial model in which incumbent locations are fixed but prices are not, instead adjusting to equilibrium levels after entry (which potential entrants understand in advance); and Eaton and Ware (1987) examine equilibrium firm counts, firm sizes, and price, using a model of sequential entry.

*Institutions, Signalling, and Status*

In the 1980s, Curt's research interests turned toward the economics of social interaction. His resulting contributions deal mainly with three topics: property rights institutions, signalling and coordination games, and status or relative position.

Curt's research on property rights grew out of his work with William White on efficiency wages, a topic Richard Lipsey discusses in Chapter 2. Eaton and White apply this analytic framework to the enforcement of property rights in situations where one agent can steal from another. In a 1986 working paper (published as Eaton and White 2002b), they consider a model where an agent is tempted to steal, with a positive probability of being caught, and the upper bound on the sanction that can be imposed is determined by the wealth of the thief. In this setting, it might be optimal to transfer some wealth to the agent because this allows a more–than-offsetting reduction in monitoring cost. Eaton and White (1991) extend this approach to a two-period model in which agents make investment decisions. In Eaton and Morrison (2003), the system oscillates between an efficient Nash equilibrium, where agents invest and retaliate against theft, and an inefficient equilibrium, where they do not invest. The efficient outcome can persist for long intervals, but repeatedly collapses due to evolutionary drift.

Curt has also made substantial contributions to the analysis of coordination and signalling games. His earliest working paper along these lines (with White, 1992) is published for the first time as Chapter 9 of this volume. This was followed by a 1995 working paper on image advertising, published as Eaton and White (2002a). In both papers, individuals of various types are matched at random. It is mutually beneficial for agents to take actions that are appropriate to the types of their partners, but types are not directly observable (for example, one might not know the political views of a stranger at a dinner party). However, people can use observable cues (such as clothing) to infer the types others represent. This leads to a complex coordination game involving many potential 'languages' that associate signals with types. Arifovic and Eaton (1995, 1998) use genetic algorithms to study the conditions under which learning converges to a Pareto-efficient signalling equilibrium in which player types are fully revealed.

The most recent theme in Curt's work on social interaction involves preferences for relative position or status. This began with Eaton and Eswaran (2003), which develops an evolutionary rationale for such preferences. In a 2009 paper, Eaton and Eswaran address the paradox that, as incomes in rich countries rise, people do not report a corresponding rise in subjective happiness. Using simple general equilibrium models involving a Veblen good – a good whose utility depends, not on absolute consumption, but on one's consumption relative to others in society – they show that rising productivity tends to reduce leisure, the consumption of other private goods, and the consumption of public goods, while disproportionately expanding consumption of the Veblen good. Utility eventually falls due to the externalities surrounding status competition, even as productivity increases.

*Industrial Organization and Spatial Economics*

Part II of this volume contains three papers in the areas of industrial organization and spatial economics. The first, by Ralph Winter (Chapter 3), is an overview of entry deterrence via contracts. Winter begins by asking: when do buyers and an incumbent supplier in a market have the incentive to enter into contracts that deter entry by other suppliers? This question ties nicely into Curt's work in the areas of strategic entry deterrence and applied contract theory. Winter's focus in answering the question is on long-term contracts and exclusivity restrictions.

Winter begins by offering a synthesis of long-term contracts that can deter entry, and uses a set of assumptions to support the early view of economists at the University of Chicago that long-term contracts voluntarily entered into cannot be anticompetitive. He summarizes Aghion and Bolton's (1987) theory of anticompetitive long-term contracts, which flow through 'transfers extracted (or externalities imposed) on the entrant,' and discusses how exclusion can be achieved by imposing different types of externalities, or transfers, on parties outside the contract: horizontal externalities among buyers, vertical externalities, externalities over time, and externalities imposed on downstream buyers from a monopoly established upstream. Winter suggests a different set of assumptions for each theory of anticompetitive contract in order to distinguish them from the Chicago 'benchmark' theory that exclusive contracts are not exclusionary. Winter also discusses some extensions of the theory and an application of the theories of exclusion to the Nielsen case that was heard by the Competition Tribunal of Canada.

In Chapter 4, Andrew Eckert and Douglas West build on their earlier work on firm survival and chain growth in the liquor store industry in Calgary and Edmonton, which the province of Alberta privatized in 1993, by examining the evolution of the liquor store industry outside Alberta's two major cities. The authors consider whether the evolution of the industry can be explained by any of three conjectures: a free entry/rapid approach to long-run equilibrium conjecture, a pre-emption conjecture, or an S-curve entry conjecture. The authors plot on a map the locations of all liquor stores in Alberta that were in business between December 1995 and December 2007 and calculate both the areas and the populations of the areas from which they drew their trade. Eckert and West essentially reject the free entry/ rapid approach to long-run equilibrium conjecture by examining changes in firm counts, the number of towns and cities containing liquor stores, and population per store over time. They also find little support for the pre-emption conjecture when they examine the entry of new chain stores in towns in which the chain was already operating. The data, however, do provide some support for one of the explanations underlying the S-curve conjecture: under entry (that is, less than the long-run equilibrium amount) and a slow approach to equilibrium. Demand uncertainty and the slow expansion of supermarket-owned liquor stores after privatization could partly explain the slow approach to equilibrium. Eckert and West calculate the trade areas of towns containing liquor stores as the nearest point sets of these towns once they are plotted on a map, from which they can easily determine trade area populations. This type of spatial analysis, which Eckert and West have used in a number of papers, is motivated by the contributions of Eaton and Lipsey to spatial competition analysis.

The third paper in Part II relates closely to Curt's research interests in spatial economics, particularly retail location. Here, Richard Arnott and Yundong Tu (Chapter 5) examine a competitive model of retail agglomeration. Individual consumers choose where to live and where to shop, and their utility is determined by both the quantity of retail goods they purchase and the variety of retail goods that are available near their chosen shopping destination. Retailers choose where to locate their retail outlets and sell goods at competitively determined prices. The incentive for stores to agglomerate comes from consumers' preferences with respect to product variety. Arnott and Tu identify parameter values consistent with two different equilibria: a symmetric monocentric equilibrium, where all retailers locate in a single central retail district and individuals live between this district and the city boundaries, and an equilibrium where there is no retail agglomeration but, instead, each consumer has his or her own 'backyard' store. In particular, the authors examine the roles of transportation costs, the intensity of taste for variety, and the rate at which benefits from variety decline with distance. They conclude by discussing how their approach might be extended to a dynamic simulation model that is currently being developed for the Los Angeles metropolitan area.

*Trade and Productivity*

Part III of the volume begins with a paper by Richard Harris and Peter Robertson (Chapter 6), who are concerned with the impact of migration and education subsidy policies on the supply of human capital in a small open economy. To examine the effect of a change in the skills composition of immigrants on human capital formation, Harris and Robertson use a multisector computable general equilibrium model of growth that includes both endogenous skills formation and a supply and demand for education. In their simulation analysis, they use Australian data and consider first the effects of an immigration increase of 10 per cent of the skilled labour force. They find that, over ten years, gross domestic product (GDP) per capita increases by 1.5 per cent, consumption by 0.9 per cent, and unskilled wages by 2 per cent, while skilled wages fall by 3.8 per cent. The increase in immigration does not increase the supply of skilled labour proportionally, however, as there is a crowding out in the domestic education sector.

In their simulation involving an increase in education subsidies, Harris and Robertson find a smaller increase in the skilled labour force than occurred with the increase in skilled migrants in the first simulation. Over the ten-year period, education output increases each year. GDP per capita grows by 0.8 per cent, but consumption per capita falls by 0.1 per cent by year 10. Although the educational subsidy increases educational investment, consumption and welfare fall. So, immigration and education programs that attempt to increase the skilled labour force might have little or no effect.

One important area of Curt Eaton's research is in the theory of product differentiation. In Chapter 7, Simon Anderson and Nicolas Schmitt examine the effects of trade policy in a two-sector setting in which goods in one sector are vertically differentiated. In particular, they explore the different effects of trade barriers in the homogeneous products sector and in the sector with vertical differentiation; they find that, when a sufficiently large trade barrier is imposed on the homogeneous products sector, the only international trade is intra-industry. In contrast, a trade barrier in the vertically differentiated sector results in only inter-industry trade. The authors view their results as consistent with the documented increase in intra-industry trade for vertically differentiated goods.

Harry Bloch, in his paper on cyclical movements in price and productivity in mining and manufacturing (Chapter 8), emphasizes certain differences between the two industries. Manufacturing, he argues, is more amenable than mining to the type of analysis Curt Eaton has carried out on imperfectly competitive markets. He suggests that the long-run equilibrium in a manufacturing industry will have price greater than marginal cost and unexploited economies of scale. In mining, he sees competition as global, with some firms operating as price takers and supplying output to the point where price equals marginal cost. As a result, he predicts that prices in mining will rise and fall procyclically, while manufacturing prices will be little affected by the business cycle. He further predicts that productivity in mining will move procyclically near the bottom of the cycle and countercyclically near the top, while productivity in manufacturing will move in a procyclical fashion.

Using mining and manufacturing price index data for Canada (for the period 1957 through 2007) and Australia (for the period 1968 through 2007), Bloch finds that prices in mining do move up and down with the business cycle, while manufacturing prices seem to be insensitive to the cycle. With respect to productivity, he finds that movements in a measure of multifactor productivity in both manufacturing and mining are generally consistent with his predictions. In discussing the trade and policy implications of his results, he suggests that the cyclical movement of the relative prices of mining products and manufacturing products can create pressure for resource reallocation that can complicate fiscal and monetary policy. In terms of trade, the procyclical movement of mining product prices favours exporting countries in the upturn and importing countries during the downturn, hence creating trade imbalances that can be inflationary during the upturn.

*Social Interaction*

Part IV of the volume begins with a previously unpublished paper by Eaton and White (1992), now presented as Chapter 9, which sets up a signalling and coordination game. This is a game of common interests in the sense that all players benefit from accurate communication and no one has an incentive to misrepresent their true type. This is followed by three papers that assume that players come in multiple types and that types cannot be observed directly by other players. In each of these papers, some players have reasons to engage in misrepresentation. For Dow and for Bekar et al. (Chapters 10 and 11), the problem is one of signalling, where informed players choose actions that may allow uninformed players to infer their types. For Arifovic and Kariavanov (Chapter 12), the problem is one of screening, where the uninformed player attempts to separate agents of different types using a menu of contracts. Part IV, and the volume, closes with a paper by Eswaran and Oxoby (Chapter 13) that drops the idea of incomplete information and focuses instead on preferences involving relative position.

The paper by Eaton and White focuses on a coordination game where players come in multiple types, are randomly matched for pair-wise interactions, and share an interest in taking actions appropriate to the types of their partners. The authors study two major ways in which this coordination problem can be solved: by repeated play of the signalling game and by image advertising by firms. They argue that, with repeated play, salient strategies lead players to converge on a perfectly revealing equilibrium, provided that sufficient weight is given to future payoffs and/or the goods used for signalling are sufficiently durable. They also argue that advertising by firms can solve the problem, although this leads to a nonconcavity in each firm's profit function and, thus, the possibility of significant entry barriers (see also Eaton and White 2002a).

In Chapter 10, Greg Dow addresses the question of why some firms are strongly hierarchical while others have more participatory structures. He argues that this variation can be traced partly to adverse selection involving the quality of entrepreneurial projects. Assuming that worker participation raises productivity but also increases the bargaining power of workers, an entrepreneur will create a participatory firm only if workers compensate him in advance for his loss of bargaining power. An entrepreneur with good projects can try to signal his or her true type by offering more worker participation. But if adverse selection is severe, in the sense that most entrepreneurs have bad projects, signalling of this sort will not work and firms will remain hierarchical despite potential productivity gains from worker participation.

Dow's concept of membership fees paid by workers in exchange for participation in the firm is reminiscent of Eaton and White's (1982, 1983) discussion of entry fees as a way to eliminate worker rents in the context of efficiency wage theory. Moreover, Dow's analysis of multiple equilibria that can be Pareto ranked echoes earlier work by Eaton and his co-authors on coordination games. In Dow's framework, different equilibria lead to different organizational outcomes. He closes by arguing that the fragility of worker beliefs accounts for an episode in the history of plywood cooperatives in the Pacific Northwest, where a loss of trust by workers in the honesty of entrepreneurs brought entry by new cooperatives to an abrupt halt.

In Chapter 11, Cliff Bekar, Greg Dow, Clyde Reed, and Josh Stine address a seemingly quite different subject: the nuclear arms race during the Cold War. The underlying theoretical structure again involves signalling, this time by an entrepreneurial state. The authors argue that the United States and the Soviet Union grossly overinvested in their nuclear arsenals relative to any conceivable estimate of what either needed to deter a first strike by the other. These investments not only involved large financial outlays, but noticeably increased the danger of accidental nuclear war. The authors argue that several standard explanations for the arms race are inconsistent with the available evidence, and that the solution to this puzzle involves the role of a large nuclear arsenal as a signal to potential allies about a superpower's willingness to take risks – in particular, the military risk of defending an ally threatened by the rival hegemon. In this view, political leaders with 'hard-line' preferences (those truly willing to take risks) invest in large arsenals in order to attract and retain allies, as long as the benefit from alliances exceeds the additional cost of accidental war. Leaders with 'soft-line' preferences, who want to avoid confrontation, may find it necessary to imitate the behaviour of hardliners.

Bekar et al. show that, in some cases, hardliners overinvest in arsenals relative to the minimum needed for deterrence, while softliners do not. However, since softliners may also imitate hardliners, this can lead to multiple equilibria with different arsenal sizes. In the latter case, the equilibria can be Pareto ranked. An equilibrium with large arsenals is clearly undesirable because the same deterrence and alliance-building effects could have been achieved with a substantially smaller risk of accidental nuclear war. Nevertheless, soft political leaders are trapped, because if they deviate to a smaller arsenal, they will be revealed as soft and lose the benefits derived from their alliances.

As we noted earlier, some of Curt Eaton's work on signalling and coordination games in the 1990s was carried out in collaboration with Jasmina Arifovic. In Chapter 12, she and Alexander Karaivanov apply the same methodology (a simulation involving genetic algorithms) to a related issue: whether it is possible for an employer to learn the optimal employment contract in an environment where workers' preferences are unknown. It is not hard to show theoretically that the optimal contract involves screening (or second-degree price discrimination), where the employer offers two contracts aimed at two different types of workers – those with a low effort cost and those with a high effort cost. In the simulation framework, however, it is remarkably difficult for employers to learn this. In most runs, employers instead converge on a single contract that excludes the high-cost workers, and they occasionally converge on a pooling contract that both types will accept. Arifovic and Karaivanov suggest that the reason involves the ruggedness of the fitness landscape, which has sharp discontinuities where the participation constraints of worker types become binding. As with the earlier research by Arifovic and Eaton, the key lesson is that learning may not lead quickly and easily to Pareto-efficient solutions.

Curt co-authored his work on status, or Veblen, goods with Mukesh Eswaran, and so, appropriately, the volume closes with a contribution on this topic by Eswaran and Rob Oxoby. One feature of status goods is that they easily yield inefficiencies. When each person tries to consume more of a status good than do others, but everyone is identical, in equilibrium everyone will have the same consumption level of the good. However, consumption of the status good is too high relative to other goods. Eswaran and Oxoby apply this insight to a two-period model and find that, for similar reasons, there is a bias toward present consumption at the expense of future consumption. They show that this leads to biased estimates of the rate of time preference (people place more weight on the future than one might naively infer from their behaviour). When the model includes a tradeoff between labour and leisure, increased productivity can lead to greater consumption rather than greater leisure, even though everyone might be better off with more leisure. Using a clever experimental design, the authors show in the laboratory that intertemporal consumption decisions are biased in the predicted direction when subjects give weight to status concerns.

*Conclusion and Acknowledgments*

The conference in honour of B. Curtis Eaton provided the opportunity for some of Canada's leading economists to prepare original papers on topics related to Eaton's work or inspired by his infectious enthusiasm for economic analysis. We are grateful to all of the contributors for their efforts, and to the friends and colleagues of Curt Eaton who attended the conference. We wish to extend our appreciation to Brenda Carrier and Darina Irvine for helping out with conference planning and administration, and to Charlene Hill, who assisted in manuscript preparation.

We are also grateful to the conference's financial sponsors, which made the conference and this book possible. The sponsors included Industry Canada, Pearson Education Canada, CRA International, and the Departments of Economics at the University of Calgary, University of Alberta, Simon Fraser University, and University of British Columbia.

REFERENCES

Aghion, Philippe, and Patrick Bolton. 1987. 'Contracts as a Barrier to Entry.' *American Economic Review* 77 (June): 388–401.
Archibald, G.C., B.C. Eaton, and R.G. Lipsey. 1986. 'Address Models of Value Theory.' In *New Developments in the Analysis of Market Structure*, edited by Joseph Stiglitz and G. Frank Mathewson. Cambridge, MA: MIT Press.
Arifovic, Jasmina, and B. Curtis Eaton. 1995. 'Coordination via Genetic Learning.' *Computational Economics* 8 (3): 181–203.
– 1998. 'The Evolution of Communication in a Sender/Receiver Game of Common Interest with Cheap Talk.' *Journal of Economic Dynamics and Control* 22 (8-9): 187–207.
Donaldson, David, and B. Curtis Eaton. 1981. 'Patience, More than Its Own Reward: A Note on Price Discrimination.' *Canadian Journal of Economics* 14 (1): 93–105.

Eaton, B. Curtis. 1972. 'Spatial Competition Revisited.' *Canadian Journal of Economics* 5 (2): 268–78.

– 2002. *Applied Microeconomic Theory: Selected Essays of B. Curtis Eaton.* Cheltenham, UK: Edward Elgar.

Eaton, B. Curtis, Diane F. Eaton, and Douglas W. Allen. 2009. *Microeconomics: Theory with Applications*, 7th ed. Toronto: Pearson Education Canada.

Eaton, B. Curtis, and Mukesh Eswaran. 2003. 'The Evolution of Preferences and Competition: A Rationalization of Veblen's Theory of Invidious Comparisons.' *Canadian Journal of Economics* 36 (4): 832–59.

– 2009. 'Well-Being and Affluence in the Presence of a Veblen Good.' *Economic Journal* 119 (539): 1088–1104.

Eaton, B. Curtis, and Richard G. Lipsey. 1975. 'The Principle of Minimum Differentiation Reconsidered: Some New Developments in the Theory of Spatial Competition.' *Review of Economic Studies* 42 (1): 27–49.

– 1976. 'The Non-Uniqueness of Equilibrium in the Löschian Location Model.' *American Economic Review* 66 (1): 77–93.

– 1977. 'The Introduction of Space into the Neoclassical Model of Value Theory.' In *Studies in Modern Economic Analysis*, edited by M.J. Artis and A.R. Nobay. Oxford: Basil Blackwell.

– 1978. 'Freedom of Entry and the Existence of Pure Profit.' *Economic Journal* 88 (351): 455–69.

– 1979a. 'Comparison Shopping and the Clustering of Homogeneous Firms.' *Journal of Regional Science* 19 (4): 421–35.

– 1979b. 'The Theory of Market Pre-emption: The Persistence of Excess Capacity and Monopoly in Growing Spatial Markets.' *Economica* 46 (182): 149–58.

– 1980. 'Exit Barriers Are Entry Barriers: The Durability of Capital as a Barrier to Entry.' *Bell Journal of Economics* 11 (2): 721–29.

– 1981. 'Capital, Commitment and Entry Equilibrium.' *Bell Journal of Economics* 12 (2): 593–604.

– 1982. 'An Economic Theory of Central Places.' *Economic Journal* 92 (365): 56–72.

– 1989. 'Product Differentiation.' In *Handbook of Industrial Organization*, edited by R. Schmalensee and R.D. Willig. Amsterdam: North-Holland.

– 1997. *On the Foundations of Monopolistic Competition and Economic Geography: The Selected Essays of B. Curtis Eaton and Richard G. Lipsey.* Cheltenham, UK: Edward Elgar.

Eaton, B. Curtis, and William G. Morrison. 2003. 'Evolutionary Stability in the Investment-Opportunism-Retaliation Game.' *Journal of Bioeconomics* 5 (1): 27–45.

Eaton, B. Curtis, and Roger Ware. 1987. 'A Theory of Market Structure with Sequential Entry.' *RAND Journal of Economics* 18 (1): 1–16.

Eaton, B. Curtis, and William D. White. 1982. 'Agent Compensation and the Limits of Bonding.' *Economic Inquiry* 20 (3): 330–43.

– 1983. 'The Economy of High Wages: An Agency Problem.' *Economica* 50 (198): 175–81.

– 1991. 'The Distribution of Wealth and the Efficiency of Institutions.' *Economic Inquiry* 29 (2): 336–50.

– 1992. 'Image Building.' Discussion Paper 92-17, Department of Economics, Simon Fraser University.

– 2002a. 'Image Advertising.' In *Applied Microeconomic Theory: Selected Essays of B. Curtis Eaton*, edited by B. Curtis Eaton. Cheltenham, UK: Edward Elgar; originally working paper, Department of Economics, Simon Fraser University, 1995.

– 2002b. 'Wealth: The Support of Institutions and the Limits of Control.' In *Applied Microeconomic Theory: Selected Essays of B. Curtis Eaton*, edited by B. Curtis Eaton. Cheltenham, UK: Edward Elgar; originally Working Paper E-86-26, Hoover Institution, 1986.

Eaton, B. Curtis, and Myrna H. Wooders. 1985. 'Sophisticated Entry in a Model of Spatial Competition.' *RAND Journal of Economics* 16 (2): 282–97.

# 2 B. Curtis Eaton's Contributions to the Economics of Information

RICHARD G. LIPSEY

One of the most significant new lines of enquiry in economic theory over the past 50 years has been the development of the economics of imperfect information. George Akerlof is generally credited with starting the modern development with his seminal article, 'The Market for Lemons: Quality Uncertainty and the Market Mechanism' (1970). The 2001 Nobel Prize, awarded to Akerlof, Michael Spence, and Joseph Stiglitz, recognized the importance of this subject and the contributions made by these three economists. In this paper, I review the many significant contributions that Curtis Eaton and several·of his co-authors have made to this literature. I discuss them chronologically and note where he seems to have been first or nearly first in some specific area.

The first article I discuss is 'Firm-Specific Human Capital: A Shared Investment or Optimal Entrapment?' (Donaldson and Eaton 1976), which first appeared in 1974 as a University of British Columbia (UBC) discussion paper. Although it does not deal with asymmetric information, the paper is interesting because it comes close to efficiency wage theory in that firms use wages that exceed their employees' marginal products to induce them to do something that the firm desires. In this case, it is to minimize voluntary quits. The basic observations being explained are wage profiles that vary with age rather than with marginal products. The standard explanation of this phenomenon at the time was due to Becker (1964), who argued that firm-specific human capital represents a joint investment by the firm and the employee. As a result, the worker accepts a lower initial wage rate as payment for education and later gets a higher wage rate as a return on his firm-specific capital. Becker argued that the sharing of investment in firm-specific human capital is designed to inhibit costly labour turnover because, if the employee quits or is fired, both the employee and the employer will not then gain the full return on the investment.

In contrast, Donaldson and Eaton (1976) argue that, although this wage profile might be evidence of human capital, it is not necessarily evidence of shared investment in it. Instead, the firm can inhibit quits by offering a rising pay scale not related to the employee's marginal product. This way, the whole profitable investment in human capital comes from the firm, allowing the return on it to accrue wholly to the firm. Since the human capital is firm specific, the employer does not need to offer a wage premium equal to the extra marginal product that the capital produces; all that is needed is a wage that is just higher than the worker's marginal product in alternative employment where this capital has no value. This is a more profitable alternative to the firm than the joint investment Becker envisioned.

The difference between Becker and Donaldson and Eaton is of some importance for policy. Becker saw 'such [compensation] devices as increasing the security of both parties in the 'shared investment' (1964, 24). In contrast, Donaldson and Eaton see devices such as non-vested pensions, deferred stock options, paid vacations which increase with an employee's tenure in a firm, the allocation of the most desired office space by seniority, and even the perquisite of a key to the executive washroom[1] are, in our interpretation, simply devices employed by the firm to maximize its return from its investment in firm-specific human capital (1976, 471–2).

They go on to observe:

> Our interpretation of job-specific human capital also calls for some scepticism towards publicly financed on-the-job training programs which are now quite common in the United States and the United Kingdom. Such programs are presumably intended to provide workers with general skills. But, to the extent that they create firm-specific skills, the public is subsidizing an investment on which the employer alone will realize a return. (472)

I have a number of observations to make regarding the Donaldson and Eaton paper. First, as already noted, their analysis comes close to the concept of the efficiency wage (although not in the face of asymmetric information). Second, in an approach that is typical of Curt's work, their analysis uses 'the simplest (competitive) models which allow us to develop our alternative interpretation. More elaborate and more realistic models could be developed, but we do not think that the elaborations (at least those which seem obvious to us) would significantly alter our interpretation' (1976, 464). Third, the analysis is clearly related to important policy issues, which is another hallmark of much of Curt's work. Fourth, if two such divergent predictions as those of Becker and Donaldson and Eaton were derived from competing theories in the natural sciences, a host of researchers could try to devise tests to choose between the two on the basis of empirical evidence. I see no such rush in the economics literature. Economists often seem more interested in developing competing theories than in figuring out how to decide among them.

'Patience, More Than Its Own Reward: A Note on Price Discrimination' (Donaldson and Eaton 1981) first appeared as a UBC discussion paper in 1979. The monopolist does not know how his groups divide but he allows them to self-select by creating two markets, one with a lower money price and a high waiting time and the other with a high price and no waiting time. This is price discrimination. It is found, the authors argue, in many places: discount days in which queues and congestion are great, discount air fares that take time to locate, inconvenient locations of price-discounting stores, in the United Kingdom public hospital beds at a price of zero but with waiting and private beds at a positive price but no waiting.

This is an early contribution to the literature on sorting, in this case when the agent does not know the characteristics of his customers but sets up an arrangement by which they sort themselves. Interestingly, in his survey article 'Silver Signals: Twenty Five Years of Screening and Signalling,' John Riley (2001) cites 118 references, only 22 of which predate Donaldson and Eaton (1981) and none of which deals with this problem of a seller's screening his buyers, although he does not cite Donaldson and Eaton (1981).

The next two papers I wish to discuss are by Eaton and William White and concern efficiency wage theory, although they do not use that term, which came into common use well after their articles were published – as far as I can determine, they were both published prior to any other modern paper on efficiency wage theory. The first was rejected by the *American Economic Review* and the second by the *Bell Journal of Economics* before being published in journals that, although of somewhat lesser prestige, were still quite widely read. Although they did receive notice at the time,[2] they went unnoted in any of the summaries of the efficiency wage literature, including in the Nobel Prize lectures by Akerlof (2001), Spence (2001), and Stiglitz (2001), despite the latter's apparently being intended as a survey of the major works in the modern literature of information economics.

The first of these papers, 'Agent Compensation and the Limits of Bonding' (Eaton and White 1982), was written in spring 1980 and published in 1982.[3] Their problem is how firms can control agents who are given a position of trust that they might violate. Until Eaton and White wrote, the solutions offered to this problem all made the agents just earn their opportunity cost in equilibrium by, for example, requiring the posting of a bond that just covered the expected value of the agent's gain if the agent cheated. Becker and Stigler (1974) suggest that agents might be paid more than their opportunity cost (called a noncompensating differential) and then have their performance monitored stochastically. If caught, they lose the wage that is set sufficiently in excess of their opportunity cost so that they are motivated not to cheat. Becker and Stigler go on to argue that the present value of this differential could be recovered by an entry fee so that agents would be indifferent between jobs that required trust and those that did not.

Eaton and White ask what no one else seems to have asked: what if the entry fee or the value of the bond exceeds the value of the agent's assets? When we consider the massive amounts that are sometimes taken by those who do violate trust, it is not difficult to imagine such situations. Eaton and White show that entry fees or bonds that exceed the agent's wealth have no effect on the agent's behaviour and, therefore, that conditions exist in which it is optimal to pay agents more than their opportunity cost. The high wage motivates the agent not to cheat but is less than the expected value of the loss to the firm if that agent does cheat. They demonstrate these possibilities in a simple one-period model in which an agent pays an entry fee to do a job and is compensated on completion of the job, contingent on the agent's not being apprehended in violation of the trust.

Eaton and White investigate several cases. In those in which the loss to the firm greatly exceeds the gain to the agent (loss of the firm's reputation could be one reason) and/or the agent's wealth is much less than the firm's potential loss, profit maximization calls for the firm to pay the agent more than his/her opportunity cost and more than the entry fee. This reduces the potential loss to the firm by more than it raises its costs. The result is a pure efficiency wage (a term not then in common use) that motivates workers to behave in ways that raise the firm's profits. This leads to an excess supply of would-be employees, allowing employers to discriminate among potential employees at zero cost to themselves, exercising their prejudices in ways that Milton Friedman long ago argued were inconsistent with profit maximization.

Earlier, some writers had suggested that firms might pay wages higher than opportunity costs because these might affect workers' productivity (for a discussion, see Stiglitz 2001, 479–80). In this case, agents earn more than their opportunity cost but no more than the value of their marginal product to the employer. To the best of my knowledge, no one had before studied the case in which it was optimal to pay a wage that is not only higher than the agent's opportunity cost, but also higher than the agent's direct marginal product to the firm.

The second of the two Eaton and White papers on efficiency wage theory, 'The Economy of High Wages: An Agency Problem' (Eaton and White 1983), was written in the fall of 1980.[4] Here they consider a situation in which an agent can vary the amount of effort he or she puts in. Other treatments of this problem had dealt with situations in which risk sharing and supervision are intermixed. Eaton and White remove risk in order to look solely at the issue of supervision. The firm then chooses one from a number of possible compensation schemes. All have the characteristic that the agent gets a standard wage unless he or she is monitored (at a cost to the firm) with probability $p$, in which case the agent gets compensation contingent on his or her actual effort. The firm desires to get a given amount of effort from the agent. Eaton and White investigate a number of possibilities, and two results stand out. First, '[a] strictly positive probability of monitoring is necessary to induce the agent to provide a positive effort (when the cat's away, with certainty, the mice will surely play)' (177). Second, if monitoring is sufficiently costly, the firm chooses to offer a compensation package that is strictly preferred to the agent's best outside alternative. Compliance – that is, providing the desired amount of effort – is a function of the wage when not monitored, $w$, and the probability, $p$, of being monitored. Because the compliance constraint is negatively sloped in $(p, w)$ space, $w$ and $p$ are substitutes in the firm's effort to induce the agent to supply the desired amount of effort. The firm can induce the agent's compliance with a high wage and a low probability of being monitored or a low wage and a high probability of being monitored. If monitoring were free, the firm would pay the agent the value of his or her opportunity cost and monitor with probability 1. But if monitoring is sufficiently costly, it will be to the firm's advantage to increase the agent's wage and reduce the probability of monitoring. Hence Eaton and White's designation, 'the economy of high wages.' This is an 'efficiency wage' result analogous to that in Eaton and White (1982) and similar comments apply.

Eaton and White also wrote 'Wealth: The Support of Institutions and the Limits of Control' (1986) and 'The Distribution of Wealth and the Efficiency of Institutions' (1991). It is unfortunate that the first was never resubmitted for journal publication after being rejected by the *American Economic Review*. Although there is overlap between the two, they are by no means identical, and the first covers some interesting cases not found in the second. Nonetheless, they deal with a common general issue: the relation of agents' wealth to the efficacy of institutions that are designed to influence behaviour. Although the authors do not emphasize this, both papers also involve asymmetric information. Influencing behaviour in the ways studied in the articles would not be a problem under perfect information because the intentions of anyone about to engage in some antisocial or otherwise undesired behaviour would be known to the relevant authorities, who would apprehend the potential wrong doer before the wrong was done.

The first article has the usual simple but highly insightful Eaton-style model. Here, an agent is tempted to commit some antisocial act – in this case, stealing an amount $T$ – while the institutions are designed to discourage the agent in an efficient manner. The agent can be persuaded not to steal by some combination of size of penalty and probability of being caught. Policing is costly to society but the penalty, being a pure transfer, is not. So, fairly obviously, the least costly method of persuasion is to set the penalty at the agent's total wealth and the probability of being caught such that the expected utility from theft is just equal to the utility of not stealing – *ceteris paribus*, the agent chooses honesty. This solution will be adopted if it is less costly to society than having no policing and accepting the social cost of the unlawful act. What might be less obvious is that, if the agent is given a wealth transfer and the penalty is increased correspondingly, compliance can be induced with a lower probability of being caught and hence the costly monitoring activity can be reduced. The agent now has more to lose from being caught, so a lower probability of apprehension leaves him or her on the same level of satisfaction. If the agent has the option of some desperate action, such as fleeing the country if caught, this reduces the maximum efficient penalty to the amount of the agent's wealth minus what he or she can salvage by fleeing. Finally, in a two-person game, it can be Pareto improving for the richer person to transfer some wealth to the poorer person. Since, in this model, only the poor steal, this reduces the rich person's chance of being robbed, which might outweigh the value of the transfer. We see here one limitation of the model, since in reality the rich often 'rob' from the poor as, for example, in the Enron and sub-prime scandals.

The second paper in this group (Eaton and White 1991) sets up another interesting model. Here, two persons produce corn (and receive some manna from heaven so that they do not starve if they have no corn). Each begins with an endowment of corn, which they divide between consumption in this period and planting to yield a larger amount of corn in the next period. They have an absolute property right over their corn in this period but a variable one over next year's crop. Agent 1's endowment of corn is always larger than agent 2's, so 2 is the potential thief and 1 the potential victim if only one agent steals. Eaton and White first show that, if there are no property rights over the planted crop, neither agent will plant as long as one seed of corn produces less than 2 seeds of crop; instead, they will consume everything in this period. The authors then go on to consider various property-right regimes that require costly enforcement. If one person steals from the other, he gets his own crop plus what he steals, assuming he is not caught. If he does get caught, he loses what he stole plus a penalty. So the variables are the size of the penalty and the probability of being caught by a costly monitoring process. Depending on the size of the two parameters and the relative wealth of the two agents, the solution can have (i) neither stealing, (ii) 2 stealing from 1, or (iii) both stealing from each other.

The analysis of these cases is interesting but takes more space than I have available here. It leads to two main conclusions. First, the relative wealth of the agents matters. For example, for certain wealth distributions, increasing the magnitude of the sanction and/or the probability of being caught can reduce overall efficiency, as measured by total corn consumption over the two periods (less planting and more consumption in the first period). Second, the distribution of wealth itself affects efficiency – there are circumstances in which, for given magnitudes of the sanction and the probability of apprehension, reducing the inequality of wealth increases total output. Of course, the proposition that the penalty should equal the agent's total wealth is not a useful guide for setting penalties when many agents with different amounts of wealth are involved. But, although nothing final can be concluded from such a simple model, the analysis does suggest possibilities for further investigation. For example, most people's intuition is that increasing the probability of being caught will raise efficiency. So it is suggestive to note that, in Eaton and White's model, this is not always so. The ability to refute a generalization is one of the great values of simple models. In this case, it shows that the belief that it is always efficient to increase the efficacy of enforcement is wrong. The next step would be to look for circumstances in which the belief is either true or false.

In what should have been a seminal article if an earlier version had not been rejected by the *Journal of Political Economy* and not resubmitted for journal publication,[5] Eaton and White (1995) take on a really interesting problem: how to analyse image advertising of goods that people consume as much to establish an identity among onlookers as for their direct utility value in consumption. An expensive car might be better to drive than a cheap one but it also advertises that the user is wealthy. An Yves Saint Laurent dress tells onlookers something about the taste and style sense of the wearer, as well as giving her direct satisfaction – and so on for many of the goods and services we consume today. Given most of the problems Eaton and his co-authors deal with in the material I have surveyed so far, I would have had some idea of how to start modelling them – although no doubt I would not have gotten near to the simple but wonderfully fruitful models that are their hallmark. But here I would not have had a clue of how to begin.

The authors do! They build a model of social interaction in which players use visual signs they call 'costumes' to signal their identity to other players. The intuition of the problem can be seen if one looks at much of life as a never-ending series of pair-wise social encounters. Before each gathering that will produce such an encounter, we decide what our type will be today – a professor, a guy on the make, a sports fan looking for someone with whom to talk sports, someone looking to sell (or buy) sex, and so on. In every encounter, players are better off if they know their partner's type and if their partner knows their type. For example, when someone like me goes into a bar and sees a Hell's Angel type, he is glad the wearer is advertising his identity by what he wears so that the likes of me can avoid him.

The encounter game has exactly these features. The model is a two-stage game in which players of several different types choose their costumes in the first stage and in the second stage have random, pair-wise encounters in which the appropriate action depends on identifying the other person's type. (The encountering players are called 'partners.') This might possibly be inferred costlessly by looking at the partner's costume or discovered at a cost by direct investigation, called policy $N$. Although players do not know which players are wearing which consumes, they do know the frequency with which each type of costume is worn by each type of player. There is an appropriate action for each player to take in each encounter, which depends on the partner's type. The payoff is highest if the type can be identified costlessly by inferring it from the consume, enabling the appropriate action, next highest if resources are used to establish the type by direct investigation (policy $N$), again followed by the appropriate action, and least if the type is estimated incorrectly from inspecting the costume, which leads to inappropriate action. So each player has two options. Option one is to infer the partner's type from costume inspection, in which case the player either gets the highest possible payoff for guessing right and taking appropriate action or the lowest possible payoff for guessing wrong and taking inappropriate action. Option two is to adopt policy $N$, taking the appropriate action, and accepting an intermediate payoff. The dominant strategy in the second stage of the game is to take action based on inferring the partner's type from his or her costume if the frequency of people of that type wearing that kind of costume is high enough and otherwise to choose strategy $N$.

In the first-stage game, players choose their costume. If each type of costume is chosen only by players of one type, the costume becomes a perfect signalling device and, in the second stage, all partners use costume inference to choose the appropriate action. This is a subgame perfect equilibrium to this two-stage game. But so is the case in which there is a distribution of players of different types who choose different costumes, so that no particular costume is a sufficiently reliable signalling device. Then, in the second stage, all partners chose alternative $N$. Mixed equilibria, in which some costumes are perfectly reliable signals while others are not, are also possible. The equilibria in which all players perfectly signal their type are Pareto dominating over all other equilibria; but since there are many others, there is a difficult coordination problem.

Eaton and White then go on to show that their version of brand advertising can solve this coordination problem. An advertiser broadcasts a message that all individuals of a particular type should buy a costume of their type, while others should not. Players might or might not hear this message, and might or might not act on it in choosing their stage-one costume and in deciding on the appropriate action in stage two.

A number of interesting conclusions emerge from the authors' analysis of this game. First, the target group for the advertising must be larger than the group to which the advertiser hopes to sell its product. This is because the costume cannot act as a signal if nonbuyers do not know its message. Second, to be effective, the advertiser must persuade intended buyers that a substantial portion of the target audience has heard and understood the message – otherwise they will not act on it. Hence, it is necessary to advertise where everyone knows the audience is large, such as during a Super Bowl game, and to repeat the advertisement many times and in different media. Third, let two firms attempt to establish the same image for their separate product – for example, sending out the message that their car is the one that will best advertise to others that the driver is rich and famous. Each firm must then saturate the market so that everyone has heard its advertising. Although I suspect this full-saturation result is an artefact of the specific model, the evidence does show that advertising is much more intense in such situations compared with those in which different firms seek to establish images that are differentiated from each other.

I have not been able to locate any other treatment of this problem. So I conclude that it is an original piece that tackles an interesting issue in a highly imaginative way, which makes it doubly unfortunate that it was not published in a widely read journal.

The general problems posed by this paper are: what are the equilibria of this encounter game, and how do they emerge and evolve? The second paper on this issue (Arifovic and Eaton 1998) uses the same general model. It tells a story in which learning is modelled in an evolutionary framework and eventually leads to an equilibrium with perfect signalling. In contrast to the previous paper, it shows, among other things, how the communication of types can evolve even in the absence of conscious efforts to promote it.

Together, these two papers specify a highly interesting and suggestive model that is applicable to all sorts of situations. The vision of both papers is about uniforms, both official and unofficial (such as biker garb), about wedding rings and engagement rings, about men wearing diamonds in their ears to signal their sexual orientation, about prostitutes who wear garb that lets everyone know what their business is.

The final paper I want to discuss is 'Incomplete Information and Migration: The Grass Is Greener across the Higher Fence' (Allen and Eaton 2005). Here, the authors are concerned with the basic observation that migrants go to the closer of two possible places much more often than can be accounted for by differentials in the cost of transport or expected earnings. When they wrote their paper, the accepted explanation was that (1) distance is a proxy for the difficulty of obtaining information, so that potential migrants have less information about the more distant location, and (2) that migrants tend to go to places for which they have more information, so (3) they tend to go to the closer location. Allen and Eaton accept proposition (1) but show that proposition (2) is wrong for risk-neutral agents, who, if income is their main concern, will on average go to the destination about which they have least information! Thus, if agents are risk neutral and if distance is a proxy for information, there is a bias in favour of the more distant destination.

Although the proof takes much space to develop, the intuition is easy. Suppose there are three locations – one's own and two possible migration destinations – and in all three, incomes are dispersed equally around a *common average* and the cost of moving from any one location to any other is zero. Also suppose there is a large number of agents, who sample incomes in the two migration destinations, calculate the mean of their individual samples, and act on that knowledge. Now, as a first step, suppose the agents have perfect information about the closer of the two migration destinations but just a sampling of incomes in the more distant one. In this event, no one will move to the closer destination because each agent knows for certain that it offers no increase in income over staying at home. For the other area, however, the distribution of individual agents' sample means will be centred on the average income ruling at home, but, for half the individuals, their own sample mean will indicate that they can obtain a higher income in the distant location and they will move.

Now, suppose agents have imperfect information about both migration destinations. In this case, the larger the size of each agent's sample from any location, the more the distribution of agents' sample means is concentrated near the true mean, until – if each agent's sample reaches a full 100 per cent enumeration of all incomes – the distribution collapses to the mean. Suppose more information becomes available about the nearer destination because each agent has a larger sample of incomes from that destination than from the more distant one. Thus, the density of the distribution of sample means will become more concentrated near the true average for the nearer area and more dispersed for the more distant area. It follows that, of the agents who think there is a small gain to be had from moving, more will go to the closer location than to the more distant one. But of those who think there is a medium to a large gain from moving, far more will go to the more distant location than to the closer one. On balance, then, more agents will move to the distant location than to the closer one, and the average expectation of income gain for those who move to the distant location will be higher than for those who go to the closer location.

Allen and Eaton then go on to show that even a modest degree of risk aversion will reverse the results. First, given two locations that promise equal incomes, migrants, on average, will choose the one for which they have more information. Second, given two locations in which one has a higher mean income than the other, as the amount of information potential migrants have about both is increased, so does the likelihood that they will choose the one with the higher income.

The authors argue that their analysis can also account for the observation that gross inflows of migrants greatly exceed net inflows. Because sampling errors always make migration look better than staying put for some agents, even when different locations offer the same average income, there will always be some movement whenever new samplings are made. This might be one reason, but I suspect that a more important one is provided by the evidence that quite a bit of migration is intended to be temporary and that such migrants mean to return to the homeland as soon as they achieve some objective, such as the acquisition of sufficient wealth with which to set up back home.[6] If so, the movement from a higher-income area to a lower one will be dominated by the return of those who came to make their 'grub stake' rather than by those whose sampling errors led them to the mistaken belief that they were moving to a higher-income area. Although theory cannot settle this issue, direct questioning of migrants could do so.

In conclusion, I want to speculate as to why the works of Eaton and his co-authors have not been cited more frequently in the literature on imperfect information, especially when they seem to me to have been the first to obtain some key results, including efficiency wage theory. I tentatively suggest some possibilities.

First, let me digress a bit to tell a story reported by Ed Mishan when he joined the staff of the London School of Economics in the mid-1950s after a sojourn at the Cowles Commission for Research in Economics. He said that, at a typical event, some young staff member would explain over coffee his great new theoretical idea that possibly also had policy implications. 'Fine,' the older staff members would say, 'now go and formalize it.' When the young staffer would return some days later, they would say, 'yes, but it is not general enough; and it can still be easily understood. Go back and make it more airtight.' This iterative process would continue back and forth until the senior staff concluded that the idea was now expressed so generally, with all special cases ruled out, no matter how unlikely they might be, that it would be intelligible to only a very few of the highly initiated, and certainly not to any policy type. It could now be published.

Although this is an extreme tale, it holds a grain of truth in that all too many economists value a high degree of formalism over less formal but more intuitive and more easily applicable treatments. In contrast, the Popperian approach on which I was raised was to use the simplest possible model that could deal with the problem at hand. This, combined with Einstein's advice that 'everything should be made as simple as possible, *but not simpler*,' could be made Curt Eaton's theme song. His models are usually simple and highly intuitive. They capture the object of his interest in formal analysis that non-specialists can (mostly) understand and where the intuition of the result is easy to extract. Possibly, this approach does not recommend itself to those who prefer the most abstract treatment possible.

With respect to the two papers on efficiency wage theory, the answer might lie in their focus. This theory was developed in the mainstream of neo-Keynesian theory that was rationalizing one of the basic assumptions of Keynesian models: that labour markets did not clear, leaving room for varying amounts of involuntary unemployment. Coming out of the micro field of industrial organization, the Eaton and White article did not emphasize the employment effects of their theory, although they did note them.

Nonetheless, as their articles were the first to demonstrate formally the possibility that employers could rationally offer wages above the market-clearing level, it seems to me that they merit a place in surveys of the development of efficiency wage theory.

Another possible reason the works of Eaton and his co-authors have not received the recognition they deserve is that Curtis is outside of the main centres of power in our subject. One can do quite useful work from the periphery, but if one is not at the very core, with powerful and influential friends, it is hard to make one's voice heard when operating outside of the box of what is generally accepted. If even George Akerlof had trouble getting his great lemons article published until powerful friends told editors they were making a great mistake by rejecting it, then people such as Curt, without that base of support, face even larger obstacles. Novel, even seminal, ideas published in less influential journals are likely to go unnoticed until taken up, or independently discovered, by someone at the centre. I speculate that had Curt been at Harvard, Yale, MIT, Berkeley, or even Michigan, his original works would have received much more attention than they actually did.[7] But I leave it to readers to make their own judgment on this contentious matter.

NOTES

1  I suspect they had just seen the movie *The Apartment*.
2  In particular, they were referenced in Yellen (1984) and Akerlof (1986).
3  There is no UBC discussion paper version of this paper as that series was inactive at the time. The paper was written while Curt and I were visiting at Yale, and I have strong memories of discussing it with him then.
4  Again there is no discussion paper version because of inactivity on that front, but this was the first thing Curt did after returning to Vancouver from Yale and before leaving to take up an appointment at the University of Toronto.
5  The version submitted to the *Journal of Political Economy*, Eaton and White (1992), was rejected on the grounds that the model was not properly closed in the second-stage game. A revised version of this article is published as Chapter 9 of this volume. The authors solved the problem with the new assumption that the technology of advertising was perfectly ordered. The revised version appeared in 1995 as a UBC discussion paper but was never resubmitted for publication; it was finally included in Eaton (2002). In a paper published in 1993, Wärneryd develops a similar game that contains only two players, two

signals, and two actions, and, importantly, no $N$-type action. Without the possibility of action $N$, the problem is simpler and not as rich in implications.

6  For example, in the 1950s, many Irish migrants to England would return home after they had earned enough to set themselves up in a business or a farm, after which they could marry, while many of the prostitutes on the streets of the high-class Mayfair district in London were French girls from provincial towns working to earn a dowry, after which they would return home to marry and lead respectable lives. See Arunachalam and Shah (2008), which nicely corroborates my anecdotal observations in London

7  Eaton's experience might be an excellent example of the behaviour of editors of top-line economic journals, as discussed by Hodgson and Rothman (1999).

## REFERENCES

Akerlof, George. 1970. 'The Market for Lemons: Quality Uncertainty and the Market Mechanism.' *Quarterly Journal of Economics* 84 (3): 488–500.

–  1986. *Efficiency Wage Models of the Labour Market*. Cambridge: Cambridge University Press.

–  2001. 'Behavioral Macroeconomics and Macroeconomic Behavior.' The Nobel Prize Lecture 2001. In *The Nobel Prizes 2001*, edited by Tore Frängsmyr. Stockholm: Nobel Foundation, 2002.

Allen, Jeremiah, and B. Curtis Eaton. 2005. 'Incomplete Information and Migration: The Grass Is Greener across the Higher Fence.' *Journal of Regional Science* 45 (1): 1–19.

Arunachalam, Raj, and Manisha Shah. 2008. 'Prostitutes and Brides?' *American Economic Review Papers and Proceedings* 98 (2): 516–22.

Arifovic, Jasmina, and B. Curtis Eaton. 1998. 'The Evolution of Type Communication in a Sender/Receiver Game of Common Interest with Cheap Talk.' *Journal of Economic Dynamics and Control* 22 (8-9): 1187–207.

Becker, Gary. 1964. *Human Capital: A Theoretical and Empirical Analysis, with Special Reference to Education*. New York: Columbia University Press.

Becker, Gary, and George Stigler. 1974. 'Law Enforcement, Malfeasance, and Compensation of Enforcers.' *Journal of Legal Studies* 3 (1): 1–18.

Donaldson, David, and B. Curtis Eaton. 1976. 'Firm-Specific Human Capital: A Shared Investment or Optimal Entrapment?' *Canadian Journal of Economics* 9 (1): 462–72. Reprinted in *Applied Microeconomic Theory: Selected Essays of B. Curtis Eaton*. Cheltenham, UK: Edward Elgar, 2002.

–  1981. 'Patience, More than Its Own Reward: A Note on Price Discrimination.' *Canadian Journal of Economics* 14 (1): 93–105. Reprinted in *Applied*

*Microeconomic Theory: Selected Essays of B. Curtis Eaton.* Cheltenham, UK: Edward Elgar, 2002.

Eaton, B. Curtis. 2002. *Applied Microeconomic Theory: Selected Essays of B. Curtis Eaton.* Cheltenham, UK: Edward Elgar.

Eaton, B. Curtis, and William D. White. 1982. 'Agent Compensation and the Limits of Bonding.' *Economic Inquiry* 20 (3): 330–43. Reprinted in *Applied Microeconomic Theory: Selected Essays of B. Curtis Eaton.* Cheltenham, UK: Edward Elgar, 2002.

– 1983. 'The Economy of High Wages: An Agency Problem.' *Economica* 50 (198): 175–81.

– 1986. 'Wealth: The Support of Institutions and the Limits of Control.' Working Paper in Economics E-86-26, Hoover Institution. Reprinted in *Applied Microeconomic Theory: Selected Essays of B. Curtis Eaton.* Cheltenham, UK: Edward Elgar, 2002.

– 1991. 'The Distribution of Wealth and the Efficiency of Institutions.' *Economic Inquiry* 29 (2): 336–50. Reprinted in *Applied Microeconomic Theory: Selected Essays of B. Curtis Eaton.* Cheltenham, UK: Edward Elgar, 2002.

– 1992. 'Image Building.' Discussion Paper 92-17, Department of Economics, Simon Fraser University.

– 1995. 'Image Advertising.' Working paper, Department of Economics, Simon Fraser University. Reprinted in *Applied Microeconomic Theory: Selected Essays of B. Curtis Eaton.* Cheltenham, UK: Edward Elgar, 2002.

Hodgson, Geoffrey M., and Harry Rothman. 1999. 'The Editors and Authors of Economics Journals: A Case of Institutional Oligopoly.' *Economic Journal* 109 (453): F165–86.

Riley, John G. 2001. 'Silver Signals: Twenty-Five Years of Screening and Signalling.' *Journal of Economic Literature* 39 (2): 432–78.

Spence, Michael. 2001. 'Signalling in Retrospect and the Informational Structure of Markets.' The Nobel Prize Lecture 2001. In *The Nobel Prizes 2001*, edited by Tore Frängsmyr. Stockholm: Nobel Foundation, 2002.

Stiglitz, Joseph E. 2001. 'Information and the Change in the Paradigm in Economics.' The Nobel Prize Lecture 2001. In *The Nobel Prizes 2001*, edited by Tore Frängsmyr. Stockholm: Nobel Foundation, 2002.

Wärneryd, K. 1993. 'Cheap Talk, Coordination, and Evolutionary Stability.' *Games and Economic Behaviour* 5 (4): 532–46.

Yellen, Janet. 1984. 'Efficiency Wage Models of Unemployment.' *American Economic Review* 74 (2): 200–05.

# PART II

---

# Industrial Organization
# and Spatial Competition

# 3 Entry Deterrence via Contracts

RALPH A. WINTER

When do buyers and an incumbent supplier in a market have the incentive to enter into contracts that deter entry by other suppliers? This chapter offers an overview of recent developments in the economic theory addressing this question. This is a natural topic for a book in honour of Curt Eaton since the topic is in the intersection of two areas of economic theory to which Curt has made important contributions: strategic models of entry and entry deterrence; and applied contract theory.[1]

Research on the topic has been active in the economic literature, especially since Aghion and Bolton (1987). And the topic is central to competition policy. Competition policy is concerned ultimately with the two kinds of possible market distortions: excessive prices and the wrong mix of products in a market. Contracts that deter entry can distort the allocation of resources in both dimensions, and competition policy often restricts contracts on the basis of exclusionary effects.[2] Yet even the theoretical possibility that contracts can have an anticompetitive exclusionary effect was, until recently, a matter of disagreement.

In this overview of contracts as entry deterrence, I focus my discussion on two types of contracts – long-term contracts and exclusivity restrictions – setting aside other potentially exclusionary contracts, such as tied sales.

Consider the theory that long-term contracts can act as an anticompetitive entry-deterrence device. The idea is that I, as a seller, sign long-term contracts with buyers in the market so that you, as a potential entrant, are less likely to enter the market since you face the additional cost of having to attract any buyers away from my contracts, which are designed to make this cost quite substantial. A reader new to the idea should be skeptical of this argument for a number of reasons. First, long-term contracts appear everywhere and are surely explained almost always as facilitating efficient economic transactions. A long-term contract is preferred to a spot transaction, for example, if a party to the transaction must make a substantial specific investment. The long-term contract can protect the return on this investment against 'hold-up' by the other party. Prior to considering the evidence in any particular case involving a long-term contract, one must believe that the contract is most likely efficient. Second, the exclusionary effect argued for in a long-term contract seems too close to the exclusion inherent in *any* economic transaction to be of concern. Once I provide the buyer the requested product at a particular price, you as a rival are pre-empted from supplying the buyer at the same price. One obviously would not want the concept of strategic entry deterrence to be so broad as to encompass any economic transaction, so the sense in which a long-term contract can deter entry is not clear *a priori*. Finally, the early Chicago school of law and economics[3] argued that buyers would not enter voluntarily into a potentially exclusionary contract without compensation by the supplier. If the compensation is enough to satisfy the buyer, then it might seem that the contract is efficient.

The economic theory that long-term contracts can act as an entry barrier is now well developed, however. In this chapter, I offer an overview of the essential elements of this theory and apply the theory to a Canadian competition policy case where long-term contracts were (correctly, I argue) struck down in competition law as anticompetitive. Parts of the chapter follow a more detailed development in Jing and Winter (2008).

*Exclusivity restrictions* go beyond long-term contracts. Contracts with these restrictions explicitly condition a transaction on a buyer's dealings with another seller: 'you can buy good A from me, providing you agree not to buy any units of A from another seller.' These contracts might appear to be more problematic than long-term contracts, but it remains for us to explain why buyers need protection against contracts they are not compelled to enter into. (Variations on exclusive dealing, such as *loyalty contracts*, are similar. Instead of restricting a buyer entirely from dealing with other sellers, loyalty contracts reward the buyer via a lower price for the buyer's entire business or a large share of the business.[4]) Exclusivity restrictions or loyalty clauses can also be offered by an incumbent to upstream suppliers.

Long-term contracts and exclusivity have a myriad possible efficiency explanations. Uncovering the motivation for and impact of a contract in a particular case requires, of course, an evaluation of the evidence against the testable implications of the possible theories of the contract. I do not offer here a list and evaluation of all possible theories of each strategy;

instead, I outline the various economic theories underlying a single explanation of these practices: entry deterrence.

My aim in presenting the theories is not to search for generality. Instead, I try to emulate Curt Eaton's research approach in stripping each model down to its simplest possible form. In the synthesis offered in the next section, this means starting with the framework of any intermediate market in which an incumbent has the opportunity to offer a contract to other market participants that deters entry. One particular set of assumptions about the structure of markets within this framework supports the early Chicago view that exclusionary contracts are not profitable. Around this 'Chicago benchmark,' I introduce various changes in market structure, each of which isolates a different channel through which the incentives for exclusionary contracts will flow. The case application of the theory is more complex than any single model, of course, and combines almost all of the channels through which the incentives flow. But a 'model of the case' that captures all of the channels at once, in a way that is more realistic than any single model outlined below, is the last thing that an applied theorist should attempt in this area. One model, one point.

### Entry-deterring Contracts: A Synthesis

The traditional view of exclusivity contracts – or what we could call the 'pre-economics' view of these contracts – was that they are anticompetitive on their face when they foreclose a substantial share of a market to rival sellers. A restriction that prohibits my buyers from purchasing from you is anticompetitive simply because it prevents you from competing. This intuition, or something similar, had some influence in competition law.[5]

Competition law has moved away from this position to become more consistent with the economic foundations. I offer an overview of these foundations in this section. I describe below the general structure of an intermediate market in which an incumbent faces the threat of entry; a benchmark set of assumptions under which the incentive for entry-deterring contracts does not arise; and various departures from this benchmark that do give rise to this incentive.

### The General Structure

An intermediate market in which an incumbent faces the risk of entry has four sets of players (see Figure 3.1):

Figure 3.1: The General Framework

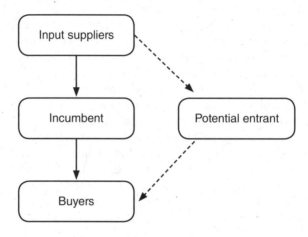

- an incumbent monopolist;
- upstream suppliers to the monopolist;
- downstream buyers from the monopolist; and
- a set of potential entrants, facing an uncertain (but common) unit cost.[6]

The monopolist can offer contracts to downstream buyers or upstream suppliers *ex ante*, before the realization of the entrants' costs. *Ex post*, the incumbent can offer prices to any buyer who is not already in a long-term contract; entrants are free to offer prices to any buyer.

I also adopt some simplifying assumptions throughout:

- upstream suppliers and the incumbent monopolist each have constant unit costs;
- the distribution of uncertain entrants' costs is smooth; and
- the payoff to each buyer depends only on the buyer's contract itself – that is, on the payment the buyer makes and quantity of the product the buyer receives.[7]

Any *ex ante* contract offers must meet participation constraints: a contract will be acceptable to a party only if it offers expected profits at least as high as could achieved by refusing the contract and waiting for whatever price obtains *ex post*. (All parties are risk neutral.) The *ex post* price will be low if entrants' realized cost is low and if entrants are competitive, for example.

*Ex ante* contracts I interpret as long-term contracts.[8] The questions of interest are whether the incumbent monopolist has an incentive to offer *ex ante* contracts to buyers or sellers – and whether these contracts are anticompetitive in the sense of resulting in a reduction in the probability of entry and a reduction in efficiency (total surplus) in the market. The answer depends on additional assumptions that one imposes on this general framework.

I start with a set of assumptions that supports the early Chicago view of exclusive contracts – that such contracts cannot be explained as anticompetitive attempts to increase profits. I then depart from this 'Chicago benchmark by introducing assumptions that can support theories of exclusive contracts, or simply long-term contracts, as anticompetitive. The object of each model, or set of assumptions, is not to present a realistic description of a market structure but rather to isolate each of four possible channels through which the incentives for exclusionary contracts flow. I simply sketch the arguments underlying various claims, and refer to Jing and Winter (2008) for a formal development. I then offer a review of extensions and further developments in the literature.

*The Chicago Benchmark*

The Chicago school of law and economics was the first to look at competition law (among other areas of the law) through the lens of economics. Its view of exclusivity restrictions in contracts was that these contracts could not be explained as an attempt by a monopolist to restrict competition and increase monopoly profits since contracts are entered into voluntarily. Suppose that buyers are identical, to rule out price discrimination, and that each buyer purchases one unit or none. If a monopolist charges buyers the full monopoly price – that is, the value of the product – then it cannot impose additional restrictions on buyers without reducing its price to compensate them. Exclusivity restrictions therefore cannot be explained as an attempt to extract more profits by suppressing competition. Observed exclusivity restrictions must be explained as means of increasing efficiency, or total surplus. Contracts always maximize the combined wealth of contractual parties.

Judge Robert Bork, who is often cited for this view, states, 'The truth appears to be that there has never been a case in which exclusive dealing or requirements contracts were shown to injure competition. A seller who wants exclusivity must give the buyer something for it. If he gives a lower price, the reason must be that the seller expected the arrangement to create efficiencies that justify the lower price' (1978, 309). The following set of assumptions, the 'Chicago benchmark,' added to our basic structure, is sufficient for the Chicago conclusion that long-term contracts of any type cannot be explained as attempts to suppress competition:

- The upstream market for inputs is competitive.
- There are many potential entrants into the intermediate market. These entrants are price takers and share a common realized cost.
- Two-part prices are feasible in contracts with buyers.

Put simply, if the incumbent monopoly is the only source of market power in the structure, contracts cannot be exclusionary. Total surplus is maximized in any market provided that, in every state of the world (here: every realization of entrants' cost), buyers purchase at marginal cost from the minimum-cost, intermediate-good supplier. Under the Chicago benchmark assumptions, this condition for total surplus maximization is achieved with no long-term contract at all because buyers will purchase at cost either from competitive entrants (if the entrants' realized cost is lower than the monopolist's unit cost) or from the monopolist at an efficient two-part price, with the variable price equal to the unit cost (if the monopolist's price is lower).

The monopolist's profit is maximized through the choice of either of two strategies: (a) no contract at all, in which case the monopolist extracts a profit *ex post* equal to the total surplus in the state of the world minus the consumer surplus that buyers could obtain by purchasing from the entrants (if the latter is positive); or (b) an *ex ante* contract in which the monopolist charges a fixed fee to each buyer equal to the expected fixed fee that the buyer would have paid in the absence of a contract. An attempt by the monopolist to extract a higher fixed fee under either strategy would violate buyers' participation constraints. Since the quantity that the buyer will purchase from the monopolist (if the buyer does so at all) is known, the *ex ante* contract is equivalent to a call option on the quantity equal to the buyer's demand at an exercise price given by the monopolist's cost. The exercise price is the monopolist's cost of producing this quantity, and the option price is the fixed fee in the two-part pricing scheme.

If we believe that the Chicago benchmark assumptions describe the world in any particular case of long-term contracts, then we would have to explain the contracts as motivated by something other than an attempt to suppress competition. This would have to be an efficiency explanation.

A simpler explanation of the connection between the set of assumptions above and the Chicago view, which highlights the logic underpinning our discussion going forward, is that, under these assumptions, the downstream buyers and the monopolist are the only agents in the model that earn a positive surplus. There can be no externalities to parties outside the contracts. Since the contractual parties are the only agents that earn a positive surplus and since they can exchange lump-sum transfers (via changes in the fixed fee), whatever contract or lack of contract is established must maximize the sum of the expected payoff to each of them. The Chicago position that contracts must maximize the wealth of contractual parties (and, therefore, that government regulation of contracts is uncalled for) would be perfectly valid in a world in which agents outside the contracting parties operate in perfectly competitive markets.

*Theories of Contracts as Entry Deterrence*

AGHION-BOLTON I
Aghion and Bolton (1987), in a classic contribution, offer a theory that shows that even simple long-term contracts can be anticompetitive. Referring to the general structure (Figure 3.1), consider the following assumptions, which we can call Aghion-Bolton I:

- The upstream market for inputs is competitive.
- There is a single entrant.
- Buyers purchase 0 units or 1 unit.

The incumbent can make an *ex ante* offer consisting of a price $p$ and a stipulated damage $d$ that is paid if the buyer exits the contract *ex post*.

The *ex post* game is Bertrand if a long-term contract has not been signed; if a long-term contract exists, the entrant *ex post* can make a take-it-or-leave-it offer to each buyer.

It is enough under these assumptions to consider a single buyer. The Aghion-Bolton structure represents a single departure from the Chicago benchmark: market power (hence the possibility of profits) on the part of the entrant. The assumption that buyers purchase 0 units or 1 unit is simplifying and makes an exclusivity restriction redundant.

Aghion and Bolton show that, under these assumptions, the incumbent and the buyer will strike a contract that deters entry even in states where entry is efficient because the entrant's cost is lower. The effect is a reduction in total surplus, with the key argument being that the *ex ante* contract will impose an externality on the entrant (which, because it makes profits in some states of the world, is vulnerable to the externality). The contract struck between only two of the three agents in the model, imposing an externality on the third, will be inefficient.

To develop this argument, note that the following is a general contract with parameters $p$, $d$.[9] The contract calls for the buyer to purchase the unit for a price $p$, and if the buyer decides *ex post* to exit the contract, the buyer pays the incumbent a stipulated damage of $d$. When the entrant's cost are low enough that it will enter the market successfully, it must offer a price low enough to attract the buyer away from the incumbent's contract – that is, a price lower than $p - d$, since $d$ represents an opportunity cost to the buyer of leaving the long-term contract. The incumbent and the buyer pair therefore recognizes that each one-dollar increase in $d$ represents a transfer to the pair in the states in which entry by the new firm is inframarginal.

We can describe the Aghion-Bolton contract in payoff-equivalent terms as follows: the buyer pays $d$ up front for the option to pay an additional $p - d$ to buy *ex post*. This is precisely a call-option contract, with exercise price $p - d$ and option price $d$.

An exercise price $p - d$ in the Aghion-Bolton call option that were exactly equal to the incumbent's unit cost $c$ would achieve maximum total surplus in the market, since it would ensure that the buyer chose to purchase from the incumbent only when the incumbent's cost were the lower of the two costs in the market. (Having the lower-cost firm produce *ex post* is the single efficiency condition in this simple model.)

The key implication of the Aghion-Bolton theory, however, is that the optimal contract – that is, the optimal call option – involves an exercise price *below* the incumbent's unit cost. A monopolist or monopsonist in any market would like to do two things: maximize surplus and maximize the share of total surplus that it captures. The buyer and seller pair lowers the exercise price below the efficient level – that is, below the incumbent's cost – because they trade off these two goals. The envelope theorem guarantees that the first-order effect on the total surplus of the drop in the exercise price below the efficient level is zero – so the contracting pair accepts the drop in the total surplus in favour of an increase in the transfer from the entrant in all inframarginal entry states of the world.[10] As Aghion and Bolton show, the incumbent-buyer pair acts exactly as a monopsonist setting an *ex ante* price to the entrant with a supply curve generated by the distribution of its uncertain cost. The exercise price set in the Aghion-Bolton call option is exactly the *ex ante* price that the pair establishes *ex ante* for the entrant's unit of supply, and just as a conventional monopsonist sets an inefficiently low price, so does the contracting pair.

With the single change in assumptions from the Chicago benchmark – market power on the part of the entrant – the optimal contract thus remains a call option, but with an exercise price *below* the efficient level, the incumbent's unit cost.

The Aghion-Bolton I model has been criticized on several grounds. It assumes away renegotiation between the contracting parties after the offer of a price by an entrant. Any model of a market with inefficiencies, however, assumes some kind of barrier to Coasian contracting to complete efficiency. A possible barrier to such contracting in general – and, as Bolton and Dewatripont (2005, 610) point out, a barrier to efficient renegotiation in their model – is asymmetric information. The model also yields the unrealistic result that the incumbent monopolist earns a higher return in the event of entry when it receives $d$ than in the event of no entry (when a high realization of the entrant's cost precludes entry), when its profit is $p - c$, where $c$ is the incumbent's unit cost.[11] This admittedly is a peculiar implication of a model that we are describing as a theory of strategic entry deterrence. And the damage level $d > p - c$ violates the constraint under the penalty doctrine of U.S. common law, which stipulates that damages not be greater than lost profits. Nonetheless, Aghion-Bolton I is exactly the right model to capture the incentive for long-term, entry-deterring contracts that flow through transfers extracted (or externalities imposed) on the entrant.

EXCLUSION VIA THE EXPLOITATION OF HORIZONTAL EXTERNALITIES
AMONG BUYERS

Consider the following alternative departure from the Chicago benchmark:

- The upstream market for inputs is competitive.
- Each buyer purchases 0 units or 1 unit and has a common value $v$ for the product.
- There are at least two entrants, sharing identical – and known – costs.
- Entrants' costs consist of a fixed cost and a constant unit cost. The fixed cost is large enough that an entrant could not cover costs by selling to any one buyer at the buyer's full value. The fixed cost, however, is not incurred until after a contract is offered by the entrant and accepted by a buyer.

- Contract offers, *ex ante* and *ex post*, are specific to each buyer – that is, price discrimination is allowed. Contracts commit the buyer to purchasing 1 unit, and the *ex ante* contract is enforced – that is, it does not include an option for the buyer to leave the contract for a stipulated damage.
- The *ex post* game pricing for uncommitted buyers is Bertrand, with price offers being made to free buyers by entrants and by the incumbent

This set of assumptions seems like a mild departure from the Chicago benchmark: the set of entrants is not a perfectly competitive set of suppliers – but it is a *contestable* set of suppliers. (Any market in which binding contracts can be struck with buyers prior to expenditure on fixed costs by suppliers is contestable.) Price will be driven down in the *ex post* pricing game to the realized average cost of supplying all buyers by an entrant (evaluated at a quantity equal to the number of free buyers) because any entrant stands ready to offer a price equal to average cost. Because entrants earn no profits, no externalities can possibly be imposed on them.

The externalities that lead to anticompetitive (that is, inefficient) contracts under this set of assumptions are *horizontal* externalities, across buyers. Because the entrants and suppliers earn zero profits whatever happens, these are the only externalities under the assumptions outlined above. The idea is that entry is possible only if there are enough buyers free of any long-term contractual obligations to cover potential entrants' fixed costs. A single buyer gains nothing from rejecting an *ex ante* contract offer if all other buyers accept the contract because that buyer alone would not be enough to attract a superior offer from an entrant. 'Accept' by all buyers is therefore a Nash equilibrium in acceptance decisions. One Nash equilibrium for the entire game – contract offer, acceptance decision, *ex post* pricing – therefore, is the offer of a long-term contract at the buyers' common value $v$. The right to make the first offer, which is assumed to flow from incumbency, allows the incumbent to extract the entire surplus in this equilibrium, even when faced with the threat of entry by a set of more efficient firms.

The idea of exploiting horizontal externalities among buyers in order to establish profitable exclusionary contracts is due to Aghion and Bolton, in section 3 of their classic 1987 paper, although Salop (1986) discusses the externalities (which he terms 'reverse free riding') in a related contractual setting. Aghion and Bolton use a model with (1) random entry costs; (2) a single entrant; and (3) contracts with each buyer that depend on whether an offer is made to another buyer. All of these elements add to the complexity of the analysis, which adopts a specific functional form; the second element, in particular, means that the model mixes in the horizontal-buyers'-externalities incentive for exclusionary contracts with the Aghion-Bolton I theory of extracting rents from the entrant. Rasmussen, Ramseyer, and Wiley (1991) adopt a model in which buyers are paid an amount *ex ante* for agreeing not to buy from the entrant (what they call a 'naked exclusion'); in which each identical buyer has a downward-sloping demand and faces a monopoly price *ex post* in the event of exclusion because the monopolist cannot commit *ex ante* to a long-term price; and in which technology is described by constant average costs past a minimum efficient scale. The authors have the clearest expression of the buyer-externality basis for exclusion in the abstract of their paper:

> Ordinarily, a monopoly cannot increase its profits by asking customers to sign agreements not to deal with potential competitors. If however, there are 100 customers and the minimum efficient scale requires serving 15, the monopoly need only lock up 86 customers to forestall entry. If each customer believes that the others will sign, each also believes that no rival seller will enter. Hence, an individual customer loses nothing by signing the exclusionary agreement and will indeed sign. Thus, naked exclusion can be profitable.

Rasmussen, Ramseyer, and Wiley claim that their model yields two possible equilibria: all buyers sign and no buyers sign. Segal and Whinston (2000) show, however, that the latter outcome is an equilibrium in the Rasmussen-Ramseyer-Wiley model only when no discrimination is possible in contract offers to buyers.[12] Whinston and Segal show that, when price discrimination is allowed, the incumbent always finds it profitable to exclude in the Rasmussen-Ramseyer-Wiley model. The prediction of exclusivity in the Rasmussen-Ramseyer-Wiley model is thus stronger than the authors recognize.

The role of price discrimination is clear in the much simpler model I outlined above, which is analysed in detail in Jing and Winter (2008). The game has three stages: in the first stage, the offer of long-term contracts by the incumbent, possibly with different prices to a subset of buyers; in the second stage, simultaneous accept or reject decisions by buyers; and, in the third stage, simultaneous price offers by potential entrants and the incumbent to free (noncommitted) buyers. The third stage is simple: the market price is the minimum of the incumbent's unit cost and the average cost of entrants, and a single supplier – an entrant, if entrants' average cost over the set of free buyers is lower than the incumbent's cost, otherwise the incumbent. After *some* sets of price offers, the set of Nash equilibria of the acceptance subgame will include enough rejections to render viable the offer by entrants of a price less than the buyers' value $v$ of the product in the *ex post* game. But we show that, for the incumbent, any such set of price offers (and rejection decisions) is dominated by a set of price offers – to enough buyers to render entry nonviable – that make 'accept' a dominant strategy for each buyer that is offered the contract. This strategy does require that the average cost of entrants over all buyers exceeds some lower bound – that is, that entrants not be too cost efficient – but this lower bound is less than the monopolist's unit cost. In other words, the first-mover advantage that we assume comes with incumbency allows the incumbent to pre-empt the competitive discipline or entry by potential entrants even when entrants are more efficient.[13]

THE EXPLOITATION OF VERTICAL EXTERNALITIES

Suppose we drop the assumption that there are many buyers, to rule out the horizontal channel for the incentive for exclusionary contracts; require the single buyer to be a contract taker or price taker, to rule out any downstream monopsony power; bring back competitive entry to rule Aghion-Bolton I (the extraction of contingent rents from the potential entrant); and also bring back the assumption of uncertain costs. This takes us back to the Chicago benchmark, with a single price-taking buyer.[14]

Now we introduce a different departure from the benchmark: the possibility of profits *upstream*, via a single-input supplier. This leaves us with the following set of assumptions:

- A single supplier provides the upstream input.
- A single price-taking downstream buyer purchases the final output.
- Entrants into the intermediate market are competitive price takers, sharing a common realization of costs.

To understand why this structure generates an incentive for entry-deterring contracts, let us start with the following obvious point. Any long-term (*ex ante*) contract an incumbent monopolist offers to an agent at another stage of a supply chain must meet the agent's individual rationality constraint if it is to be accepted. This constraint depends on the probability of entry; the threat of relying on entry is the only source of power the agent has to extract some share of rents in the contract. Any sort of entry-deterring strategy that the incumbent has adopted elsewhere in the supply chain will relax this individual rationality (IR) constraint and allow the monopolist to collect a larger share of the rents – that is, to charge a higher price in the *ex ante* contract. *When the entry-deterring strategy elsewhere in the supply chain is itself a long-term contract, the two contracts are complementary, each serving to relax the IR constraint in the other by reducing the probability of entry.*

Jing and Winter (2008) develop this argument formally, showing that the dual-contracting strategy indeed dominates single or no-contracting strategies. The effect is that entry fails to occur even in some states of the world where it would be efficient. The pair of vertical externalities working along the supply chain is analogous to the set of horizontal externalities in the horizontal externalities model: the single buyer and single upstream supplier would be better off rejecting the offer, but find it individually optimal to accept the exclusionary contract.

EXTERNALITIES OVER TIME

All three theories of contracts as entry deterrence adopt the Aghion-Bolton perspective of characterizing anticompetitive (inefficient) contracts in terms of the externalities imposed on parties outside the contract – that is, extracting transfers from these extracontractual agents. But these are all static, or nearly static, models. In many of the most prominent cases of exclusionary conduct, it is clearly the *dynamic* effects of exclusion that are the most important and contentious. In the various cases against Microsoft and Intel, the static models cannot capture the allegations. The arguments in these cases revolve around the theme that the dominant firm is benefiting from excluding rivals, not just for the additional profit that it can extract from current technology, but also for the gains from protecting or solidifying the firm's position in the technology race so that it can reap the rewards of profit in future markets.

The theories outlined above all have a simple temporal structure: the incumbent pre-empts future entry by offering contracts prior to the entrants' having an opportunity to enter. *Ex post*, the only 'state variable' that affects the current market equilibrium is the set of long-term contracts to which agents are committed. In reality, exclusionary contracts affect current market shares, which affect a firm's rate of product and process innovation, which, in turn, affects future costs, products, and market shares. The impact of market shares on innovation stems from at least two features of markets and innovation: learning by doing – that is, the enhanced rate of product improvement and cost reduction that is possible for a firm that invests in the knowledge required for current production – and greater flow of internal capital. Innovation tends to be financed much more with internal capital than other expenditures, for good reason.

This dynamic gives rise to a new set of externalities that can explain exclusionary contracts, beyond those in the theories outlined so far. When a buyer and an incumbent dominant firm enter into an exclusive contract in a dynamic setting with innovation, they impose a cost on *future buyers* in the market. The reduction in market share of the incumbent's rival (possibly to zero) increases the probability that the incumbent will discover the next stage of the technology and, therefore, that the incumbent will obtain a larger market share in the future. The next generation of buyers bears the cost of this. The current buyer and dominant firm, as a team, extract rents from future buyers via the exclusionary contract. The pair would also extract rents from the future rival, but this effect is already captured in the Aghion-Bolton model. Without commenting on the merits of any particular case, I note that, in high-tech markets, the distortions arising from the dampening of competition in the race for new technology could have a much greater social cost than distortions in prices.[15]

The idea that exclusive dealing might be used to foreclose a market to a rival supplier because of a transfer to the supplier from noncontractual parties in another market, separated in time, is due to Bernheim and Whinston (1998). They analyse exclusive dealing at a retailer, and consider a model in which two retail markets develop sequentially and in which manufacturers must serve more than one market to achieve the necessary economies. Exclusion may occur in this model because, as Bernheim and Whinston explain, exclusion affects the degree of competition among manufacturers in the second market and, therefore, the amount of rents that the second retailer (which is not a party to the contract) is able to extract in the second market. The exclusionary contract is a means by which the contractual parties extract rent from the future retailer.

Gilbert (2000) considers various models of exclusive dealing that also incorporate dynamic efficiency effects, especially on the incentive of a rival firm to enter into a future market. The fundamental externalities at work in Gilbert's theory are dynamic externalities.

EXCLUSIONARY CONTRACTS AS INSTRUMENTS FOR HORIZONTAL COMBINATION

None of the theories developed above, nor the Aghion-Bolton perspective, should distract us from perhaps the simplest of all theories of anticompetitive, exclusionary contracts. Suppose that there is a fixed number of upstream suppliers of the essential input that compete on price and that there are complete barriers to entry into the production of more of the input. Suppose, further, that the incumbent and the rival (which might already be in the market) offer very close substitutes. Then, in the entire industry, absent any exclusive contracts, the total economic profits are very small because of competition in both the intermediate and the upstream markets. If the incumbent purchases the exclusive rights to all upstream suppliers, however, then a monopoly is created at that stage of production – just as if all the suppliers had merged. With a monopoly at one stage of production in a supply chain, it might be possible to realize full monopoly profits for the entire supply chain.

Of course, the purchaser of exclusive rights to upstream inputs must deal with the potential problem of hold out, whereby each upstream supplier and the downstream rival generally have the incentive to strike a contract for the exchange of exclusive rights at a price higher than that offered by the incumbent monopolist if the two downstream products are not perfect substitutes. (For example, if there are ten symmetric upstream suppliers, the most that the incumbent could pay for the exclusive rights to each supplier would be one-tenth of monopoly profits downstream, but this amount might be less than the profits that a rival would earn as a duopolist with the rights to a single upstream firm.) But hold-out problems arise in many kinds of economic transactions, from corporate takeovers to land development, and are resolved at least to some extent in practice.

The externality leading to inefficiency in this theory is simply the cost imposed on downstream buyers from the monopoly established upstream. Monopolization through exclusive contracts carries the same cost to buyers as monopolization through other means. The efficiency cost of the contracts is the monopoly distortion in prices.

**Extensions and Related Developments**

*Renegotiation*

In each theory of exclusionary contracts presented so far, there is necessarily an incentive to renegotiate the contract *ex post*. Each setting results in the possibility of production by the incumbent even when it was not the lower-cost producer. This is the sense in which there is anticompetitive entry deterrence. In any market setting where there is inefficiency, there is scope for negotiation or contracting to reach the first best allocation of resources (Coase 1960). If parties could renegotiate costlessly, the inefficiency would disappear.

In the Aghion-Bolton model, for example, when the realized entrant's cost, $c_e$ is in $(p - d, c)$, then the entrant would buy from the incumbent, since paying the exercise price of the call option, $p - d$, is better for the buyer than paying the entrant. But if the entrant were to offer a price in $(p - d, c)$, then, for the buyer-incumbent pair, accepting the entrant's offer is the lowest-cost means of obtaining the product, and the two will renegotiate the contract if possible. As Masten and Snyder (1989) first observed, the Aghion-Bolton prediction of entry deterrence disappears if renegotiation is introduced into the model. Similarly, in the vertical-externality theory, if the buyer and seller could get together *ex post* and negotiate with an entrant and renegotiate with the incumbent, the *ex post* inefficiency would disappear.

The vulnerability of these models to renegotiation does not negate their value as a theoretical basis for hypotheses in competition law cases. Contract theory, starting with the simplest principal-agent model, is full of assumptions of no renegotiation. More to the point, the context of each case must be examined to understand whether renegotiation is plausible. In a case such as *Nielsen*, which I discuss below, renegotiation of all contracts to eliminate *ex post* inefficiencies would be inconceivable, and the value of the portfolio of theories in delineating the sources of incentive for exclusionary contracts stands [16]

Nonetheless, it is valuable to ask whether the Aghion-Bolton model can be extended in a way that leaves the prediction robust to renegotiation. This is among the questions Spier and Whinston (1995) address. They introduce into the model an investment by the incumbent in specific assets. This investment, which is noncontractible, takes place after the incumbent and the buyer sign the contract and has the effect of reducing the incumbent's unit cost. The Spier-Whinston model has the following timing: the incumbent and buyer sign a contract $(p, d)$; the incumbent undertakes specific investment, $r$, which results in cost of production $c(r)$; the entrant makes an offer, $p_e$ to the buyer; the incumbent and the buyer renegotiate their contract; and, finally, the buyer chooses which contract to accept and the agreed-upon transaction takes place.

Spier and Whinston show that, in this model, the Aghion-Bolton prediction of inefficient entry deterrence is restored. Two observations are key to understanding this result. First, anticipating the possibility of renegotiation, the entrant makes an offer equal to the incumbent's cost, $c(r)$, in all states where its own realized cost is lower. The incumbent-buyer pair therefore anticipates a marginal benefit of investment equal to the reduction in the entrant's price, $\partial c/\partial r$, in all states in which the entrant's realized cost is lower. The pair again extracts rent from the entrant, in all inframarginal entry states, through an increase in investment, $r$, if they can write a contract that induces one of them, the incumbent, to make the investment. Note that because the benefit of rent extraction is a private, not a social, benefit, the contracting pair has an incentive to induce an excessive level of specific investment. The second observation is that the contracting pair can indeed induce higher specific investment: an increase in the damage component, $d$, of the contract increases the share of the gains from renegotiation accruing to the incumbent because it represents a transfer of contractual rights from the buyer to the incumbent – rights for which the incumbent must then be compensated in the renegotiation.

In short, renegotiation in the basic Aghion-Bolton model negates the effect of anticompetitive entry deterrence, but the presence of noncontractible specific investment by the incumbent restores the effect. Note that, conditional on the investment by the incumbent, entry is efficient in the Spier-Whinston model: entry occurs only if the entrant's realized cost is less than $c(r)$. The entire entry-deterrence effect is through the inducement of excessive specific investment.

*Competition among Downstream Buyers*

Throughout the discussion, starting with the basic framework, I have assumed that there are no direct externalities among buyers' choice of contract. That is, the payoff to each buyer depends only on the contract struck between the buyer and the incumbent, or between the buyer and the entrant, depending on which of these sellers supplies the buyer[17] This is plausible if buyers are final consumers; in the literature prior to Fumagalli and Motta (2006), this is the standard assumption, despite the fact that all major exclusive dealing cases are in intermediate markets.

Fumagalli and Motta consider the case of an intermediate market in which downstream buyers are suppliers that compete intensively in the downstream market. A single buyer supplying this downstream market, if it purchases from an upstream entrant at a low cost, can expand its output downstream to capture a large share of this market, taking advantage of its low input price. This translates into a substantial derived demand by the single downstream firm for the upstream input at a price lower than the incumbent's cost if the single downstream firm is the only buyer from the entrant upstream. The result is that even the single buyer is enough to support entry into the upstream market. The potential for using exclusive contracts in an anticompetitive way crucially depends on the intensity of competition in downstream markets. Fumagalli and Motta conclude that, if competition in downstream markets is intense, exclusive dealing will not be an instrument for foreclosure.

Fumagalli and Motta's argument rests on an assumption that intense competition downstream – which one could describe alternatively as very high elasticity of firm demand downstream – is sufficient for a high elasticity upstream. In other words, an entrant that offers a price to a single buyer that is lower than the price available from the incumbent will face a large demand, and one that is sufficient to cover its costs. Recall, however, the Hicks-Marshall determinants of the factors that determine the elasticity of derived demand (Marshall's 'four laws of the elasticity of derived demand'). The elasticity of final product demand is only one such factor. Others are the proportion of the factor expenditure in total expenditure on inputs, the substitutability of the factor with other factors, and the elasticity of supply of the other factors. In the case I outline below (in which there are two levels of exclusionary contracts), the downstream competing suppliers are grocery manufacturers and the intermediate input is marketing information about the products. For a company such as General Mills, for example, the expenditure on marketing information is a small proportion of total cost. Hence Marshall's 'third law of the elasticity of derived demand' applies and, despite competition downstream, the elasticity of derived demand is not necessarily high. The various economic theories of exclusionary contracts are not negated by competition downstream.

*Common Law Constraints on Breach Penalties*

Simpson and Wickelgren (2007) observe that, under U.S. common law, each party to a contract has the option of performing its contractual duties or breaching the contract and paying expectation damages, which are the profit that the other party was anticipating from the contract. Stipulated penalties, in other words, cannot exceed lost profits. This constraint, Simpson and Wickelgren argue, implies that the horizontal buyers' externalities theory developed by Aghion-Bolton, Rasmussen-Ramseyer-Wiley, and Segal-Whinston cannot hold when buyers are final consumers. On the other hand, Simpson and Wickelgren claim that, when breach with expectation damages is an available option, exclusive contracts can deter entry if buyers are downstream competitors. In other words, the law against excessive stipulated damages (the 'penalty doctrine' in contract law) reverses the understanding from the literature after Fumagalli and Motta (2006), which had been that exclusionary contracts are possible when buyers are final consumers but not when they are downstream competitors.

The common law constraint against excessive penalties, however, is easily circumvented. Instead of a contract in which the buyer makes no payment prior to its signing, as the literature assumes, the parties can simply adjust the contract so that the buyer makes a one-time payment up front. This is most clearly developed in the Aghion-Bolton model, where the buyer pays damages $d > p - c$ in the optimal contract, thus violating the common law limit on damages. But the buyer and seller can circumvent the constraint by having the buyer pay a fixed fee *ex ante*, $d$, for the right to purchase at a price $p - d$. In other words, the contracting pair can adjust the timing to match the call option contract that I described as equivalent to the Aghion-Bolton contract. No law requires a refund of a price paid by a buyer that finds a better deal. The same argument applies to the horizontal buyers' externalities theory of exclusionary contracts.

In short, the economic theory of incentives for exclusionary contracts remains intact, whether downstream buyers are final consumers or intermediate suppliers. These contracts are designed to transfer rents from non-contracting parties to a contracting party, and the various theories are usefully categorized into the five types of externalities or transfers that can explain the practice. I turn next to a case application of the theories.

**Case Application: *Nielsen***

The background to the *Nielsen* case[18] involved the market for information obtained from infrared checkout scanners in ten regional Canadian grocery store chains – including market shares, estimates of elasticities of demand and responsiveness of product sales to various promotion strategies, and projections of the impact of various marketing strategies – and sold to large downstream grocery producers such as General Mills, Kellogg, and Proctor and Gamble.[19] In the summer of 1986, at a time when Nielsen was the incumbent monopolist in the market,[20] Information Resources Incorporated (IRI) of Chicago attempted to enter the Canadian market. IRI and Nielsen had operated as a duopoly in the United States, with approximately equal market shares.

Evidence in the case showed that upstream raw data inputs were complementary, in the sense that a full range of data from grocery chains across the country was an important source of value in the downstream product. Evidence also showed that, conditional upon the same raw data inputs, the Nielsen and IRI products (or potential products, in terms of the Canadian market) were similar but not identical – a feature one can label as low inherent product differentiation. In short, upstream products were complementary; downstream products were substitutes.

The case involved a challenge by the Canadian competition authority, the Director of Investigation and Research (now called the Commissioner of Competition), of two sets of Nielsen contracts. Nielsen had entered into five-year exclusive contracts with all of the upstream grocery suppliers of scanner data in 1986, which contained liquidated damage clauses and prohibited the sale of scanner data to any other party.[21] With these exclusive contracts in place, IRI did not find it profitable to enter, and Nielsen maintained its monopoly over this period. With the threat of entry starting in 1985, Nielsen had also entered into long-term (three-to-five-year) contracts with a set of downstream buyers (grocery product manufacturers); until then, at least in those contracts entered as evidence, Nielsen's downstream contracts had been evergreen ones that were terminable on eight months' notice. The challenge of both sets of contracts by the Director of Investigation and Research before the Canadian Competition Tribunal was successful, and both sets were struck down, largely on the basis of arguments developed below.[22]

An explanation of Nielsen's upstream contracts might start with the assumption that I have carried throughout this paper: that the incumbent has an inherent first-mover advantage in offering contracts. This assumption, however, is less defensible in the context of contracts with upstream-input suppliers than with buyers – and, as a factual matter, IRI was the first to offer the contracts to upstream suppliers. Consider a bidding contest between two downstream firms over the rights (exclusive or not) to upstream inputs. Assume, as in *Nielsen*, that the bidding must take the form of simple payments for the rights, conditioned on whether the rights are exclusive or not – rather than competition on the basis of contracts, as in the Bernheim-Whinston (1998) model of exclusive rights at a single downstream retailer. Jing and Winter (2008) show that, if a pure strategy equilibrium exists in this model (taking, as Bernheim and Whinston do, the Pareto-dominant equilibrium among any multiple Nash equilibria as the equilibrium concept), the equilibrium satisfies the Bernheim-Whinston condition of maximizing the sum of aggregate profits. In the case of strong product *substitutability* downstream and input *complementarity* upstream, this means that the equilibrium in the bidding game allocates all inputs to a single downstream firm.[23] The substitutability/complementarity condition holds in the set of the upstream and downstream markets in *Nielsen* and, as the theory predicts, the rights to all inputs were won by a single firm. Under the conditions of this case, a downstream monopoly is the inevitable outcome of bidding for rights to upstream inputs. The Competition Tribunal accepted this argument, and nullified the exclusive contracts.

The effect of the bidding 'for the right to be the monopolist' is that much of the prospective rents from the downstream monopoly were shifted upstream to the owners of the scare resources, the scanner data. Only to the extent that Nielsen had an asymmetric advantage in the bidding game would it be able to share in the rents.

Some of the most interesting strategic interactions in the contest for the rights to upstream inputs involved dynamics, going beyond our assumption of simultaneous bids. The bids were not simultaneous. In fact, IRI, the entrant, had secured all but one of the suppliers of raw data in long-term contracts that would have self-destructed if insufficient suppliers had been signed up. The final supplier was then in a position to command a high bid for its raw data. Nielsen won the contest for acquiring the final supplier's data, and IRI's exclusive contracts unravelled. After Nielsen had won all the exclusive contracts, with identical five-year contracts, it faced a repeat of the bidding contest with IRI in 1991, with the monopoly rents again flowing upstream to the owners of the scarce inputs. Nielsen then renegotiated a contract with a major supplier, thus using staggered contracts that re-established the power of incumbency and shifted the share of prospective rents in any future exclusive contracts back downstream to itself. Why would a major supplier engage in recontracting, staggered contract terms, and a shift in the share of rents back downstream? The answer lies clearly in contract externalities. The recontracting supplier would bear only part of the cost to suppliers of the shift in the share of rents and so the recontracting served to extract rents from the other upstream suppliers.

The downstream contracts with buyers matched the predictions of the economic theory that I have outlined. The terms of these contracts jumped from less than one year (terminable on a few months' notice) to three to five years as soon as IRI attempted to enter the industry. Nielsen's internal documents read as if the management had just read an early version of Aghion and Bolton (1987). These documents indicated that the strategic purpose of the shift in contract lengths was to deter the entry of IRI by 'locking up' customers in long-term contracts that contained liquidated damages payable to Nielsen if customers terminated them. Nielsen did not induce all customers to sign long-term contracts; instead, it targeted the Canadian subsidiaries of U.S. customers of IRI, since Nielsen was most vulnerable to the loss of these clients.

The horizontal buyers' externalities theory applies here because each client would view the probability of IRI's entering – an event with positive value for the client – as almost unaffected by its own decision to accept the long-term contract. Only a small 'bribe' in terms of a lower price would be necessary to induce the client to sign the contract. The Aghion-Bolton theory applies here as well: the liquidated damages clause was not very costly to the downstream customer because damages would not be paid if IRI did not enter and the client were forced to remain with Nielsen anyway. More to the point, if IRI did enter (an event that would be essentially exogenous to the client), then, since the firm had small or zero marginal cost and would be negotiating prices with each client separately, much of the liquidated damages would be passed on to it.

Finally, a vertical externality also applies. The fact that Nielsen as the incumbent was able to strike the downstream contracts gave it an advantage over IRI in the upstream bidding game for the exclusive rights to the data: IRI's willingness to pay for the upstream data was surely reduced by the disadvantage it faced in overcoming the long-term contracts downstream. Those contracts thus imposed a negative externality, and extracted a transfer, from upstream suppliers in allowing Nielsen to win the upstream game with lower bids.

In short, three of the five theories of entry-deterring contracts were at play in the case: the horizontal collective action theory, the Aghion-Bolton theory of extracting rents from the potential rival, and the vertical externalities theory.

## Conclusion

Exclusive contracts are ubiquitous. A McDonald's franchisee must sell exclusively McDonald's products. An executive at Ford Motor Company cannot moonlight for General Motors. And a professor on sabbatical research leave cannot take a full-time teaching job at another university. Efficiency rationales for many exclusivity contracts are clear.[24] Efficiency rationales for long-term contracts, especially in protecting specific investment, are even more obvious. In any antitrust case on exclusionary practices, evidence for anticompetitive and efficiency uses must be analysed and the burden of proof must rest on the side of intervention.

In this chapter, I outlined the economic theory on one side of the case: why participants in a market might enter contracts that achieve anticompetitive entry deterrence. I started with a simple principle from contract theory: a contract must be explained as being in the interests of all contractual parties. The Aghion-Bolton perspective follows immediately: contract inefficiencies must be traceable to an externality or transfer imposed on agents outside the contract, to the benefit of parties inside the contract.[25] Incentives to adopt anticompetitive, entry-deterring strategies in the form of long-term contracts or exclusivity contracts can arise because of any of five different externalities or transfers imposed on parties outside the contracts. I synthesized the economic theory of these contracts by isolating each of the five sources of the incentive for entry-deterring contracts with a different set of assumptions. Each set of assumptions represents a different departure from a Chicago benchmark under which exclusive contracts are not exclusionary. The application of the theory to the *Nielsen* case illustrates the interaction of three of the five incentives outlined in the theory.

## NOTES

1 Curt Eaton's contributions to the entry literature include strategic models of entry (Eaton 1976; Eaton and Lipsey 1978, 1979a, 1979b, 1980, 1981; Eaton and Ware 1987; and Eaton and Wooders 1985). His contributions to applied contract theory are seen throughout his career, with the most fundamental contributions being Eaton and White (1982, 1983) and Eaton and Koss (1997).

2 See, for example, *Standard Oil Co. of Cal. v. United States* 337 U.S. 293 (1949); *Tampa Electric Co. v. Nashville Coal Co.* 365 U.S. 320 (1961); *U.S. v. Waste Management* (1996); *U.S. v. Microsoft* (1995 *Consent Decree*); *Canada ( Director of Investigation and Research ) v. The D & B Companies of Canada Ltd.* (1995), 64 C.P.R. (3d) 216 (Comp. Trib.) ('Nielsen'); and the matter currently involving Intel before the European Commission.

3 I am referring here especially to the oral tradition in the Chicago Law School associated with Aaron Director and including Robert Bork.

4 For example, the European Commission investigation into Intel's practices included a Statement of Objections sent to Intel on 26 July 2007 that the Commission's preliminary view was that Intel had infringed the EC Treaty rules on abuse of a dominant position (Article 82) with the aim of excluding its main rival, AMD, from the x86 Computer Processing Units (CPU) market (European Commission Press Release, 27 July 2007). Intel's practices to which the Commission objected included offering original equipment manufacturers' (OEMs') rebates provided that the OEMs sourced all or the great majority of their products from Intel, as well as payments to induce an OEM either to delay or to cancel the launch of a product line incorporating an AMD-based CPU.

5 See, for example, *Standard Oil Co. v. United States ( Standard Stations ) 337 U.S. 293 ( 1949 )* and *Tampa Electric.*

6 For some of the models below, the entrants' common costs are known.

7 This assumption rules out downstream externalities in the contracts established. If downstream buyers were competing firms, then a buyer's payoff would depend on the contracts (for example, prices) offered to other buyers.

I set aside this possibility in the analysis but discuss the extension below. Note that, in one of the models reviewed below, externalities distort buyers' acceptance decisions – but this is because the externalities affect each buyer's price and quantity. The assumption is that a buyer's preference is over his or her own price and quantity.

8  That is, the single element of real-world long-term contracts that I incorporate is the fact that these contracts are signed prior to spot-market contracts.

9  The following contract is general under the assumption that it cannot depend on the entrant's cost; for example, the cost is unobservable.

10  I describe the contracting pair as cooperatively maximizing its own wealth through increased transfers from the entrant. More precisely, the transfers are captured by the incumbent through the payment of the damage $d$. But this is irrelevant; it is clearer just to think of the contracting pair as maximizing its combined wealth.

11  The fact that $d > p - c$ follows from the fact that the exercise price $p - d$ is less than $c$.

12  The analysis of Rasmussen, Ramseyer, and Wiley (1991) is inconsistent, as they allow for price discrimination at some places in the development but not in others.

13  Because of the fixed costs of technology and the contestability nature of the market, the competitive discipline is entirely in the form of potential competition. Of course, this discipline might well be strong in the absence of exclusionary contracts.

14  The assumption of a single firm upstream and a single firm downstream also serves to rule out another conventional channel for exclusionary contract incentives: the offer of exclusive contracts to all firms at one stage of a vertical supply chain so as to ensure a monopoly at that stage (and, therefore, full monopoly profits for the system). This theory of horizontal combination through vertical contracts is ruled out because the assumptions guarantee there is a single firm upstream whatever contracts are signed.

15  The simplest formal model that isolates the externality on future buyers and the rival involves a market that operates over two periods: in the first, the incumbent has the right to make a long-term contract prior to the emergence of a rival; in the second, costs (or the probability of successful innovation) that, for either firm, depend on the firm's first-period market share. A structure of contestable entrants, or a competitive fringe, would isolate the externality on future buyers from the Aghion-Bolton externality on the rival. For a similar model, in the context of tying contracts as exclusionary, see Choi and Stefanidis (2001).

16 The horizontal buyers' externalities theory of exclusionary contracts is less vulnerable to the criticism that the equilibrium is not renegotiation proof, because the negotiation required would be across buyers, and there are costs, including legal constraints, for collective negotiation of terms with a supplier.

17 There are, of course, indirect externalities in acceptance decisions. For example, in the horizontal buyers' externalities theory, each buyer's payoff depends on the acceptance decisions of the other buyers.

18 *Canada (Director of Investigation and Research) v. The D & B Companies of Canada Ltd. (1995), 64 C.P.R. (3d) 216 (Comp.Trib.),*

19 The product is also sold back to retailers for their own purposes, especially to assist in inventory accounting, though I ignore this aspect here. Note also that the flow of information from 'upstream' to 'downstream' is the opposite direction of the flow of the main product in the industry, groceries.

20 I refer to Nielsen as the incumbent because it was established in the broad market for market-tracking services, but in fact scanner-based information products were in development in the mid-1980s. Nielsen introduced the full scanner-based information product in 1988, after the main events on which the case focused.

21 In fact, Nielsen and IRI competed for upstream data inputs on the basis of exclusive contracts.

22 I was the expert witness for the Director of Investigation and Research in this case.

23 The strong substitutability downstream favours the allocation of all inputs to one firm to avoid profit-decreasing price competition downstream; complementarity of inputs clearly favours the allocation of all inputs to the active firms, rather than a mix of exclusive allocations to two firms, so as to maximize the market value of the final products.

24 The most frequently argued efficiency explanations for exclusive dealing are the prevention of free riding of various sorts (see Marvel 1982) and the creation of dedicated agents.

25 Note that this proposition, while true in the settings I have outlined here, is not perfectly general. Aghion and Hermalin (1990) develop a model in which legal restrictions on a contract can improve the welfare of the parties to the contract. If a party has an opportunity in the contractual relationship to signal its type, forgoing this opportunity is impossible. But signalling can be inefficient. *Ex ante* (before the type is known and the contract entered into), all agents might be better off if their future ability to signal within the contractual relationship is constrained by a legal restriction on the contract.

REFERENCES

Aghion, Philippe, and Benjamin Hermalin. 1990. 'Legal Restrictions on Private Contracts Can Enhance Efficiency.' *Journal of Law, Economics and Organization* 6 (2): 381–409.

Aghion, Philippe, and Patrick Bolton. 1987. 'Contracts as a Barrier to Entry.' *American Economic Review* 77 (3): 388–401.

Bernheim, B. Douglas, and Michael Whinston. 1998. 'Exclusive Dealing.' *Journal of Political Economy* 106 (1): 64–103.

Bolton, Patrick, and Mathias Dewatripont. 2005. *Contract Theory.* Cambridge, MA: MIT Press.

Bork, Robert H. 1976. *The Antitrust Paradox: A Policy at War with Itself.* Chicago: University of Chicago Press.

Choi, Jay, and Christodoulos Stefanadis. 2001. 'Tying, Investment, and the Dynamic Leverage Theory.' *RAND Journal of Economics* 32 (1): 52–71.

Coase, Ronald. 1960. 'The Problem of Social Cost.' *Journal of Law and Economics* 3 (1): 1–44.

Eaton, B. Curtis. 1976. 'Free Entry in One-Dimensional Models: Pure Profits and Multiple Equilibria.' *Journal of Regional Science* 16 (1): 21–33.

Eaton, B. Curtis, and Patricia Koss. 1997. 'Co-Specific Investments, Hold-up, and Self-Enforcing Contracts.' *Journal of Economic Behavior and Organization* 32 (3): 457–70.

Eaton, B. Curtis, and Richard G. Lipsey. 1978. 'Freedom of Entry and the Existence of Pure Profit.' *Economic Journal* 88 (351): 455–69.

– 1979a. 'Comparison Shopping and the Clustering of Homogeneous Firms.' *Journal of Regional Science* 19 (4): 421–35.

– 1979b. 'The Theory of Market Preemption: The Persistence of Excess Capacity and Monopoly in Growing Spatial Markets.' *Economica* 46 (182): 149–58.

– 1980. 'Exit Barriers Are Entry Barriers: The Durability of Capital as a Barrier to Entry.' *Bell Journal of Economics* 11 (2): 721–29.

– 1981. 'Capital, Commitment and Entry Equilibrium.' *Bell Journal of Economics* 12 (2): 593–604.

Eaton, B. Curtis, and Roger Ware. 1987. 'A Theory of Market Structure with Sequential Entry.' *RAND Journal of Economics* 18 (1): 1–16.

Eaton, B. Curtis, and William D. White. 1982. 'Agent Compensation and the Limits of Bonding.' *Economic Inquiry* 20 (3): 330–43.

– 1983. 'The Economy of High Wages: An Agency Problem.' *Economica* 50 (198): 175–81.

Eaton, B. Curtis, and Myrna Wooders. 1985. 'Sophisticated Entry in an Address Model of Monopolistic Competition.' *RAND Journal of Economics* 16 (2): 277–92.

Fumagalli, Chiara, and Massimo Motta. 2006. 'Exclusive Dealing and Entry, when Buyers Compete.' *American Economic Review* 96 (3): 785–95.

Gilbert, Richard. 2000. 'Exclusive Dealing, Preferential Dealing, and Dynamic Efficiency.' *Review of Industrial Organization* 16 (2): 167–84.

Jing, Ran, and Ralph A. Winter. 2008. 'Exclusionary Contracts.' Working paper, University of British Columbia.

Marvel, Howard P. 1982. 'Exclusive Dealing.' *Journal of Law and Economics* 25 (1): 1–25.

Masten, Scott, and Edward A. Snyder. 1989. 'The Design and Duration of Contracts: Strategic and Efficiency Considerations.' *Law and Contemporary Problems* 52 (1): 63–85.

Rasmussen, Eric, Mark J. Ramseyer, and John S. Wiley, Jr. 1991. 'Naked Exclusion.' *American Economic Review* 81 (5): 1137–45.

Salop, Steven C. 1986. 'Practices that (Credibly) Facilitate Oligopoly Co-ordination.' In *New Developments in the Analysis of Market Structure,* edited by Joseph E. Stiglitz and G. Frank Mathewson. Cambridge, MA: MIT Press.

Segal, Ilya R., and Michael Whinston. 2000. 'Naked Exclusion: Comment.' *American Economic Review* 90 (1): 296–309.

Simpson, John, and Abraham Wickelgren. 2007. 'Naked Exclusion, Efficient Breach, and Downstrea m Competition.' *American Economic Review* 97 (4): 1305–20.

Spier, Kathryn E., and Michael D. Whinston. 1995. 'On the Efficiency of Privately Stipulated Damages for Breach of Contract: Entry Barriers, Reliance and Renegotiation.' *RAND Journal of Economics* 26 (2): 180–202.

# 4 The Spatial Evolution of Alberta's Privatized Liquor Store Industry

ANDREW ECKERT AND DOUGLAS S. WEST

In a 1977 paper, Eaton and Lipsey discussed the research program they had initiated several years previously and identified two themes: that economic activity is a spatial phenomenon, and that it is characterized by physical and temporal indivisibilities. Incorporating these assumptions into economic models allowed Eaton and Lipsey to produce a series of papers that enhanced our understanding of structure and conduct in real markets. Commencing with extensions of the hotelling model (Eaton and Lipsey 1975), they further employed spatial competition analysis to help us understand the formation of shopping centres (Eaton and Lipsey 1979a, 1982) and the possibilities for strategic locational behaviour on the part of firms (Eaton and Lipsey 1979b). Their work was clearly motivated by their personal observations of structure and conduct in retail markets. Perhaps because of their desire to fashion theories that explained what they observed, their theories of pre-emption and central places have generated testable implications that have been examined in papers by West (1981) and West, Von Hohenbalken, and Kroner (1985), respectively.

Eaton and Lipsey's applied spatial analysis also provided some of the theory underlying empirical examinations of spatial predation (Von Hohenbalken and West 1984); retail demand in rural Saskatchewan (Wensley and Stabler 1998); and competition among gas stations (Netz and Taylor 2002; Eckert and West 2005), airlines (Borenstein and Netz 1999), fertilizers (Shaw 1982), computers (Stavins 1995), microprocessors (Swann 1985), and chemical products (Lieberman 1987) in space.

One body of empirical literature in which location should have a prominent role concerns industry evolution and firm survival. Surprisingly, however, much of this literature is formally spaceless.[1] Given this shortcoming in the literature and the established importance of location in understanding market structure and conduct in various industries, we included a number of spatial variables in our econometric analysis of firm survival and chain growth in Alberta's privatized liquor store industry (Eckert and West 2008). Using annual observations of the names and locations of all liquor stores operating in Calgary and Edmonton from December 1995 to December 2005, we found that location – in particular, whether a liquor store is located in a shopping centre or near a supermarket – is associated with the store's survival. Building on that earlier work, in this paper we examine the evolution of Alberta's privatized retail liquor store industry, with particular focus on the industry in towns and cities other than Calgary and Edmonton. We wish to determine whether that evolution can be explained by one of three conjectures: a free entry/rapid approach to long-run equilibrium, pre-emption, or S-curve entry.

In the course of examining these conjectures, we derive stylized facts regarding how the liquor store industry outside of Calgary and Edmonton has evolved. To anticipate our results, there is little support for the first two conjectures. We find that the liquor store industry took longer to evolve to what might be its long-run equilibrium in locations than would be expected if such evolution had been constrained only by retail space limitations and government delays. With respect to pre-emption, there is some evidence that neighbour relations matter in the expansion of liquor store chains, but that expansion took considerably longer than might have been expected. The data are more consistent with the S-curve entry conjecture – in particular, with delayed entry to learn about the market and the population necessary to support new stores.

In the next section, we summarize the theoretical predictions we examine in this paper. We follow this by describing the data we used in the empirical analysis, and by reporting summary statistics. We then present the empirical results. In the final section, we present a summary and concluding remarks.

**Industry Evolution in a Privatized Spatial Market**

Prior to September 1993, all full-service liquor stores in Alberta were owned and operated by the provincial government through the Alberta Liquor Control Board (ALCB). At the time of the announcement (on 2 September 1993) that liquor retailing in Alberta would be privatized, there were 205 ALCB stores, 47 of which were in the province's two largest cities (Edmonton and Calgary). There were also 53 private wine and cold beer stores, 35 of which were in Edmonton and Calgary.[2] In all, 153 Alberta cities and towns were served by ALCB stores; in 146 of them, there was just a single store.

In privatizing liquor retailing in Alberta, the government adopted a model whereby beverage alcohol was to be sold in liquor stores that had 90 percent of their sales in beer, wine, and liquor products. Under the *Alberta Gaming and Liquor Act*, stores were to be operated as separate from any affiliated business, with no cross marketing or joint advertising permitted.[3] The government also mandated uniform wholesale prices: all liquor stores in Alberta would have access to the same wholesale price list, which is permitted to change every two weeks. Retailers would not be allowed to negotiate discounts with suppliers, but they would be permitted to set their own retail prices.

The privatization of liquor retailing in Alberta gives us a unique opportunity to study the evolution of a retail industry that became, without prior warning, 'up for grabs.'[4] While we have already studied the factors that contribute to the survival of liquor stores and firms in Edmonton and Calgary and the growth of retail chains (Eckert and West 2008), it is not clear that the industry will evolve in a similar way in the province's smaller cities, towns, and rural areas. The rest of Alberta offers a large number of local markets of varying sizes where the industry evolution could play out in different ways. Economic theory suggests several alternative conjectures regarding the characteristics of this evolution.

*Conjecture 1: Free entry, and a noncooperative and nonstrategic game.* Under this conjecture, firms compete to enter the market, and entry continues until an additional entrant expects negative profits from entering. The market quickly reaches a long-run equilibrium, given the size of the population and the costs of owning and operating a store.

This conjecture assumes that, once privatization was announced and a licensing process put in place, there were no impediments to applying for a licence and entering each market. Implicit in the conjecture is the assumption that the number of stores a market can support is known and that entry occurs 'quickly' until this number is reached. There is no initial over- or under-entry in a market.

There is some question of how quickly a market reaches its equilibrium store count. Although entry might be facilitated by the acquisition of an existing ALCB store, the government permitted the licensing of new stores. If there are no store vacancies or if a town is contemplating new zoning regulations for private liquor stores, entry might be delayed. At the time of privatization, the Alberta government did not come to a firm decision about whether supermarket firms would be licensed to sell liquor in their stores or even be allowed to own separate liquor stores nearby. It was not until August 1994 that the minister announced that grocery stores would not be allowed to sell beverage alcohol from their stores for at least another five years (see Laxer et al. 1995, 5), although they were permitted to own and operate separate liquor stores, and the first of these was licensed in 1995. Nevertheless, it should not take long to open a new liquor store once the decision is made to enter a market, even if a new store must be built. (Its profitability is another matter.) Certainly, one would expect an equilibrium to be reached under Conjecture 1 within five years.

A second possible explanation for the way in which the industry has evolved has similarities to Conjecture 1, but focuses more on the identities of the firms that will actually enter and expand in the market:

> *Conjecture 2: Spatial pre-emption.* Here, firms will pre-empt the market by acquiring multiple locations for liquor stores in the same town once free entry is permitted or by acquiring locations in neighbouring towns.

This conjecture is motivated by Eaton and Lipsey's (1979b) result that it will always pay an incumbent firm to pre-empt the market before it pays a new entrant to enter.[5] By doing so, the incumbent can charge the joint profit-maximizing prices and select the joint profit-maximizing locations. Note that the result assumes the incumbent firm has sunk capital costs, while all the costs of potential entrants are avoidable. In the liquor store setting, unlike the supermarket setting (see West 1981), sunk costs might be low enough to make pre-empting the market a more difficult proposition. Pre-emption, however, implies that neighbour relations matter insofar as explaining the spatial distribution of a firm's ownership of stores is concerned, and entry should occur quickly after licensing of stores begins.[6]

Given that all full-service liquor stores were government owned at the time of privatization, there were no real incumbent private owners or operators of liquor stores. In rural areas, however, there were 49 privately owned 'agency stores' – that is, a general merchandise store permitted to sell beverage alcohol from an area in the store. Also, 532 hotels were licensed to sell liquor products from off-sales outlets, and 18 stores outside Calgary and Edmonton were licensed as wine stores or cold beer stores (Alberta Liquor Control Board 1994, 10–12). So there were some incumbent private retailers of liquor in the market, and they would have had some of the requisite expertise to operate a liquor store. Still, to observe perfect pre-emption in many of the towns that had government liquor stores, a liquor store owner would have had to be the first to obtain licences for multiple liquor stores in a given town, as well as in surrounding towns capable of supporting them, but there was nothing preventing other potential liquor store owners from applying for licences at the same time. Later in the paper, we look for evidence consistent with the pre-emption conjecture, while not expecting to observe perfect pre-emption in any market.

The first two conjectures predict that liquor store entry will have taken place quickly after the privatization announcement. There is, however, a body of empirical literature documenting lengthy periods of evolution toward equilibrium, at least for new manufacturing industries (see, for example, Gort and Klepper 1982). Thus, a third conjecture that might explain the evolution of the liquor store industry is as follows:

> *Conjecture 3: The S-curve.* Under this conjecture, the number of competitors in a new industry increases slowly at first, then speeds up, and finally converges to an equilibrium level (possibly then declining at the end of the industry's life cycle).

Several theoretical explanations have been proposed for the observation of the S-curve in manufacturing industries. These include (1) a coordination problem among potential entrants that can result in initial over- or under-entry (see Cabral 1993); (2) under-entry that occurs from uncertainty over the market-demand function (see Rob 1991; Vettas 1997); and (3) delayed entry so that firms can learn from the experiences of initial entrants (see Jovanovich and Lach 2001).

At the time of privatization, potential entrants could have learned something about demand by examining the sales of the ALCB stores. This, in conjunction with the incentive to enter early to capture the best locations, could have weakened the incentive to delay entry, as reflected by an S-curve. However, a coordination problem for new entrants could have existed, given that liquor store markets were put up for grabs at the same time. Also, the population that ultimately would be necessary to support a new liquor store and that a new store would capture might have been revealed over time.

In addition, there was some demand uncertainty for new entrants since they did not know at the time of privatization when supermarkets would be licensed to sell liquor, or whether they would be allowed to sell beverage alcohol in their stores.[7] They also did not know the prices that supermarket chains would charge, since these depend on unknown demands and costs, or how these prices might affect the sales of rivals located nearby.[8] The government also announced that there would be a five-year review of the effects of privatization, after which changes in the rules and regulations affecting liquor stores might be made.[9] Finally, it is possible that some established liquor stores in shopping centres could lose their leases if the supermarket located in the shopping centre wanted to operate the liquor store.[10]

It follows from this discussion that each explanation of a possible S-curve describing new entry in the liquor store industry might have some validity. We present evidence in support of the S-curve conjecture later in the paper.

One further consideration in the industry evolution literature relates to the number of firms that a market can support. This number depends on how competitive conduct really is as a function of the number of firms in the market, and it varies across markets and over time, assuming it takes different amounts of time for firms to assess the competitiveness of the market. In a 1991 paper, Bresnahan and Reiss examine the effects of entry in concentrated markets, looking in particular at the number of doctors, dentists, druggists, plumbers, and tire dealers in 202 isolated local markets in the early 1980s, and at the relationship between population and the number of firms in each town. Calculating ratios of successive per-firm-population-entry thresholds, they find that these ratios decline with the number of firms, but that the decline stops at N = 3. They conclude that post-entry competition increases at a rate that decreases with the number of incumbents, but that most of this increase comes with the entry of the second and third firms.[11]

Bresnahan and Reiss chose towns that were at least 20 miles from the nearest town of 1,000 people or more, and they eliminated towns that are part of clusters of towns or that are within 100 miles of a city of 100,000 people or more. They did this so that the town population would provide a reasonable estimate of market population, though we use a different approach to estimating trade area population in our analysis of liquor stores in Alberta.

In a more recent paper, Dunne et al. (2007) study entry and exit patterns of dental and chiropractic establishments in 750 small geographic markets in the United States at five-year intervals from 1977 to 2002. They find that the effect of an increase in the number of establishments on average profits is not strong, consistent with a competitive effect of increasing establishment numbers that diminishes rapidly with an increase in this number.

It can be argued that population per store need not increase with the number of stores in a town for at least two reasons. First, Eaton and

Lipsey's (1978) result with respect to freedom of entry and the existence of pure profit implies that firms could make profits in a town without inducing entry. There will be a range of populations per store that is consistent with equilibrium in the market. However, we should still see a certain population-per-store threshold hit before entry occurs, assuming the market has adjusted to a post-privatization equilibrium. Second, firms might collude tacitly when only a small number of them serve a town, reducing the competitive effect that might otherwise exist with two or three firms serving the market.[12] We look at data on population per store in towns with different numbers of liquor stores below.

### The Market and the Data

The data set we use in our analysis consists of annual observations of the names, locations, and licence holders of all liquor stores operating in Alberta from December 1995 to December 2007, as reported by the ALCB and the Alberta Gaming and Liquor Commission. At the start of the period, there were 604 private liquor stores in Alberta; by the end, the count had increased to 1,081.

As the pre-emption hypothesis relates to the expansion of retail chains, we need to identify them in our data. The data provide two ways to do this. First, if two stores have the same name, we regard them as members of the same chain. Second, we regard two stores as part of the same chain if the licence holder is the same, even if the names differ.

As our interest centres on how quickly equilibrium is achieved in liquor store markets outside Calgary and Edmonton, we require some measures to help us determine this. One such measure is population per store, but this raises the question of how to calculate a store's trade area, where some portion of it can extend into rural areas outside of the town in which the store is located. To address this, we calculate, for each year of our sample, trade areas of all towns and cities containing one or more liquor stores in that year. On the assumptions that all stores are identical and charge the same price, that distances are Euclidean, and that consumers minimize shopping costs, a town's trade (or catchment) area is the nearest point set that contains all points that are closer to that town than to any other town on the map.[13]

All towns and cities containing liquor stores are represented by points on the map at the centre of the town or city. This leads to the calculation of trade areas of towns surrounding the cities of Calgary and Edmonton that can capture some of those cities' populations. We exclude the Calgary and Edmonton trade areas, as well as the adjacent trade areas of neighbouring towns, from much of the empirical analysis in the next section. For all other towns and cities, we calculated trade area populations as follows. First, we collected population data by enumeration area for the 1996 census, and population data by dissemination area for the 2001 and 2006 censuses. We used these data to compute a population for each trade area for each of the three census years. For example, for 1996, for each trade area, we identified each intersecting enumeration area and the proportion of the enumeration area contained in the trade area; we then assigned the trade area this proportion of the enumeration area's population. Finally, we summed these populations to get a population for the trade area. We applied a similar method using dissemination areas for the 2001 and 2006 censuses. For years other than census years, we estimated population using linear interpolation.

Figure 4.1 shows the trade areas of all towns and cities in Alberta outside Calgary and Edmonton and surrounding areas that contained liquor stores as of December 2007. The map also indicates those trade areas that contained just one liquor store (the white trade areas), two liquor stores (the light grey areas), and three or more liquor stores (the dark grey areas).[14] (Note that Edmonton and Calgary and surrounding areas are shaded black.) Perhaps not surprisingly, large areas in northwestern and northeastern Alberta were served by a single liquor store, although hotel off-sales and general merchandise stores might have been located in these areas as well. Also, some areas had clusters of trade areas containing a single liquor store; perhaps these are areas where liquor stores were able to exploit more market power, especially if the distances between towns are more than a few kilometres. Depending on the size of population and expected growth of population in a single-store trade area, entry might look attractive. But there is still the question of the competitive effect of entry (see Bresnahan and Reiss 1991), which could have an impact on the timing of entry. We present evidence on this in the next section.

**Liquor Store Industry Evolution in Alberta: Results**

*Approach to Long-run Equilibrium*

The first conjecture to be examined is that, given free entry after privatization, liquor store markets adjust quickly to a long-run equilibrium. To examine this conjecture, we look at changes in the store count over time, in the number of towns and cities that contain liquor stores, in population per store, and in the firm count.

Figure 4.1: Trade Areas of Towns and Cities with Liquor Stores, Alberta, 1995

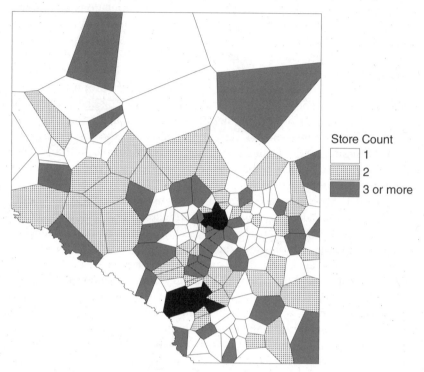

Black shaded area represents Calgary and Edmonton and surrounding areas

When privatization was introduced in September 1993, there were 205 ALCB stores and 53 licensed wine and cold beer stores in the province. By 1995, there were 604 liquor stores (a 134 per cent increase); in 1998, there were 732 (a 21 per cent increase over 1995), and in 2007, 1,089 (a 49 per cent increase over 1998). Outside Calgary and Edmonton and surrounding areas, the number of stores increased from 342 in 1995 to 394 in 1998 (a 15 per cent increase) and then to 524 in 2007 (a 33 per cent increase). Net additions to the number of stores have occurred every year since privatization, but the large percentage increases in the store count more than five years after privatization suggests that there was not a rapid approach to long-run equilibrium.

We can examine Conjecture 1 further by looking at changes in the number of towns and cities containing liquor stores and the population per

Figure 4.2: Average Population per Store, Alberta, 1995–2007

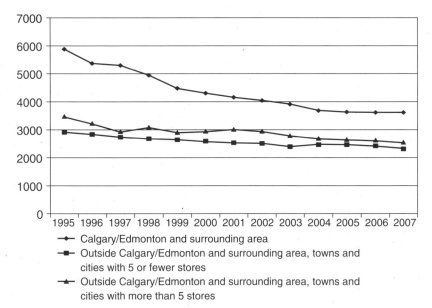

— Calgary/Edmonton and surrounding area
— Outside Calgary/Edmonton and surrounding area, towns and
cities with 5 or fewer stores
— Outside Calgary/Edmonton and surrounding area, towns and
cities with more than 5 stores

store over time. With respect to the former, there was a clear flattening in the city and town count between 2004 and 2007. Just prior to privatization, 155 towns and cities were served by ALCB stores; by 1995, that number had increased to 176, and rose every year but one up to 2003, when it peaked at 215. After 2003, however, the number varied between 209 to 215, falling in two years and rising in two years.

Figure 4.2 illustrates changes in population per store in Calgary and Edmonton and surrounding areas, in towns with five or fewer stores, and in towns and cities with more than five stores. We broke the towns and cities outside Calgary and Edmonton into two categories in case they exhibited different patterns of evolution, with the larger towns and cities behaving more like Alberta's two largest cities. Note that, in Calgary and Edmonton and surrounding areas, the population per store decreased more or less continuously until 2006. The curve suggests a flattening in population per store beginning in 2004. The other two curves start out with much lower populations per store than the one for Calgary and Edmonton, and they do not decline as steeply as the latter curve, though they both still show a tendency to convergence.

Figure 4.3: Firm Counts, Alberta Liquor Stores, 1995–2007

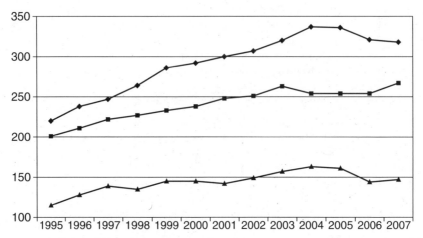

-•- Calgary/Edmonton and surrounding area
-■- Outside Calgary/Edmonton and surrounding area, towns and cities
   with 5 or fewer stores
-▲- Outside Calgary/Edmonton and surrounding area, towns and cities
   with more than 5 stores

Note that the large difference in the 2007 population per store between Calgary and Edmonton (3,619) and towns with five or fewer liquor stores (2,329) could reflect the lower costs of owning and operating liquor stores in small-town Alberta.

Figure 4.3 shows how the number of firms changed over time in the same categories as in Figure 4.2. In Calgary and Edmonton and surrounding areas, the firm count increased more or less continuously until 2004, whereupon it more or less levelled off, while it peaked a year earlier for towns with five or fewer stores.[15] The rising store count and flattening firm count reflects both the opening of new stores by independents and chains and the loss of firms through the acquisition by larger chains of smaller chains and independents.

The data on towns and cities served by liquor stores, population per store, and firm counts are not consistent with Conjecture 1, but they are consistent with the approach of a long-run equilibrium by 2003–04, ten years after privatization. We consider explanations of this result as part of our assessment of Conjecture 3.

While many of the statistics considered above suggest that long-run equilibrium was achieved approximately by 2007, one feature of the industry that continued to change was the proportion of chain stores. In Calgary and Edmonton and surrounding areas, 24 per cent of stores were part of a chain in 1995, rising to 42 per cent in 2001, and to 53 per cent in 2007. Outside Calgary and Edmonton, 18 per cent of stores were members of a chain in 1995, 18 per cent again in 2001, and 32 per cent in 2007. Clearly, chain stores grew first in the large cities and only more recently in smaller cities and towns. This increase was due partly to the expansion of a chain called the Liquor Depot and partly to the growth of chains associated with supermarkets. Liquor Depot's expansion came through the acquisition of smaller established chains and independents and the opening of new stores in growing neighbourhoods of cities. In December 1995, Liquor Depot had 11 stores, but by May 2008, it had 171. Between December 2007 and May 2008 alone, it acquired five independent stores and four from other chains and opened five new stores, with plans for six more.[16]

One reason for the growth of chains could be pre-emptive behaviour on the part of incumbent firms. We turn to a consideration of that hypothesis next.

*Pre-emption*

According to Conjecture 2, firms pre-empt the market by acquiring multiple locations for stores in the same town once free entry is permitted, or by acquiring locations in neighbouring towns. As part of our examination of this conjecture, we constructed Table 4.1, which treats 1995 as the initial observation of the location of privatized liquor stores, and then tabulates where new entry occurred. Column 2 reports, for each year, the total number of new stores established in towns and cities outside Calgary and Edmonton and surrounding areas. Column 3 shows the total number of chain store entries. Note that chain stores as a percentage of total entries did not rise above 23 per cent until 2004, but rose to between 33 and 41 per cent over the next four years – results that are consistent with the rising proportion of chain stores over time. Still, the numbers suggest that pre-emption by incumbent firms does not explain the majority of entries. From 1996 to 2007, chains accounted for 23 per cent of total entries.

Column 4 shows the extent to which chain store entries occurred in towns where other stores in the same chain were already operating. In the first few years, this occurred relatively frequently; it dropped over the next five years but rose again in three of the four years after that. These numbers provide some evidence to support the importance of location and proximity to members of the same chain in explaining the towns chosen for chain store entry; overall, however, chains did not pre-empt a large

Table 4.1
Liquor Store Chain Entry, Alberta, 1996–2007

| Year | Entry | Chain Entry | Chain Entry in Same Town as Existing Chain | Chain Entry in Town Adjacent to One with Existing Chain | Chain Entry Elsewhere | Entering Chain's Percentage of Town Store Count (average) | Entry in Trade Areas with or Adjacent to Chains | Entrants Entering Towns as Only Store in the Town |
|------|-------|-------------|---------------------------------------------|----------------------------------------------------------|-----------------------|-----------------------------------------------------------|--------------------------------------------------|---------------------------------------------------|
| 1996 | 44 | 4 | 3 | 1 | 0 | 29 | 37 | 15 |
| 1997 | 50 | 11 | 4 | 0 | 7 | 25 | 38 | 15 |
| 1998 | 23 | 3 | 2 | 0 | 1 | 23 | 20 | 7 |
| 1999 | 33 | 6 | 1 | 2 | 3 | 34 | 27 | 13 |
| 2000 | 25 | 5 | 2 | 3 | 0 | 32 | 22 | 8 |
| 2001 | 27 | 2 | 0 | 0 | 2 | 14 | 21 | 9 |
| 2002 | 27 | 5 | 1 | 0 | 4 | 30 | 25 | 7 |
| 2003 | 38 | 8 | 2 | 1 | 5 | 27 | 34 | 7 |
| 2004 | 32 | 13 | 6 | 3 | 5 | 19 | 31 | 1 |
| 2005 | 17 | 7 | 2 | 2 | 3 | 28 | 16 | 5 |
| 2006 | 27 | 9 | 5 | 2 | 3 | 23 | 24 | 1 |
| 2007 | 36 | 14 | 7 | 2 | 6 | 33 | 36 | 6 |
| Total | 379 | 87 | 35 | 16 | 39 | 27 | 331 | 93 |

number of markets – only 35 of 88 chain entries between 1996 and 2007 were in the same town as an existing chain.

In column 5, we look for evidence that chain stores attempted to pre-empt locations for new stores in adjacent trade areas. With the exception of 2000, when four of six chain store entries were in towns adjacent to ones containing members of the same chain, the numbers are low, never accounting for more than a third of chain entries. Between 1996 and 2007, only 17 of 88 chain store entries were in towns adjacent to ones with an existing chain.

Column 7 shows the extent to which an entering chain had a dominant presence in a particular city or town. In each year, on average, the entering chain did not achieve majority status in any town, and only in 2000 did the entering chain begin to approach dominant firm status in a town, on average. Column 8 shows the number of occasions on which a chain store could have taken advantage of a pre-emption opportunity; in fact, the vast majority of these opportunities were exploited by independents.

Finally, column 9 displays the number of times in each year that the entering store was the only store in that town that year. Occupying a one-store town is one way to pre-empt and perhaps permit the firm to exploit more market power than it would have been able to by locating in the same town as other liquor stores. In 1999, 38 per cent of entries were of this type, but the percentages were smaller for all other years. The small numbers toward the end of the sample could reflect the declining number of sites that would allow a single new liquor store to enjoy some spatial dominance: only one of 32 entering stores in 2004 and one of 27 in 2006 were in a town where it was the only liquor store.

We conclude that the pre-emption conjecture finds little support in the data. It could be that putting the entire retail liquor store industry up for grabs at the same time made the cost of pre-empting liquor store markets too high.

*The S-curve Conjecture*

Conjecture 3 is that the number of competitors in a new industry increases slowly at first, then speeds up, and converges on an equilibrium level (then possibly declining at the end of the industry's life cycle). In fact, the number of liquor stores in our sample did not increase slowly at first, perhaps because existing government-owned liquor stores could be converted quickly to private operations.[17] As we have noted, prior to privatization in September 1993, there were 205 ALCB stores and 53 licensed wine and cold beer stores in the province. By March 1994, there were 380 private liquor stores, with the number rising to 535 by November 1994. Still, the S-curve literature offers several explanations of delayed entry that could slow the approach to a long-run equilibrium.

First, there can be a coordination problem among potential entrants that leads to either under- or over-entry. To examine the extent of over-entry, we looked at the number of towns that had store counts in 2007 that were below their maximum and found that, of the 230 towns or cities that had liquor stores in at least one of the post-privatization sample years, 37 (16 per cent) had none by 2007 and all but three of the 37 had just one store. Of the remaining 193, 156 (81 per cent) had as many stores in 2007 as at their maximum; only seven of these towns lost more than one store.

To control for the length of time over which the maximum store count might be breached, we looked at the number of towns and cities that had a higher store count in 1995 than in 2000, and found that 13 (7 per cent) out of 185 did so. Another 10 had stores in 1995 but not in 2000. These numbers do not provide any compelling evidence of over-entry.

With respect to under-entry, we have already discussed the evidence that the store counts and firm counts were increasing in towns and cities up to ten years after privatization, while population per store was decreasing. There was under-entry in this sense, but instead of a problem of coordination, this could be due to uncertainty about market demand or difficulty in learning about the market from the experience of other entrants.

Table 4.2, which reports the frequency distribution of stores by town and trade area population for 2007, provides some evidence consistent with a learning explanation for industry evolution. Both Eaton and Lipsey (1978) and Bresnahan and Reiss (1991) would expect there to be a range of population sizes capable of supporting a particular number of stores. For example, 8 towns or cities with a trade area population of less than 1,000, 32 with a trade area population of between 1,000 and 2,000, and 42 with a trade area population of between 2,001 and 4,000 had a single store. This suggests that the population might have to reach 4,000 before a second store will enter. However, an additional 13 towns and cities with a trade area population above 4,000 also had only one liquor store.[18] At the same time, 32 towns with a trade area population of less than 4,000 supported two liquor stores. It could be that, while the industry was approaching the equilibrium, it was still not quite there, as additional entry could occur in towns that seemed to have the population necessary to support it.[19]

In terms of the findings of Bresnahan and Reiss (1991), it could be that to go from one liquor store to two requires a town of more than double the population because of the price competition created by the introduction of the second store. Although some of the data in Table 4.2 are consistent with this finding, we cannot rule out alternative explanations for the store distribution in the table.

A second way in which evidence consistent with a learning explanation for industry evolution might be found is by examining how the proportion of the 2007 store count reached in each year changed over time for towns and cities with and without ALCB stores in 1993. At the time of privatization, towns with ALCB stores would have had more certain expected liquor sales and resident expertise in how to run a store, not to mention an available site in which to operate a private store. Figure 4.4 plots the proportion of the 2007 store count reached in each year from 1995 to 2007 for towns and cities with five or fewer stores that had ALCB stores and those that did not. The figure shows that more than 80 per cent of the 2007 store count for towns and cities with ALCB stores in 1993 was achieved by 1995, and that proportion increased only slowly thereafter. Many of those towns would have had one ALCB store that quickly converted to a private store shortly after privatization. In towns and cities without ALCB stores in 1993, only 34 per cent of the 2007 store count was reached by 1995, with a steady increase after that. These results are consistent with the learning-about-demand and learning-from-earlier-entrant explanations for the S-curve.

Table 4.2
Liquor Store Counts in Towns and Cities of Different Sizes, Alberta, 2007

| Stores | Population | | | | | | | |
|---|---|---|---|---|---|---|---|---|
| | 0–1,000 | 1,001–2,000 | 2,001–3,000 | 3,001–4,000 | 4,001–5,000 | 5,001–6,000 | 6,001–10,000 | Over 10,000 |
| 1 | 8 | 32 | 22 | 20 | 5 | 6 | 2 | 0 |
| 2 | 0 | 5 | 12 | 12 | 6 | 4 | 6 | 2 |
| 3 | 0 | 1 | 0 | 2 | 3 | 1 | 4 | 3 |
| 4 | 0 | 0 | 0 | 0 | 1 | 1 | 5 | 2 |
| 5 | 0 | 0 | 0 | 0 | 1 | 0 | 2 | 6 |
| 6–10 | 0 | 0 | 0 | 0 | 0 | 0 | 2 | 11 |
| More than 10 | 0 | 0 | 0 | 0 | 0 | 0 | 0 | 6 |
| Total | 8 | 38 | 34 | 34 | 16 | 12 | 21 | 30 |

Figure 4.4: Proportion of 2007 Store Count Reached in Each Year, Towns and Cities with 5 or Fewer Stores, Alberta, 1995–2007

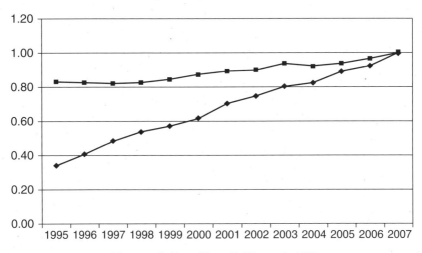

We can also look at the number of cases in which a former ALCB store was being operated in a town in December 1995 (41) relative to the number of ALCB towns with five or fewer stores in 2007 (99). Since more than 80 per cent of the 2007 store count for towns and cities with ALCB stores in 1993 was achieved by 1995, we conclude that what matters insofar as an ALCB town's getting a private liquor store is not simply having had an available ALCB store to privatize but also the available expertise to run a liquor store, as well as more information about local demand.

A third way in which evidence consistent with the learning explanation for industry evolution might be found is by examining how the proportion of the 2007 store count reached in each year changed over time for towns and cities (with no more than five liquor stores) that were near those containing major chain supermarkets. Recall that, in 1994, there was uncertainty about whether supermarkets would be allowed to sell beverage alcohol in their stores or, instead, to own separate liquor stores. By the end of that year, some of this uncertainty was resolved, and the picture became clearer still after the five-year review of privatization. Nevertheless, the entry of new liquor stores in towns that were close to those with major supermarkets might have been delayed by fears that supermarket-owned stores would have significant negative effects on their business (because of pricing, advertising, and the ability to exploit the supermarket/liquor store complementarity). As it turned out, towns with trade areas adjacent to those containing major supermarkets reached 56 per cent of their 2007 store count by 1995, compared with 66 per cent for towns not adjacent to those with supermarkets. This result is consistent with expectations, but the difference is not large, and remains relatively small over time.

To examine further the role different factors played in the delayed entry of stores into different towns, we conducted a basic probit analysis. The dependent variable is given by $I_{95i}$, which equals 1 if town i had reached its final 2007 store count by December 1995. The probability that $I_{95,i}$ equals 1 for town i is given by $F(\beta X_i)$, where $F(\ )$ is the cumulative distribution function for a standard normal random variable, and $X_i$ is a list of observations for town i on variables expected to influence the speed with which the town reached its final store count. The variables used are:

$ALCB_i$   = 1 if town i had an ALCB store in 1993;

$Supermarket_i$ = 1 if the town had a major supermarket chain in it or within 30 kilometres;

$Growth_i$   = the percentage growth of the population of the town's 2007 trade area from 1995 to 2007;

$Pop95_i$      = the population of the 2007 trade area of the town as of 1995; and

$Density_i$      = the number of towns within 30 kilometres.

The coefficient on $ALCB_i$ is expected to be positive; the presence of an ALCB store in a town in 1993 is expected to increase knowledge about the characteristics of the local market, indicate the presence of local skills in liquor retailing, and indicate an immediately available location for a liquor store. We constructed the variable $Supermarket_i$ using the 1994 Yellow Pages for Alberta, and identified Canada Safeway, Real Canadian Superstore, IGA Garden Market, and Save-On as the major supermarket chains. The coefficient on $Supermarket_i$ is expected to have a negative sign, as the presence of a major supermarket chain is expected to be associated with greater uncertainty about the profitability of opening a liquor store in a town or in one nearby. The coefficient on $Growth_i$ is expected to have a negative sign, as areas exhibiting large growth might have been more likely to increase their store counts after 1995 if potential liquor retailers did not anticipate it. The coefficient on $Pop95_i$ is expected to have a negative sign since, although a large town might achieve most of its store count quickly, the final one or two stores might require longer to appear. The coefficient on $Density_i$ is expected to have a negative sign, as the increased presence of towns nearby indicates greater competition from outside the town, implying less profitable entry opportunities.

We estimated the model over the sample of all towns with liquor stores as of December 2007 outside Calgary and Edmonton and surrounding areas and that had no more than five stores at any point in the sample. The estimated probability that town i had reached its final store count by 1995 is given by (standard errors are given in parentheses):

$$F\left( \begin{array}{cccccc} 1.42^* ALCB_i & -0.07\, Supermarket_i & -0.34\, Growth_i & -0.0002^*\, Pop95_i & +0.05 Density_i & -0.14 \\ (0.25) & (0.33) & (0.33) & (0.0001) & (0.06) & (0.23) \end{array} \right),$$

where * indicates statistical significance at the 1 per cent level. Note that the only coefficients that are statistically significant at standard levels are for the $ALCB$ and $Pop95$ variables, with the expected sign. In terms of magnitude, setting other variables equal to their sample means, the presence of an ALCB store in a town is associated with a 0.52 increase in the probability that a town will achieve its final store count by 1995.

The results do not provide evidence to support a relationship between the speed of market evolution and the nearby presence of a major supermarket chain. One possible explanation is that since the major supermarket chains are largely found only in major centres, this variable might be picking up some offsetting relationship between the speed of evolution and proximity to large centres. Finally, the model does not support a relationship between the speed of evolution and population growth or town density.

We estimated a large number of additional specifications to explore the robustness of these results. We re-estimated the model using as the dependent variable, first, whether the town had achieved its final store count by each year from 1996 to 1999; and, second, whether the town had achieved 75 percent of its final store count by the second year. We also estimated models in which the density variable was removed and in which *Pop95* was replaced by the town's 2007 store count.

The main finding – that of a negative and significant coefficient on *ALCB* – is strongly robust to alternative specifications. The main change in the results across specifications is that, in some cases, the coefficient on *Supermarket* was significant with the expected sign, giving some weak support for the hypothesis that proximity to a major supermarket chain increased uncertainty and delayed liquor store entry.

### Summary and Concluding Remarks

It has been more than 30 years since Eaton and Lipsey embarked on their research program to incorporate space into the neoclassical model of value theory. Their work, focused as it was on explaining what we might observe empirically, has led to some theoretical extensions and to a handful of papers that attempt to test their theoretical propositions, and to a larger set of empirical papers that have been influenced by their spatial models.

One body of literature that seems particularly in need of spatial extensions is the industry evolution literature. Understanding how real industries evolve over time seems to require an appreciation of the role space can play in determining the equilibrium that will eventually be achieved.

Building on earlier work that incorporated a number of spatial variables in an econometric analysis of firm survival and chain growth in the privatized liquor store industry in Calgary and Edmonton, this paper examined the evolution of that industry outside those two major cities. We wished to determine whether or not the industry evolution could be explained by one of three conjectures: a free entry/rapid approach to long-run equilibrium, pre-emption, or S-curve entry.

We plotted the locations of all liquor stores in Alberta from December 1995 to December 2007 in each year, and calculated their trade areas and trade area populations. We examined Conjecture 1 by studying changes in the liquor store and firm counts over time, changes in the number of towns and cities containing liquor stores, and changes in population per store. All of the results are inconsistent with a rapid approach to equilibrium, as suggested by Conjecture 1.

To examine the pre-emption conjecture, we looked for evidence that chain entry was occurring in towns occupied by members of the same chain or in towns adjacent to ones with the same chain. The data, however, do not provide much support for this conjecture.

Finally, we considered the different explanations underlying the S-curve conjecture. We did not find support for the existence of a coordination problem that led to initial over-entry; rather, the evidence is more consistent with under-entry and a slow approach to equilibrium, perhaps due in part to demand uncertainty because of the slow expansion of supermarket-owned liquor stores. We also find that whether or not a town had an ALCB store prior to privatization could have had an impact on how quickly it reached its final store count, possibly because there was less demand uncertainty, more available expertise, and an available liquor store site in towns that contained ALCB stores. A regression analysis largely supports these findings, and significant in explaining a town's having reached its 2007 store count by 1995 were the presence of an ALCB store prior to privatization and the 1995 population of its trade area.

The findings we present in this paper – particularly the length of time required for the industry to evolve to a final equilibrium structure – are important for governments that are considering the privatization of liquor retailing. Our results suggest that the results of early studies of the effects of Alberta's privatization, such as ALCB (1994), were premature. Instead, a view of the structure of liquor retailing in the province almost ten years after privatization reveals a more complete picture of how the industry evolved and, in some dimensions, is continuing to do so.

NOTES

1 Space does play a role in a subset of the industry evolution and firm survival literature. See, for example, Miron (2002); Aguirregabiria and Vicentini (2006); Seim (2006); Jia (2008); and Holmes (2008).

2 Prior to privatization, retail liquor sales were permitted in licensed general merchandise stores (with an area in the store carved out for liquor sales) serving rural areas and hotel off-sales. These retail formats were continued after

privatization, but we do not examine them here since they are qualitatively different than full-service class D liquor stores.

3  Supermarkets have been fined for violations of the separate business requirement, but the fines have been small.

4  West (2003) examines the economic effects of Alberta's liquor store privatization, including the effects on prices, store locations, product selection, government revenues, wages and employment, but industry evolution is not the focus of that study.

5  Eaton and Lipsey (1979b) also derive a pre-emption-by-new-entrant result: provided the incumbent firm does nothing to block entry, new entrants will pre-empt the market by entering at a time when their present values are zero. Note that this result assumes there is already an incumbent firm in the market.

6  Aguirregabiria and Vicentini (2006) also construct a model to study spatial pre-emption. They note that economies of density might provide another explanation for why chain stores choose to expand by selecting locations close to existing stores. On the importance of economies of density and industry evolution, see Jia (2008) and Holmes (2008). Other possible explanations for chain formation include exploitation of scale economies in advertising and administration, taking advantage of limited time offers provided by liquor suppliers, and exploiting management expertise (see Raymond James Equity Research – Canada 2005, 24). Exploring such explanations, however, is beyond the scope of this paper

7  There were also concerns that supermarkets would not operate their liquor stores as separate businesses, as required by the *Alberta Gaming and Liquor Act*. To address some of these concerns, in 1997 the Alberta Gaming and Liquor Commission carried out an audit of two Real Canadian Liquorstores associated with the Real Canadian Superstore chain and found that the two stores were operating within government rules. See 'Superstore gets OK for 8 liquor shops,' *Edmonton Journal*, 24 July 1997, p. A2.

8  One of the supermarket-owned liquor store chains that began entering the market in 1996 was associated with a discount supermarket and quickly developed a reputation for charging lower prices. Lindsey and West (2003) look at how low pricing by this chain might affect rival liquor stores. They find that price responses by rivals can be insignificant and that only rivals located very close by are much affected by the low prices charged by the supermarket-owned chain. They also find that 'rivals located some distance from the predator can raise their prices if their losses are concentrated with remote, and correspondingly price elastic, consumers' (p. 580).

9  Some of the issues that were to be considered during the five-year review are discussed in Gray (1998).

10 However, since a supermarket is the main anchor of many shopping centres below the regional level, it could have some leverage with the landlord or even an ownership interest in the centre.

11 Other papers have also studied population thresholds of entry; see, for example, Berry and Reiss (2007).

12 This possibility is also considered by Bresnahan and Reiss (1991) and Berry and Reiss (2007).

13 We used the Alberta provincial boundary to bound trade areas on the periphery. Towns with liquor stores in British Columbia and Saskatchewan largely were located far enough from the provincial boundary as to have little effect on the trade area populations of towns within Alberta.

14 In general, the trade area can include a number of stores that exceeds the number of firms. There were also two trade areas, Lethbridge and Medicine Hat, where one of the neighbouring town's trade areas picked up some of the population that clearly belonged to the other. We reassigned these populations to avoid the creation of outliers.

15 We counted some of the same firms in each time series since chains might have had stores in all three categories.

16 Included in this total is Liquor Depot's acquisition of a chain called Liquor Barn.

17 In fact, of the 2005 ALCB stores, 115 were converted to private operations.

18 Of course, it is always possible that some of the trade area population estimates over- or underestimate actual catchment area populations of liquor stores.

19 It is also the case that the demand for liquor stores in a town depends not just on the population, but also on such factors as the age distribution of the population, the closeness of neighbouring towns, and the local taste for alcohol.

## REFERENCES

Aguirregabiria, V., and G. Vicentini. 2006. 'Dynamic Spatial Competition between Multi-Store Firms.' Working paper, Department of Economics, University of Toronto.

Alberta Liquor Control Board. 1994. 'A New Era in Liquor Administration: The Alberta Experience.' St. Albert, AB: Alberta Liquor Control Board, December.

Berry, S., and P. Reiss. 2007. 'Empirical Models of Entry and Market Structure.' In *Handbook of Industrial Organization*, vol. 3, edited by M. Armstrong and R. Porter. Amsterdam: Elsevier.

Borenstein, S., and J. Netz. 1999. 'Why Do All the Flights Leave at 8 am? Competition and Departure-Time Differentiation in Airline Markets.' *International Journal of Industrial Organization* 17 (5): 611–40.

Bresnahan, T.F., and P.C. Reiss. 1991. 'Entry and Competition in Concentrated Markets.' *Journal of Political Economy* 99 (5): 977–1009.

Cabral, L. 1993. 'Experience Advantages and Entry Dynamics.' *Journal of Economic Theory* 59 (2): 403–16.

Dunne, T., S. Klimek, M.J. Roberts, and Yi Xu. 2007. 'Entry and Exit in Geographic Markets.' Working paper, Pennsylvania State University.

Eaton, B. Curtis, and Richard G. Lipsey. 1975. 'The Principle of Minimum Differentiation Reconsidered: Some New Developments in the Theory of Spatial Competition.' *Review of Economic Studies* 42 (1): 27–49.

– 1977. 'The Introduction of Space into the Neoclassical Model of Value Theory.' In *Studies in Modern Economic Analysis*, edited by M.J. Artis and A.R. Nobay. Oxford: Basil Blackwell.

– 1978. 'Freedom of Entry and the Existence of Pure Profit.' *Economic Journal* 88 (351): 455–69.

– 1979a. 'Comparison Shopping and the Clustering of Homogeneous Firms.' *Journal of Regional Science* 19 (4): 421–35.

– 1979b. 'The Theory of Market Pre-emption: The Persistence of Excess Capacity and Monopoly in Growing Spatial Markets.' *Economica* 46 (182): 149–58.

– 1982. 'An Economic Theory of Central Places.' *Economic Journal* 92 (365): 56–72.

Eckert, A., and D.S. West. 2005. 'Price Uniformity and Competition in a Retail Gasoline Market.' *Journal of Economic Behavior and Organization* 56 (2): 219–37.

– 2008. 'Firm Survival and Chain Growth in a Privatized Retail Liquor Store Industry.' *Review of Industrial Organization* 32 (1): 1–18.

Gort, M., and S. Klepper. 1982. 'Time Paths in the Diffusion of Product Innovations.' *Economic Journal* 92 (367): 630–53.

Gray, Ian. 1998. 'Taking the Government Out of Business.' *Vendor Magazine* 4 (Convention): 7–8.

Holmes, T.J. 2008. 'The Diffusion of Wal-Mart and Economies of Density.' NBER Working Paper 13783. Cambridge, MA: National Bureau of Economic Research.

Jia, P. 2008. 'What Happens when Wal-Mart Comes to Town: An Empirical Analysis of the Discount Retailing Industry.' *Econometrica* 76 (6): 1263–1316.

Jovanovic, B., and S. Lach. 2001. 'Entry, Exit, and Diffusion with Learning by Doing.' *American Economic Review* 79 (4): 690–99.

Laxer, G., D. Green, T. Harrison, and D. Neu. 1994. 'Out of Control: Paying the Price for Privatizing Alberta's Liquor Control Board.' Edmonton: Canadian Centre for Policy Alternatives.

Lieberman, M.B. 1987. 'Excess Capacity as a Barrier to Entry: An Empirical Appraisal.' *Journal of Industrial Economics* 35 (4): 607–27.

Lindsey, C.R., and D.S. West. 2003. 'Predatory Pricing in Differentiated Products Retail Markets.' *International Journal of Industrial Organization* 21 (4): 551–92.

Miron, J.R. 2002. 'Löschian Spatial Competition in an Emerging Retail Industry.' *Geographical Analysis* 34 (1): 34–61.

Netz, J., and B.A. Taylor. 2002. 'Maximum or Minimum Differentiation? Location Patterns of Retail Outlets.' *Review of Economics and Statistics* 84 (1): 162–75.

Raymond James Equity Research – Canada. 2005. 'Liquor Stores Income Fund.' Vancouver, 5 July.

Rob, R. 1991. 'Learning and Capacity Expansion under Demand Uncertainty.' *Review of Economic Studies* 58 (4): 655–75.

Seim, K. 2006. 'An Empirical Model of Firm Entry with Endogenous Product-Type Choice.' *RAND Journal of Economics* 37 (3): 619–40.

Shaw, R.W. 1982. 'Product Proliferation in Characteristics Space: The U.K. Fertiliser Industry.' *Journal of Industrial Economics* 31 (1-2): 69–91.

Stavins, J. 1995. 'Model Entry and Exit in a Differentiated-Product Industry: The Personal Computer Market.' *Review of Economics and Statistics* 77 (4): 571–84.

Swann, G.M.P. 1985. 'Product Competition in Microprocessors.' *Journal of Industrial Economics* 34 (1): 33–54.

Vettas, N. 1997. 'Entry and Exit under Demand Uncertainty.' *Economics Letters* 57 (2): 227–34.

Von Hohenbalken, B., and D.S. West. 1984. 'Predation among Supermarkets: An Algorithmic Locational Analysis.' *Journal of Urban Economics* 15 (2): 244–57.

Wensley, M.R.D., and J.C. Stabler. 1998. 'Demand-Threshold Estimation for Business Activities in Rural Saskatchewan.' *Journal of Regional Science* 38 (1): 155–77.

West, D.S. 1981. 'Testing for Market Preemption Using Sequential Location Data.' *Bell Journal of Economics* 12 (1): 129–43.

– 2003. *The Privatization of Liquor Retailing in Alberta.* Vancouver: Fraser Institute.

West, D.S., B. Von Hohenbalken, and K. Kroner. 1985. 'Tests of Intraurban Central Place Theories.' *Economic Journal* 95 (377): 101–17.

# 5 Shopper City

RICHARD ARNOTT AND YUNDONG TU[1]

One of the authors of this paper recently has participated in the development of a large-scale, microeconomic metropolitan simulation model (tentatively called METRO-LA) that aims to forecast transportation, land use, and pollution in the Los Angeles metropolitan area. One of the many modelling questions that have arisen is how retail location should be modelled at such a geographic scale. The literature on retail location that is most familiar to economists is strategic firm location theory/spatial competition theory, to which Curtis Eaton has made distinguished contributions, many in co-authorship with Richard Lipsey.[2] Models in this literature solve for the Nash equilibrium of a game among firms, with locations, prices, and perhaps entry as strategy variables. With space interpreted as geographic space, this literature has provided many insights into the location and pricing of firms; and with space interpreted as characteristics space, into product differentiation. But spatial competition theory is not well suited to the analysis of retail location on a broad geographical scale. For one thing, attempting to solve for the Nash equilibrium of a game among thousands of firms, with many different types of consumer goods, is intractable. For another, firm location theory is partial equilibrium in nature, taking the location of consumers as given, but a satisfactory model of land use needs to take into account the simultaneous location equilibrium of firms and households. For yet another, land rent is ignored in spatial competition theory but in an urban setting plays an essential role in location choice.

There is also a large literature on retail location outside economics, in marketing and in geography and regional science. The bulk of the marketing literature on retail location looks at the topic from the perspective of either the individual retail firm or the individual shopper. The former examines the most profitable location of a single retail firm or shopping centre, often taking into account strategic interaction with other retail firms.[3] The latter examines the individual's decision about where to shop.[4] The geography/regional science literature on the subject, for which Harris (1985) provides an excellent review, examines the spatial distribution of retail activities within a city or region, drawing on central place theory (see, for example, Berry 1967), the Lowry model (Lowry 1964, 1967; Goldner 1971), and spatial interaction theory (Wilson 1970, 1974). This branch of the literature does not incorporate prices and markets, and does not treat agglomeration economies, at least not explicitly.

This paper looks at retail location from the perspective of a general equilibrium model of location and land use, with agglomeration economies in retailing, adapting the approach developed by Fujita and Ogawa (1982), who solve for the simultaneous location equilibrium of firms and households in a city. The Fujita-Ogawa model is essentially competitive. Each firm decides where to locate, taking prices, rents, household location, and other firm locations as given, and produces under constant returns to scale. The economies of scale that give rise to agglomeration are external to the individual firm. Closer proximity to other firms makes a firm more productive: firms learn from other firms, incur lower transport costs in intermediate goods exchange, and have access to a broader labour pool. In deciding where to locate, a firm trades off the higher productivity of more proximate locations against the higher wages and rents there. Each individual makes two location decisions – where to live and where to work – taking prices, rents, wages, firm location, and the location of all other households as given. In deciding where to live, the individual trades off the higher commuting cost of a less central location against the lower land rent; and in deciding where to work, the individual trades off a higher wage at a more central location against the higher commuting cost.

Equilibrium obtains when, by changing location, no firm can increase its profits and no household can increase its utility. In equilibrium, land and labour markets clear at all locations, and land goes to that use which bids the most for it. Since there are economies of scale, there might be multiple equilibria, corresponding to different location patterns. One possible equilibrium is monocentric, in which all firms are located at the city centre, with residences surrounding them; another possible equilibrium is completely mixed, with firms and households co-locating at all urban locations; another has three centres; and so on.

Four parameters are particularly important in determining which location patterns are equilibria: commuting cost per unit distance, the spatial decay rate – that is, the exponential rate at which benefits from proximity to other firms decay with distance – the population, and a parameter characterizing the intensity of agglomeration economies in production. When, for instance, the spatial decay rate is large and commuting costs are moderate, there are equilibria with many small employment centres. Also, as the urban population increases, subcentring occurs.

In this paper, we adapt the Fujita-Ogawa model by having firms sell differentiated retail goods rather than produce. In order to highlight the basic economics, we make the model as simple as possible. Agglomeration economies occur via individuals' taste for product variety rather than via external economies of scale in production; in particular, stores have an incentive to co-locate in a shopping centre since doing so raises the *effective variety* there, which makes shopping there more attractive. Each of the identical individuals receives an endowment of a generic good, which she spends on her lot, transportation for shopping, and the differentiated retail goods. She decides where to live, trading off rent against transport cost, and where to shop, trading off the greater variety against the higher price and likely higher transport cost of shopping at a larger centre. Using only land, competitive retail firms transform the generic good into differentiated retail goods and sell them. Thus, individuals and stores compete in the land market. If population and shopping transport costs are low, if the taste for variety is high, and if the benefit one store derives from proximity to other stores falls off moderately rapidly with distance, then there exists a monocentric equilibrium, with all stores at a single, central shopping centre. If shopping transport costs are high and if the taste for variety is low, then an equilibrium exists in which stores and residences are intermixed. The model is called 'Shopper City' since individuals do nothing but shop and enjoy consuming their differentiated retail goods on their lots.

A companion paper, Arnott and Erbil (2008), enriches this model, developing a computable static general equilibrium (CGE) model with agglomeration in both retailing and production. The CGE model is standard (allowing for labour and capital, as well as land, in retail goods production, intermediate and wholesale goods production, structures of variable density, multiple types of retail goods, multiple household groups, commodity transportation, and so on) except that it treats residential location, household transportation for commuting and shopping, and agglomeration economies in both production and retailing.

When completed, METRO-LA will have the same model structure, except that it will be dynamic. History dependence will be incorporated through durable structures and the transmission of industry- and zone-specific location potentials and zone-specific indices of effective varieties from one period to the next. The present will be linked to the future via property markets, with property values being determined under perfect foresight.

In the next section, we lay out the basic model. We then derive the parameter restrictions such that a monocentric equilibrium exists, and perform the same exercise for a completely mixed urban configuration. The paper ends with concluding comments.

## A Description of the Model

Our model adapts Fujita and Ogawa (1982), replacing agglomeration economies in production with agglomeration economies in retailing.

### Geography, Population, and Transportation

$N$ identical individuals live in the city. Each resides on a lot of size $S$ and requires $s$ units of retail land area.[5] Thus, the residential area is $NS$, the retail area $Ns$, and the total urban area $N(S + s)$. The city is long and narrow, of unit width. The central location is taken to be the origin, and both $x$ and $y$ are used to index location. The boundaries of the city are $-N(S + s)/2$ and $N(S + s)/2$. Every day each individual makes a return journey from her home to the shopping location[6] of her choice at a transport cost of $t$ per unit distance.

### Tastes

Each individual derives utility from differentiated retail goods and her lot. Since lot size is fixed, utility can be treated as a function only of differentiated consumer goods. The utility she receives from retail goods is a function of the quantity she purchases, $Q$, as well as the effective variety, $v$:

$$U = u(Q, v) = Qv. \tag{1}$$

The multiplicative form is chosen to simplify the algebra. The effective variety for a shopper who travels to location $y$ to shop is measured as:

$$v(y) = 1 + k \int_{-b}^{b} a(x) \exp\{-\alpha|x - y|\} dx, \tag{2}$$

where $a(x)$ is the proportion of land at $x$ that is used by stores, $k$ is a parameter indexing the intensity of taste for variety or the degree of variety, and $\alpha$ is the exponential rate of spatial attenuation of benefits from variety. Thus, effective variety is additive in the contribution to effective variety over locations, and the contribution to effective variety of a store at location $x$ to a shopper who travels to location $y$ to shop decreases exponentially in the distance between $x$ and $y$. Observe that the effective variety offered by a completely isolated store is normalized to be unity. Note also that (2) is a reduced-form specification, only implicitly taking into account search costs. Equation (2) is the same as the Fujita-Ogawa location potential function,[7] except for the addition of the 1.

*Individual Choice*

Each individual decides where to reside, $x$, and where to shop, $y$, so as to maximize utility, given by (1) and (2), subject to the budget constraint

$$Y - R(x)S - p(y)Q - t|x - y| = 0, \tag{3}$$

where $Y$ is exogenous income (endowment of the generic good), $R(x)$ is the rent function at $x$, $p(y)$ is the retail price function relating the retail price to shopping location, and $t$ is transport cost per unit distance.

*Land Ownership and Alternative Land Uses*

All land rents accrue to absentee landlords. Land not in urban use is employed in agriculture at a rent of $R_a$.

*Retail Technology*

Retailing is characterized by constant returns to scale. An atomistic store at $x$ purchases the generic good from households, transforms it into differentiated retail goods, which it then sells at the competitively determined retail price $p(x)$. Stores incur, in addition, a fixed cost per unit area $K$, which can be interpreted as capital costs, as well as land rent. Thus, the profit function per unit area is

$$\pi(x) = [p(x) - 1]Q(x) / s - K - R(x). \tag{4}$$

$Q(x)$ is the equilibrium quantity of retail goods purchased by an individual who shops at $x$ and $1/s$ is the number of individuals who shop at $x$, so that $Q(x)/s$ is the retail sales volume at $x$.

Equilibrium is defined to be a location pattern, described by $a(x)$, the proportion of land in retail use at $x$; $a^-(x)$, the proportion of land in residential use at $x$; $b$, the city boundary; a retail price function $p(x)$; and a rent function $R(x)$, such that all markets clear, no store can increase its profits per unit area by changing location, and no individual can increase her utility by changing either her residential or her shopping location. In equilibrium, all urban land is developed, so that $a(x) + a^-(x) = 1$ for $x \in [-b, b]$.

The constructive procedure to solve for equilibrium is the same as that employed by Fujita and Ogawa. For each qualitatively different location pattern, one solves for the set of parameter values consistent with the equilibrium conditions. To illustrate the procedure, the next section derives the set of parameter values consistent with a symmetric monocentric equilibrium, in which stores occupy the central area and on both sides residential lots extend from the outer boundary of the retail area to the city boundary, beyond which land is used in agriculture. We then derive the set of parameter values consistent with a completely mixed equilibrium, in which each individual purchases at a backyard store.

One might reasonably object to our specification of agglomeration economies in retailing. If one were to ask store owners why one location is more attractive than another, the first thing they likely would mention is customer volume. In our model, in contrast, store owners differentiate locations according to the competitive price. We defend our specification on three grounds: first, it is in keeping with our competitive assumptions;[8] second, if the model were extended to allow for variable structural density, shopping volume would be higher at locations with greater shopping variety; and, third, it is our impression that retail prices do differ significantly over locations.[9]

### A Monocentric Urban Configuration

In a monocentric urban configuration, the city is symmetric around the origin. Letting $f$ denote the distance of the retail-residential boundary from the city centre, the retail area, which extends from $-f$ to $f$, is flanked by two residential areas, one extending from $-b$ to $-f$, the other from $f$ to $b$. To simplify, where applicable, the right-hand side of the city shall be considered, for which the location index is positive. Thus:

$$f = Ns/2 \qquad b - f = NS/2 \qquad b = N(S + s)/2. \qquad (5)$$

This is a convenient point at which to record some properties of the effective variety function, (2):

For $x \in [0, f]$:

$$v(x) = 1 + k\int_{-f}^{x} \exp\{-\alpha(x-y)\}dy + k\int_{x}^{f} \exp\{-\alpha(y-x)\}dy > 0$$

$$v'(x) = k(\exp\{-\alpha(x+f)\} - \exp\{-\alpha(f-x)\}) < 0$$

$$v''(x) = -k\alpha(\exp\{-\alpha(x+f)\} + \exp\{-\alpha(f-x)\}) < 0. \tag{6}$$

For $x \in (f, b]$:

$$v(x) = 1 + k\int_{-f}^{f} \exp\{-\alpha(x-y)\}dy = 1 + (k/\alpha)(\exp\{-\alpha(x-f)\} - \exp\{-\alpha(x+f)\})$$

$$v'(x) = -k(\exp\{-\alpha(x-f)\} - \exp\{-\alpha(x+f)\}) = -\alpha(v(x)-1) < 0$$

$$v''(x) = -\alpha v'(x) > 0. \tag{7}$$

Also,

$$v(0) = 1 + (2k/\alpha)(1 - \exp\{-\alpha f\}), \quad v(f) = 1 + (k/\alpha)(1 - \exp\{-2\alpha f\})$$

$$v(b) = 1 + (k/\alpha)\exp\{-\alpha NS/2\}(1 - \exp\{-2\alpha f\}). \tag{8}$$

Thus, on the right-hand side of the city, the effective variety function declines monotonically with distance from the city centre, is positive everywhere, and is concave in the retail area and convex in the residential area.

The approach taken to solve for the monocentric equilibrium is essentially the same as that employed by Fujita and Ogawa. First, solve for the retail bid-rent function and the residential bid-rent function, taking as given two endogenous parameters: the equilibrium level of utility and the equilibrium retail price at the retail-residential boundary. Second, apply two equilibrium conditions to determine the two endogenous parameters, first that the retail bid rent equals the residential bid rent at the retail-residential boundary and, second, that the residential bid rent equals the agricultural bid rent at the urban boundary. Finally, check that the solution is consistent with the final equilibrium condition that 'land goes to that use which bids the most for it'; specifically, check that the retail bid rent exceeds the residential bid rent everywhere in the retail area, and that the residential bid rent exceeds the retail bid rent everywhere in the residential area.

*The Retail Bid-Rent Function*

The retail bid rent at $x$, $\Phi(x)$, is the maximum amount a retail firm is willing to bid in rent per unit area of land at $x$, which is the amount that drives its profits to zero. Thus, the retail bid rent at $x$ equals revenue minus non-land costs, the cost of wholesale goods plus the fixed cost:

$$\Phi(x) = [p(x) - 1]Q(x)/s - K. \tag{9}$$

In equilibrium, all identical individuals receive the same level of utility, $U^*$. Furthermore, $U = Qv$, so that

$$Q(x) = U^* / v(x). \tag{10}$$

Substituting (10) into (9) yields

$$\Phi(x) = [p(x) - 1]U^* / (sv(x)) - K. \tag{11}$$

*The Residential Bid-Rent Function*

The residential bid rent, $\Psi(x,U)$, is the maximum amount an individual residing at $x$ is willing to pay in rent per unit area of land, consistent with utility $U$. For the moment, consider the residential bid-rent function only in the residential area. Since, in equilibrium, all individuals are indifferent as to where they shop in the retail area, without loss of generality the individual who shops at $f$ is considered. The residential bid-rent function for $x \in (f, b)$ is

$$\Psi(x,U) = (Y - p(f)U / v(f) - t(x - f))/S. \tag{12}$$

The individual at $x$ spends $t(x - f)$ in shopping transport costs, and when she shops at $f$ has to spend $p(f)U/v(f)$ to achieve utility $U$, leaving $Y - p(f)U/v(f) - t(x-f)$ to spend on lot rent. Observe that, over the residential area, the residential bid rent varies with residential location so as to offset transport costs, that the residential bid-rent curve is linear in $x$, and that with fixed lot size the sum of the expenditures on transport costs and lot rent is constant across residential locations, which leaves a constant amount left over to spend on the differentiated retail goods. Thus, over the residential area, individual expenditure on differentiated retail goods is independent of both residential and shopping location. We consider later the form of the residential bid-rent function in the retail area.

### Equal Rent Conditions

One of the equal rent conditions is that the residential bid rent equals the agricultural bid rent at the city boundary:

$$R_a = \Psi(b,U) = (Y - p(f)U / v(f) - t(b - f)) / S. \tag{13}$$

Since transport costs at the urban boundary, as well as the boundary location are known, this equation can be solved for the equilibrium expenditure on differentiated retail goods:

$$p(f)U / v(f) = Y - t(b - f) - R_a S = Y - tNS / 2 - R_a S. \tag{14}$$

The other equal rent condition is that the residential bid rent equals the retail bid rent at the retail-residential boundary:

$$\Phi(f) = [p(f) - 1]U / (sv(f)) - K = (Y - p(f)U / v(f)) / S = \Psi(f,U), \tag{15}$$

which can be rewritten as

$$[p(f)U / v(f)][1 / s + 1 / S] = U / (sv(f)) + K + Y / S. \tag{16}$$

Substituting (14) into (16) and rearranging yields

$$U^* = v(f)\{(Y - [tNS / 2 + R_a S][1 + s / S] - Ks\}, \tag{17}$$

which gives the equilibrium level of utility $U^*$ as a function of exogenous parameters and $v(f)$, which can be calculated using (5) and (8). The causality underlying (17) is complicated by the endogeneity of the retail price function. Knowing the location of the city boundary and the rent there determines the equilibrium residential bid-rent curve (equations (12) and (13)). In the standard monocentric city model, knowing the equilibrium residential bid-rent curve permits determination of the equilibrium utility level, but here it permits us to determine only the equilibrium expenditure on retail goods. Since the equilibrium residential bid rent at the retail-residential boundary is known, the equal rent condition gives the equilibrium retail bid rent there. Knowing the retail bid rent there, as well as the equilibrium expenditure on the differentiated retail goods, permits determination of the equilibrium retail price at that location. Knowledge of the equilibrium expenditure $p(f)U/v(f)$, the equilibrium retail price, and the effective variety at that location then permits determination of the equilibrium level of utility, $U^*$. From (14) we obtain

$$p^*(f) = (Y - tNS/2 - R_aS)v(f)/U^*, \tag{18}$$

which gives the equilibrium $p(f)$ as a function of exogenous parameters.

*Completing the Solution*

Thus far, we have solved for the following: the equilibrium residential bid-rent function in the residential area, the equilibrium level of utility, and the equilibrium retail price and retail bid rent at the retail-residential boundary. It remains to solve for the complete equilibrium residential bid-rent, retail bid-rent, and retail price functions.

At whatever retail location $x$ an individual shops, in equilibrium she receives utility $U^* = Q^*(x)v(x)$ from consumption of the differentiated retail goods, yielding $Q^*(x) = U^*/v(x)$. Furthermore, in equilibrium, an individual who shops at location $x$ in the retail area and lives in the residential area spends $tNS/2 + R_aS + t(f - x)$ on her lot rent, leaving $Y - tNS/2 - R_aS - t(f - x)$ to spend on the retail good. Thus, $p^*(x)Q^*(x) = Y - tNS/2 - R_aS - t(f - x)$. Combining these results yields

$$p^*(x) = [Y - tNS/2 - R_aS - t(f - x)]v(x)/U^*$$

$$= [Y - R_aS - t(b - x)]v(x)/U^* \text{ for } x \in [0,f]. \tag{19}$$

To derive the retail price function in the residential area, consider a store at location $y$ in the residential area. Only individuals who live further away from the city centre than $y$ would patronize this store. Such an individual who lives at $x > y$ pays $R_aS + t(b - y)$ in lot rent and transport cost, leaving $Y - R_aS - t(b - y)$ to spend on retail goods. Thus, $p^*(y)Q^*(y) = Y - R_aS - t(b - y)$. Combining this result with $Q^*(x) = U^*/v(x)$ and with (19) gives

$$p^*(x) = [Y - R_aS - t(b - x)]v(x)/U^* \text{ for } x \in [0,b]. \tag{20}$$

Notice that the retail price function is the product of two terms. The first, in square brackets, which is increasing in $x$, reflects the reduced transport cost associated with less accessible shopping locations; the second, which is decreasing in $x$, reflects the reduced product variety at less accessible locations. As a result, the retail price function may be either increasing or decreasing in $x$.

Having solved for the equilibrium retail price function, it is straightforward to solve for the equilibrium retail bid-rent function:

$$\Phi^*(x) = [p^*(x) - 1]U^* / (sv(x)) - K. \tag{21}$$

Notice that this function is a product of two terms. The first term, the retail markup, might be either increasing or decreasing in $x$; the second term, the quantity purchased, is increasing in $x$. Consequently, the equilibrium retail bid-rent function might be either increasing or decreasing in $x$.

The equilibrium residential bid-rent function for residential locations has already been solved for. To solve for the function in the retail area, consider an individual who resides in the retail area, $x \in [0,f)$. Although she is indifferent between shopping at her residential location and at any location closer to the city centre, assume that she shops at her residential location. There, she consumes a lot of size $S$, receives a level of utility $U^* = Q^*(x)v(x)$ from retail goods, and spends $p^*(x)Q^*(x)$ on them. Thus, for $x \in [0,f]$:

$$\Psi^*(x,U) = (Y - p^*(x)U^* / v(x)) / S = R_a + t(b - x)) / S \text{ (using (20)).} \tag{22}$$

Expressed in terms of exogenous parameters, from (12), (19), (20), and (22), the equilibrium residential bid-rent function is

$$\Psi^*(x,U) = R_a + t(b - x)) / S \text{ for } x \in [0,b], \tag{23}$$

which is linearly decreasing in $x$. And, using (20), and (21), the equilibrium retail bid-rent function expressed in terms of exogenous parameters and $v(x)$ is

$$\Phi^*(x) = [Y - R_a S - t(b - x)] / s - U^* / (sv(x)) - K \text{ for } x \in [0,b]. \tag{24}$$

As noted earlier, the retail bid-rent function may be either positively or negatively sloped. Also,

$$\text{sgn}[d^2\Phi^*(x) / dx^2] = \text{sgn}[v''v - 2(v')^2]. \tag{25}$$

From (6) it follows that $\Phi^*(x)$ is concave in the retail area. In the residential area, from (7), $v''v - 2(v')^2 = -\alpha^2(v-1)(v-2)$, so that the retail bid-rent function is concave at those residential locations for which $v > 2$ and convex where $v < 2$.

*Checking that the Solution Is Indeed a Monocentric Urban Configuration*

For the solution to characterize a monocentric urban configuration, it must be the case that the residential bid rent exceeds the retail bid rent everywhere in the retail area and that the retail bid rent exceeds the residential bid rent everywhere in the retail area. Since the residential bid-rent curve is linear while the retail bid-rent curve is concave in the retail area and can change curvature only once in the residential area, from concave to convex as $x$ increases, it follows that these two conditions are satisfied if, first, the retail bid rent exceeds the residential bid rent at the city centre, and, second, if the residential bid rent exceeds the retail bid rent at the urban boundary. The former condition, which we term the first inequality, is

$$\Phi(0) = [Y - R_a S - tb] / s - U^* / (sv(0)) - K > R_a + tb / S = \Psi(0). \quad (26)$$

The latter condition, which we term the second inequality, is that

$$\Phi(b) = [Y - R_a S] / s - U^* / (sv(b)) - K < R_a = \Psi(b). \quad (27)$$

These conditions can be simplified by using the equilibrium condition that the residential and retail bid rents are the same at the retail-residential boundary:

$$\Phi(f) = [Y - R_a S - t(b - f)] / s - U^* / (sv(f)) - K = R_a +$$

$$t(b - f) / S = \Psi(f). \quad (28)$$

Combining (26) and (28), the first inequality reduces to

$$(U^* / s)(1 / v(f) - 1 / v(0)) - tf / s > tf / S. \quad (29)$$

Substituting out for $f$ and for $U^*/v(f)$ using (17), this inequality reduces to

$$\{(Y - R_a(s + S) - Ks\}[1 - v(Ns / 2) / v(0)]$$

$$> [tN(s + S) / 2](1 + s / S - v(Ns / 2) / v(0)). \quad (30)$$

Note that, as intuition suggests, the first inequality is easier to satisfy the lower is unit transport cost. Now consider the second inequality. Combining (27) and (28) yields the inequality

$$(U^* / s)(1 / v(b) - 1 / v(f)) - t(b - f) / s > t(b - f) / S. \quad (31)$$

Substituting out for f and for $U^*/v(f)$ using (17), this inequality reduces to

$$\{(Y - R_a(s+S) - Ks\}[v(Ns/2)/v(N(s+S)/2) - 1]$$

$$> [tN(s+S)/2]v(Ns/2)/v(N(s+S)/2). \tag{32}$$

The second inequality, too, is easier to satisfy the lower is unit transport cost. That both inequalities are easier to satisfy the lower is unit transport cost implies that a monocentric urban configuration is 'more likely' to be an equilibrium, the lower is unit transport cost, as intuition would suggest. Note that the exogenous parameters in the above inequalities are $Y$, $t$, $N$, $S$, $s$, $K$, $\alpha$, and $k$.

Throughout the paper, we consider a single numerical example. The following parameter values are employed: $N = 2 \times 10^4$, $S = 2 \times 10^{-5}$ $mile$, $s = 10^{-5}$ $mile^2$, $k = 10^9$\$$/mile^2$, $Y = 3 \times 10^4$\$, $t = 2700$\$$/mile$, $R_a = 3.2 \times 10^6$\$$/mile^2$, $\alpha = 10$, and $k = 0.6$. With these parameters, both a monocentric equilibrium and a completely mixed equilibrium exist.

Figure 5.1 plots the equilibrium spatial configuration, and effective variety, retail price, and rent, as functions of location, with these parameter values. The graphs are as expected. The top panel shows that the retail district, marked as BD, is at the city centre, and flanked by residential areas, marked as RA. The effective variety function declines monotonically from the city centre with an inflection point at the retail-residential boundary, between a concave region inside the retail-residential boundary and convex regions outside it. The retail price function is concave on each side of the retail area (as was derived above) and has its maximum away from the city centre. The rent function is the upper envelope of the equilibrium retail bid-rent curve and the equilibrium residential bid-rent curve. In the example, the retail bid-rent function is concave on each side of the city centre and achieves the maximum away from the city centre. The residential bid rent falls off linearly from the city centre.

Figure 5.2, panel A, plots the set of $(\alpha, t)$ for which a monocentric urban configuration exists. The other parameters are held fixed at their base case values. The area below the dashed line satisfies the first inequality and that below the solid line the second inequality. The shaded area is the region in which both inequalities are satisfied, and in which therefore a monocentric urban equilibrium exists.[10] Consider first holding $\alpha$ fixed and raising the unit transport cost until a monocentric equilibrium fails to exist. There are two cases to consider. If the first inequality is violated, the residential bid rent at the city centre exceeds the retail bid rent there, so that, with the supposed

Figure 5.1: A Monocentric Urban Configuration

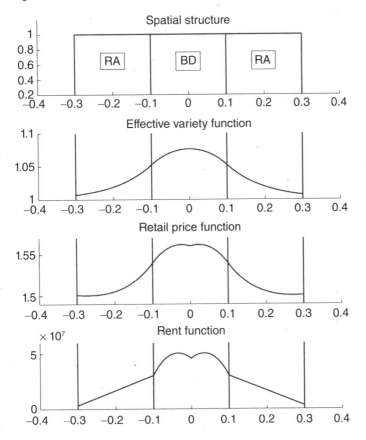

rent function, an individual can achieve a higher utility at the city centre than in the residential area. If the second inequality is violated, the retail bid rent at the urban boundary exceeds the residential bid rent there, so that it would be profitable for a firm to relocate from the retail area to the urban boundary. Next, consider holding $t$ fixed and varying $\alpha$ – the rate of decay of the benefit in terms of effective variety from proximity to other stores. At very low levels of $\alpha$, with a monocentric urban configuration effective variety would decline so slowly with distance from the city centre that the benefit to the individual from shopping at a more central location would be more than offset by the higher travel costs. At high levels of $\alpha$, with a monocentric urban configuration, effective variety declines so rapidly with distance from the city centre that a store could profit by moving from the retail area to the urban boundary.

Figure 5.2, panel B, plots the set of ($LogN,k$) for which a monocentric urban configuration exists. The other parameter values are held at their base case levels. Holding population fixed, a monocentric equilibrium exists when the preference for variety is sufficiently strong; otherwise, an individual would not find it worthwhile to travel to a more central location to do her shopping. Now hold $k$ fixed. For low levels of population, the rate at which effective variety increases with proximity to the centre does not increase sufficiently to justify travelling to shop. At high levels of population, it is profitable for a single store to relocate to the urban boundary.

## A Completely Mixed Urban Configuration

In a completely mixed urban configuration, retail and residential land uses are interspersed so that each individual essentially has a store in his backyard. In this section, we determine the set of parameter values for which this configuration is an equilibrium. Note that the completely mixed urban configuration and the monocentric urban configuration are extreme cases: in one, stores are as centralized as possible; in the other, they are as decentralized as possible. Intuition therefore suggests that the parameter set for which equilibria of both types exist may be empty, as it is in Fujita and Ogawa (1982).

The city extends from $-b$ to $b$, with $b = N(S + s)/2$, with a proportion $s/(s + S) = a$ of the land at each location being allocated to retail and the rest to residential use. The effective variety function is the same as for the monocentric city configuration, except that $a(x) = a$ throughout the urban area, rather than equalling 1 in the retail area and 0 in the residential area as was the case in the monocentric urban configuration. Thus, for $x \in [0,b]$:

$$v(x) = 1 + ka \int_{-b}^{x} \exp\{-\alpha(x - y)\}dy + ka \int_{x}^{b} \exp\{-\alpha(y - x)\}dy > 0$$

and

$$v'(x) = ka(\exp\{-\alpha(x + f)\} - \exp\{-\alpha(f - x)\}) < 0$$

$$v''(x) = -ka\alpha(\exp\{-\alpha(x + f)\} + \exp\{-\alpha(f - x)\}) < 0. \tag{33}$$

Figure 5.2: Equilibrium Conditions for a Monocentric Urban Configuration

*A. The Set of (α,t)*

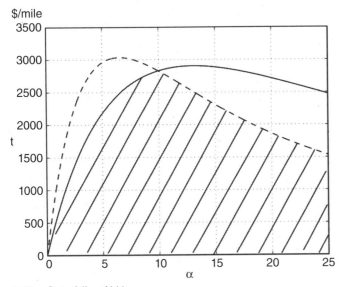

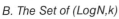

*B. The Set of (LogN,k)*

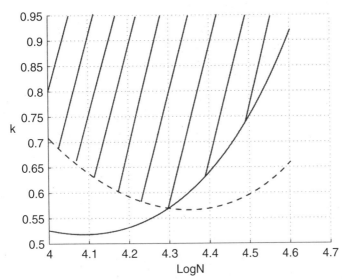

Also,

$$v(0) = 1 + (2ka / \alpha)(1 - \exp\{-\alpha b\})$$

$$v(b) = 1 + (ka / \alpha)(1 - \exp\{-2\alpha b\}). \tag{34}$$

Thus, the effective variety function declines monotonically from the city centre and is concave throughout the city.

For the retail bid-rent function, equations (9) through (11) continue to apply.

For the residential bid-rent function, everyone shops at their backyard store and therefore incurs no transport costs. Thus,

$$\Psi(x,U) = (Y - p(x)U / v(x)) / S. \tag{35}$$

For equal rent conditions, since retail and residential land co-exist at all urban locations, in equilibrium,

$$\Phi(x) = \Psi(x) = R(x) \text{ for } x \in [0,b],$$

where $R(x)$ is the rent function, or

$$[p(x) - 1]U / (sv(x)) - K = (Y - p(x)U / v(x)) / S. \tag{36}$$

Rewrite (36) as

$$p(x) = [1 + (Ks + Ys / S)v(x) / U] / (1 + s / S). \tag{36'}$$

Also, in equilibrium at the city boundary, both the retail and residential bid rents equal the agricultural bid rent:

$$Y - p(b)U / v(b) = R_a S. \tag{37}$$

Substituting (37) into (36') evaluated at $x = b$ yields

$$U^* = v(b)[Y - R_a(s + S) - Ks], \tag{38}$$

which gives the equilibrium level of utility in terms of exogenous parameters.

Substituting (38) into (36') would give an expression for $p(x)$ in terms of only $v(x)$ and exogenous parameters. Now, insert (36') into (35) to give the rent function:

$$R(x) = \{Y - [U^* / v(x) + (Ks + Ys / S)]\} / (s + S). \tag{39}$$

The condition for the existence of a completely mixed configuration is that the rent function has a slope with absolute value less than $t / S$, since otherwise it would be worthwhile for some individuals to commute inwards to shop. Now,

$$R'(x) = U^* v'(x) / [v^2(x)(s + S)]. \tag{40}$$

Since $d(v'(x) / v^2(x)) / dx = (1 / v^2)(vv'' - 2(v')^2) < 0$ from (33), $|R'(x)|$ takes on its highest value at $x = b$. Thus, the condition for the existence of a completely mixed urban configuration is that $-U^* v'(b) / v^2(b) < t(s + S) / S$ or, using (33), (34), and (38), that

$$[Y - R_a(s + S) - Ks][ks(1 - \exp\{-2\alpha N(s + S) / 2\}) / (s + S)]$$

$$> t(1 + s / S)[1 + (ks / \alpha)(1 - \exp\{-2\alpha N(s + S) / 2\}) / (s + S)]. \tag{41}$$

Two features of the inequality bear note. Most importantly, there exists some critical level of $t$, $\hat{t}(Y, R_a, S, s, k, N)$, above which a completely mixed urban configuration exists and below which it does not. Also, the conditions for such a configuration are more stringent the higher is per capita 'net endowment,' $Y - R_a(s + S) - Ks$.

We now return to the numerical example. Figure 5.3 plots the spatial structure, and effective variety, retail price, and rent, as functions of location. The graphs are as expected. The top panel shows that the spatial structure, marked ID, is uniform over the city. The effective variety, retail price, and rent functions decline monotonically with distance from the city centre and are concave.

Figure 5.4, panel A, plots the set of $(\alpha, t)$ for which a completely mixed urban equilibrium exists. The other parameters are held at their base case levels. With this spatial configuration, only one inequality needs to be satisfied. The set of parameter pairs satisfying the inequality, and for which, therefore, a completely mixed urban equilibrium exists, is indicated by the

Figure 5.3: Completely Mixed Urban Configuration

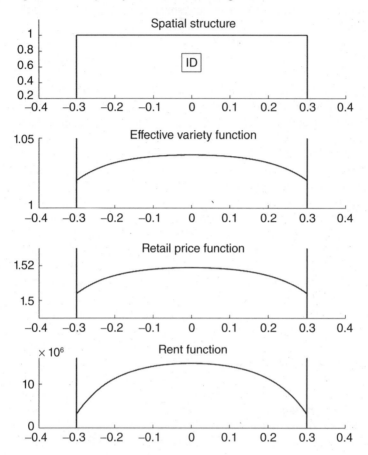

cross-hatched area. Consider first holding $\alpha$ fixed and lowering the unit transport cost. Below a critical level of the unit transport cost, a completely mixed urban equilibrium does not exist since, at some locations at least, an individual can improve her utility by shopping at a more central location that offers greater product variety. Consider next holding $t$ fixed and varying $\alpha$. For low levels of $\alpha$, effective variety does not fall off sufficiently rapidly with distance from the city centre to make travel to shop at more central locations, with greater retail variety, worthwhile, while for higher levels of $\alpha$ effective variety does fall off sufficiently rapidly to make it worthwhile.

Figure 5.4, panel B shows the region in ($LogN,k$) space for which a completely mixed urban configuration exists. When the taste for variety is sufficiently high, there are some locations at which effective variety and the taste for variety increase sufficiently rapidly with proximity to the city centre to justify travel to shop, and for which therefore a completely mixed equilibrium does not exist.

Figure 5.5 displays the region of ($\alpha,t$) space for which both the monocentric and completely mixed equilibria co-exist. A monocentric equilibrium exists in the region below the dashed and solid line and a completely mixed urban equilibrium in the region above the dash-dot line. In the small cross-hatched region, which is centred on the parameter values of the numerical example, both types of equilibria co-exist. We have already provided some intuition for the shapes of the regions in this space for which each of the two equilibria exist. Start at the point in the cross-hatched area corresponding to the values of $t$ and $\alpha$ in the numerical example, and move SE to the area where neither type of equilibrium exists. The monocentric equilibrium ceases to exist since the first inequality is violated – with a monocentric urban configuration, an individual can achieve a higher level of utility at the centre than in the residential area. The completely mixed equilibrium ceases to exist since, in the completely mixed configuration, it becomes worthwhile for the individual at the urban boundary to travel a small distance toward the city centre to shop; the cost of travel falls and the benefit increases.

Now, instead, move SW to the area where neither type of equilibrium exists. The monocentric equilibrium ceases to exist since the second inequality ceases to be satisfied – with a monocentric urban configuration, it becomes profitable for a single store to move from the retail area to the urban boundary; the decrease in the spatial decay rate of proximity benefits causes the difference in the effective variety at the retail location compared with the urban boundary to fall, and this effect more than offsets the increased attractiveness of shopping in the retail area due to the decline in transport costs. The completely mixed equilibrium ceases to exist because, in a completely mixed urban configuration, it becomes worthwhile for the individual at the urban boundary to travel a small distance toward the city centre; the cost of travel falls by more than the benefit does.

Figure 5.6 displays the region of ($LogN,k$) space in which the two types of equilibria exist. A monocentric equilibrium exists in the region above the dashed and solid line and a completely mixed equilibrium in the region below the dash-dot line. In the small cross-hatched region, which is centred on the parameter values of the numerical example, both types of equilibria co-exist. Start at the point in the cross-hatched area with the values of $k$

Figure 5.4: Equilibrium Conditions for a Completely Mixed Urban Configuration

*A. The Set of (α,t)*

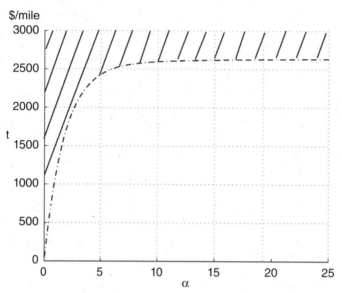

*B. The Set of (LogN,k)*

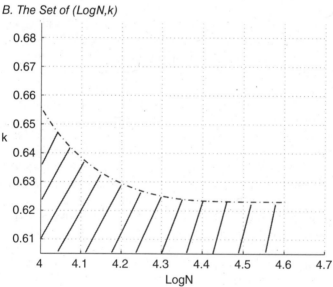

Figure 5.5: Equilibrium Condition for the Set of $(\alpha,t)$ for a Monocentric, Completely Mixed Urban Configuration

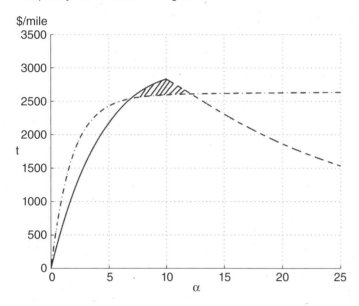

and $N$ in the numerical example. Holding population fixed, in the completely mixed urban configuration, with an increase in the taste for variety that the benefit from shopping closer to the city centre increases, resulting in the completely mixed equilibrium failing to exist; and with a decrease in the taste for variety in the monocentric urban configuration, either an individual can increase his utility by living at the city centre or it becomes profitable for a store to relocate to the urban boundary. The explanation for how the existence of the two types of equilibria depends on population, holding fixed the taste for variety, is left to the reader.

We have considered two qualitative spatial configurations, the monocentric and the completely mixed, but there are many other possibilities, including the incompletely mixed and the duocentric. The procedures for determining the parameter set for each of these other configurations are variations of the procedures developed for the monocentric and completely mixed configurations.

**Concluding Comments**

In this paper, we have developed a competitive model of retail agglomeration. While the model is very simple, the simplifying assumptions are not

Figure 5.6: Equilibrium Condition for the Set of (LogN,k) for a Monocentric, Completely Mixed Urban Configuration

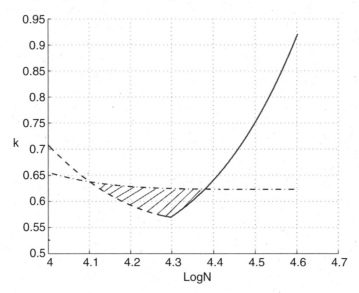

substantive in the sense that the same approach can – and will – be applied in the dynamic, competitive general equilibrium simulation model of the LA Metropolitan Area, tentatively named METRO-LA, which builds on Alex Anas's RELU-TRAN model for Chicago (Anas and Liu 2007), and in the development of which Anas and Arnott are participating. In these concluding comments, we describe briefly how this paper's model could be extended for this application.

One module of the LA model solves for the temporary (static) equilibrium for each period. Each period inherits a stock of properties (vacant land and land with structures on it) indexed by type and zone, as well as location potentials indexed by industry type and zone, and the effective varieties indexed by zone. The temporary equilibrium is like a static Arrow-Debreu competitive equilibrium with (commodity) transport costs,[11] except that: first, each household consumes property at only one location and incurs transport costs, for commuting from its chosen residential location to its chosen work location, for shopping, recreational activities, and so on;[12] second, retail goods are distinguished from wholesale goods; third, the economy is endowed with structures, as well as conventional factors of production; and fourth, agglomeration economies in production and retailing are treated via industry-specific location potential functions and an effective variety function.[13] A temporary equilibrium is characterized by a market-clearing set of prices and the corresponding allocation. The location potential functions and effective variety function can be solved for from the location pattern of the temporary equilibrium of one period and then treated as exogenous in determining the next period's temporary equilibrium.

The second module links the time periods. The present is linked to the past via the inheritance of real properties, location potential functions, and the effective variety function.[14] The present is linked to the future via real property markets. Economic agents have perfect foresight, and the market value of a property equals the expected present discounted value of future net rents.[15] Between periods, developers make profit-maximizing conversion decisions, building on vacant land, demolishing structures, allowing some existing properties to deteriorate and rehabilitating others, and so on, which moves the property stock forward from one period to the next.[16] Currently, the demography of the model is exogenous, but the aim is to make it responsive to economic conditions. The base industries grow according to the time path of export prices, which are taken as exogenous.

Despite the higher complexity of the LA model, the economics of retail agglomeration are essentially the same as those described in this paper. The essential component is the effective variety function, which relates the attractiveness to individuals of shopping at different locations to the spatial distribution of stores. Taking the spatial pattern of retail location, as reflected in the effective variety function, and of retail prices as given, individuals choose where to shop, trading off the greater variety of retail goods at larger shopping centres against the higher prices there and (for most individuals) the higher transport costs of travelling to a larger centre. Stores choose where to locate trading off the higher price they can charge at a larger centre against the higher rent they must pay there and in equilibrium make zero profits. The spatial pattern of retail prices, as well as the retail and residential bid-rent functions and the effective variety function, adjust simultaneously to clear the location-specific markets for retail goods as well as the location-specific land markets.

NOTES

1  Richard Arnott would like to thank Daniel Chen for his excellent research assistance in preparing a literature survey on retail location (Chen 2007) and participants at the Conference in Honour of B. Curtis Eaton and at the

Macroeconomics, Real Estate and Public Policy Workshop, Istanbul, for helpful comments, especially John Quigley for reminding us of the Lowry model. Yundong Tu would like to thank the Edward J. Blakely Center for Sustainable Suburban Development for financial assistance.

2  These include Eaton (1976); Eaton and Lipsey (1975, 1979, 1982); and Eaton and Wooders (1985).

3  There is a vast literature on the subject. Some well-known papers include Huff (1964, 1966); Craig, Ghosh, and McLafferty (1984); Weisbrod, Parcells, and Kern (1984); Brown (1989, 1993); Drezner and Drezner (1996); and Clark, Bennison, and Pal (1997). Kohsaka (1984) is representative of papers that look at optimal shopping centre location.

4  The literature on this topic is less extensive. Three well-known papers are Cadwaller (1975); Bell, Ho, and Tang (1998); and Bucklin, Gupta, and Siddarth (1998).

5  An earlier version of the paper employs the more realistic assumption that physical sales volume per unit area is fixed. With this assumption, however, the algebra is considerably more complex and little additional insight was obtained.

6  Trip frequency could be endogenized by adding home inventory costs. An individual residing at a location that is less accessible to shops would travel less frequently to shop and keep a larger inventory of goods at home.

7  $v(x)$ could be termed the retail location potential function, but this term is used in the earlier literature (for example, Lowry 1964) to refer to the profitability of a location to a store, whereas $v(x)$ refers to the attractiveness of a location from the perspective of a customer.

8  Our model could be adapted without difficulty so that retailers are monopolistically competitive rather than perfectly competitive, but the treatment of other industry structures (except monopoly, which is unrealistic) would result in intractability.

9  This is difficult to document because of sales, discounts, and product choice. Consider, for example, goods that have a suggested retail price. A store owner could lower his average markup on such goods by selling them at a deeper discount, selling them at the discounted price a greater proportion of the time, having deeper and more frequent store-wide sales, and choosing to sell those goods for which the ratio of the suggested retail price to the wholesale price is lower. The higher price of groceries in ghetto locations is documented. Labour economists have used the McDonald's wage to measure intrametropolitan spatial variation in wages. Perhaps the same could be done for product prices.

10 In Fujita and Ogawa (1982), in contrast to this paper, one of the inequalities implies the other. The region in which both inequalities hold has the same

qualitative shape as in Figure 5.2, panel A. We suspect that the difference derives primarily from a difference in the assumed form of the spatial decay function. In our paper, the effective variety at an isolated store is unity; in Fujita and Ogawa, in contrast, the productivity of an isolated firm is zero.

11 Each household maximizes its utility and each firm maximizes its profits, taking prices as fixed. There is potentially an arbitrarily large but finite number of types of individuals and of retail and intermediate goods.

12 In the Arrow-Debreu model, the assumption of convex preferences would result in households diversifying their housing consumption over locations, and people transport costs are not treated.

13 An industry-specific location potential function can depend on proximity to firms in other industries as well to firms in the same industry, and similarly for a retail-good-type-specific index of effective variety.

14 In the model of the paper, the effective variety function is determined as part of the static equilibrium, taking as given the qualitative spatial configuration. In a corresponding dynamic model, effective variety as a function of location could be calculated as part of that period's temporary equilibrium, taking as the starting point in the computation the equilibrium effective variety function from the previous period, which would generate some history dependence in the location pattern. METRO-LA assumes instead that the locational potential functions and effective variety functions calculated from one period's temporary equilibrium are taken as exogenous in the next period's temporary equilibrium. This (substantive) simplifying assumption is made to reduce computational costs.

15 A nonstationary, infinite horizon model obviously cannot be solved exactly with a computer, which has finite computational ability; the model must be truncated somehow. In the LA model, the truncation is done by assuming that, at some terminal time, the economy's property values correspond to those of a stationary equilibrium.

16 Individual utilities and developer conversion costs are treated as idiosyncratic (in particular, the logit algebra is employed) so as to smooth adjustment, which facilitates computation.

## REFERENCES

Arnott, R., and C. Erbil. 2008. 'Competitive Retail Agglomeration.' Mimeographed.

Bell, D., T.-H. Ho, and C. Tang. 1998. 'Determining Where to Shop: Fixed and Variable Costs of Shopping.' *Journal of Marketing Research* 35 (3): 352–69.

Berry, B. 1967. *Geography of Market Centers and Retail Distribution*. Englewood Cliffs, NJ: Prentice-Hall.

Brown, S. 1989. 'Retail Location Theory: The Legacy of Harold Hotelling.' *Journal of Retailing* 65 (4): 450–70.

– 1993. 'Retail Location Theory: Evolution and Evaluation,' *International Review of Retail, Distribution and Consumer Research* 3 (2): 185–229.

Bucklin, R., S. Gupta, and S. Siddarth. 1998. 'Determining Segmentation in Sales Response across Consumer Purchase Behaviors.' *Journal of Marketing Research* 35 (2): 189–97.

Cadwaller, M. 1975. 'A Behavioral Model of Consumer Spatial Decision Making.' *Economic Geography* 51 (4): 339–49.

Chen, D. 2007. 'Optimal Retail Location Theory and Shopping Trip Behavior: A General Summary and Literature Review.' Mimeographed.

Clark, I., D. Bennison, and J. Pal. 1997. 'Towards a Contemporary Perspective of Retail Location.' *International Journal of Retail and Distribution Management* 25 (2): 59–69.

Craig, S., A. Ghosh, and S. McLafferty. 1984. 'Models of the Retail Location Process: A Review.' *Journal of Retailing* 60 (1): 5–36.

Drezner, T., and Z. Drezner. 1996. 'Competitive Facilities: Market Share and Location with Random Utility.' *Journal of Regional Science* 36 (1): 1–15.

Eaton, B.C. 1976. 'Free Entry in One-Dimensional Models: Pure Profits and Multiple Equilibria.' *Journal of Regional Science* 16 (1): 21–33.

Eaton, B.C., and R.G. Lipsey. 1975. 'The Principle of Minimum Differentiation Reconsidered: Some New Developments in the Theory of Spatial Competition.' *Review of Economic Studies* 42 (1): 27–49.

– 1979. 'Comparison Shopping and the Clustering of Homogeneous Firms.' *Journal of Regional Science* 19 (4): 421–35.

– 1982. 'An Economic Theory of Central Places.' *Economic Journal* 92 (365): 56–72.

Eaton, B.C., and M.H. Wooders. 1985. 'Sophisticated Entry in a Model of Spatial Competition.' *RAND Journal of Economics* 16 (2): 282–97.

Fujita, M., and H. Ogawa. 1982. 'Multiple Equilibria and Structural Transition of Non Monocentric Urban Configurations.' *Regional Science and Urban Economics* 12 (1): 161–96.

Goldner, W. 1971. 'The Lowry Model Heritage.' *Journal of the American Planning Association* 37 (2): 100–10.

Harris, B. 1985. 'Urban Simulation Models in Regional Science.' *Journal of Regional Science* 25 (4): 545–67.

Huff, D. 1964. 'Defining and Estimating a Trading Area.' *Journal of Marketing* 28 (3): 34–8.

– 1966. 'A Programmed Solution for Approximating an Optimum Retail Location.' *Land Economics* 42 (3): 293–303.

Kohsaka, H. 1984. 'An Optimization of the Central Place System in Terms of Multipurpose Shopping Trips.' *Geographical Analysis* 16 (3): 250–68.

Lowry, I.S. 1964. *A Model of Metropolis*. Memorandum RM-4035-RC. Santa Monica, CA: RAND Corporation.

– 1968. *Seven Models of Urban Development: A Structural Comparison*. Urban Development Models Special Report 97. Washington, DC: Highway Research Board, National Research Council.

Weisbrod, G., R. Parcells, and C. Kern. 1984. 'A Disaggregated Model for Predicting Shopping Area Market Attraction.' *Journal of Retailing* 60 (1): 65–83.

Wilson, A. 1970. *Entropy in Urban and Regional Modeling*. London: Pion.

– 1974. *Urban and Regional Models in Geography and Planning*. New York: Wiley.

# PART III

## Trade and Productivity

# 6 The Interaction between Education, Skilled Migration, and Trade

RICHARD G. HARRIS AND PETER E. ROBERTSON

The subject of this paper is the interaction between migration and human capital. These are both fields in which Curt Eaton has made important contributions – albeit under very different assumptions regarding information completeness and market structure.[1] Likewise, our central research question will be familiar to any of Curt's students – that is, how do individuals respond to the institutions they face? Specifically, in this paper, the central question is, how do individuals adjust their education decisions to changes in skilled immigration in a small, open economy?

Over the past decade, flows of skilled labour from developing to developed countries have increased dramatically, in part related to the increased global supply of labour, particularly with the opening of China, India, and the former Soviet bloc (see Salt 1997; Freeman 2006; International Monetary Fund 2007). In addition, there has been a sharp shift in demand for skilled immigrants in developed market economies. Many developed countries, including Australia, Canada, the United Kingdom, and Germany, have sought to take advantage of the foreign supply of skilled workers by tailoring their immigration programs to attract workers with skills (Cobb-Clarke 2004).[2] With the Kennedy-Rodino *Immigration Act of 1990* and immigration reform currently being considered at various levels of government, the United States has also moved toward skilled migration policies.[3]

An extensive literature on the effects of skilled migration exists – from the perspective of both host and source countries. With respect to the host country, much of the focus is on the effects on factor returns and policies that provide incentives to attract 'brains.' There is relatively little research, however, on the effects of increased skilled labour inflows on economic growth or human capital accumulation. Developing analytically tractable models that are useful to policy-makers in looking at these dynamic issues is a major research challenge. In this paper, we present one such model, with a specific application to education and immigration policy in Australia.

The model we develop focuses on two interaction effects of skilled labour migration within an open economy. The first is the effect of migration on the endogenous production of human capital. Changes in the returns to human capital have an effect on both the supply and the demand for education. Over time, the dynamic accumulation response of the stock of skilled labour to policies that either stimulate the supply of human capital (such as education subsidies) or the demand for human capital (such as changes in immigration quotas) will affect growth and factor returns. Second, both migration and education policies are influenced by the causal linkages among trade, factor endowments, and factor prices, as emphasized in traditional trade theory. A highly open economy can import indirectly the services of skilled labour by increasing the import of skills-intensive goods. The traditional model predicts that, in open economies, changes in the supply of factor endowments has little effect on factor returns but a large effect on the composition of output and trade. But even small, open economies have significant nontradable sectors that will tend to dampen this quantity response.

We focus on Australia as an advanced, small, highly open economy in which there has been a dramatic increase in skilled visa migrants in the past decade and substantial public support for tertiary education. The main result of the policy simulations suggests that a change in the composition of migration toward highly skilled labour has a substantial crowding-out effect on the education sector in the host country.

The rest of the paper proceeds as follows. In the next section, we discuss the policy background. We then lay out the model and discuss the results of calibrated simulations that contrast education and migration as means of enhancing human capital accumulation. The paper ends with concluding comments.

## Policy Background

The U.S. literature on immigration has been quite tentative in endorsing skilled immigration as beneficial to that country. In particular, Borjas (2006) emphasizes some negative impacts of skilled immigration on skilled wages and the crowding out of university places by foreign students.[4] Borjas (1995) also emphasizes that the national welfare gains from immigration are very small.[5]

In Australia, however, where the points system has been in place since the 1970s, the literature on skills-based immigration is more sanguine. In particular, a number of studies have indicated that the points system has contributed to better labour market outcomes for migrants (see Withers 1987; Cobb-Clarke and Connolly 1997; Miller 1999).[6]

Within the broad immigration literature, however, there has been relatively little discussion on the longer-term effects of skilled immigration on the human capital supply in the host country.[7] As an interesting point of contrast, standard models in the 'brain drain' literature recognize that the outflow of migrants increases the incentive for human capital investment among workers in the source country (see Bhagwati and Hamada 1974; McCulloch and Yellen 1975).[8] The flip side of this – that higher skilled immigrant inflows may crowd out education in the host country – has received very little attention.[9] Clearly, however, it is an important issue in terms of understanding how the mix of skilled workers in the immigration program affects the structure of the economy and the distribution of factor incomes.

### The Skilled Visa Program in Australia

Between 1990 and 1995, Australia halved the intake of permanent migrants from 120,000 per year to around 60,000. Between 2000 and 2006, however, the intake more than doubled to 140,000 immigrants per year. The remarkable feature of this change is that, while the number of family visa entrants stayed roughly constant at the 1999 level, the number of people entering under the skilled migrant quota increased dramatically (see Productivity Commission 2006). This change in composition can be seen in Figure 6.1.[10]

The expansion of the skilled visas category implies an increase in the average skill level of immigrants. According to the Productivity Commission, approximately 65 per cent of those entering under this category had a bachelors degree or equivalent, or higher. Although this is a high fraction, it is clear that the total intake of skilled visa migrants overstates the impact on domestic skill levels and on the ratio of skilled workers in the labour force. To gain a clearer picture of this, we consider the net flow of migrants who stated that they had a skilled occupation. These data, presented in Figure 6.2, reveal that the increase in the net inflow of skilled migrants was due almost entirely to a net increase in professional occupations.[11]

In terms of the impact on the labour supply in the economy, the inflow of skilled immigrants increased from 0.10 to 0.15 per cent of the labour force per year in the mid-1990s to 0.28 per cent of the labour force in 2004–05. In terms of numbers, it amounted to 15,000 professionals per year over the period 1996–2005, or 20,000 per year over the period 1999–2005. As we

Figure 6.1: Program Immigration Flows, Australia, 1989–2006

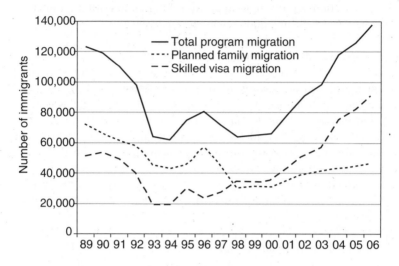

Sources: Birrell, Rapson, and Smith 2006; Productivity Commission 2006.

Figure 6.2: Net Flows of Skilled Immigrants Stating an Occupation, Australia, 1996–2005

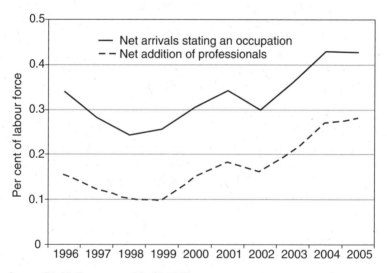

Source: Birrell, Rapson, and Smith 2006.

noted above, however, this increase in professionals mainly represented a change in the composition of immigration flows, as the total number of migrants between 1995 and 2006 remained relatively constant.

## Immigration and Skills Formation

To consider the effect of a change in the skills composition of immigration on human capital formation, we employ a multisector computable general equilibrium model. The model has been employed elsewhere to quantify the interactions between trade and economic growth (see Harris and Robertson 2007b). In particular, it incorporates endogenous skills formation with both a supply and a demand for education. The education sector produces skilled workers after a given schooling period. This section describes the human capital dynamics of the model, which also incorporates the possibility of skilled immigration.

First, we let the working population, or labour force, at time $t$ be denoted $P_t$. The additions to the labour force have two sources: births and net immigrant flows. Let $m_t = M_t / P_t$ be the net immigration rate. Then, allowing for retirements, the net increase in the labour force is

$$P_{t+1} = (1 + b_t + m_t - d_t)P_t, \tag{1}$$

where $b_t$ is the birth rate and $d_t$ is the retirement rate. Thus, once migrants enter the economy, they form part of the representative household and have similar birth and death rates to those of the native-born population. At a point in time, the labour force is defined in terms of skilled labour, $LS$, unskilled labour $LU$, and students, $H$:

$$P_t = LS_t + LU_t + H_t. \tag{2}$$

The population that is not skilled can either work as unskilled labour or go to school. The stock of skilled labour thus depends on past schooling decisions by unskilled workers and the skills levels of past migrant flows. We denote the number of migrants who are skilled as $\gamma_t M_t$, where $\gamma_t$ is the fraction of skilled migrants and is assumed to be an exogenous policy instrument. Thus, increasing the skilled migrant intake can be interpreted as a change in $\gamma_t$.

The second source of skilled labour is the flow of students graduating each year and entering the skilled labour force. Thus, we have $E_t = H_t / \varsigma$, where $H_t$ is the stock of students, $E_t$ is the flow of graduates, and $\varsigma$ is number of years in school. This identity ignores the fact that, during periods of substantial growth and a very long schooling period, the number of graduates as a fraction of the stock of students would not be constant. However, provided the period of advanced schooling is not too long, the relationship will hold fairly closely.[12] The updating equation for skilled labour is then

$$LS_{t+1} = LS_t + H_t / \zeta + \gamma M_t - d\, LS_t. \tag{3}$$

*The Steady State*

It is useful to consider briefly the steady-state constraints on migration and schooling flows. The ratio of skilled labour to population, $\lambda = LS_t / P_t$, must be constant on a steady-state path and, hence, $LS_t$ must grow at the long-run population growth rate. Likewise, on a steady-state path, the birth rate, $b$, retirement rate, $d$, and net migration rate, $m$, must be constant. Thus, dividing equation (3) by $LS_t$ and re-arranging gives

$$\frac{H / \zeta + \gamma M}{LS} = b + m, \tag{4}$$

which shows that, on a steady-state path, the growth rate of human capital, $LS$, from migration and education must be constant. From this we can see that, on a steady-state path, with an increase in the skills intensity of the migrant population, $\gamma$, and no change in the total population growth rate, $b + m$, then either there must be an increase in $LS$ or the annual flow of graduates, $H / \zeta$, must fall. Note, however, that this places no restriction on the long-run endogenous stock of skilled labour relative to other factors, such as capital or land. Equation (4) holds irrespective of the nature of the dynamics – that is, whether they are forward looking or recursive.[13]

Given that $M / LS = m / \lambda$ is also constant on a steady-state path, we can determine the required steady-state ratio of investment in schooling for any given demographic and policy variables:

$$\frac{H}{LS} = (b + m - \gamma m / \lambda)\zeta \equiv \sigma. \tag{5}$$

*The Stock of Skilled Labour during a Transition*

To model the transitional pattern of investment in schooling, we consider a representative household with members who are receiving schooling, either domestically or abroad. The foreign-educated immigrants arrive exogenously from the household's view, since this is determined by the government's immigration quota, which we assume to be binding at all times.

Given this arrival of skilled (and unskilled) immigrants, the household maximizes the present value of total labour incomes subject to on-the-job training costs faced by skilled labour. This is given by

$$\sum_{t=0}^{\infty} \frac{1}{(1+\rho)^t} [u_{s,t} \, LS_t - u_t \, C(H_t, LS_t) + u_{u,t} \, LU_t - p_{e,t} \, A_{s,t} H_t], \qquad (6)$$

where $u_{s,t}$ is the after-tax skilled wage, $u_{u,t}$ is the after-tax unskilled wage, $p_{s,t}$ is the consumer price of education, $A_{s,t}$ is a technology parameter determining the quantity of education required to produce a skilled graduate, $\rho$ is the discount rate that households apply to education decisions, and $C(H_t, LS_t)$ is the training-costs function, which plays the same rule as installation costs in the more general neoclassical model of investment. Education is 'purchased' by households that choose to become skilled from a competitive education sector at price $p_e$; educational subsidies are reflected in the difference between the production cost of education and the price paid by individuals who receive schooling.

We assume that on-the-job training costs apply only to native-born graduates, not to immigrants. This can be justified on the basis that skilled immigrants are selected according to particular 'skills shortages' and will often have work experience.[14]

Noting that, on a steady-state path, we have $H = \sigma LS$, we assume that the adjustment costs function takes the form

$$C = \frac{\alpha (H_t - \sigma \, LS_t)^2}{2 \, LS_t}. \qquad (7)$$

Thus, the size of the training cost depends on deviations from the steady-state growth path. The household's objective is to maximize equation (6) subject to (1), (2), and (3). As shown in the appendix, this gives the following demand function for education, which is expressed as a demand for the stock of students relative to the current stock of skilled labour:

$$\frac{H_t}{LS_t} = \left( \frac{\Pi_t / \zeta - u_{u,t} - p_{e,t} \, A_{s,t}}{\alpha \, u_{s,t}} \right) + \sigma, \qquad (8)$$

where $\alpha$ is a parameter of the training-cost function and $\Pi_t$ is the Lagrange multiplier associated with the constraint (3) and can be interpreted as the value of an additional unit of skilled labour. Equation (8) thus shows that, during a transition, variation in the demand for students due to immigration depends only on prices. In particular, it depends on the asset value of skilled labour relative to the current wage rate, $\Pi_t / u_{s,t}$, the relative unskilled wage, $u_{u,t} / u_{s,t}$, and the costs of education.

Further, note that the adjustment-cost parameter $\alpha$ enters in the dominator. Thus, if the level of adjustment costs is large, the term in brackets tends to be smaller and $H_t / LS_t$ tends to be constant. Conversely, if $\alpha$ is small, $H_t / LS_t$ might deviate a long way from the steady-state level during a transition.

On the supply side, education services are produced by a nontraded competitive industry that supplies these services at a supply price, $p_e$. Education is treated as a 'nontraded' good in that its price is determined by equating the supply and demand for education within the domestic economy. The production function for domestic education services is given by

$$y^e = \min\left[M^e, f^e(v^e)\right], \tag{9}$$

where $v^e$ is a vector of factors employed in the education sector. This production function is constant returns in the vector of domestic factors, $v^e$, and in intermediate goods input aggregate, $M^e$, which is defined by

$$M^i = \min_{j=1,..n}\left[\frac{Y_{ji}}{a_{ji}}\right]. \tag{10}$$

Dual to the value-added function, $f^e(v^e)$, is a unit-cost function, $c^e(w)$, where $w$ is the vector of factor returns. Factor demands are given by Shepherd's lemma applied to $c^e(w)$, which are then multiplied by the level of educational output, $y_e$ to give total demand. Note that, in equilibrium, price equals cost in the education sector, so that

$$p_e = (1 - s^e)\left[c^e(w^e)\sum_j a_{je} p^j\right], \tag{11}$$

where the demand price, $p_e$ is net of any education subsidy provided at rate $s^e$, and $p^j$ is the price of intermediate inputs from sector $j$. The total amount of educational output is given by

$$y_e = A_s H. \tag{12}$$

Thus, the output of the educational sector is measured in units of person schooling per year (or students per year), efficiency adjusted. As economy-wide technical change occurs through time, more schooling output is required to produce skilled workers. This is to conform with the dynamic equations relating changes in schooling into units of skilled labour supply. In the model, $y_e = A_s H$ grows at the overall rate of exogenous total factor productivity growth; one interpretation of this is that, as the level of technical progress increases, it is increasingly costly to produce a unit of 'skilled labour.' Note that we do not model the effect of an increase in the length of the schooling period – which is another alternative. Rather, the length of required schooling stays constant but the resources devoted to schooling per student increase as technological progress occurs.

As education is an investment decision and the alternative to becoming educated is to work as an unskilled worker, there is necessarily a long-run arbitrage relationship between skilled and unskilled wages. Thus, it can be shown that the long-run skill premium is tied down in this model to the cost of education and various growth and return parameters. Let

$$\Delta \equiv \frac{1+g}{(1+\rho)-(1-d)(1+g)}.$$

Then, in a steady-state equilibrium, it is necessarily the case that skilled wages, $u_s$, and unskilled wages, $u_u$, satisfy

$$\hat{u}_s = \frac{(\hat{u}_u + p_e)\zeta}{\Delta} + \hat{u}_u,$$

where $\hat{u}_s = u_s / A_s$, $\hat{u}_u = u_u / A_u$ are the wages in terms of efficiency units.[15] This is an important restriction on long-run factor returns and the demand price of education, which must hold in addition to the traditional Stolper-Samuelson restrictions relating factor returns to product prices. It is important to emphasize that, in both the short and long run, investment in education is distorted in three ways relative to a full social optimum, and that these distortions are constant across all simulations. First, there is a tax wedge as wage income is taxed. Second, there are private discount rates on education decisions that are higher than those on other types of capital accumulation. Third, due to subsidies, the private cost of education is below the marginal cost of the production of education.

### Increasing Skilled Labour by Migration versus Education

To capture broadly the changes in Australian immigration policy over the past decade, we consider the implications for the initial skilled labour force of a 10 per cent increase in the targeted intake of skilled immigrants. Over the longer term, this increase comes at the expense of the family visa program, with little change in the total flow of immigrants. Thus, in the experiments we consider, the total migration rate, $m$, is assumed to be constant since we focus on the skills composition of immigrants rather than on the total number of immigrants. The experiment, therefore, is to increase the fraction of skilled immigrants, $\gamma$, while holding the migration rate, $m$, and birth rate, $b$, constant.

It is useful to consider these changes in proportion to the relative stocks of students and skilled workers in Australia. The model is calibrated to an assumed a steady-state path in 2000. One stylized fact regarding the Australian stock of graduates is that it is not on a steady-state path. As Dolman, Parham, and Zheng (2007) document, $LS/P$ in Australia is approximately 20 per cent while in the United States it is 30 per cent, but in Australia's case the stock is growing faster, with a larger fraction of younger workers than older workers having a bachelor's degree. With retirements, Australia should reach a steady state similar to that of the United States in about 2030. This means that, in Australia, the ratio of graduates to skilled labour, $H/LS$, is falling as the stock is accumulating. Thus, the steady-state ratios in the benchmark are calibrated using current U.S. ratios, which differ slightly from those in Australia.

We begin by exploring the impact of an unannounced increase in skilled immigrants that lasts ten years. Each year, the intake of new skilled immigrants is about three-tenths of 1 per cent of the total labour force and is constant over the entire ten-year period. After the tenth year, immigration policy reverts to its former composition between the skilled and unskilled.

The calibration of the increased migration is implemented in the following way. The rate of skilled migration is increased for ten years and then returns to the benchmark rate. Recall that the skilled migration rate is $\gamma m = \gamma M/P$, where $M$ is the total of skilled immigrants and $P$ is the labour force. The change in $\gamma$ is chosen so that there is a cumulative increase of skilled immigrants over ten years equal to 10 per cent of the *initial stock* of skilled labour, $0.01\,LS_0$. Thus, the change in the skilled migration rate, $\gamma' - \gamma$, solves

$$\sum_{t=1}^{10} (\gamma' - \gamma)\, m_t P_t = 0.01\, LS_0.$$

With a constant population, this would just give $(\gamma' - \gamma)\, m = 0.003$. Because the population is growing, however, the required value of $\gamma$ is slightly lower and equal to an increase in the labour force of $(\gamma' - \gamma)\, m = 0.0028$.

As can be seen from Figure 6.2, this assumed increase in the annual flow of skilled immigrants is approximately equal to the inflow of professionals in 2005. Moreover, since this increased from an approximate inflow rate of 0.001 of the labour force, this increase in skilled migration represents a shock that is not disproportional to recent actual increases in skilled migrants. Note also that total immigration flow in every year is assumed to be fixed. Thus, unskilled immigration implicitly falls and the policy has no net effect on the total size of either the population or the labour force.

*Results of Increased Skilled Migration*

Table 6.1 reports the results of this unanticipated change in skilled immigrant flows for some key variables. It can be seen that the increase has a fairly substantial effect on consumption and gross domestic product (GDP), with GDP per capita rising by 1.5 per cent and consumption by 1.0 per cent over ten years. It is widely recognized that these are poor welfare measures, however, since they average the effect over both the native-born and immigrants. In particular, much of the 'gain' in GDP will be captured by migrants as payment for their labour. Likewise, it has often been pointed out that the gain to the native-born will also depend on the composition of foreign debt, the structure of the tax system, and the distribution of public assets and public debt. The aim of the current analysis, therefore, is to consider, not the welfare effects, but the effects on different groups within the economy.

Bearing these factors in mind, it nevertheless can be seen that the effect on GDP mainly reflects the increase in factor supplies. This is presumably the aim of policy, and the increase reflects the skills level of the migrants, all of whom may be thought of in this experiment as professionals relative to the domestic labour force.

Following Krusell et al. (2000), we assume that the production functions exhibit capital-skill complementarity. Hence, exogenous increases in the supply of skilled labour are assumed to raise the marginal product of each type of capital. Table 6.1 shows that the increase in skilled workers is associated with a 4.1 per cent increase in machinery and equipment capital and a 3.5 per cent increase in structural capital relative to the stock of unskilled labour. Hence, the increase in GDP reflects substantial accumulation decisions of domestic residents. Thus, while it is difficult to make welfare inferences, it is clear that skilled immigration generates economic growth.

This accumulation of capital – both human and nonhuman – delivers benefits to skilled and unskilled labour in the longer term. In particular, unskilled wages rise by 2.1 per cent over the ten-year period, though skilled wages fall by 3.8 per cent. This wage rate effect is in line with studies such as those of the Productivity Commission (2006) and Econtech (2006).[16]

Table 6.1
Effect of Migration Policy

| | Year 1 | Year 5 | Year 10 | Year 100 |
|---|---|---|---|---|
| | (percentage change) | | | |
| Real GDP per capita | 0.1 | 0.8 | 1.5 | 0.0 |
| Real consumption per capita | 0.1 | 0.5 | 1.0 | 0.0 |
| Investment in machinery and equipment | 1.6 | 1.7 | 1.2 | 0.0 |
| Investment in structures | 1.3 | 1.3 | 0.8 | 0.0 |
| Investment in housing | 1.0 | 0.7 | 0.2 | 0.0 |
| Real return to machinery and equipment | 0.3 | 0.4 | 0.7 | 0.0 |
| Real return to structures | 0.1 | 0.5 | 1.1 | 0.0 |
| Real return to housing | 0.1 | 0.3 | 0.7 | 0.0 |
| Real skilled wages | −0.1 | −1.7 | −3.8 | 0.0 |
| Real unskilled wages | −0.4 | 0.7 | 2.1 | 0.0 |
| Land rents | 0.1 | 0.4 | 0.9 | 0.0 |
| Resource rents | −0.1 | 0.4 | 0.7 | 0.0 |
| Skill premium | 0.3 | −2.4 | −5.8 | 0.0 |
| Education output relative to GDP | −7.6 | −7.0 | −3.5 | 0.0 |
| $LS/LU$ | 0.7 | 2.6 | 7.1 | 0.0 |
| Internal exchange rate (traded versus nontraded) | 0.1 | 0.3 | 0.5 | 0.0 |
| Terms of trade | −0.1 | −0.1 | 0.0 | 0.0 |
| Openness | 0.1 | −0.2 | −0.6 | 0.0 |
| Relative price of education ($p_e/w_u$) | 0.2 | −1.4 | −3.6 | 0.0 |
| Machines per unskilled worker | −0.7 | 1.5 | 4.1 | 0.0 |
| Structures per unskilled worker | −0.7 | 1.1 | 3.5 | 0.0 |
| Residential per unskilled worker | −0.7 | 0.8 | 2.8 | 0.0 |
| Students | −7.5 | −6.3 | −2.1 | 0.0 |
| Cumulative sum grads (% of labour force) | −0.1 | −0.5 | −0.9 | −1.4 |
| Industry output | | | | |
| Agriculture | −0.1 | −0.4 | −0.9 | 0.0 |
| Minerals | −0.1 | 0.0 | −0.1 | 0.0 |
| Low-tech | 0.7 | 1.6 | 2.2 | 0.0 |
| Intermediate manufacture | 0.2 | 1.0 | 1.6 | 0.0 |
| Durables | 1.5 | 4.4 | 6.5 | 0.0 |
| Traded services | 0.3 | 1.1 | 1.9 | 0.0 |
| Construction | 0.9 | 1.3 | 1.4 | 0.0 |
| Nontraded services | 0.3 | 0.8 | 1.3 | 0.0 |
| Public | 0.2 | 1.4 | 2.8 | 0.0 |
| Housing | 0.0 | 0.3 | 0.5 | 0.0 |
| Education | −7.5 | −6.3 | −2.1 | 0.0 |

The policy has some significant effects on the education sector but, surprisingly, relatively small effects on the overall composition of the labour force. In particular, the expansion of skilled immigration does not raise the skilled labour supply proportionally. As Table 6.1 shows, there is, on announcement of the policy, an immediate fall in the stock of students – and, hence, of education output – of 7.5 per cent. This represents a substantial crowding out of the domestic education sector. After ten years, the skilled labour stock increases only by approximately 5 per cent compared with the target of 10 per cent of the skilled labour force (equivalent to 3 per cent of the total labour force). This shortfall is due to the cumulative effect of the fall in education investment as student enrolments fall. Unskilled labour supply falls by 2 per cent, so $LS/LU$ increases by 7.1 per cent. The cumulative loss in graduates after ten years adds up to 0.9 per cent of the initial labour force, or approximately 3 per cent of the initial *skilled* labour force.

Trade plays two important roles with respect to labour markets in this model. First, with given terms of trade, factor prices are 'pinned' down in part by the factor-price equalization, or Stolper-Samuelson conditions. Second, importing (or exporting) skills-intensive goods is a substitute for importing (or exporting) skilled labour. This implies that output composition changes will be the most important channel through which factor markets clear – which is very different from the Ricardian or specific-factors framework. This gives rises to significant 'Rybczinski' effects, where changes in relative factor supplies have large effects on the composition of output and, thus, trade. Hence, increasing the supply of skilled relative to unskilled labour should result in an expansion of output in skills-intensive sectors.

As it turns out, increasing the number of skilled migrants is positive for manufacturing sectors – particularly durables – and bad for education and agriculture; we noted above the large negative effect on education output. The strong increase in durables is a dual consequence of its relative skills intensity plus the 'knock-on' physical accumulation of capital, given the complementarity of skills and capital. Australia has a significant comparative advantage in agriculture, a large sector that makes intensive use of physical capital. The net effect of increasing the skills composition of the labour force, however, is to contract agriculture, largely because that sector has to compete with durables for physical capital. Also, there is a competitiveness effect as the increase in unskilled wages reduces the competitiveness of the agriculture sector. It is somewhat surprising that the services sector does not bear a larger part of the adjustment, given its relative size and skills intensity. In a closed economy, increasing the supply of skilled labour would be expected to expand the services sector. Clearly, the response in small, open economies is much different, with a large amount

Table 6.2
Calibration of Education Subsidy

| Description | Value |
|---|---|
| Skilled labour as a fraction of labour force (%) | 30.0 |
| Number of students (% of labour force) | 6.0 |
| Target number of graduates per year (10% over 10 years) | 3.0 |
| Number of years of schooling required for graduation | 4.0 |
| Total annual cost of new scholarships (% of GDP) | 0.4 |
| Current education spending (% of GDP) | 2.2 |
| Annual increase in education spending (% of current spending) | 20.0 |
| New subsidy (% of supply price) | 20.0 |

of adjustment accommodated through changes in the relative composition of output across traded goods industries.

*Increasing Skilled Workers though Increases in Education Subsidies*

An increase in public support for higher or tertiary education is the usual policy advocated to enhance stocks of human capital. We model such policies generically as increases in education subsidies, specifically to higher education. To make the policy experiment comparable with the preceding skilled immigration experiment, the total value of the subsidies is calibrated to be equal to additional funding for student places sufficient to raise the stock of skilled labour by 10 per cent relative to the benchmark. The cost of a scholarship is valued at the average cost of a degree (calculated as total annual spending / total students, multiplied by the number of years for a degree). The subsidies are imposed for ten years and then removed. Thus, the target is to increase the flow of graduates by 1 per cent each year for ten years so that the total funding over ten years is sufficient to fund a 10 per cent increase in graduate places.

As Table 6.2 shows, this implies a 20 per cent increase in total public and private education spending each year over the ten-year period. This, in turn, implies a subsidy of 20 per cent. This subsidy is added to the existing subsidies and taxes in the benchmark. The education price is $p_e$. Given that the flow rate of graduates is increased by 1 per cent each year, the annual subsidy cost is the target number of graduates multiplied by the supply cost, or $p_e 0.1\ Ls\zeta$. Dividing this cost by current spending gives the new subsidy rate as s = 0.2.[17]

The principal results from increased education subsidies are given in Table 6.3. Note that the target number of graduates is 3 per cent of the labour force; in this experiment, however, the cumulative sum of graduates rises only

Table 6.3
Effect of Increased Education Subsidies

|  | Year 1 | Year 5 | Year 10 | Year 100 |
|---|---|---|---|---|
|  | (percentage change) | | | |
| Real GDP per capita | 0.2 | 0.5 | 0.8 | 0.0 |
| Real consumption per capita | −0.1 | −0.2 | −0.1 | 0.0 |
| Investment in machinery and equipment | 0.3 | 0.8 | 1.0 | 0.0 |
| Investment in structures | 0.6 | 0.8 | 0.7 | 0.0 |
| Investment in housing | −0.2 | 0.0 | 0.2 | 0.0 |
| Real return to machinery and equipment | −0.3 | 0.1 | 0.2 | 0.0 |
| Real return to structures | −0.2 | 0.1 | 0.4 | 0.0 |
| Real return to housing | −0.2 | −0.2 | −0.1 | 0.0 |
| Real skilled wages | 0.2 | −0.8 | −1.6 | 0.0 |
| Real Unksilled wages | 0.2 | 0.7 | 1.2 | 0.0 |
| Land rents | −0.2 | −0.2 | −0.1 | 0.0 |
| Resource rents | −0.3 | 0.0 | 0.3 | 0.0 |
| Skill premium | −0.1 | −1.5 | −2.7 | 0.0 |
| Education output relative to GDP | 5.4 | 5.1 | 5.1 | 0.0 |
| $LS/LU$ | 0.5 | 2.0 | 3.6 | 0.0 |
| Internal exchange rate (traded versus nontraded) | 0.6 | 0.7 | 0.8 | 0.0 |
| Terms of trade | −0.1 | 0.0 | 0.0 | 0.0 |
| Openness | −0.1 | −0.1 | −0.2 | 0.0 |
| Relative price of education ($p_e/w_u$) | −10.5 | −11.2 | −12.0 | 0.0 |
| Machines per unskilled worker | 0.5 | 1.2 | 2.3 | 0.0 |
| Structures per unskilled worker | 0.5 | 1.2 | 2.1 | 0.0 |
| Residential per unskilled worker | 0.5 | 0.9 | 1.5 | 0.0 |
| Students | 5.6 | 5.5 | 3.6 | 0.0 |
| Cumulative sum grads (% of labour force) | 0.1 | 0.4 | 0.9 | 0.7 |
| Industry output | | | | |
|   Agriculture | −0.4 | −0.7 | −0.9 | 0.0 |
|   Minerals | −0.3 | −0.1 | 0.0 | 0.0 |
|   Low tech | −0.3 | 0.1 | 0.6 | 0.0 |
|   Intermediate manufacture | −0.6 | −0.1 | 0.4 | 0.0 |
|   Durables | −1.5 | 0.7 | 2.4 | 0.0 |
|   Traded services | −0.3 | 0.0 | 0.4 | 0.0 |
|   Construction | 0.0 | 0.2 | 0.5 | 0.0 |
|   Nontraded services | −0.2 | −0.1 | 0.1 | 0.0 |
|   Public | −0.2 | 0.3 | 0.9 | 0.0 |
|   Housing | 0.0 | −0.1 | 0.0 | 0.0 |
|   Education | 5.6 | 5.5 | 5.9 | 0.0 |

to 0.9 per cent of the labour force after ten years. Thus, less than one-third of the target level is actually reached as a result of the subsidy, which points to the strong importance of feedback effects on the demand for education as unskilled wages rise and skilled wages fall in response to relative supply changes. The overall skilling of the labour force is more modest than was the

case with the migration policy: the ratio of skilled to unskilled labour, $LS/LU$, rises by 3.6 per cent as opposed to 7.1 per cent in the migration case.

Education output increases by approximately 5 to 6 per cent each year. By the tenth year, GDP per capita rises by 0.8 per cent but consumption per capita falls slightly. Thus, the overall the effect on welfare, as measured by consumption, is negative. Education subsidies increase GDP because of a large increase in educational investment, but this comes at the expense of consumption.

With the exception of education, the sectoral effects are much smaller than in the immigration policy case. There is a small increase in the overall capital intensity of production, and durables production also increases but by a smaller amount than in the previous case. Interestingly, once again the agriculture sector contracts.

**Conclusion**

To summarize, we examined the effects of a change in the composition of the flow of immigrants versus increasing subsides to educations as a policy response to perceived skills shortages. The policy background is the increase in professionals entering Australia under the expansion of the skilled visa program that has occurred since 2000. Our focus was on the effects on factor markets and the accumulation of factor supplies. The main questions of interest are effects on growth, the wages of skilled and unskilled workers, and the composition of output changes across sectors.

We find that, in the case of the increased intake of skilled migrants, there is substantial crowding out of the domestic education sector. Intuitively, skilled immigrants depress wages in skilled occupations, but the dynamic analysis shows that this wage depression also reduces the incentive to attain higher education. Nevertheless, the aggregate benefits, in terms of both GDP and consumption, of increased skilled immigration are positive. In the case of increased subsidies to education, there is a large positive effect on the size of the education sector, but the overall effect on increasing skill levels in the labour force is more modest than was the case with increasing skilled immigration. Moreover, the consumption effect of increased education subsidies is negative. These divergent consumption results essentially reflect the consumption of the savings from higher education tuition by the native-born. The theme of this analysis, however, has been on the distributional impacts of skilled immigration, as it is well known that the redistributive effects are large relative to the net welfare gains.

Our results contrast with those in the existing literature, which emphasizes the effects of immigration on wages. We find that, with endogenous supplies of skilled labour, the effects of skilled immigration on the wages of skilled labour are mitigated, and that there is a supply response with a reduction in the domestic production of skilled labour. This implies, however, that the burden of adjustment falls on the education sector. Moreover, we find that this 'crowding-out' effect might be large, representing a large negative impact on the education sector. Most of the adjustment across sectors occurs in the tradables sector, with an increase in sectors that are intensive in the use of skilled labour – particularly durables manufacturing.

The analysis indicates that skilled immigration programs might not have the desired effect of raising the skills intensity of the labour force, or might do so only in a limited way. Moreover, it suggests that, in the absence of other policies, the burden of adjustment falls on the education sector, rather than on the wages of skilled labour. In contrast, increasing the skills composition of the labour force through increased support of higher education, while leading to an increase in the size of the education sector, has negative welfare effects due to the increased costs of investing in human capital. Targeted increases in the skills composition are much more modest than simple impact analysis would suggest due to feedback effects of wage changes on the demand for education.

Most countries use a combination of both types of policies in response to perceived skills shortages. It is clear that both are likely to raise the wages of the unskilled and to reduce the wages of the skilled, while leading to positive growth effects. Overall, however, to the extent that skilled migrants represent the acquisition of relatively low-cost human capital relative to expensive domestic production of human capital, one should expect strong competition for skilled migrants among open industrial economies.

## NOTES

1  See, for example, Donaldson and Eaton (1976); and Allen and Eaton (2005).

2  According to Antecol et al. (2003), a 'points system' for screening a substantial portion of immigrant applicants was introduced in Canada in the late 1960s and a similar system was introduced in Australia in the early 1970s.

3  See Antecol, Cobb-Clark, and Trejo (2003); 'Immigration Reform Stuck in the Senate,' *The Economist*, 14 June 2007.

4  Borjas (2006) finds that foreign students studying in the U.S. reduce expected earnings on domestic students by 3-4 per cent. Borjas (2004) finds that foreign students crowd out domestic student enrolments across institutions.

5  However, Chellaraj, Maskus, and Mattoo (2004) find that skilled immigrants stimulate innovation in the United States. Likewise, Ottaviano and Peri (2006) and Peri (2007) argue that, empirically, immigrants to the United States tend

to have different skills than those of domestic labour and, hence, do not compete directly in the same labour market. Gang and Rivera-Batiz (1994) make a
similar point, although they find that complementarities between different
types of labour are very weak.

6  As Cobb-Clarke and Connolly (1997) note, skills levels under the points system also depend on external factors – in particular, on the immigration policies of other countries; see also Withers (1987).

7  For example, recent reports by the Productivity Commission (2006) and
Econtech (2006) are perhaps representative of the literature by modelling the
accumulation of physical capital as endogenous but leaving the accumulation
of skills as an exogenous variable.

8  More recent models, such as those of Mountford (1997), Beine, Docquier,
and Rapoport (2001), and Stark and Wang (2002), include human capital
externalities such that the expansion of education investment in the home
country may have positive net positive benefits. For a survey of this literature,
see Commander, Kangasniemi, and Winters (2004).

9  The possibility of crowding out, however, has been acknowledged in the literature. Examples include Chapman and Withers (2002) and Corden (2003).
A rare empirical study is Baker and Wooden (1992); they investigate, but
dismiss, the proposition that immigration acts as a deterrent to employer-
sponsored training programs for domestic workers in Australia.

10 The official reason given for this policy – to address the 'skills shortage' –
has been widely commented on in Australia. Alternative explanations include
political economy motives, such as a response to the growth lobby. As discussed above, however, there is a general view that skilled immigrants are
more desirable, as they contribute more to the Australian economy, although
it is widely argued that the aggregate gains for the native-born from immigration are likely to be small (see Borjas 1995). Thus, it is perhaps more interesting to consider the distributional effects of skilled immigration – in particular,
its effect on the wages of native-born skilled workers, on sectoral output
shares, and on the education sector.

11 As Birrell, Rapson, and Smith (2006) note, this will exclude onshore immigrants – students who undertook education in Australia and subsequently
obtained a visa, as most of them (93 per cent) did not state an occupation
when they applied for their visa.

12 The relationship also assumes that all students are native-born. Foreign students
are a large fraction of the university student population in Australia, however,
and increasingly choose to work in Australia. The main focus of Australia's
skilled migration policy, however, has been on offshore immigrants with particular skills. Hence, we assume that all skilled migrants, $m$, arrive from abroad.

13  It is worth noting that some recent literature has emphasized the differences in factor services supplied by immigrant labour and domestic labour. This literature mainly refers to unskilled labour, however. There is no evidence to suggest that, for example, immigrant doctors perform different services than domestically trained doctors.

14  On the other hand, it can be argued that immigrants also face significant training costs associated with language barriers and achieving local certification. An alternative assumption is that both immigrants and local graduates face symmetric on-the-job training costs. As Harris and Robertson (2007a) show, this does not have a large quantitative effect on the results, but tends to lead to more crowding out of education.

15  The wages, thus measured in efficiency units – that is, scaled by the labour productivity variables, $A_u$ and $As$ – are constant in the steady state.

16  For example, the Productivity Commission (2006) finds that a doubling of the skilled visa intake would call for a 10 per cent fall in the wages of professionals.

17  For a 10 per cent increase over ten years, the subsidy rate can be calculated as

$$ s = \frac{p_e\ 0.1\ Ls\ \zeta}{10\,p_e\ H} = \frac{0.01\ Ls\ \zeta}{H}. $$

Since $Ls/H = 5$ and $\zeta = 4$, we have $s = 0.2$.

## REFERENCES

Allen, J.M., and B.C. Eaton. 2005. 'Incomplete Information and Migration: The Grass Is Always Greener across the Higher Fence.' *Journal of Regional Science* 45 (1): 1–19.

Antecol, H., D.A. Cobb-Clark, and S.J. Trejo. 2003. 'Immigration Policy and the Skills of Immigrants to Australia, Canada and the United States.' *Journal of Human Resources* 38 (1): 192–218.

Baker, M., and M. Wooden. 1992. 'Immigration and Its Impact on the Incidence of Training in Australia.' *Australian Economic Review* 98 (2): 39–53.

Beine, M., F. Docquier, and H. Rapoport. 2001. 'Brain Drain and Economic Growth: Theory and Evidence.' *Journal of Development Economics* 64 (1): 275–89.

Bhagwati, J.N., and K. Hamada. 1974. 'The Brain Drain, International Integration of Markets for Professionals and Unemployment.' *Journal of Development Economics* 1 (1): 19–42.

Birrell, B., V. Rapson, and T.F. Smith. 2006. 'Australia's Net Gains from International Skilled Movement: Skilled Movements in 2004-05 and Earlier Years.' Melbourne: Monash University, Centre for Population and Urban Research.

Borjas, G.J. 1995. 'The Economic Benefits from Immigration.' *Journal of Economic Perspectives* 9 (2): 3–22.
– 2004. 'Do Foreign Students Crowd Out Native Students from Graduate Programs?' NBER Working Paper 10349. Cambridge, MA: National Bureau of Economic Research.
– 2006. 'Immigration in High-Skill Labor Markets: The Impact of Foreign Students on the Earnings of Doctorates.' NBER Working Paper 12085. Cambridge, MA: National Bureau of Economic Research.
Chapman, B., and G. Withers. 2002. 'Human Capital Accumulation: Education and Immigration.' Working Paper 452. Canberra: Australian National University, Centre for Economic Policy Research.
Chellaraj, G., K.E. Maskus, and A. Mattoo. 2004. 'The Contribution of Skilled Immigration and International Graduate Students to U.S. Innovation.' University of Colorado. Mimeographed.
Cobb-Clark, D.A. 2004. 'Selection Policy and the Labour Market Outcomes of New Immigrants.' Discussion Paper 1380. Bonn, Germany: Institute for the Study of Labor.
Cobb-Clark, D.A., and M.D. Connolly. 1997. 'The Worldwide Market for Skilled Immigrants: Can Australia Compete?' *International Migration Review* 31 (3): 670–90.
Commander, S., M. Kangasniemi, and L.A. Winters. 2004. 'The Brain Drain: Curse or Boon? A Survey of the Literature.' In *Challenges to Globalization*, edited by R. Baldwin and L.A. Winters. Chicago: University of Chicago Press.
Corden, W.M.. 2003. '40 Million Aussies? The Immigration Debate Revisited.' Inaugural Richard Snape Lecture, 30 October 2003. Melbourne: Productivity Commission.
Dolman, B., D. Parham, and S. Zheng. 2007. 'Can Australia Match US Productivity Performance?' Staff working paper. Melbourne: Productivity Commission.
Donaldson, David, and B. Curtis Eaton. 1976. 'Firm-Specific Human Capital: A Shared Investment or Optimal Entrapment?' *Canadian Journal of Economics* 9 (1): 462–72.
Econtech. 2006. 'The Economic Impacts of Migration: A Comparison of Two Approaches.' Report Prepared for the Department of Immigration and Multicultural Affairs. Canberra.
Freeman, R.B. 2006. 'Labor Market Imbalances: Shortages, or Surpluses, or Fish Stories?' Paper presented to the Boston Federal Reserve Economic Conference, Global Imbalances – As Giants Evolve, Chatham, MA, 14–16 June.
Gang, I.N., and F.L. Rivera-Batiz. 1994. 'Labor Market Effects of Immigration in the United States and Europe: Substitution vs. Complementarity.' *Journal of Population Economics* 7 (2): 157–75.

Harris, R.G., and P.E. Robertson. 2007a. 'The Dynamic Effects of Skilled Labour Targeting in Immigration Programs.' Australian Conference of Economists, University of Tasmania, Hobart.
– 2007b. 'The Dynamic Effects of the US Productivity Boom on Australia.' *The Economic Record* 83 (S1): S35–S45.
International Monetary Fund. 2007. *World Economic Outlook: Spillovers and Cycles in the Global Economy.* Washington, DC: IMF.
Krusell, P., L. Ohanian, J.-V. Ríos-Rull, and G. Violante. 2000. 'Capital-Skill Complementarity and Inequality: A Macroeconomic Analaysis.' *Econometrica* 68 (5): 1029–53.
McCulloch, R., and J.L. Yellen. 1975. 'Consequences of a Tax on the Brain Drain for Unemployment and Income Inequality in Less Developed Countries.' *Journal of Development Economics* 2 (3): 249–64.
Miller, P.W. 1999. 'Immigration Policy and Immigrant Quality: The Australian Points System.' *American Economic Review* 89 (2): 192–7.
Mountford, A. 1997. 'Can a Brain Drain Be Good for Growth in the Source Economy?' *Journal of Development Economics* 53 (2): 287–303.
Ottaviano, G.I.P., and G. Peri. 2006. 'Rethinking the Effects of Immigration on Wages.' NBER Working Paper 12497. Cambridge, MA: National Bureau of Economic Research.
Peri, G. 2007. 'Immigrants' Complementarities and Native Wages: Evidence from California.' NBER Working Paper 12956. Cambridge, MA: National Bureau of Economic Research.
Productivity Commission. 2006. *Economic Impacts of Migration and Population Growth.* Melbourne: Productivity Commission.
Salt, J. 1997. 'International Movements of the Highly Skilled.' OECD Social, Employment and Migration Working Paper 3. Paris: Organisation for Economic Co-operation and Development.
Stark, O., and Y. Wang. 2002. 'Inducing Human Capital Formation: Migration as a Substitute for Subsidies.' *Journal of Public Economics* 86 (1): 29–46.
Withers, G. 1987. 'Immigration and Australian Economic Growth.' In *The Economics of Immigration*, edited by Paul Miller and Lyle Baker. Canberra: Australian Government Publishing Service.

# 7 Differentiated Products, International Trade, and Simple General Equilibrium Effects

SIMON P. ANDERSON AND NICOLAS SCHMITT

Several papers[1] have shown that, over the past 20 years, the share of intra-industry trade in vertically differentiated products has increased significantly at the expense of both one-way trade and intra-industry trade in horizontally differentiated products. This phenomenon was first identified for trade flows among members of the European Union (where vertical intra-industry trade is about 40 per cent of total trade) and more recently for a wide range of country pairs (Fontagné, Freudenberg, and Gaulier 2006). Although the methodology adopted to separate trade into vertically and horizontally differentiated products based on unit prices is largely ad hoc, this phenomenon is still surprising as most models would predict that, when countries open their borders, the prices of differentiated products converge, suggesting that, if anything, the share of intra-industry trade in horizontally differentiated products should increase at the expense of other forms of trade.

A number of papers have attempted to explain this phenomenon by investigating how differences in endowments affect the different types of trade (see, for instance, Cabral, Falvey, and Milner 2007). In this paper, we propose a model with a simple explanation for these empirical observations: that they are due to general equilibrium effects associated with a deeper degree of trade liberalization in the differentiated products sector (the manufacturing sector) than in the homogeneous product sector (the nonmanufacturing sector). Thus, we argue that this shift in the composition of trade does not depend on the nature of intra-industry trade (horizontal versus vertical) but is due to the allocation of resources, especially within vertically differentiated industries.

The literature on intra-industry trade has focused most of its attention on imperfect competition, whether with monopolistic competition or with oligopoly. In the case of vertically differentiated products, most papers are cast in an oligopolistic environment (see, for example, Gabszewicz and Thisse 1980; Shaked and Sutton 1983). This literature is useful insofar as strategic considerations among firms play an important role, including the determination of product characteristics. If trade liberalization tends to increase the extent of horizontal and vertical differentiation among products (as suggested by Schmitt 1995; and Boccard and Wauthy 1998), prices generally still converge with lower barriers to trade. Moreover, these models are ill equipped to address the type of broad shifts uncovered by the above empirical papers, as they are shown to hold for a wide range of sectors.

An alternative approach is the one proposed by Falvey and Kierzkowski (1987) and Flam and Helpman (1987). They set their analysis in a general equilibrium model with two perfectly competitive sectors, one producing a homogeneous product and the other one producing a continuum of product qualities. Cast in a two-country environment, Flam and Helpman look at North-South trade in the presence of technical progress or population growth. In contrast, Falvey and Kierzkowski show that imperfect competition and economies of scale are not needed to generate intra-industry trade, and that conventional forces such as differences in technology and in factor endowments between two countries are consistent with intra-industry trade, provided this trade is in vertically differentiated products.

In this paper, we adopt a similar formulation to that of Falvey and Kierzkowski. However, whereas they look at the pattern of trade in a world without barriers to trade, we investigate how trade policy determines the pattern of trade and the composition of trade between two countries. In particular, we build a simple general equilibrium model in which the *intra*-industry trade pattern in differentiated producers is indeterminate in the absence of any friction between two countries even though the *inter*-industry trade pattern is well defined (there is a difference in factor endowment and/ or country size). We then introduce an international barrier to trade in each sector to show that well-defined patterns of trade emerge. In particular, depending on the importance of the sector-specific transport cost, one can generate inter-industry trade only (there is no intra-industry trade in quality goods), intra-industry trade only (there is no trade in the homogeneous product), or both types of trade. This allows us to look at the effect of trade liberalization on the composition and pattern of trade.

We find that, when the homogeneous product sector receives some protection, trade liberalization in vertically differentiated products increases intra-industry trade at the expense of inter-industry trade. We further show that such trade liberalization is consistent with diverging average prices of exports and imports, at least if the trading countries are not too similar. Essentially, a barrier to trade in nonmanufacturing decreases trade between the two countries and increases the price of the factor used in both sectors (labour) in the capital-abundant country. This generates intra-industry trade in vertically differentiated products, as the capital-abundant country still exports quality products but prefers importing such products using relatively more labour. Hence, the recently observed increase in intra-industry trade of vertically differentiated products might be attributed to the general equilibrium implications of asymmetric trade liberalization in the two sectors. Thus, the pattern and composition of trade rely on traditional forces (endowments, country size), not on imperfect competition and economies of scale.

The implications of the model are also consistent with the recent empirical literature on international trade at the firm level, whether it is the fact that not all firms export (Bernard et al. 2003), the important role of the 'extensive margin' for international trade (that is, the range of exported products), or that a richer country exports higher-priced products (Schott 2004; Hummels and Klenow 2005). These results are obtained without relying on models with fixed costs of production or export.

This paper is related to Curtis Eaton's work since it makes product differentiation a central issue of the analysis. In addition, as in most of his work on the subject, each consumer buys just one unit of the differentiated product. However, instead of disagreeing among themselves about the marginal utility of differentiated products (horizontal differentiation), consumers agree about their ranking (vertical differentiation).[2]

The paper is organized as follows. In the next section, we propose the model and derive the free trade equilibrium. We then consider separately the effects of an international barrier to trade in the manufacturing and the nonmanufacturing sectors. This is followed by a characterization of the pattern and composition of trade for arbitrary levels of barriers to trade, and an investigation of the effects of trade liberalization on the pattern and composition of trade. The paper ends with a conclusion and an appendix.

## The Model

Our model is based on that of Mussa and Rosen (1978). Consider two countries, $H$ and $F$, each of which has two sectors of production, manufacturing, $M$, and nonmanufacturing, $N$. Sector $N$ could be agriculture, services, or even basic manufacturing, while we think of $M$ as being high manufacturing, where quality matters most. Both sectors are perfectly competitive. Production in $N$ uses labour only according to

$$N_i = \frac{L_i^N}{a_i}, \quad i = H, F,$$

where $L_i^N$ is the total number of units of labour used in $N$, and $a_i$ is the number of units of labour required to produce one unit of $N$ in country $i$. Production of the manufacturing good requires both labour and capital. The cost of producing one unit of the quality good is

$$c_i(q) = w_i + r_i m_i(q),$$

where $m_i(q)$ is the number of units of capital necessary to produce one unit of the good with quality $q$. Thus, this unit necessitates one unit of labour and $m_i(q)$ units of capital. We assume that $m_i(q)$ is a continuous and strictly convex function of $q$ ($m_i' > 0$, $m_i'' > 0$). Also, $m_i(0) > 0$, so that some units of capital are necessary even at the 'zero' quality level. Since the technology in the $M$ sector exhibits perfect complementarity between capital and labour, the production function in country $i$ for a good with quality $q$ is

$$Q_i(q) = Min[l_i^Q, \frac{k_i^Q}{m_i(q)}],$$

where $l_i^Q$ ($k_i^Q$) is the minimum number of units of labour (capital) necessary to produce $Q_i$ units of the product with quality $q$ in $i$.

On the demand side, we assume that consumers value differently their marginal utility of quality. A consumer's (indirect) utility is given by

$$U = v(q) + y = \theta q - p(q) + y, \tag{1}$$

where $\theta$ is the marginal utility of quality, assumed to be uniformly distributed over $[0, \bar{\theta}]$ with $D_i$ ($i = H, F$) consumers at every point, $p(q)$ is the price of the quality good bought by the consumer, and $y$ represents total spending on good $N$. It is apparent from equation (1) that each consumer buys one unit of the quality product.

For the time being, assume that country $F$ is relatively capital abundant, with respect not to labour but to the number of consumers of quality products. This is because labour has no influence on the pattern of trade in this model. Whoever is not employed in the manufacturing sector is employed in the nonmanufacturing sector at a constant marginal productivity, and nonmanufacturing does not use any capital.

The model has two types of gains from trade: the first is the standard gain from comparative advantage between the two countries; the second is a gain in product diversity. Since tastes differ, consumers are, on average, better off when they consume a wider range of qualities and when, given $\theta$, they consume higher-quality products.

### Free Trade with Identical Technologies

Suppose that labour productivity and the technology to produce quality goods are the same in both countries; hence, $m_H(q) = m_F(q)$. Also, without loss of generality, assume that $a_H = a_F = 1$. We also treat $N$ as the numéraire product so that $p_N = 1$. The model is now a Heckscher-Ohlin trade model.

With perfect competition in the manufacturing sector, $p(q) = c(q)$, so that the indirect utility function (1) can be rewritten as

$$U = \theta q - w - rm(q) + y. \tag{2}$$

A consumer with marginal utility of quality $\theta$ selects the differentiated product satisfying $\theta = rm'(q)$ or,

$$q = \gamma(\frac{\theta}{r}), \tag{3}$$

where the function $\gamma$ corresponds to $(m')^{-1}$. Assuming that buying a quality product brings nonnegative utility, we require $v(q) = \theta q - w - m(q) \geq 0$. The consumer who buys the lowest-quality product $\hat{q}$ also has the lowest marginal utility for quality $(\hat{\theta})$. For $\hat{\theta} > 0$, it is determined by $v(\hat{q}) = rm'(\hat{q})\hat{q} - w - rm(\hat{q}) = 0$, where $\hat{q} = \gamma(\hat{\theta}/r)$. The highest-quality product is such that $\bar{q} = \gamma(\bar{\theta}/r)$. Hence, the set of product qualities is $\Omega \varepsilon [\hat{q}, \bar{q}]$.

Figure 7.1 illustrates the range of qualities supplied by each country in free trade. The marginal cost curve, $c(q)$, is drawn for $w$ and $r$ and it is the same for both countries. The consumer who is indifferent between buying and not buying a quality product is found at the tangency between the (linear) indifference curve $v(q) = 0$ and $c(q)$, while the consumer who buys the highest-quality product is found at the tangency between the indifference curve (with slope $\hat{\theta}$) and $c(q)$. All the product qualities between these two limits are consumed in both countries.

Figure 7.1: The Basic Setup

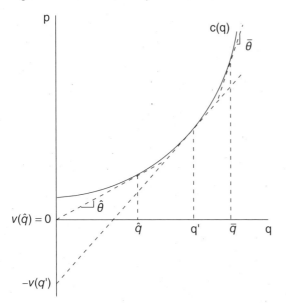

To characterize the free trade equilibrium, two additional elements are needed: the factor prices and the balance-of-trade condition. When both countries are incompletely specialized, free trade equalizes factor prices across countries. Denoting by $w$ and $r$ the free trade price of labour and capital, respectively, $w = 1$, since $a_H = a_F = 1$, and $p_N = 1$. The international price of capital is determined by the equality between the demand for and supply of capital:

$$K_H + K_F = \int_{\hat{\theta}_H}^{\bar{\theta}} D_H m[\gamma(\theta / r)] d\theta + \int_{\hat{\theta}_F}^{\bar{\theta}} D_F m[\gamma(\theta / r)] d\theta,$$

where $D_i$ is the density of consumers in country $i$ ($i = H, F$), $\hat{\theta}_i$ satisfies $\hat{\theta}_i \gamma(\hat{\theta}_i / r) - w - rm[\gamma(\hat{\theta}_i / r)] = 0$, and $\hat{\theta}$ is the upper bound of $\theta$. Note that, given our assumptions, $\hat{\theta}_H = \hat{\theta}_F = \hat{\theta}$. The demand for capital is downward sloping since, given $\theta_i$, an increase in $r$ decreases product quality – that is, $\partial q / \partial r < 0$ in equation (3) – and thus the demand for capital necessary to produce the quality good.

What about the balance of trade? When $D_H = D_F$, the total number of consumers is exactly the same in both countries, so that the capital content of total consumption is also the same in both countries. Since country $F$ has relatively more units of capital, trade can be balanced only if, through international trade, $F$ is a net exporter of capital and country $H$ is a net exporter of labour. Hence, $F$ is a net exporter of quality products and $H$ is an exporter of product $N$. Intra-industry trade in quality products is possible, but the free trade pattern of intra-industry trade is indeterminate.

When $D_H > D_F$, the overall pattern of trade is the same as when $D_H = D_F$ since, *a fortiori*, country $F$ must export quality goods to satisfy the demand in $H$. It is only when $D_H < D_F$ that international trade might be eliminated or the overall pattern of trade reversed, since country $H$ could become capital abundant relative to the number of consumers of quality goods. Hence, in the absence of barriers to trade, the pattern of inter-industry trade is such that country $F$ is a net exporter of quality products whenever

$$\frac{K_F}{D_F[\bar{\theta} - \hat{\theta}_F]} > \frac{K_H}{D_H[\bar{\theta} - \hat{\theta}_H]},$$

where $D_i[\bar{\theta} - \hat{\theta}_i]$ represents the number of consumers of quality products in country $i$. Since each consumer buys only one unit of the quality product, only the total number of them matters. And since labour plays no role, the only determinant of the inter-industry pattern of trade is the relative comparison of the size of the supply of capital with respect to the size of the demand for quality products.

### A Barrier to Trade in One Sector

We now show that trade frictions not only determine the pattern and the composition of trade between the two countries but, more important, that they have very different effects depending on whether the barrier to trade affects only the nonmanufacturing or the manufacturing sector. To see this, let the specific trade friction $t_N$ or $t_M$ affect international exchanges in sector $N$ or $M$. We model it as a symmetric international transport cost (where the transportation is carried out by country $H$) but we could easily adapt the model so as to be a specific tariff.

#### A Barrier to Trade in Manufacturing

The effect of introducing a barrier to trade in the manufacturing sector is to increase the price of imported quality goods by $t_M$ in both countries. Clearly, since imported products are, on impact, more expensive than domestic variants, consumers in both countries buy only domestic variants. Since capital is fully employed in both countries, the complete substitution to domestic quality products must imply that the price of capital must increase in country $H$ (on impact, there is an excess demand for capital in $H$ since, under free trade, it is a net importer of quality products) and fall in country $F$ (since there is an excess supply of capital in this country). This has one key consequence: in the trade equilibrium with positive $t_M$, country $F$ never buys any quality good from country $H$. In effect, the combination of a positive $t_M$ and a higher price of capital relative to country $F$'s make country $H$'s entire range of quality goods more expensive than any domestic quality product in country $F$. Hence, if there is an equilibrium with international trade in the presence of positive $t_M$, it cannot exhibit intra-industry trade.

The pattern of trade is easy to determine. Recall that an increase in $t_M$ increases $c(q)$ equally irrespective of $q$, whereas an increase in the price of capital increases high-quality products relatively more than low-quality products, as the former require more units of capital. Since only country $H$'s consumers can possibly buy country $F$'s products, we need to compare $c_F(q) + t_M$ and $c_H(q)$. There are three possibilities: $c_F(q) + t_M < c_H(q)$ for all $q$, $c_F(q) + t_M > c_H(q)$ for all $q$, or $c_F(q) + t_M < c_H(q)$ for high $q$ only. The first inequality is inconsistent with an equilibrium, as $K_H$ would be unemployed. The second inequality is also inconsistent with a trade equilibrium since it implies that country $H$ does not import any product from country $F$, violating its balance of trade. Only the third possibility is consistent with an international equilibrium. It is illustrated in Figure 7.2. Consumers in country $F$ buy only domestic quality products since its price of capital is lower than in country $H$. Consumers in country $H$ buy low-quality products from domestic producers and import high-quality products from country $F$ in exchange for $N$. They prefer high-quality products from $F$ because the lower price of capital there makes them cheaper than in $H$.

Result 1 then follows:

*Result 1*: If a specific barrier to trade distorts trade in differentiated products, inter-industry trade is the only pattern of trade. Moreover, the relatively capital-abundant country ($F$) exports high-quality products to the relatively consumer-abundant country ($H$) in exchange for the homogeneous product.

In Figure 7.2, the range of domestic qualities consumed in country $F$ is given by $[\hat{q}_F, \bar{q}]$. Country $H$'s consumers buy domestic quality products over the range $[\hat{q}_H, \tilde{q}_H]$ and they buy foreign quality products over the

Figure 7. 2: A Barrier to Trade in Manufacturing

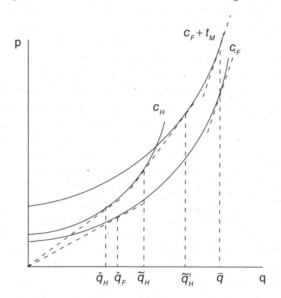

range $[\tilde{q}_H',\bar{q}]$. Since, for country $H$, the net value of these imports is equal to the area below $c_F$ over the range $[\tilde{q}_H',\bar{q}]$, it must also correspond to the value of exports of nonmanufacturing products.

Result 1 is different from that of Falvey (1981), who considers the effect of protection in the quality-product sector *given* the existence of intra-industry trade in this sector. This is achieved by assuming different tech-nologies to produce the quality goods in the two countries. In our model, however, technologies are identical in the two countries, and Result 1 shows that a trade friction in the quality sector does not, by itself, generate intra-industry trade.

### A Barrier to Trade in Nonmanufacturing

Consider now the effect of a barrier to trade, $t_N$, in the nonmanufacturing sector of both countries. Since, under free trade, country $F$ imports $N$, $t_N$ increases the price of imports of nonmanufacturing products in this coun-try to $1 + t_N$. Since $N$ requires only labour, the domestic price of $N$ in coun-try $F$ is equal to $w_F$, so that there is no import of this product in $F$ if $w_F < 1 + t_N$. Suppose, however, that it is the case (that is, that $t_N$ is high enough).

Clearly, a trade equilibrium, if it exists, exhibits intra-industry trade in vertically differentiated products.

What, then, is the pattern of trade? As in the previous case, there are three candidates: $c_H(q) < c_F(q)$ for all $q$, $c_H(q) > c_F(q)$ for all $q$, or $c_H(q) < c_F(q)$ for some range of quality. The first two cases are inconsistent with an intra-industry trade equilibrium (neither country $H$ nor country $F$ would buy foreign variants). Not surprisingly, intra-industry trade is possible only when $c_H(q) < c_F(q)$ for part of the quality range. While the price of labour has no reason to change in country $H$ (it is equal to the price of the numéraire), $w_F$ increases in country $F$ since it no longer imports any non-manufacturing products. This increases both the cost of production and the price of quality products in country $F$, inducing consumers in both countries to substitute away from quality goods produced in country $F$ into quality goods produced in country $H$. Since there is a direct link between the change in the demand for products and that for capital, these changes must be accompanied by an increase in $r_H$ and a fall in $r_F$. These changes in factor prices occur so as to satisfy both the balance-of-trade condition and the equality between the demand for and supply of capital in both countries. Since the changes in $r$ affect the high-quality products more than the low-quality products, $c_H(q) < c_F(q)$ for low-quality products while the converse holds for high-quality products. Result 2 summarizes the discussion:

*Result 2*: When $t_N$ is high enough, the only international trade equilibrium exhibits intra-industry trade. When $\dfrac{K_F}{D_F[\bar{\theta} - \hat{\theta}_F]} > \dfrac{K_H}{D_H[\bar{\theta} - \hat{\theta}_H]}$,

country F specializes in high-quality products and country H specializes in low-quality products.

Figure 7.3 illustrates this case. Consumers in both countries consume the same range of qualities ($[\hat{q}_i, \tilde{q}_i]$ and $[\tilde{q}_i', \bar{q}_i]$) since there is no barrier to trade in the manufacturing sector, but country $F$ produces and exports the upper range of product qualities, while country $H$ produces and exports the lower range. When the number of potential consumers is the same in both countries, the value of trade is proportional to the area below each curve, so that, for trade to be balanced, the range of quality produced in $F$ must be smaller than in $H$.

The model has simple and clear-cut predictions of the composition of trade since a positive barrier to trade in the manufacturing sector generates

Figure 7.3: A Barrier to Trade in Nonmanufacturing

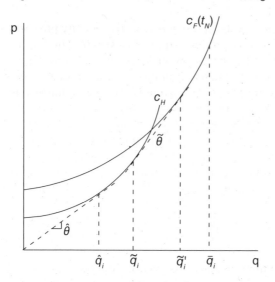

only inter-industry trade, while a sufficiently high barrier to trade in non-manufacturing generates only intra-industry trade. One can already antici-pate an important result: if trade liberalization occurs in the manufacturing sector but not in nonmanufacturing, intra-industry trade in vertically dif-ferentiated products becomes relatively more important. We now charac-terize the different trade equilibria for arbitrary but feasible values of $t_M$ and $t_N$ so as to trace the effects of trade liberalization on the composition and pattern of trade.

### Characterization of the Trade Equilibria

For the remainder of the paper, we assume that, in both countries, $m(q) = e^{\alpha q}$, where $\alpha > 0$ is a parameter determining the slope of the function. Utility maximization then requires – see equation (3) – that $\theta = r_i \alpha e^{\alpha q}$, where we now allow $r$ to be different between countries. Hence,

$$q = ln\left(\frac{\theta}{\alpha r_i}\right)^{\frac{1}{\alpha}}, i = H, F.$$

Assuming that $t_N \geq 0$ and $t_M \geq 0$, we start by characterizing the equilibrium with inter-industry trade alone.

*Inter-industry Trade Equilibrium*

This equilibrium is characterized by country $F$ exporting quality products to and importing homogeneous products from country $H$. For this to occur, $w_H = 1$ and $w_F = 1 + t_N$. Country $H$'s consumers, who are indifferent between imported product quality $\tilde{q}_H'$ and domestic product quality $\tilde{q}_H$, have a willingness to pay for quality $\tilde{\theta}_H$ (see Figure 7.2). This willingness is determined by $v(\tilde{q}_H) = v(\tilde{q}_H')$ and thus by

$$\tilde{\theta}_H \tilde{q}_H - (1 + r_H e^{\alpha \tilde{q}_H}) = \tilde{\theta}_H \tilde{q}_H' - (1 + t_N + t_M + r_F e^{\alpha \tilde{q}_H'}). \tag{4}$$

Since utility maximization implies $\tilde{q}_H = ln(\tilde{\theta}_H / \alpha r_H)^{1/\alpha}$ and $\tilde{q}_H' = ln(\tilde{\theta}_H / \alpha r_F)^{1/\alpha}$, equation (4) becomes

$$\tilde{\theta}_H = \frac{\alpha(t_N + t_M)}{ln\ r}, \tag{5}$$

where $r = r_H / r_F$. The minimum quality consumed in country $i$, $\hat{q}_i$, corresponds to $v(\hat{q}_i) = 0$ and so to $\hat{\theta}_i \hat{q}_i - (w_i + r_i e^{\alpha \hat{q}_i}) = 0$. Since $\hat{q}_i = ln(\hat{\theta}_i / \alpha r_i)^{1/\alpha}$ then $\hat{\theta}_i$ satisfies

$$\hat{\theta}_i ln\left(\frac{\hat{\theta}_i}{\alpha r_i}\right)^{\frac{1}{\alpha}} - w_i - \frac{\hat{\theta}_i}{\alpha} = 0, \quad i = H, F. \tag{6}$$

The maximum quality consumed is the same for consumers of both countries; it is given by $\bar{q} = ln(\bar{\theta} / \alpha r_F)^{1/\alpha}$.

With inter-industry trade, it is easy to find the equilibrium price of capital in each country. Since capital in country $H$ is entirely used in products consumed domestically, $r_H$ is determined by

$$K_H = \int_{\hat{\theta}_H}^{\tilde{\theta}_H} D_H e^{\alpha q(\theta)} d\theta = \int_{\hat{\theta}_H}^{\tilde{\theta}_H} D_H \frac{\theta}{r_H} d\theta = \frac{D_H}{2\alpha r_H}(\tilde{\theta}_H^2 - \hat{\theta}_H^2), \tag{7}$$

where $\tilde{\theta}_H$ is given by (5) and $\hat{\theta}_H$ by equation (6). In country $F$, capital is used in products consumed domestically and exported, so that $r_F$ is determined by

$$K_F = \int_{\hat{\theta}_H}^{\bar{\theta}} D_H e^{\alpha q(\theta)} d\theta + \int_{\hat{\theta}_F}^{\bar{\theta}} D_F e^{\alpha q(\theta)} d\theta = \frac{1}{2\alpha r_F}[D_H(\bar{\theta}^2 - \tilde{\theta}_H^2) + D_F(\bar{\theta}^2 - \hat{\theta}_F^2)], \tag{8}$$

where $\tilde{\theta}_H$ is given by (5) and $\hat{\theta}_F$ by equation (6).

The balance of trade requires that the value of trade be equalized. Since $t_N$ and $t_M$ represent international transport costs and country $H$ transports the products, then, from country $H$'s point of view, the balance of trade condition is

$$\int_{\tilde{\theta}_H}^{\bar{\theta}} D_H (w_F + r_F e^{\alpha q(\theta)}) d\theta - N_t (1 + t_N) = 0. \tag{9}$$

The first term represents the value of the quality products imported by country $H$; the second term represents the value of the nonmanufacturing products exported by country $H$, including the transport cost paid by country $F$. Since $w_F = 1 + t_N$, then, after integration,

$$N_t = D_H (\bar{\theta} - \tilde{\theta}_H) \left[ 1 + \frac{\bar{\theta} + \tilde{\theta}_H}{2\alpha(1 + t_N)} \right]. \tag{10}$$

The equilibrium with inter-industry trade only is determined by equations (5), (6), (7), (8), and (10). Since equation (6) is used for $i = H$ and $i = F$, there are six equations solving respectively for $\tilde{\theta}_H$, $\hat{\theta}_H$, $\hat{\theta}_F$, $r_H$, $r_F$, and $N_t$ given the exogenous variables.

*Intra-industry Trade Equilibrium*

Now consider the equilibrium with intra-industry trade only, where both $t_N$ and $t_M$ are positive. For this equilibrium to hold, $w_F < 1 + t_N$, since it should be cheaper for country $F$ to produce nonmanufacturing goods than to import them. In country $H$, the willingness to pay of consumers who are indifferent between domestic and foreign products, $\tilde{\theta}_H$, is determined by $v(\tilde{q}_H) = v(\tilde{q}'_H)$, and thus by $\tilde{\theta}_H \tilde{q}_H - (1 + r_H e^{\alpha q(\tilde{\theta}_H)}) = \tilde{\theta}_H \tilde{q}'_H - (w_F + t_M + r_F e^{\alpha q'(\tilde{\theta}_H)})$. Solving for $\tilde{\theta}_H$,

$$\tilde{\theta}_H = \frac{\alpha(w_F + t_M - 1)}{\ln r}. \tag{11}$$

Similarly, country $F$'s consumer who are indifferent between imports and domestic products satisfy $v(\tilde{q}_F) = v(\tilde{q}'_F)$, and thus $\tilde{\theta}_F \tilde{q}_F - (1 + t_M + r_H e^{\alpha q(\tilde{\theta}_F)}) = \tilde{\theta}_F \tilde{q}'_F - (w_F + r_F e^{\alpha q'(\tilde{\theta}_F)})$. Solving for $\tilde{\theta}_F$,

$$\tilde{\theta}_F = \frac{\alpha(w_F - t_M - 1)}{\ln r}. \tag{12}$$

Consumers in country $i$ who are indifferent between buying and not buying a quality product satisfy $v(q(\hat{\theta}_i)) = 0$. Since the lowest quality corresponds to a domestic (foreign) product for country $H$'s (respectively, country $F$'s) consumers, $\hat{\theta}_i$ ($i = H, F$) satisfies, respectively,

$$\hat{\theta}_H ln \left( \frac{\hat{\theta}_H}{\alpha r_H} \right)^{\frac{1}{\alpha}} - 1 - \frac{\hat{\theta}_H}{\alpha} = 0, \text{ and } \hat{\theta}_F ln \left( \frac{\hat{\theta}_F}{\alpha r_H} \right)^{\frac{1}{\alpha}} - 1 - t_M - \frac{\hat{\theta}_F}{\alpha} = 0. \tag{13}$$

With intra-industry trade, the stock of capital in each country is used for domestic consumption and exports of quality products. The rental price of capital, $r_H$, respectively $r_F$, is determined by

$$K_H = \int_{\hat{\theta}_H}^{\hat{\theta}_H} D_H e^{\alpha q(\theta)} d\theta + \int_{\hat{\theta}_F}^{\hat{\theta}_F} D_F e^{\alpha q(\theta)} d\theta = \frac{1}{2\alpha r_H}[D_H(\tilde{\theta}_H^2 - \hat{\theta}_H^2) + D_F(\tilde{\theta}_F^2 - \hat{\theta}_F^2)];$$

$$K_F = \int_{\hat{\theta}_H}^{\bar{\theta}} D_H e^{\alpha q(\theta)} d\theta + \int_{\hat{\theta}_F}^{\bar{\theta}} D_F e^{\alpha q(\theta)} d\theta = \frac{1}{2\alpha r_F}[D_H(\bar{\theta}^2 - \tilde{\theta}_H^2) + D_F(\bar{\theta}^2 - \tilde{\theta}_F^2)]. \tag{14}$$

For trade to be balanced, the value of exports of quality products must be equal to the value of imports of quality products. Thus, from country $H$'s point of view,

$$\int_{\hat{\theta}_H}^{\bar{\theta}} D_H(w_F + r_F e^{\alpha q(\theta)}) d\theta - \int_{\hat{\theta}_F}^{\tilde{\theta}_F} D_F(1 + t_M + r_H e^{\alpha q(\theta)}) d\theta = 0. \tag{15}$$

The above condition can be interpreted as determining $w_F (w_H = 1)$ given the values of the other variables, since $w_F$ must be high enough to make sure that $H$'s demand for $F$'s high-quality products is low enough for its value to be equal to its exports of low-quality products. Rearranging equation (15),

$$w_F = \frac{D_F}{D_H(\bar{\theta} - \tilde{\theta}_H)} \left[ (1 + t_M)(\tilde{\theta}_F - \hat{\theta}_F) + 12\alpha(\tilde{\theta}_F^2 - \hat{\theta}_F^2) \right] - \frac{1}{2\alpha}(\bar{\theta} + \tilde{\theta}_H) < 1 + t_N. \tag{16}$$

Equations (11), (12), (13), (14), and (16) determine the equilibrium with intra-industry trade only (that is, $\tilde{\theta}_H$, $\tilde{\theta}_F$, $\hat{\theta}_H$, $\hat{\theta}_F$, $r_H$, $r_F$, and $w_F$) for given values of the exogenous variables.

*Trade Equilibrium with Both Regimes*

The third possible equilibrium has both inter- and intra-industry trade and is thus a combination of the two previous equilibria. Since there is trade in nonmanufacturing products, necessarily, $w_F = 1 + t_N$. It is then easy to derive the willingness to pay of consumers indifferent between buying domestic and foreign products. Indeed, just substitute $w_F$ by $1 + t_N$ in equations (11) and (12) to get

$$\tilde{\theta}_H = \frac{\alpha(t_N + t_M)}{\ln r} \quad \text{and} \quad \tilde{\theta}_F = \frac{\alpha(t_N - t_M)}{\ln r}. \tag{17}$$

The consumers buying the lowest-quality products are still captured by equation (13) since, in equilibrium, consumers from both countries buy these products from country $H$.

Interest rates in each country are then determined by equating the supply of and demand for capital in each country. Since capital is used to produce quality goods only, equation (14) still determines $r_H$ and $r_F$. The balance of trade, however, is different than in the previous cases. With both inter- and intra-industry trade, it is

$$\int_{\tilde{\theta}_H}^{\bar{\theta}} D_H(w_F + r_F e^{\alpha q(\theta)})d\theta - \int_{\tilde{\theta}_F}^{\hat{\theta}_F} D_F(w_H + t_M + r_H e^{\alpha q(\theta)})d\theta - N_t(1+t_N) = 0. \tag{18}$$

The first term represents the value of country $F$'s exports while the latter two terms represent the value of its imports of quality products, nonmanufacturing products, and transportation. Since $w_F = 1 + t_N$ and $w_H = 1$, then, after integration,

$$N_t = \frac{1}{1+t_N} \left\{ D_H[(1+t_N)(\bar{\theta} - \tilde{\theta}_H) + \frac{1}{2\alpha}(\bar{\theta}^2 - \tilde{\theta}_H^2)] - \right.$$

$$\left. D_F[(1+t_M)(\tilde{\theta}_F - \hat{\theta}_F) + \frac{1}{2\alpha}(\tilde{\theta}_F^2 - \hat{\theta}_F^2)] \right\}. \tag{19}$$

The equilibrium $\tilde{\theta}_H$, $\tilde{\theta}_F$, $\hat{\theta}_H$, $\hat{\theta}_F$, $r_H$, $r_F$, and $N_t$ is determined by equations (13), (14), (17), and (19).

The three equilibria are illustrated in the space $(t_M, t_N)$ in Figure 7.4. It is divided in four regions (see the appendix for a precise characterization). In region I, there is no trade when both $t_N$ and $t_M$ are sufficiently high. When $t_N$ and $t_M$ are both low enough for trade to exist, there is inter-industry only. This is the Heckscher-Ohlin region, where the trade barriers, particularly $t_N$ are not high enough to distort each country's comparative advantage. In region II, intra-industry trade emerges alongside inter-industry trade: $t_N$ is now high enough to make wages in country $F$ – and

Figure 7.4: Equilibrium Types of Trade

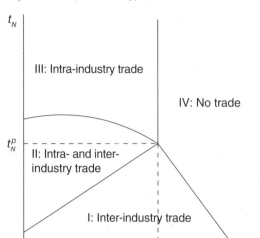

thus the price of quality products in country $F$ – high enough for consumers there to import some quality products from $H$. Since $r_H > r_F$, they do so only for low-quality products. In region III, $t_N$ is too high to sustain trade in nonmanufacturing products, so that a trade equilibrium is consistent only with intra-industry trade. In region IV, the barriers to trade are high to sustain no international trade.

Two additional points are worth noting. First, $t_N^p$ and $t_M^p$ are the lowest prohibitive barriers to trade in each sector. Second, consistent with our earlier analysis, complete free trade exhibits only inter-industry trade.

**Trade Liberalization**

There are obviously many possible paths to trade liberalization. But if $t_M$ decreases more than $t_N$, it is apparent from Figure 7.4 that, along such a path, intra-industry trade emerges if it does not already exist, and increases if it already exists. In order to capture the degree of intra-industry trade, the Grubel-Lloyd index is an obvious measure. Since there is only one sector with differentiated products, the index is simply

$$IIT \equiv 1 - \frac{|X_q - M_q|}{X_q + M_q},$$

where $X_q$ (respectively, $M_q$) is the value of exports (respectively, imports) of quality products for one of the two countries. Since $0 \leq IIT \leq 1$ (with $IIT = 0$ corresponding to inter-industry trade only and $IIT = 1$ to intra-industry only), $IIT$ is equal to 0 in region I, between 0 and 1 in region II, and equal to 1 in region III. Thus, the only ambiguity is the value of $IIT$ in region II. Accordingly, $X_q$ and $M_q$ for country $H$ in region II are:

$$X_q = \int_{\hat{\theta}_F}^{\tilde{\theta}_F} D_F(w_H + t_M + r_H e^{\alpha q(\theta)})d\theta = D_F[(1+t_M)(\tilde{\theta}_F - \hat{\theta}_F) + \frac{1}{2\alpha}(\tilde{\theta}_F^2 - \hat{\theta}_F^2)];$$

$$M_q = \int_{\tilde{\theta}_H}^{\bar{\theta}} D_H(w_F + r_F e^{\alpha q(\theta)})d\theta = D_H[w_F(\bar{\theta} - \tilde{\theta}_H) + \frac{1}{2\alpha}(\bar{\theta}^2 - \tilde{\theta}_H^2)].$$

We are also interested in the terms of trade in quality products to see whether intra-industry trade becomes more similar or more dissimilar when its volume increases. The terms of trade are found by computing the ratio of the average prices of exports and imports of quality products for one of the countries. For country $H$, the country transporting the products, the terms of trade are equal to

$$P = \frac{\bar{p}_x}{\bar{p}_m} = \frac{\dfrac{\displaystyle\int_{\hat{\theta}_F}^{\tilde{\theta}_F} D_F(w_H + t_M + r_H e^{\alpha q(\theta)})d\theta}{D_F(\tilde{\theta}_F - \hat{\theta}_F)}}{\dfrac{\displaystyle\int_{\tilde{\theta}_H}^{\bar{\theta}} D_H(w_F + r_F e^{\alpha q(\theta)})d\theta}{D_H(\bar{\theta} - \tilde{\theta}_H)}} = \frac{2\alpha(1+t_M) + \tilde{\theta}_F + \hat{\theta}_F}{2\alpha w_F + \bar{\theta} + \tilde{\theta}_H}.$$

$P$ is valid only when there is intra-industry trade ($IIT > 0$) – and, thus, in regions II and III. Note that, for country $H$, $P < 1$, as it exports low-quality products. A fall in $t_M$ has a direct effect that decreases $P$ further below 1, as well as a number of indirect effects through the changes in $w_F$, $\tilde{\theta}_H$, $\tilde{\theta}_F$, and $\hat{\theta}_F$.

We use simulations to compute the Grubel-Lloyd Index ($IIT$) and the terms of trade ($P$) in regions II and III for different parameters. We concentrate our attention on one issue: how $P$ and $IIT$ change with lower $t_M$ and $t_N$. Changes in $P$ are associated with changes in average quality in the trade of differentiated products, and IIT tells us the relative importance of intra-industry trade with respect to total trade. We are particularly interested in determining some of the circumstances under which $IIT$ increases and $P$ either decreases (reflecting more vertical differentiation in the trade of country $H$) or increases (reflecting less vertical differentiation in the trade of $H$). In all these simulations, $\alpha = .35$.

Table 7.1
$IIT$ and $P(K_H = D_H = D_F = 1)$

| | $K_F = 1.2$ | | | | | $K_F = 2$ | | | |
|---|---|---|---|---|---|---|---|---|---|
| Region | $t_N$ | $t_M$ | $IIT$ | $P$ | Region | $t_N$ | $t_M$ | $IIT$ | $P$ |
| II | .2 | 0 | .97 | .78 | II | 1.5 | 0 | .84 | .585 |
| | | .01 | .96 | .76 | | | .1 | .83 | .586 |
| | | .03 | .92 | .71 | | | .2 | .78 | .586 |
| | | .05 | .39 | .67 | | | .3 | .43 | .586 |
| | .3 | 0 | .97 | .76 | | 2 | 0 | .89 | .541 |
| | | .01 | .97 | .76 | | | .1 | .91 | .547 |
| | | .03 | .97 | .72 | | | .2 | .92 | .553 |
| | | .05 | .94 | .69 | | | .3 | .93 | .558 |
| | | .07 | .71 | .67 | | | .4 | .52 | .563 |
| | .5 | 0 | .99 | .73 | | 2.5 | 0 | .93 | .504 |
| | | .01 | .99 | .72 | | | .1 | .97 | .512 |
| III | .6 | 0 | 1.0 | .71 | III | 3 | 0 | 1.0 | .463 |
| | | .04 | 1.0 | .7 | | | .1 | 1.0 | .5 |
| | | .08 | 1.0 | .67 | | | .2 | 1.0 | .529 |
| | | .12 | 1.0 | .65 | | | .3 | 1.0 | .549 |

Table 7.1 shows that, given $t_N$ and relatively similar countries, lower $t_M$ generally increases $IIT$ and $P$. Hence, as the share of intra-industry trade increases at the expense of one-way trade, the average quality of the differentiated goods traded by each country becomes more similar. Making country F more capital abundant with respect to country $H$ (Table 7.1) or increasing the consumer population of country $H$ (Table 7.2) makes $P$ decrease with trade liberalization in the quality sector. Since $IIT$ rises when $t_N$ is relatively high, trade liberalization leads in both instances to more intra-industry trade and to more international vertical differentiation.

When trade liberalization occurs in nonmanufacturing alone (lower $t_N$), $IIT$ falls and $P$ increases. This outcome should be expected, since lower $t_N$ boosts trade in nonmanufacturing products. The fact that $P$ increases is because trade liberalization in nonmanufacturing generates smaller differences in wages between the two countries, resulting in more similar average quality produced and traded by the two countries. In other words, international vertical differentiation generally decreases with trade liberalization in nonmanufacturing.

Our results confirm that more vertical differentiation in trade is consistent with trade liberalization, provided the nonmanufacturing sector has a high enough level of distortion $t_N$ and countries are not identical in terms of their endowment and/or number of consumers.

Table 7.2
IIT and P ($D_F = K_H = 1$)

| | | $D_H = 1.7, K_F = 1.2$ | | |
|---|---|---|---|---|
| Region | $t_N$ | $t_M$ | IIT | P |
| II | 1.5 | 0 | ·.798 | .625 |
| | | .06 | .775 | .622 |
| | | .12 | .716 | .621 |
| | | .18 | .537 | .619 |
| | 2.0 | 0 | .841 | .575 |
| | | .06 | .842 | .577 |
| | | .12 | .834 | .579 |
| | | .18 | .802 | .581 |
| | | .24 | .665 | .582 |
| | 2.2 | 0 | .887 | .533 |
| | | .04 | .899 | .536 |
| III | 3 | 0 | 1.0 | .458 |
| | | .06 | 1.0 | .486 |
| | | .12 | 1.0 | .511 |
| | | .18 | 1.0 | .533 |
| | | .24 | 1.0 | .549 |
| | | .3 | 1.0 | .561 |

## Conclusion

We have shown that the empirically observed increase in the share of intra-industry trade in vertically differentiated products with respect to one-way trade is consistent with a simple general equilibrium model in which trade liberalization is more extensive in the manufacturing than in the nonmanufacturing sector.

A reasonable alternative explanation for this observation is the large increase in the volume of international trade in intermediate products. More firms now rely on parts and services produced by geographically distinct units, giving rise to trade in intermediate and final products that would not exist without vertical international specialization in production. Recent evidence suggest that the share of trade due to vertical specialization in production is as high as 50 percent for small countries (see Hummels, Rapoport, and Yi 1998; Yi 2003).

Could the fragmentation of production explains the shift in the nature of intra-industry trade? It is surely a contributing factor but it is not obvious that it is the main cause. First, one would expect that foreign direct investment

(FDI) to be highly correlated with intra-industry trade in vertically differentiated products for the fragmentation of production to be the driving force. In fact, Fontagné, Freudenberg, and Péridy (1997) find that FDI is positively correlated with the three forms of trade. Even if the effect of FDI is higher on intra-industry than on inter-industry trade, the literature finds no particular link between FDI and trade in vertically differentiated products. Second, one would expect vertical fragmentation to take place in sectors where multinational corporations are important, since there is a large share of company-specific products in total parts and components trade. This would imply a link between sectors where multinationals are important and the increase in trade in vertically differentiated products. This is not what the literature generally finds, however, since the increase in the share of intra-industry trade in vertically differentiated products has occurred in *all* manufacturing sectors, irrespective of their market structure. Of course, it is ultimately an empirical issue as to which explanation is valid; to our knowledge, this research has not yet been undertaken. Another possibility that no one has investigated is the role of income distribution (see Choi, Hummels, and Chong 2006) and thus whether recent changes in income distributions across countries might help to explain the rise in trade of vertically differentiated products.

Clearly, more study is needed to understand the causes of this change in the composition of international trade. The implications for welfare or for policy are not the same if the underlying cause is a fundamental change in the production process or if, as we have argued, it can be explained by comparative advantage and asymmetric sectoral trade liberalization.

## Appendix

In this appendix, we derive the equilibrium conditions for the limits of each trade configuration and, thus, the frontiers in Figure 7.4. Along the frontier between regions I and IV, there is no trade; thus, $N_t = 0$. With equation (10), $\tilde{\theta}_H = \bar{\theta}$; thus, with equation (5),

$$\bar{\theta} = \frac{\alpha(t_N + t_M)}{\ln r}, \tag{A.1}$$

while (7) and (8) become

$$K_H = \frac{D_H}{2\alpha r_H}(\bar{\theta}^2 - \hat{\theta}_H^2) \quad \text{and} \quad K_F = \frac{D_F}{2\alpha r_F}(\bar{\theta}^2 - \hat{\theta}_F^2). \tag{A.2}$$

The frontier between regions I and IV is determined by equations (6), (A.1), and (A.2). These five equations determine $\hat{\theta}_H$, $\hat{\theta}_F$, $r_H$, $r_F$, and $t_M$ for given values of $t_N$, $K_H$, $K_F$, $D_H$, $D_F$, $\alpha$, and $\bar{\theta}$.

The frontier between regions I and II defines the limit for intra-industry trade. Since this type of trade exists as soon as country $F$'s consumers buy quality products from country $H$, it must be true that, along this frontier, $\tilde{\theta}_F = \hat{\theta}_F$. Using equation (7),

$$\hat{\theta}_F = \frac{\alpha(t_N - t_M)}{\ln r}.$$

$$(A.3)$$

Note that, since $\hat{\theta}_F > 0$ – see equation (6) – then $t_N > t_M$. The frontier between regions I and II is then determined by equations (5), (6), (7), (8), and (A.3). They determine, respectively, $\tilde{\theta}_H$, $\hat{\theta}_H$, $\hat{\theta}_F$, $r_H$, $r_F$, and $t_M$ for given values of $t_N$, $K_H$, $K_F$, $D_H$, $D_F$, $\alpha$, and $\bar{\theta}$. Note that equation (10) also determines $N_t$ residually.

The frontier between regions II and III is characterized by $N_t = 0$ and the existence of intra-industry trade. Hence, using equation (19),

$$D_H\left[(1+t_N)(\bar{\theta} - \tilde{\theta}_H) + 12\alpha(\bar{\theta}^2 - \tilde{\theta}_H^2)\right]$$
$$= D_F\left[(1+t_M)(\tilde{\theta}_F - \hat{\theta}_F) + 12\alpha(\tilde{\theta}_F^2 - \hat{\theta}_F^2)\right].$$

$$(A.4)$$

This also implies from equation (16) that $w_F = 1 + t_N$. Hence, the frontier between regions II and III is determined by equations (13), (14), (17), and (A.4), which determine, respectively, $\hat{\theta}_H$, $\hat{\theta}_F$, $r_H$, $r_F$, $\tilde{\theta}_H$, $\tilde{\theta}_F$, and $t_M$.

Finally, the frontier between regions III and IV has no intra-industry trade and thus is characterized by $\tilde{\theta}_H = \bar{\theta}$ and $\hat{\theta}_F = \tilde{\theta}_F$, since country $H$'s (respectively, $F$'s) consumers import high-quality (respectively, low-quality) products. Using equations (11) and (12), this implies

$$\bar{\theta} = \frac{\alpha(w_F + t_M - 1)}{\ln r},$$

$$(A.5)$$

and

$$\hat{\theta}_F = \frac{\alpha(w_F - t_M - 1)}{\ln r}.$$

$$(A.6)$$

This also means that the capital market condition reduces to equation (A.2). Hence, equations (6), (A.2), (A.5), and (A.6) determine, respectively, $\hat{\theta}_H$, $r_H$, $r_F$, $w_F$, and $t_M$. Note that this system of equations is independent of $t_N$.

Finally, to see why the four frontiers intersect at the same point in Figure 7.4, observe that, at this point, $w_F = 1 + t_N$, so that equations (A.5) and (A.6) are the same as (A.1) and (A.3), respectively. Since $\bar{\theta} = \tilde{\theta}_H$ and $\tilde{\theta}_F = \hat{\theta}_F$, equation (14) is identical to (A.2). Hence, this point is determined by equations (13), (A.1), (A.2), and (A.3) and these six equations are consistent with the equilibrium in regions I, II, and III. They determine, respectively, $\hat{\theta}_H$, $\hat{\theta}_F$, $t_N^p$, $r_H$, $r_F$, and $t_M^p$, given $K_H$, $K_F$, $D_H$, $D_F$, $\alpha$, and $\bar{\theta}$.

## NOTES

1  See, for instance, Abd-el-Rahman (1991); Greenaway, Hine, and Milner (1995); Fontagné, Freudenberg, and Péridy (1997); Greenaway, Milner, and Elliott (1999); Blanes and Martin (2000); and Gullstrand (2002).
2  Eaton has worked with this approach in two papers: Eaton and Lipsey (1987) and Eaton and Harrald (1992).

## REFERENCES

Abd-el-Rahman, Kamal. 1991. 'Firms' Competitive and National Comparative Advantage as Joint Determinants of Trade Composition.' *Weltwirtschaftliches Archiv/Review of World Economics* 127 (1): 83–97.

Bernard, Andrew, Jonathan Eaton, Jensen Bradford, and Samuel Kortum. 2003. 'Plants and Productivity in International Trade.' *American Economic Review* 93 (4): 1268–90.

Blanes, Jose, and Carmela Martin. 2000. 'The Nature and Causes of Intra-Industry Trade: Back to Comparative Advantage Explanation, the Case of Spain.' *Weltwirtschaftliches Archiv/Review of World Economics* 136 (3): 423–41.

Boccard, Nicolas, and Xavier Wauthy. 1998. 'Import Restraints and Quality Choice under Vertical Differentiation.' CORE Discussion Paper 9818. Louvain, Belgium: Université catholique de Louvain, Centre for Operations Research and Econometrics.

Cabral, Manuel, Rod Falvey, and Chris Milner. 2007. 'Vertical Intra-Industry Trade and Differences in Endowments: Revisiting the Empirical Evidence.' Universidade do Minho. Mimeograph.

Choi, Yo Chul, David Hummels, and Chong Xiang. 2006. 'Explaining Import Variety and Quality: The Role of the Income Distribution.' NBER Working Paper 12531. Cambridge, MA: National Bureau of Economic Research.

Eaton, E. Curtis, and Richard G. Lipsey. 1987. 'Product Differentiation.' In *Handbook of Product Differentiation*, edited by R. Schamlensee and R. Willig. Amsterdam: North-Holland.

Eaton, E. Curtis, and Paul Harrald. 1992. 'Price versus Quantity Competition in the Gabszewicz-Thisse Model of Product Differentiation.' In *Market Strategy and Structure*, edited by A. Gee and G. Norman. New York: Harvester Wheatsheaf.

Falvey, Rod. 1981. 'Commercial Policy and Intra-Industry Trade.' *Journal of International Economy* 11 (4): 495–511.

Falvey, Rod, and Henryk Kierzkowski. 1987. 'Product Quality, Intra-Industry Trade and (Im)perfect Competition.' In *Protection and Competition in International Trade*, edited by H. Kierzkowski. Oxford: Basil Blackwell.

Flam, Harry, and Elhanan Helpman. 1987. 'Vertical Product Differentiation and North-South Trade.' *American Economic Review* 77 (5): 810–22.

Fontagné, Lionel, Michel Freudenberg, and Guillaume Gaulier. 2006. 'A Systematic Decomposition of World Trade into Horizontal and Vertical IIT.' *Weltwirtschaftliches Archiv/Review of World Economics* 142 (3): 459–75.

Fontagné, Lionel, Michel Freudenberg, and Nicolas Péridy. 1997. 'Trade Patterns Inside the Single Market.' Working Paper 97-07. Paris: Centre d'études prospectives et d'informations internationales.

Gabszewicz, Jean, and Jacques-François Thisse. 1980. 'Entry (and Exit) in a Differentiated Industry.' *Journal of Economic Theory* 22 (2): 327–38.

Greenaway, David, Robert Hine, and Chris Milner. 1995. 'Vertical and Horizontal Intra-Industry Trade: A Cross Industry Analysis for the United Kingdom.' *Economic Journal* 105 (433): 1505–18.

Greenaway, David, Chris Milner, and Robert Elliott. 1999. 'UK Intra-Indusry Trade with the EU North and South.' *Oxford Bulletin of Economics and Statistics* 61 (3): 365–84.

Gullstrand, Joakim. 2002. 'Does the Measurement of Intra-Industry Trade Matter?' *Weltwirtschaftliches Archiv/Review of World Economics* 138 (2): 317–39.

Hummels, David, and Peter Klenow. 2005. 'The Variety and Quality of a Nation's Exports.' *American Economic Review* 95 (3): 704–23.

Hummels, David, Dana Rapoport, and Yi Kei-Mu. 1998. 'Vertical Specialization and the Changing Nature of World Trade.' *Federal Reserve Bank of New York Economic Policy Review* (June): 79–99.

Mussa, Michael, and Sherwin Rosen. 1978. 'Monopoly and Product Quality.' *Journal of Economic Theory* 18 (2): 301–17.

Schmitt, Nicolas. 1995. 'Product Imitation, Product Differentiation and International Trade.' *International Economic Review* 36 (3): 583–608.

Schott, Peter. 2004. 'Across-Product vs. Within-Product Specialization in International Trade.' *Quarterly Journal of Economics* 119 (2): 647–78.

Shaked, Avnar, and John Sutton. 1983. 'Natural Oligopolies.' *Econometrica* 51 (5): 1469–83.

Yi Kei-Mu. 2003. 'Can Vertical Specialization Explain the Growth in World Trade?' *Journal of Political Economy* 111 (1): 52–102.

# 8 A Tale of Two Cities: Cyclical Movements in Price and Productivity in Mining and Manufacturing

HARRY BLOCH

Over the past several decades, Curtis Eaton has been at the forefront of a revolution in microeconomic theory. This revolution has shifted the focus of analysis from the general equilibrium of competitive economies to the dynamics of strategic interaction in partially localized markets. In the process, imperfect competition has replaced perfect competition as the primary focus of research in microeconomics.

The argument developed in this paper is that imperfectly competitive analysis of the type expounded in Curtis's research is particularly appropriate for analyzing long-run equilibrium in manufacturing. In this equilibrium, firms operate with price greater than marginal cost, substantial fixed costs, and unexploited economies of scale. I also argue, however, that this model is not appropriate for mining firms. A different pattern of competition in mining is attributed to the structural conditions of heterogeneous resource deposits that are used to produce standardized products, which are often sold in well-organized global markets. At least some mining firms appear to operate as price takers, with price equal to marginal cost and no unexploited economies of scale.

The focus of this study is on disequilibrium – in particular, the adjustment to cyclical shocks for an economy in which markets of the two types described above co-exist. Associated with the dichotomy in long-run equilibrium between mining and manufacturing is a difference in the short-run responsiveness of supply, which, in turn, implies differences in the price and quantity effects of supply and demand shocks. As a result, demand shocks are expected to lead to procyclical movements in the price of mining products relative to the price of manufactures.

In addition to implying that demand shocks affect prices differently across the mining and manufacturing sectors, the analysis suggests that demand shocks have different effects on productivity in the two sectors. Productivity in manufacturing is expected to be procyclical. In mining, however, the cyclical behaviour of productivity is more complicated. At the bottom of the business cycle, productivity is expected to be procyclical, but during booms, such as that experienced recently, productivity is expected to be countercyclical.

Markets for mine products tend to be global, with many products actively traded on organized commodity exchanges, while manufacturing markets tend to be segmented by country due to product differentiation and trade barriers.[1] Nonetheless, both markets can be observed in countries with both a globally integrated mining sector and a substantial manufacturing sector. Both Australia and Canada fit these requirements and have sectoral data for prices and multifactor productivity that extend back into the 1960s. These data are used to examine whether the dichotomy in competition in mining and manufacturing explains the pattern of cyclical movements in prices and productivity in the two sectors.

The remainder of the paper is organized as follows. The next section discusses competitive conditions between mining and manufacturing, resulting in the dichotomy indicated above. This is followed by an examination of cyclical movements in the prices of mining and manufacturing products in Australia and Canada. I then focus on productivity, again using data from mining and manufacturing in Australia and Canada to illustrate the working of adjustments to cyclical shocks. The final section provides some observations on implications of cyclical movements in the relative prices and productivity between miners and manufacturers for inflation and the distribution of income.

## Competitive Conditions

### Manufacturing

A key feature of Curtis's analysis of imperfect competition is the localization of competition – for example, through spatial separation (as in Eaton 1972; Eaton and Lipsey 1975; and Eaton and Wooders 1985) or through production differentiation (as in Eaton and Lipsey 1989). The localization of competition means that the market facing individual firms is imperfect and the firms face downward-sloping demand for their product, even when there are large numbers of producers in the industry. When combined with free entry of firms, as in Eaton (1976) or Eaton and Lipsey (1978), this leads toward equilibrium with unexploited economies of scale.

Another argument for the existence of unexploited economies of scale that Curtis analyses is the effort of incumbents to deter entry. Building on the seminal work of Spence (1977), Eaton and Lipsey (1979, 1980, 1981) examine conditions under which firms make strategic investments in capacity as a means of influencing entry decisions. While the case for using excess capacity as a deterrent to entry in these papers is shown to be less strong than in naive models of entry deterrence, the possibilities of unexploited economies and of economic profit in equilibrium remain.

Curtis's theoretical work on competition suggests an important distinction for empirical research – namely, the distinction between the effect of imperfect competition on economic profits and the effect on the ratio of price to marginal cost. Many of the models presented in Curtis's work analyze forward-looking equilibrium with free entry. Under at least some conditions, this equilibrium is often characterized by economic profits that approach 0 for incumbent firms. Yet, the corresponding ratio of price to marginal cost almost always exceeds 1. Thus, imperfect competition in the sense that price exceeds marginal cost need not imply economic profit.

Further support for the importance of the distinction between economic profit and the ratio of price to marginal cost as measures of the imperfection of competition is given by Sutton's (1991, 1998) application of game theory to the analysis of market structure. Sutton argues that firm expenditures on sunk cost items, such as advertising and research and development, affect the equilibrium outcome of the dynamic game. While Sutton's focus is on outcomes in terms of market structure, there are implications for outcomes in terms of economic profit and the ratio of price to marginal cost. In particular, sunk cost expenditures are covered by revenues in equilibrium, which implies, with constant marginal production cost generally assumed, that price exceeds marginal cost even when economic profit is zero.

Strong empirical support for a degree of imperfection of competition is found in studies that directly estimate the degree of market imperfection in manufacturing industries. Iwata (1974) and Applebaum (1982) estimate a cost function and the degree of imperfect competition in the context of simultaneous equations for an industry's cost function, input demand functions, and profit-maximizing price. Iwata, applying his method to estimating the degree of conjectural variation for Japanese glass manufacturers, finds a ratio of price to marginal cost in the range of 2.0 to 2.5. Applebaum finds a low ratio of price to marginal cost in the U.S. rubber and textiles industry in the order of around 1.05, a moderate ratio of price to marginal cost of about 1.25 for the electrical machinery industry. and a high ratio of about 3 in the tobacco industry.[2]

Hall (1988) provides a method of estimating the imperfection of competition in terms of the ratio of price to marginal cost, which is of particular relevance to the focus on productivity analysis in this paper. Hall infers the value of the ratio of price to marginal cost from observations on the Solow residual, measured by the difference between the real value of output growth and the weighted average growth in input usage. Using this method, Hall estimates that ratio of price to marginal cost in U.S. manufacturing is somewhat greater than 2 for durable goods and somewhat greater than 3 for non-durable goods, with a greater range of values for more disaggregated industries.

Hall (1990) notes that his procedure for inferring estimates of the ratio of price to marginal cost depends on the identifying restrictions imposed in estimation. One such restriction is constant returns to scale. He examines the validity of this restriction by inferring estimates of the elasticity of scale from the measure of the Solow residual based on cost and input price data rather than on output and input data. He finds evidence of substantial economies of scale in most manufacturing industries, and suggests that this is consistent with a type of monopolistic competition equilibrium with price equal to average cost but greater than marginal cost.

A substantial literature has followed Hall's basic approach. The results generally have supported the conclusion that there is imperfect competition in terms of price exceeding marginal cost in U.S. manufacturing, but the estimates of the margin are substantially lower when output is measured in gross terms rather than value added (see, for example, Domowitz, Hubbard, and Petersen 1988). Particularly convincing is the work of Roeger (1995), who relies on the difference between primal and dual productivity measures, and estimates the ratio of price to marginal cost across U.S. manufacturing industries to be between 1.15 and 2.75.

The general representation of competition in manufacturing that emerges from both the theoretical and empirical literature is one of imperfect competition, with price exceeding marginal cost to varying degrees across individual industries. There is no consensus on whether firms are able to earn economic profit in long-run equilibrium, in part due to the prevalence of sunk costs that reflect the efforts of incumbent firms to deter entry and protect their market positions.[3] To the extent that average cost is thereby elevated above marginal cost, profit is reduced while imperfect competition is sustained. Importantly for the analysis later in this paper of cyclical movements in productivity, this implies that incumbent firms generally operate with unexploited economies of scale on the downward-sloping portion of their average cost curves.

*Mining*

The modern economic theory of production and firm behaviour is meant to be universal and does not distinguish among manufacturing, mining, or any other economic activity. This universality applies to Curtis's analysis of imperfect competition and the other theoretical developments discussed above. However, particular assumptions in these analyses are problematic when applied to mining.

Perhaps most problematic of the standard assumptions in the analyses of imperfect competition is that all producers have identical cost functions, at least in the long run. This assumption is generally justified by producers' having equal access to best-practice production methods and being able to acquire the inputs to production of equivalent quality at equal prices. There is no clear basis for expecting mining and manufacturing firms to have different access to technology, but not all mining firms are able to acquire the identical inputs due to the heterogeneity of the nonrenewable resource inputs that are essential to mining activity.[4]

The heterogeneity of nonrenewable resource inputs suggests a constraint on the ability of firms to reproduce indefinitely, negating the assumption of free entry that is common in models of endogenous market structure, such as those of Eaton and Ware (1987) or Sutton (1991). In addition to the heterogeneity of natural resource inputs, there is fixity in their location. This interferes with the endogenous location mechanism that is central to Curtis's analysis of spatial competition. Thus, modern developments in the theory of imperfect competition are not directly applicable to the mining sector.

In the context of the old structure-conduct-performance (SCP) approach to analysing market power, the impediment to free entry would be associated with the heterogeneity of natural resource inputs, which would be seen as contributing to the imperfection of competition. Likewise, the fixity of location of production activity would contribute to the imperfection of competition by limiting the degree to which producers can relocate production to provide competition. However, the application of game theory to other problems of market structure and competition has demonstrated that many inferences from the SCP approach need to be modified.[5]

Extension of the game theoretic approach to competition in mining is complicated by the absence of an obvious closure condition that is equivalent to the zero-profit restriction associated with free entry in manufacturing.[6] A further complication is that incumbent firms and new entrants would have different cost levels associated with the heterogeneous resource, which is likely to affect their strategic interaction. Until the analysis is undertaken, it is hazardous to speculate about the degree of competition that would prevail in equilibrium. Thus, theory does not yet provide a guide to specifying conditions of competition in the mining sector.[7]

The empirical literature on competition in mining is sparse. Ellis and Halvorsen (2002) point to the difficulties associated with heterogeneous natural resource inputs as an impediment. Without a measure of the economic cost of the natural resource inputs used up during a production period, cost measures exclude the cost of these inputs. Ellis and Halvorsen argue that ignoring the cost of natural resource inputs leads to misspecification in estimating market power in mining.

Ellis and Halvorsen overcome the absence of a measure of the user cost of natural resources by estimating a model that incorporates an implicit user cost for natural resource inputs. They use an integrated system of cost function, input share equations, and a pricing equation similar to that applied to manufacturing by Iwata (1974), Applebaum (1982), and Morrison (1992), aside from including terms for the amount of input mined and cumulative extraction. The model is applied to data for Inco, then the world's leading nickel producer. Their estimates imply substantial market power, with the average markup of price over marginal cost on the order of 150 per cent.

Slade (2004) finds evidence of market power for a broader sample of large firms in nonferrous mining and refining by examining the relationship among profits, risk, market share, cumulative exhaustion, and a time trend for panel data. Slade provides no quantification of the effect of market power due to the indirect method she uses to test for it, but she notes that the level of market concentration ranges from fairly competitive to only moderately concentrated. This implies that the effect of concentration on firm behaviour is at most modest.

Adelman's research on competition in the world petroleum industry provides evidence of a divergence in the exercise of market power across firms (see Adelman 1993; Adelman and Watkins 2008). Essentially, the argument is that the world supply of petroleum is dichotomous: the Organization of Petroleum-Exporting Countries (OPEC) acts as a cartel, restricting supply so that price substantially exceeds production cost, while non-OPEC producers expand capacity and production until expected price is equal to marginal cost.

Price-taking behaviour is also assumed, explicitly or implicitly, in studies of mining production. For example, Ellerman, Stoker, and Berndt (2001) explain the time path of productivity in the U.S. coal mining industry by linking investment and mine closure decisions to the time path for coal prices. Tilton and Landsberg (1999) give a similar explanation for the time path of productivity in the U.S. copper mining industry. They do not explicitly test perfectly competitive behaviour, but the behaviour they observe is consistent with that of at least marginal producers that disregard any effect of their decisions on market price.

The theoretical and empirical basis for characterizing competition in the mining sector is weak and certainly less compelling than in the case of manufacturing. Yet, the treatment of marginal supply as coming from price-taker firms is pervasive. Thus, the working hypothesis adopted for the analysis below is that the supply response of mining firms to demand shocks comes from price-taking firms. These firms might be perfectly competitive, part of a competitive fringe, or even part of a Bertrand-type oligopoly.

## The Business Cycle and Prices in Mining and Manufacturing

Mining and manufacturing are linked together through the use of mine products as raw materials in manufacturing. This means that shocks to one sector affect the demand or supply conditions of the other. In particular, demand or supply shocks in the manufacturing sector that lead to changes in output levels or input substitution are reflected in demand shocks to the mining sector. Further, demand or supply shocks to the mining sector that lead to changes in mine output are reflected in supply shocks to the manufacturing sector.

Importantly, the transmission of shocks between mining and manufacturing occurs at the global level. For example, the substantial expansion of industrial production in China over recent years has transmitted a positive demand shock to the markets for mine products across the world, not just in China. The resulting rise in global prices of mine products appears as a negative supply shock to manufacturers worldwide, even though the initiating demand shock might have affected only a few countries.

Given the characterization of competition in manufacturing developed above, demand shocks have an ambiguous impact on prices. With marginal cost held constant, price varies with the ratio of price to marginal cost. Neither theory nor empirical evidence provides a clear indication as to whether the price-cost margin responds positively or negatively to demand shocks.[8] Thus, it is reasonable to treat manufacturing prices as generally insensitive to demand shocks, so that fluctuations in price reflect the effect of supply shocks. Indeed, if the price-cost margin is constant, the effect of a supply shock on price is equal to its effect on marginal cost. These effects can be localized if the supply shocks are specific to a particular industry and/or country.[9] Alternatively, domestic prices might be affected by supply shocks that reflect changes in technology generally available to producers (for example, new capital goods) or worldwide changes in the prices of inputs, including mine products. Thus, domestic price movements for manufacturing products might reflect either domestic or global influences.

Supply shocks to individual mining operations will be reflected in changes in the quantity of mine products produced at given prices. This implies that the effect on world markets for mine products depends on the mine operation's being of substantial size or there being many operations affected by the same shock. The latter might occur where mine operations are heavily concentrated in a particular region and shocks involve factors that affect all firms, such as weather, labour strikes, or political unrest. Also, shocks associated with technology or prices of purchased inputs, such as energy, might be expected to affect world prices noticeably. Many supply shocks, however, are idiosyncratic to isolated operations and affect either domestic or global prices only minimally.

If, as suggested above, the incremental supply of mine products comes from mining firms that behave as price takers, demand shocks can significantly affect quantities produced only through their influence on world market prices. Since the main use of mine products is as raw materials for industry, fluctuations in world industrial production are an obvious source of demand shocks that are of sufficient magnitude to have a noticeable effect on mining prices. Further, to the extent that fluctuations in industrial production are manifestations of the world business cycle, there are corresponding demand shocks to mining that lead to procyclical movements in the prices of mine products. Thus, movements in both domestic and global prices of mine products are expected to reflect the effect of the world business cycle.

Figure 8.1 shows price indexes for mining and manufacturing in Australia for the period 1968/69 through 2006/07, along with the ratio of the two price indexes, also expressed as an index number. Corresponding indexes are shown in Figure 8.2 for Canada for the period from 1957 through 2007. The indexes are annual data for the available series, with the broadest possible grouping of products in each sector. Details of the composition and sources for the data are provided in the data appendix.

Analysis suggests that prices in mining rise and fall with the ups and downs of the world business cycle, while manufacturing prices are relatively insensitive to either domestic or world business cycle influences. The pattern for Australia is that manufacturing prices increase continually, albeit at a rate that varies somewhat over the years. In contrast, mining

Figure 8.1: Price Indexes for Mining and Manufacturing, Australia, 1968/69–2006/07

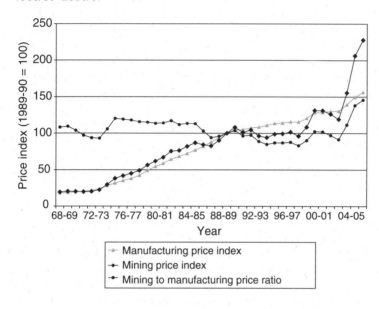

Figure 8.2: Price Indexes for Mining and Manufacturing, Canada, 1957–2007

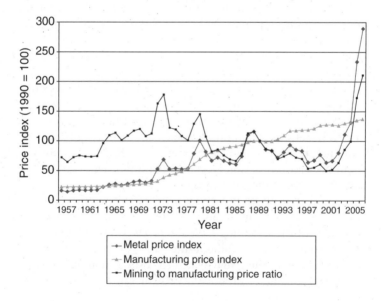

prices exhibit a high degree of volatility, particularly in recent years. The pattern of prices for Canada exhibits similar characteristics.

The ratio of mining prices to manufacturing prices within a country serves as a particularly useful indicator of world business cycle effects, as it minimizes the influence of country-specific influences that affect both manufac- turing and mining prices, especially changes in foreign-exchange rates. For both Australia and Canada, there are two periods of high values for the price ratio, as shown in Figures 8.1 and 8.2, respectively. The first is from the mid-1970s through the early 1980s (with a dip between 1975 and 1981 that is more pronounced in Canada than in Australia) and the second in the past few years, especially since 2003. These reflect the cumulative effect of periods of sustained above average growth in world industrial production leading up to the two major commodity price booms of the past half-century.[10]

In between the two booms, the period from the early 1980s through the early years of the current century is one of depressed values of the price ratio in both countries, with a recovery in common in the late 1980s, for Canada alone at the end of the 1970s, and for Australia and, to a slight extent, Canada at the end of the 1990s. The low values of the price ratio reflect relatively sluggish growth in the world economy, with incipient booms punctuated by the stock market crash of 1987 and the combination of the Asian financial crisis of 1997 and the terrorist attacks on the United States in 2001. The 1990s were particularly negative for the price ratio, as world industrial growth was particularly sluggish prior to the China boom.

## Cyclical Movements in Productivity

*Costs and Productivity*

In this section, I extend the analysis of the effect of the business cycle from prices to productivity, again building on the differences in competition identified earlier. Productivity measures reflect the amount of output pro- duced relative to the input used in production. The simplest measure is the ratio of output to input when only a single input is used in the production of a single output or when a single output and input are isolated from other inputs and outputs in a partial productivity measure, such as meas- ures of labour productivity. Broader measures of productivity, such as indexes of multifactor productivity, tell us the ratio of an index of multiple outputs to an index of multiple inputs used in production.

The earlier analysis focused on costs, rather than directly on productiv- ity. However, productivity is inversely related to cost per unit of output. If input prices are held constant, a productivity rise of, say, 10 per cent should be reflected in requiring 10 per cent less input per unit of output, and the average cost associated with those inputs would fall by 10 per cent. The formal relationship is conveniently expressed as

$$MFP_t / MFP_0 = [AC_0 / w_0] / [AC_t / w_t],$$ (1)

where $MFP$ is an index of multifactor productivity, $AC$ is a measure of the unit cost for inputs used in producing the outputs included in the $MFP$ index, and $w$ is an appropriately weighted index of prices of the inputs.[11] Thus, multifactor productivity is inversely related to the appropriately deflated average cost.

In the analysis of the conditions of competition in manufacturing, theory and evidence suggest that manufacturing firms generally are operating with unexploited economies of scale on the downward-sloping portion of their average cost curves. This means that demand shocks can be expected to lead to procyclical movements in output and countercyclical movements in deflated average cost. From equation (1), demand shocks are then expected to lead to procyclical movements in multifactor productivity in manufacturing.[12]

In the analysis of the conditions of competition in mining, the marginal supply of mine products is taken to come from price-taker firms. Demand shocks then lead to procyclical movements in output, price, and marginal cost. The movement in average cost and productivity depends on the stage of the business cycle. At the bottom of the cycle, price and marginal cost will be below average cost and a rise in output will lead to falling average cost and rising productivity. At the top of the cycle, price will be above average cost and the reverse relationships occur. Thus, demand shocks have a nonlinear relationship to productivity, with productivity moving in a procyclical manner during the low part of the cycle and a countercyclical manner during the high part.[13]

*Productivity movements in Australia and Canada*

Figure 8.3 shows the path over time for multifactor productivity (MFP) for both the manufacturing and mining sectors in Australia from 1968/69 to 2006/07 along with the ratio of prices in mining and manufacturing, while Figure 8.4 shows the corresponding data for Canada for the period 1961 through 2006. The MFP values are shown on an inverted right-hand scale to reflect the inverse relationship between productivity and average cost as indicated in equation (1). The length of the period in each country is dictated by the availability from government agencies of sectoral estimates of multifactor productivity. Details of the data and sources are given in the data appendix.

Figure 8.3: Ratio of Price Indexes and Multifactor Productivity for Mining and Manufacturing, Australia, 1968/69–2006/07

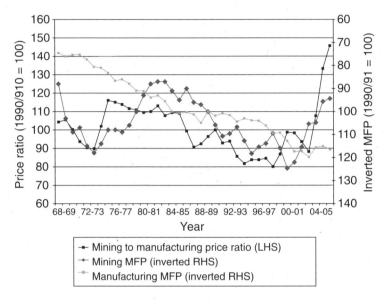

Figure 8.4: Ratio of Price Indexes and Multifactor Productivity for Mining and Manufacturing, Canada, 1961–2006

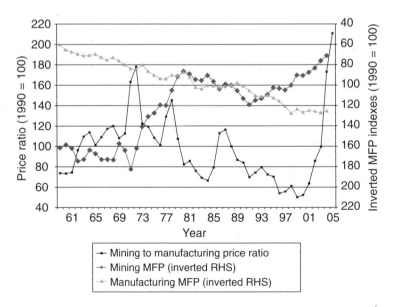

The pattern of MFP movements for manufacturing in Canada is similar to that in Australia, except that the two episodes of negative or nil MFP growth both started earlier in Canada, 1979 for the first episode and 2001 for the second. Also, there was a subperiod of growth in MFP from 1982 to 1985 in the midst of the 1979 to 1991 run of negative or nil growth. The earlier start to the latest period of MFP stagnation can be tied to the negative shock of the 2001 terrorist attacks on the United States, as the Canadian economy is so closely tied to the U.S. economy. However, the overriding influence in Canada, as in Australia, is the effect of a positive shock in the terms of trade, which pushed up the local currency and negatively affected domestic manufacturers that export or compete with imports. The earlier start to the first episode might reflect a quicker use of monetary and fiscal policy to deal with rising inflation, with the interruption from 1982 to 1985 reflecting a softening in the policy regime.

The pattern of movements in manufacturing MFP in both Australia and Canada fit the hypothesis that domestic demand shocks lead to procyclical MFP movements around a long-run trend of MFP growth[14] – at least, negative deviations from trend MFP growth can be related to negative domestic demand shocks. Further, the somewhat different timing of the deviations between Australia and Canada corresponds with the special circumstances of each country, while the overall similarity in pattern reflects the common external influences on both economies, especially their common role as exporters of primary commodities.[15]

Figure 8.3 shows that productivity in mining is characterized by substantial volatility in Australia, while Figure 8.4 gives a similar picture for Canada. Further, the patterns are similar, with productivity experiencing substantial declines from the mid-1970s through the early 1980s (shown by upward movement for the inverted productivity measure in the figures), followed by improvements from the early 1980s through the mid-1990s, then declining again from around 2000 onward. The similarity in patterns suggests a common causal factor and one that has a general effect across different subsectors of mining, so that the similar patterns occur despite the different mix of mining activity in the two countries.

The analysis in the previous section identified the world business cycle as the common causal factor behind movements in mining prices relative to manufacturing prices in both Australia and Canada. Further, it was noted that, during booms, when mining prices are above average cost, productivity moves countercyclically with demand shocks, while during substantial slumps, when prices are below average cost, mining productivity moves procyclically.

Based on the ratio of mining to manufacturing prices, Figures 8.3 and 8.4 show two boom periods; the mid-1970s through the early 1980s and the past few years, especially since 2003/04. Mining productivity declined substantially in both Australia and Canada during both booms, which fits with the expectation that positive demand shocks decrease productivity during booms. However, the positive demand shock in the first boom arguably had abated well before 1983, when the first signs of improvement in mining productivity occurred in both countries. One possible explanation is that productivity movements lag demand shocks due to the generally long gestation period for mining projects.

The ratio of mining prices to manufacturing prices was clearly below average during the 1990s in both Australia and Canada, indicating sluggish world business conditions. During that decade, the price ratio and productivity generally moved in opposite directions, perhaps shown more clearly in Figure 8.3 for Australia than in Figure 8.4 for Canada. As the productivity scale is inverted, this implies procyclical movements in productivity when the depressed price ratio is taken as the indicator that price was below average cost for mining firms. This pattern fits the expectation that mining productivity is procyclical when business conditions are sluggish.

**Conclusions and Implications**

The analysis presented in this paper indicates a dichotomy in the conditions of competition between mining and manufacturing. Long-run equilibrium in manufacturing occurs when price is higher than marginal cost and unexploited economies of scale. Further, competition is expected to be at least partially localized to the domestic economy. In mining, at least some firms operate as price takers and supply output up to the point where marginal cost equals price in the long run and competition is global.

As a result of the dichotomy, prices in mining are expected to rise and fall procyclically with the world business cycle, while manufacturing prices are not expected to be much affected by either the domestic or world business cycle. Further, productivity in mining is expected to have a nonlinear relation with the world business cycle, moving procyclically near the bottom of the cycle and countercyclically near the top of the cycle. In contrast, manufacturing productivity is expected to be procyclical with domestic business cycles regardless of the phase of the cycle.

Data from Australia and Canada show that the prices of mine products move directly with the world business cycle, while manufacturing prices have no clear relationship to either domestic or global business conditions.

As a result, the ratio of the prices of mine products to those of manufactures is procyclical with global economic conditions. Multifactor productivity in the manufacturing sectors of both Australia and Canada appears to move procyclically with domestic economic conditions. Productivity in the mining sector is clearly countercyclical with world economic conditions during the high part of the business cycle, but appears to be procyclical when world industrial production is below trend growth.

The cyclical movements in prices and productivity have important implications for countries, such as Australia and Canada, that are substantial exporters of mine products and have substantial manufacturing sectors. The opposing cyclical movements in productivity for mining and manufacturing during booms are at least partially offsetting, meaning that the cyclical behaviour of aggregate productivity diverges from the positive reaction to demand shocks that is expected for industrialized countries without large mining sectors. More important, the cyclical movement of relative prices of mine products and manufactures creates pressure to reallocate resources in the domestic economy, which leads to difficulties for domestic policy-makers who are trying to use monetary and fiscal instruments to control inflation and unemployment.

For the world economy, the procyclical movement in mine product prices leads to a cyclical pattern for the terms of trade, favouring countries that export mining products in boom times and countries that import such products in downturns. This creates imbalances in trade flows and capital accounts. Further, the structural imbalance caused by changes in the terms of trade contributes to global inflationary pressures during worldwide booms (see Bloch et al. 2007).

Understanding the effect of demand shocks on productivity is also important for interpreting long-run trends in resource exhaustion. The recent drop in mining productivity is illustrative. The pattern shown in Figures 8.3 and 8.4 suggests this is a countercyclical reaction to a period of abnormally high growth in world industrial production, stimulated by unexpected growth in China, India, Russia, and Brazil. On this interpretation, productivity will recover (and mine product prices will decline relative to prices of manufactures) once the positive demand shock abates. Alternatively, the fall in productivity (and increase in relative prices) could be interpreted as a sign of the adverse effect of the depletion of mining resources, with the implication that the relative price increases are permanent. Although some commentators seem convinced of the latter interpretation, the historical experience of Australia and Canada over the past half-century is more consistent with the former.

# APPENDIX

## Australia

*Prices (1968/69–2006/07)*

MINING

Derived aggregate output price index for eight mining sectors – coal mining, oil and gas extraction, iron ore mining, other metal ores (including bauxite), copper ore mining, mineral sand mining, and silver-lead-zinc ore mining – produced by the Productivity Commission in reply to a special request for data. The base year is aligned with manufacturing to fiscal year 1989/90 = 100.

MANUFACTURING

Data are from Australian Bureau of Statistics, *Producer Price Indexes, Australia, Index Numbers – Manufacturing Division*, cat. 6427.0. Quarterly data are adjusted to the annual fiscal year (base year 1989/90 = 100).

*Productivity (1968/69–2006/07)*

MINING

Australia, Productivity Commission, 'Statistical Annex to Supplement to Inquiry Report: Modelling the Regional Impacts of National Competition Policy Reforms,' in *Impact of Competition Policy Reforms on Rural and Regional Australia* (Canberra, September 1999), table B.10, Index of Total Factor Productivity Growth by Mining Industry, 1968/69–1989/90 (1989/90 = 100). The index for total mining is estimated by aggregating the output-weighted measures of productivity growth by industry and adopting average relative output weights. This series is combined with Australian Bureau of Statistics, *Experimental Estimates of Industry Multifactor Productivity*, cat. 5260.0.55.002, table 1, Gross Value-Added-Based Multifactor Productivity Indexes, Mining, 1989/90–2006/07. The base year is aligned with Table B.10 in the previous source (1989/90 = 100).

MANUFACTURING

Australia, Productivity Commission, Manufacturing Industry Productivity Estimates, Multifactor Productivity, 1968/69–1989/90 (1989/90 = 100). This series is combined with Australian Bureau of Statistics, Experimental Estimates of Industry Multifactor Productivity, cat. 5260.0.55.002, table 1, Gross Value-Added-Based Multifactor Productivity Indexes, Manufacturing,

1989/90–2006/07. The base year is aligned with Productivity Commission estimates (1989/90 = 100).

## Canada

*Prices (1961–2007)*

MINING

Natural Resources Canada, *Metal Price Index* (1997 = 100), based on prices and volumes of six minerals: copper, nickel, zinc, lead, gold, and silver (domestic production only). The base year is aligned with productivity indices (2002 = 100).

MANUFACTURING

Statistics Canada, v3822562, table 329-0038: Industry Price Indexes, by NAICS, Canada, All Manufacturing (index, 1997=100) [P6253]. The base year is aligned with productivity indices, 2002 = 100).

*Productivity (1961–2006)*

MINING

Statistics Canada, v41712883, table 383-0021: Multifactor Productivity in the Aggregate Business Sector and Major Sub-sectors, Canada, Multifactor Productivity, Mining and Oil and Gas Extraction [21] (index, 2002 = 100).

MANUFACTURING

Statistics Canada, v41712886, table 383-0021: Multifactor Productivity in the Aggregate Business Sector and Major Sub-sectors, Canada, Multifactor Productivity; Manufacturing [31-33] (index, 2002 = 100).

## NOTES

1  Slade (2004) treats markets for mine products as global in examining the effect of market concentration on profitability, while Bloch and Olive (2003) provide evidence of the national segmentation of markets for manufactures.
2  Both Iwata and Applebaum assume constant returns to scale technology and an absence of fixed inputs, implying constant marginal costs of production. These assumptions are problematic in terms of examining cyclical productivity movements, as they make average cost equal to marginal cost and, hence, impose an

insensitivity of productivity to demand shocks. However, the assumptions are relaxed in a study by Morrison (1992) of Canadian, Japanese, and U.S. manufacturing, which still reports evidence that price exceeds marginal cost in each country.

3  Bhattacharya and Bloch (2000) provide evidence that advertising inhibits the lowering of industry concentration that would otherwise be associated with increasing market size.

4  Heterogeneity occurs in other categories of inputs, but the usual reasoning is that supplies of any particular type of physical capital are indefinitely expandable and that the skills mix of the labour force is malleable in the long run. A more problematic category of input is organizational capability, but this category is generally ignored in the analysis of competitive conditions.

5  An excellent example is given in Eaton and Lipsey (1980).

6  A zero-profit condition for equilibrium can be applied to the marginal producer, but this leaves the number of producers and their relative size to be determined by the distribution of the natural resource in terms of the cost of extraction for equivalent product.

7  Sutton's (1991, 1998) endogenous-market-structure approach is not directly applicable. Mining products are predominantly sold as intermediate products to well-informed buyers, so advertising is unlikely to be effective as a sunk cost to deter entry. The use of technology to create niche markets is more promising, but examples of successful application in mining are limited.

8  The theoretical arguments and evidence on cyclical movements in the price-cost margin are reviewed in Bloch and Olive (2001). The evidence presented there suggests that, in U.S. manufacturing, the price-cost margin is insensitive to demand in low-concentration industries and somewhat countercyclical in high-concentration industries. However, Bloch and Olive (2003) find that, across four major industrial economies (the United States, the United Kingdom, Japan, and Germany), demand has a positive effect on the price-cost margin, especially in high-concentration industries. Other evidence on cyclical variation in price-cost margins is similarly mixed.

9  Bloch and Olive (2003) examine the determinants of manufacturing prices in 24 industries across the United States, the United Kingdom, Japan, and Germany and find that direct variable costs have a positive effect on prices across all industries and all countries.

10  Bloch and Sapsford (2000) estimate that a World Bank index of nonfuel commodity prices rises by about 1.5 percent for every 1 percent rise in the International Monetary Fund index of world manufacturing production.

11  If there is only a single input to production, the input price index is replaced by the price of the single input.

12  The procyclical movement of aggregate productivity in industrialized countries is a stylized fact of macroeconomics, according to Basu and Fernald (2001), who point to the expansion of durable goods manufacturing as particularly important in explaining this cyclicality.

13  If mining firms earn zero economic profit on average, there should be equal periods of procyclical and countercyclical relationships to demand shocks.

14  Kaldor (1967) attributes a positive relationship between output growth and productivity growth in manufacturing to the existence of increasing returns to scale. This is broadly consistent with the interpretation presented in this paper. However, my analysis is based on long-run equilibrium with unexploited economies of scale existing for manufacturing firms with substantial fixed costs. Expansion of the market might result in an increased number of firms or increased expenditures on sunk costs to prevent entry. In such circumstances, the increase in productivity following a demand shock might be only temporary.

15  See Bloch, Dockery, and Sapsford (2006) for a comparative analysis of the effect of the world primary commodity price cycle on the exchange rate and inflation rate in Australia and Canada.

REFERENCES

Adelman, M.A. 1993. *The Economics of Petroleum Supply*. Cambridge, MA: MIT Press.

Adelman, M.A., and G.C. Watkins. 2008. 'Reserve Prices and Mineral Resource Theory.' *Energy Journal* 29 (Special Issue): 1–16.

Applebaum, Ellie. 1982. 'The Estimation of the Degree of Oligopoly Power.' *Journal of Econometrics* 19 (2-3): 287–99.

Basu, Susanto, and John Fernald. 2001. 'Why Is Productivity Procyclical? Why Do We Care?' In *New Developments in Productivity Analysis*, edited by C.R. Hulten, E.R. Dean, and M.J. Harper. Chicago: University of Chicago Press for the National Bureau of Economic Research.

Bhattacharya, Mita, and Harry Bloch. 2000. 'The Dynamics of Industrial Concentration in Australian Manufacturing.' *International Journal of Industrial Organization* 18 (8): 1181–99.

Bloch, Harry, A. Michael Dockery, C. Wyn Morgan, and David Sapsford. 2007. 'Growth, Commodity Prices, Inflation and the Distribution of Income.' *Metroeconomica* 58 (1): 3–44.

Bloch, Harry, A. Michael Dockery, and David Sapsford. 2006. 'Commodity Prices and the Dynamics of Inflation in Commodity-Exporting Countries: Evidence from Australia and Canada.' *Economic Record* 82 (S1): S97–S109.

Bloch, Harry, and Michael Olive. 2001. 'Pricing Over the Cycle.' *Review of Industrial Economics* 19 (1): 99–108.

– 2003. 'Influences on Pricing and Markup in Segmented Manufacturing Industries.' *Journal of Industry, Competition and Trade* 3 (1-2): 87–107.

Bloch, Harry, and David Sapsford. 2000. 'Whither the Terms of Trade? An Elaboration of the Prebisch-Singer Hypothesis.' *Cambridge Journal of Economics* 24 (4): 461–81.

Domowitz, Ian, R. Glenn Hubbard, and Bruce C. Petersen. 1988. 'Market Structure and Cyclical Fluctuations in U.S. Manufacturing.' *Review of Economics and Statistics* 70 (1): 55–66.

Eaton, B. Curtis. 1972. 'Spatial Competition Revisited.' *Canadian Journal of Economics* 5 (2): 268–78.

– 1976. 'Free Entry in One-Dimensional Models: Pure Profits and Multiple Equilibria.' *Journal of Regional Science* 16 (1): 21–33.

Eaton, B. Curtis, and Richard G. Lipsey. 1975. 'The Principle of Minimum Differentiation Reconsidered: Some New Developments in the Theory of Spatial Competition.' *Review of Economic Studies* 42 (1): 27–49.

– 1978. 'Freedom of Entry and the Existence of Pure Profit.' *Economic Journal* 88 (351): 455–69.

– 1979. 'The Theory of Market Pre-emption: The Persistence of Excess Capacity and Monopoly in Growing Spatial Markets.' *Economica* 46 (182): 149–58.

– 1980. 'Exit Barriers Are Entry Barriers: The Durability of Capital as a Barrier to Entry.' *Bell Journal of Economics* 11 (2): 721–9.

– 1981. 'Capital, Commitment and Entry Equilibrium.' *Bell Journal of Economics* 12 (2): 593–604.

– 1989. 'Product Differentiation.' In *Handbook of Industrial Organization*, edited by R. Schmalensee and R.D. Willig. Amsterdam: North-Holland.

Eaton, B. Curtis, and Roger Ware. 1987. 'A Theory of Market Structure with Sequential Entry.' *RAND Journal of Economics* 18 (1): 1–16.

Eaton, B. Curtis, and Myrna H. Wooders. 1985. 'Sophisticated Entry in a Model of Spatial Competition.' *RAND Journal of Economics* 16 (2): 282–97.

Ellerman, D., T.M. Stoker, and E.R. Berndt. 2001. 'Sources of Productivity Growth in the American Coal Industry.' In *New Developments in Productivity Analysis*, edited by C.R. Hulten, E.R. Dean, and M.J. Harper. Chicago: University of Chicago Press for the National Bureau of Economic Research.

Ellis, Gregory M., and Robert Halvorsen. 2002. 'Estimation of Market Power in a Nonrenewable Resource Industry.' *Journal of Political Economy* 110 (4): 883–99.

Hall, Robert E. 1988. 'The Relation between Price and Marginal Cost in U.S. Industry.' *Journal of Political Economy* 96 (5): 921–47.

- 1990. 'Invariance Properties of Solow's Productivity Residual.' In *Growth, Productivity, Unemployment: Essays to Celebrate Bob Solow's Birthday*, edited by Peter Diamond. Cambridge, MA: MIT Press.

Iwata, Gyoichi. 1974. 'Measurement of Conjectural Variation in Oligopoly.' *Econometrica* 42 (5): 947–66.

Kaldor, Nicholas. 1967. *Strategic Factors in Economic Development*. Ithaca, NY: Cornell University Press.

Morrison, Catherine J. 1992. 'Unraveling the Productivity Growth Slowdown in the United States, Canada and Japan: The Effects of Subequilibrium, Scale Economies and Markups.' *Review of Economics and Statistics* 74 (3): 381–93.

Roeger, Werner. 1995. 'Can Imperfect Competition Explain the Difference between Primal and Dual Productivity Measures? Estimates for U.S. Manufacturing.' *Journal of Political Economy* 103 (2): 316–30.

Slade, Margaret. 2004. 'Competing Models of Firm Profitability.' *International Journal of Industrial Organization* 22 (3): 289–308.

Spence, A. Michal. 1977. 'Entry, Capacity, Investment and Oligopolistic Pricing.' *Bell Journal of Economics* 8 (2): 534–44.

Sutton, John. 1991. *Sunk Costs and Market Structure*. Cambridge, MA: MIT Press.

- 1998. *Technology and Market Structure*. Cambridge, MA: MIT Press.

Tilton, John E., and Hans H. Landsberg. 1999. 'Innovation, Productivity Growth and Survival of the U.S. Copper Industry.' In *Productivity in Natural Resource Industries*, edited by R. David Simpson. Washington, DC: Resources for the Future.

# PART IV

## Social Interaction

# 9  Image Building

B. CURTIS EATON AND WILLIAM D. WHITE

The economist's vision of the individual is founded on the notion of private consumption goods. If asked, for example, to think about two women sitting down to have lunch together, most economists would think of the relationship between each woman and her food as a purely private one; in the economist's eye, what one woman has for lunch has no bearing on the other's well-being. Garlic aside, this is a sensible working hypothesis for many sorts of consumer choices.

There is, however, another sort of choice for which the fiction of private consumption goods is definitely not sensible. When one of those curious fellows from the City of London puts on his bowler hat and grabs his black umbrella, he is at least as concerned about the image he is projecting to other people (that is, what they make of him) as he is about keeping his head warm and dry. Similarly, when you look at yourself in the mirror – when buying a new suit or getting dressed for a job interview, for example – your behaviour reflects more a concern for the image you project than a purely private relationship between you and your clothes. Engagement and wedding rings provide more obvious examples of goods that are worn primarily for the image they project. It is decisions about these sorts of goods – which we call *visible goods* – that are the focus of this paper.[1]

We propose to take these sometimes amusing, always interesting, and at times important decisions seriously. Our goal is to begin the development of an economic theory of *image building*. Our starting point is the observation that, in a wide range of situations, from social gatherings to job interviews, the outcomes of personal interactions depend heavily on the appropriate matching of hard-to-observe individual characteristics. The novel twist is to apply signalling notions to explore how *images* projected by choices of *visible goods* might help to solve these matching problems.

Several generic problems exist with any type of signalling (see Spence 1974; Frank 1988). One problem is that establishing a signalling equilibrium might involve complex coordination problems of its own. There is thus an issue of derivation; the process by which signals originate demands investigation. A second problem is that hand in hand with mutually beneficial signalling can come opportunities for dissembling (that is, fraud), which can lead signalling to unravel.

In this paper, we assume an environment in which there is no motive for fraud. Thus, while we recognize that issues of fraud are important in many circumstances (see Carr and Landa 1983), these circumstances do not arise in our model. The central thrust of our analysis is that, when visible goods serve as signals, consumers' choices of these goods are interdependent. We argue that this has implications not only for the theory of consumer choice, but also for the role of advertising. We consider two broad questions. Do plausible conditions exist in which visible goods come to serve as type signals in social interactions? Are there opportunities for firms to facilitate this process profitably through *image advertising*?

The idea that consumption choices are sometimes interdependent is familiar. However, interdependence typically has been considered in a context of directly interdependent utility functions – the consumption of one consumer enters the utility function of another, for example. Altruism and conformity are the obvious examples (see Wintrobe 1983; Jones 1984). In the absence of directly interdependent utility functions, standard models of consumer choice and advertising assume that behaviour is purely private. Consider, for instance, standard paradigms of advertising. At least three functions are identified: to inform consumers directly about product attributes (see Nelson 1974); to serve an indirect informational function, where, for example, by investing in advertising, a firm conveys commitment to a product (see Klein and Leffler 1981; Kilhlstrom and Riordan 1984;); and to enhance product attributes through an *affective* process by creating pleasurable associations with the consumption of a product (see Cafferata and Tybout 1989).

In all three cases, the contribution of advertising is private. Failure to reach a potential customer might lose a sale, but it has no effect on sales to others. In our analysis, utility functions are independent because individuals interact in social situations. Information as to type is valuable in these social interactions, hence individuals attempt to signal their type by their choices of visible goods. This, of course, generates interdependent demands for goods that are used as signals. We show that, through image advertising, firms have both the ability and an incentive to facilitate signalling.

Interestingly, an image-advertising campaign that does not reach most of the consumers in the relevant market will fail to create an accepted image and, hence, will have minimal effect on demand for the advertised good. We argue, among other things, that the resulting nonconcavity of profit as a function of amount spent on advertising is perhaps a substantial barrier to entry.

In the next section, we begin by outlining a model of social interaction in which individuals use visible goods as clues about the underlying characteristics of other individuals. This model is the heart of our theory. We then embed it in a two-stage model in which individuals choose their visible goods in the first stage and interact in the second. There are many equilibria of this one shot, static game and, hence, a nasty coordination problem. Then, we examine a dynamic version of the model and identify possibly salient strategies that lead eventually to a perfect signalling equilibrium. Finally, we argue that image advertising can solve the coordination problem, and close with a discussion of our findings.

A brief discussion of terminology might be useful at this point. One obvious question is what exactly we mean by an *image*. Clearly, this is a slippery concept, more easily illustrated than defined. Nevertheless, it is our view that powerful messages are often conveyed by choices as divergent as footwear (athletic shoes versus wingtips), beverage (carrot juice, light beer, or neat scotch), or means of transport (foot, public transport, chauffeured car). Accordingly, it seems constructive to think about the image-projecting dimensions of such choices. Purely informational symbols offer a more direct way to convey relevant information (through identification badges, for example). But if visible goods are already performing a signalling role, there might be no efficiency gain associated with substituting purely informational symbols for visible goods and no means of coordinating the switch, particularly if the desire to signal is contextual (in the form of, say, social gatherings or business encounters) and the consumption of particular goods (such as beverages or mode of dress) is associated with these contexts. Moreover, the incorporation of symbols such as flags, peace signs, and organizational logos as decorative motifs into consumption goods tends to blur this distinction.

A second issue is the use of the term *image advertising*. In the trade press, image advertising is used to refer to virtually any type of advertising that seeks to influence the images consumers associate with products (as opposed to conveying cognitive information). It thus encompasses affective advertising as well as image creation. In the formal analysis presented in this paper, however, we focus solely on signalling aspects.

## A Model of Social Interaction

The basic unit of social interaction in our model is an *encounter*, and these encounters take place in the context of *congregations*. A congregation is just a collection of individuals, called players, who wander about randomly bumping into each other. In any congregation, there are a number of different player types and a number of players of each type, and players know only their own type. When two players bump into each other, an event we call an encounter, they interact in some way: they might have a conversation about politics, sport, or business, they might immediately part because they perceive that they have no common interests, they might play a game of darts, or any number of other things. In any encounter, the appropriate actions depend on the types of the two players; hence, there is scope for type signalling. We index player types by *t*, and denote the number of different types by *M*.

We are not concerned with the precise nature of encounters, so we do not attempt to describe them in detail. However, one assumption regarding them is crucial: in any encounter, knowledge of the other player's type is mutually valuable. That is, in an encounter involving, say, players *i* and *j*, the payoffs to both *i* and *j* from the encounter are higher if player *i* (respectively, *j*) knows *j*'s (respectively, *i*'s) type.

The payoffs in any interaction are governed by the *presumptions*, also called actions, that each player makes about the type of the other player involved in the encounter. Although there are many player types, and hence many possible presumptions regarding type, only three sorts are payoff relevant: a player's presumption about the other's type might be *accurate*, which we denote by *A*; it might be *inaccurate*, which we denote by *I*; or the player might make *no presumption*, which we denote by *N*. No presumption, or *N*, is a neutral action intended to capture, for example, the flavour of the cautious chit-chat about politics that we use when we are uncertain just what the other person's political leanings are, and are concerned not to offend.

Table 9.1 presents the payoff matrix for an encounter between an arbitrary pair of players. The first element in each cell of the matrix is the row player's payoff and the second is the column player's payoff. Our basic hypothesis – that accurate presumptions facilitate, and inaccurate presumptions frustrate, social interaction – is captured in the following assumption:

*Basic payoff assumption*: For both players, an accurate presumption (*A*) is better than no presumption (*N*), and no presumption (*N*) is better than an inaccurate presumption (*I*).

Table 9.1
Payoffs for a Typical Encounter

|  |  | Column Player's Actions | | |
|---|---|---|---|---|
|  |  | *A* | *N* | *I* |
| Row Player's Actions | *A* | *a, a* | *b, d* | *y, g* |
|  | *N* | *d, b* | *e, e* | *z, h* |
|  | *I* | *g, y* | *h, z* | *w, w* |

Accordingly, in Table 9.1, both players' payoffs decrease as we move from left to right along any row, or from top to bottom down any column.

The analysis is somewhat simplified if we adopt the following symmetry and independence assumptions:

*Symmetric payoffs*:
$a = a, b = b, c = c, y = y, e = e, z = z, g = g, h = h, w = w.$

*Independence*:
The increase in a player's payoff associated with changing the player's own action from $I$ to $N$, or from $I$ to $A$, is independent of the other player's action. In addition, the increase in a player's payoff associated with changing the other player's action from $I$ to $N$, or from $I$ to $A$, is independent of the player's own action.

With no loss of generality we can set $w = w = 0$. We then have the payoff structure in Table 9.2. Obviously, the following inequalities hold:

$$g > h > 0; \tag{1.1}$$

$$y > z > 0. \tag{1.2}$$

The key payoff assumption is that social interactions are more productive when they are mutually informed. Accordingly, the best possible outcome in any encounter occurs when both presumptions are accurate and the worst when they are inaccurate. When this assumption is satisfied, no one has an incentive to attempt fraudulent signalling. Clearly, the assumption is appropriate for many, but not all, sorts of social interaction.

In any encounter, each player attempts to infer the other's type on the basis of the visible goods – a bowler hat, a wedding ring, a brocade vest,

Table 9.2
Payoffs for the Revised Game

|  |  | Column Player's Actions | | |
| --- | --- | --- | --- | --- |
|  |  | A | N | I |
| Row Player's Actions | A | $g+y, g+y$ | $h+y, g+z$ | $y, g$ |
|  | N | $g+z, h+y$ | $h+z, h+z$ | $z, h$ |
|  | I | $g, y$ | $h, z$ | $0, 0$ |

green hair, a power tie – worn by the other player. The image that a player projects in any real social situation is, of course, dependent on the mix of visible goods displayed by the player. For simplicity, we do not structure the image-building problem in this way. Rather, we think of players as wearing just one visible good – a garment of some specific color, for example. This involves no real loss of generality, since we could think of each distinct combination of visible goods as sending a different signal, and it does simplify the exposition.

*Equilibrium of the Encounter*

Now consider a specific congregation, and suppose that there are $S$ distinct visible goods, or signals, represented in the congregation, and index these signals by $s$. At this point, we are not concerned about how the signals themselves were chosen; that problem will occupy us below. We assume that $S \geq M$ (the number of distinct player types). Let $P(t,s)$ denote the proportion of players sending signal $s$ who are type $t$. Any column of the $M$-by-$S$ matrix defined by $P(t,s)$ is then a frequency distribution of the types wearing good $s$. Define $T(s)$ as follows:

$$T(s) \equiv \arg\max P(t,s). \tag{2}$$

For convenience, we suppose that there are no ties. So the function $T(s)$ gives us the unique player type that has the highest frequency in the set of players sending signal $s$. Obviously, given some specific signal $s$, the best guess regarding the type of a player sending signal $s$ is $T(s)$.

Define the function $F(s)$ as follows:

$$F(s) \equiv P(T(s),s), \tag{3}$$

where $F(s)$ is the frequency of player type $T(s)$ – that is, the frequency of the most frequent player type in the set of players sending signal $s$. We assume that all players know both their own type and the frequency distribution $P(t,s)$, and that no player knows any other player's type.

It is then a simple matter to find the Bayesian-Nash equilibrium in any encounter. In an encounter involving players $i$ and $j$, player $i$'s first problem is to infer $j$'s type. Given that $j$ is sending signal $s$, $i$ will infer that $j$ is most likely to be type $T(s)$ and will attach probability $F(s)$ to this event. Player $i$'s second problem is to choose whether to make a presumption regarding $j$'s type, or to make no presumption (take action $N$). If $i$ makes a presumption, it will be that $j$ is type $T(s)$; this presumption will be accurate with probability $F(s)$ and inaccurate with probability $1 - F(s)$. The expected payoff associated with this presumption will exceed the payoff associated with action $N$ (no presumption) if

$$F(s) [u + y] + [1 - F(s)]u > u + z, \qquad (4)$$

where $u$ depends on $j$'s action: $u$ is equal to 0 if $j$ makes an inaccurate presumption, $g$ if $j$ makes an accurate presumption, or $h$ if $j$ makes no presumption. But (4) reduces to

$$F(s) > z/y. \qquad (5)$$

Hence, the action that maximizes $i$'s payoff is independent of $j$'s action. So, in any encounter, player $i$ has the following dominant strategy: (i) if $F(s) \geq z/y$, presume the player is type $T(s)$; (ii) if $F(s) < z/y$, make no presumption. As a matter of convenience, we suppose that player $i$ chooses the presumptive action when $F(s) = z/y$. Recall that both $y$ and $z$ are positive, and that $y$, the bonus associated with an accurate presumption as opposed to an inaccurate one, exceeds $z$, the bonus associated with no presumption as opposed to an inaccurate one. Hence, $z/y$ is greater than 0 and less than 1. Given the more general payoff structure in Table 9.1, player $i$ does not necessarily have a dominant strategy, so it is the independence assumption that gives us a dominant strategy for any one player. The symmetry assumption gives us identical dominant strategies for all players in all encounters.

Of course, both players in every encounter see the problem of choosing an action in exactly this way. Hence, there is a dominant-strategy equilibrium in every encounter. It is instructive to compare the payoffs that different players expect in any series of encounters in a congregation. Consider then a player of type $t$ sending signal $s$, whom we will call player $(t,s)$. To compare payoffs, we can distinguish three classes of players. Player $(t,s)$ is in class 1 if $F(s) \geq z/y$ and if $T(s) = t$; in any encounter involving player $(t,s)$, the other player's dominant strategy is to presume that player $(t,s)$ is of type $t$, and this presumption is accurate. Player $(t,s)$ is class 2 if $F(s) < z/y$; in any encounter involving player $(t,s)$, the other player's dominant strategy is to make no presumption. Finally, player $(t,s)$ is in class 3 if $F(s) \geq z/y$, and if $T(s) = t^*$, not equal to $t$; in any encounter involving player $(t,s)$, the other player's dominant strategy is to presume that player $(t,s)$ is of type $t^*$, and this presumption is inaccurate.

Since player $(t,s)$'s dominant strategy in any encounter is independent of the signal she is sending, in any series of encounters her payoff is (i) smallest if she is in class 3, since the other player makes an inaccurate presumption regarding her type; (ii) larger if she is in class 2, since the other player makes no presumption regarding her type; and (iii) largest if she is in class 1, since the other player makes an accurate presumption regarding her type. So the players who do best in any congregation are those who send a strong signal that is consistent with their type.

### Choice of a Signal for One Congregation

Now we step back and look at the equilibria of the expanded game that is created when we allow players to choose the signal they send in some congregation. In this and subsequent sections, for simplicity, we assume that players do not perceive the impact their own choice of a visible good has on the frequency distribution, $P(t,s)$. In effect, we assume that a large number of players buy each visible good, so that a switch by one player from one good to another has no perceptible influence on $P(t,s)$.

We suppose that there is a large number of different visible goods for sale and that no player has yet bought one, and then look at a two-stage game in which each player chooses to buy one of the available visible goods in the first stage and then uses that good as a signal in a congregation game in the second stage. We also assume that the number of players in the congregation that will occur in stage 2 is large relative to the number of visible goods. Visible goods have, we suppose, an inherent value in use (unrelated to their potential value as signals) that is identical for all goods and all players. We also assume that the prices of the available goods are identical and less than the common value in use. Then, in stage 1, all players will buy some visible good, so the only question is: which one? Given the sequential structure of the expanded game, the appropriate equilibrium concept is subgame perfection. There are three different types of subgame perfect equilibrium in this two-stage game and many equilibria of each type, and hence a significant coordination problem.

At one extreme are all the equilibria that involve no (effective) signalling. Suppose that player choices of visible goods are such that $F(s) < z/y$ for all $s$.

Then, in all encounters, both players will choose to make no presumption about the other's type (both will choose action $N$). Further, although each player would be better off in all encounters if she could signal her type, there is no way of doing so. There are, obviously, many nonsignalling equilibria. In any of them, in all encounters, each player's payoff is $h + z$. Further, in all these equilibria, all goods are equally attractive to all players, since the goods have no value as signals and their prices and values in use are identical.

At the other extreme are all the equilibria in which all players effectively signal their type. Suppose that player choices of visible goods are such that $F(s) = 1$ for all goods that are bought by some players. Then, in all encounters, both players know with certainty the type of the other player and make the corresponding, accurate presumptions. Since this generates the highest possible payoff in all encounters, these choices of goods constitute an equilibrium. There are, obviously, many perfect signalling equilibria. In any of them, in all encounters, each player's payoff is $g + y$. Given any configuration of encounters in the second-stage congregation, any of the perfect-signalling equilibria Pareto-dominate any of the nonsignalling equilibria. In any perfect-signalling equilibrium, a player of some specific type $t$ is indifferent to all goods $s$ such that $T(s) = t$ (since they all serve equally well as signals), and she strictly prefers any of these goods to any good such that $T(s)$ is not equal to $t$ (since none of these goods will accurately signal the player's type). So, in addition to its value in use, a good that signals a player's type also has value as a signal to that player.

Mixed equilibria in which some players manage to signal their type and others do not are also possible. Suppose that player choices of visible goods are such that, for some goods, $F(s) = 1$, and for others, $F(s) < z/y$. Then, players who buy the first sort of good will be sending perfect signals regarding their type, and those who buy the second sort will be sending no effective signal. For this situation to constitute an equilibrium, we must suppose, in addition, that all players who could send a perfect signal do so. As is the case in any nonsignalling equilibrium, all the players who are not sending perfect signals would like to, but cannot. Given any configuration of encounters in the second-stage congregation, any of these mixed equilibria Pareto-dominates any of the nonsignalling equilibria, and in turn is Pareto-dominated by any of the perfect-signalling equilibria. All goods that do not serve as type signals are equally attractive to players who cannot signal their type, and are strictly preferred to goods that do serve as type signals. As in a perfect-signalling equilibrium, any player who can signal her type is indifferent to all goods that allow her to signal, and she strictly prefers any of these goods to all goods that do not serve to signal her type.

It is worth noting that all three sorts of equilibria are possible with the more general payoff structure described in Table 9.1. The independence and symmetry assumptions we added to get the payoff structure in Table 9.2 simplify the analysis and exposition, but do not drive the main results.

Obviously, there is a very nasty coordination problem in this model. In fact, in the one-shot framework we have been looking at, it seems overwhelmingly likely that real choices would not be equilibrium choices. In the next two sections, we examine how this coordination problem might be solved. First, we consider a dynamic game framework in which players attend an infinite series of congregations and buy imperfectly durable visible goods that act as signals in these repeated congregations. We identify some arguably salient strategies that lead eventually to a situation in which all players manage to signal their type accurately. Then, we see how firms might help players to solve the coordination problem through image advertising.

## A Dynamic Game with Repeated Congregations

We argue that, in a repeated, dynamic game framework, there exist salient, history-dependent strategies that effectively solve the coordination problem we saw in the static game. To demonstrate this, we consider a framework in which congregations occur in every period. All players participate in all congregations, so the number of players and the mix of types of players are identical in all congregations. Visible goods are durable but not perfectly so, and hence need to be replaced from time to time. Specifically, there is a constant probability $q$, $0 < q < 1$ that any good wears out in any period. Consequently, in each period, some players will need to buy a new good, so we now have a dynamic game.

As an initial condition, we suppose that all players are endowed with visible goods of various descriptions. We assume that the number of visible goods represented in the initial distribution is larger than the number of different player types. The initial condition might be generated, for example, by a random, uncoordinated selection of goods by players. There is a large number of players of each type, so we need not concern ourselves with the possibility of repeated encounters between the same players in different congregations.

The fact that the perfect-signalling equilibria Pareto-dominate the others suggests that eventually one of them will prevail. The difficulty is, of course, that there is a very large number of them and no obvious way of coordinating choices of the players so as to produce a perfect-signalling equilibrium. We resolve this problem by identifying what are, arguably, salient history-dependent strategies. For simplicity, we focus on strategies that depend only on initial conditions.

We identify for each player a possibly salient *target good*. These target goods are identified by reference to the frequency distribution $P(t,s)$ that describes the initial distribution of player types over goods. Obviously, we assume that this initial distribution is known by all players. In addition, we assume that all players are able to track the evolution over time of this frequency distribution and that they use the evolving frequency distribution to select the dominant actions in their encounters (as described in the previous section). We show that play of the dynamic game converges to a perfect-signalling equilibrium and that the strategies we identify sometimes constitutes a Nash equilibrium of the dynamic game.

For the time being, we suppose that all players simply use their current good until it wears out. Of course, they might choose to replace it before it wears out, if by doing so they could signal their type. We will have something to say about this possibility below, but for now we ignore it.

Given $P(t,s)$, we can partition the set of goods into two subsets. In the first subset are all goods for which $F(s) \geq z/y$, and in the second are all goods for which $F(s) < z/y$. We call any good in the first subset a *signalling good*, and any good in the second subset a *nonsignalling good*.

To identify target goods, it is useful to distinguish three categories of player. In category 1 are all the lucky players for whom there exists one or more signalling goods that signal their own type. When their good wears out, these players have a clear short-run incentive to choose one of these signalling goods – the target good, or the salient choice, would seem to be the signalling good for which $F(s)$ is largest.

Category 2 is composed of all the players (i) for whom there exists no signalling good that signals their own type and (ii) for whom there exists one or more nonsignalling good for which $T(s)$ is the player's own type. The target or salient good for any of these players is the one satisfying restriction (ii) for which $F(s)$ is largest.

Category 3 is composed of all the players for whom there exists no signalling good that signals their own type and for whom there exists no nonsignalling goods for which $T(s)$ is the player's own type. Of course, there might be no players in category 3, but if there are, we can use the following algorithm to identify target goods for them. First, eliminate all player types for whom we have already identified a target good and all goods that have been identified as target goods. Then, compute the normalized frequency distribution, $P^*(t,s)$, for all remaining types $t$ and goods $s$, and use these normalized frequencies to compute

$$T^*(s) \equiv \arg\max P^*(t,s) \tag{6}$$

and to define $F^*(s)$:

$$F^*(s) \equiv P^*(T^*(s), s). \tag{7}$$

Now partition the set of remaining player types into two subsets. In the first subset are all player types $t$ for whom there is at least one good $s$ for which $T^*(s) = t$, and in the second are all types for whom there is no such good. For each player type in the first subset, the target good is the good for which $F^*(s)$ is largest. If the second subset is empty, then a target good has been identified for all players. If the second subset is not empty (if there remain types for which no target good has yet been identified), return to first step above.

These target goods can now be used to define a set of *target strategies* for the dynamic game. In any period, a randomly determined subset of players will be in the market for visible goods. Our target strategies prescribe that each player buy her target good whenever she is in the goods market, and they prescribe the dominant actions that we found in the second section in all encounters. Clearly, this set of strategies converges to one of the perfect-signalling equilibria. Indeed, convergence is complete when all players who do not initially own their target good have replaced their initial good.

In addition, provided that future payoffs are not discounted too highly and that goods are sufficiently durable, these target strategies are Nash-equilibrium strategies of the dynamic game. Consider first any player in category 1. The target good for any such player is a good that successfully signals her own type, given the initial frequency distribution, and if other players are pursuing their target strategies the target good will continue to signal her type. Consequently, at no point in this dynamic game can one of these players improve her payoff for even one period by buying some other good.

For players in categories 2 and 3, the following awkward possibility can arise during the dynamic adjustment process induced by the target strategies we have identified: given the initial frequency distribution, there is no signalling good for any of these players. Their target good, of course, eventually will come to signal their type, but it is possible that some good other than their target good might for a time come to signal their own type. For players in category 3, there is another awkward possibility: that their own target good might for a time come to signal some other player type. When and if either possibility arises, there is a clear short-run incentive for these players to buy a good other than their target good. But long-run incentives tend to counteract these short-run incentives. In particular, if players do not discount the future too highly and/or if goods are sufficiently durable and expensive, so that today's choice of a visible good locks a player into that good for an expected period of time that is sufficiently long, then the payoff-maximizing strategy is to buy the target good.

So far, we have ignored the possibility that players choose to replace their goods before they wear out. We do not analyse in detail the dynamic game in which this sort of behaviour is permitted, but one extreme possibility is instructive. If $y$ is large enough relative to $z$, and if visible goods are cheap enough, then the following are equilibrium strategies: if the good owned by a player in the initial allocation is not that player's target good, then the player should buy her target good immediately; when a player's good wears out, she should replace it with her target good. In this case, type signalling is valuable ($y$ is large relative to $z$) and not expensive (since visible goods are cheap); accordingly, the model converges to a perfect-signalling equilibrium in just one period.

Whether the target goods we have identified are, in fact, salient is, of course, an empirical question, and it could be addressed using carefully defined experiments. The salience of the specific target goods we have singled out is not really the issue on which we want to focus. Rather, we want to raise the broader question of whether, in the dynamic context we have set out, it is reasonable to think that the model would converge to a perfect-signalling equilibrium. Like the question of salience, this one can also be examined experimentally. Our belief is that the model would converge to such an equilibrium. In particular, when $y$ is significantly greater than $z$, it seems almost inconceivable that it would get stuck in one of the Pareto-inferior equilibria or that it would fail to converge to any equilibrium.

### Firms and Visible Consumption Goods

This theory of the demand for visible goods, or image goods, has a number of implications for the behaviour of the firms that supply such goods. In particular, we argue that firms that produce visible goods have both the means, through image advertising, and, depending on the costs of such advertising, the incentive to solve the coordination problem that bedevils this game. The implied theory of image advertising has some interesting implications for entry into the market for visible goods and provides a novel perspective on the social value of brand copyright.

### Solving the Coordination Problem via Image Advertising

Here we examine a four-stage game that is an elaboration of the two-stage game we looked earlier. Players initially have no visible goods. In stage one of the game, firms choose which goods to develop and whether to engage in image advertising; in stage two, players choose whether to accept or reject the images that firms are trying to create for their goods; in stage three, players choose which visible good to buy; in stage four, players participate in a congregation where their visible goods might serve as type signals.

We suppose that it costs the firm $D$ to develop a product and $A$ to create an image for it. As in the previous section, all visible goods have an identical use value for all players, and the prices of all goods that are developed are identical and less than their value in use. For convenience, we also assume that a firm (or firms) outside the model offers for sale an *imageless good*, for which it is impossible to create a well-defined image by wearing it. This device allows us to ignore some awkward, but uninteresting, possibilities that otherwise arise. Initially, we ignore the possibility that two or more different firms develop the same good.

Image advertising and image creation are quite simple in our model. At a cost of $A$, a firm that produces good $G$ can announce to all players that, in stage three, only players of type $t$ will buy it. The crucial question is: will players accept this image? Imagine, then, a situation in which one or more firms attempt to create an image for their goods in this way. If all players accept this image, then their consumption decisions will validate it. That is, given that all players accept the image, in the equilibrium of the stage-three subgame in which players buy visible goods, players will buy a good with an image that is accurate for them if such a good is available, and they will never buy a good with an image that is inaccurate for them (because the imageless good is a preferred option). But this means that, in the stage-two subgame, the unanimous acceptance of such an image is itself an equilibrium, for if all players other than player $i$ accept it, player $i$'s best response is to accept it as well: if player $i$ does not accept the image, she might be led to buy a good with an image that is inaccurate for her or fail to buy a good with an image that is accurate for her; if she does accept the image, she will make no such mistakes. There are, of course, other equilibria of the subgame in which players choose to accept or reject the images firms are trying to create. However, the salient equilibrium seems to be the one in which all images are accepted, since this equilibrium facilitates type signalling, which is valuable to all players. We conclude, then, that all images will be accepted by all players.

Now consider firms' decisions in stage one. Equilibrium decisions in this first stage are fairly clear: given the number of type $t$ players, firms will develop and advertise enough goods with a type $t$ image so that the expected net revenue another good with image $t$ would garner in the stage-three subgame would not be sufficient to cover the development and advertising costs for that good. Hence, if there are enough players of each type, firms will give players the opportunity to buy a good with an image that is tailor made for their type, leading to a perfect-signalling equilibrium. If, however, the number of players of certain types is small, there will be no image good produced for them, and they will not be able to perfectly signal their type. (Since these players have the opportunity to buy the imageless good, they will never buy a good with an image that is inaccurate for them.) We conclude, then, that firms have both the means to solve the players' coordination problem perfectly and the incentive to do so if there are enough players of each type and/or if the costs of developing and advertising a good are small enough.

When we assumed that no two firms developed the same good, we finessed a fairly obvious free-rider problem. If we permit (perfect) cloning, then the equilibrium of this fourth-stage game is somewhat different. If one firm develops and creates a type $t$ image for its product (at a cost of $D + A$), it must anticipate that other firms will clone its product (at a cost of $D$ per firm) and free ride on the image it created. Indeed, in equilibrium, there would be enough clones so that an additional free rider could not cover its development costs. But it is then possible that the firm that spent $A$ to create the image in the first place will not be able to cover its costs. Suppose, for example, that $A > D$, and let $R$ be the net revenue from sales to type $t$ players. Suppose, too, that if $n$ firms produce a product with a type $t$ image, they share equally the net revenue, $R$. If the firm that developed the product and created its image is to cover its costs, we require that $R/n > A + D$. For an additional clone to find development unprofitable, we require that $R/(n + 1) < D$. When $A > D$, there is no positive integer $n$ for which both inequalities are satisfied, and so no firm has an incentive to develop an image good for players of type $t$. Hence, in the equilibrium associated with perfect cloning, firms might have no incentive to solve the players' coordination problem. It is clear, then, that cloning can give rise to a market failure in which firms fail to create images for their products. This is a market failure because such images solve the players' collective coordination problem.

Firms can and do use various devices to frustrate this image free riding. The prominence on clothing of alligators and polo ponies and prominently displayed brand names such as Gucci and Porsche – images that are subject to copyright protection – seem to be a rational, and socially valuable, response by firms to frustrate free riders.

## Entry

Earlier, we used a dynamic version of our model to argue that salient strategies exist that eventually produce a perfect-signalling equilibrium; and immediately above, we argued that firms have an incentive to provide, via image advertising, goods that serve as type signals. Accordingly, in our discussion of entry, we assume that all existing goods have well-defined images and that there is at least one good that signals each player type. In this world, to enter this market successfully, firms must somehow establish an image for their good. In our four-stage model, we assumed that a firm could get its image message to all players by spending a fixed amount $A$ on image adverting. In our discussion of entry, we abandon this simplifying assumption and use the more realistic one that the cost of communicating the firm's image message to $n$ players is an increasing function of $n$.

Clearly, in this framework, new visible goods somehow must acquire an image: since goods have value to players as signals in such a market, a good that has no well-defined image might appeal to no one. In our model, where values in use and prices of all visible goods are identical, an imageless good certainly would appeal to no one. There seem to be two broad possibilities for creating such an image: cloning and image advertising. Cloning is a familiar strategy – several brands of jeans appear to be free riding on the Levi's image, for example – and efforts to frustrate it are also familiar. And image advertising is, of course, a familiar aspect of the world of Madison Avenue.

Our model also suggests that effective image advertising might be very expensive. To be effective, the firm must convince its intended customers that most of the people with whom they interact accept the projected image. That is, it must convince some people that most people accept the good's image. To achieve this result, at a minimum it would seem to be necessary to convince some people that most people have been exposed to the image. Moreover, unless this is, in fact, substantially true, firms risk loss of creditability through inadvertent purchases of a good by those who do not fit the desired image.

The most effective, and often perhaps the only, way to achieve this result seems to be saturation advertising – an expensive proposition. Put another way, a small amount spent on image advertising is likely to be totally ineffective, because it will not convince anyone that most people accept the intended image. Hence, the need to create an image might constitute a significant barrier to entry. Contrast this with informational advertising. To induce an individual to buy a product because it is cheaper, or of higher quality, the advertiser must get the relevant message to that individual and to no one else. This implies, given reasonable assumptions about the technology of getting the desired information to individuals, that there will be constant or diminishing returns to informational advertising. In contrast, our theory suggests that there are significant increasing returns to image advertising.

**Discussion**

In this paper, we have examined how individuals employ visible image goods to signal hard-to-observe characteristics in social interactions. It is evident that circumstances exist in which substantial efficiency gains might arise from such signalling. But it is also evident that substantial coordination problems exist in achieving signalling equilibrium.

We argue that these coordination problems create profitable opportunities for firms to create images for their goods through advertising. There are, it seems, substantial increasing returns associated with image advertising. To be effective, broad acceptance of a product's image is required. To accomplish this, saturation advertising might be necessary. Consequently, to enter a market in which image advertising is important, large upfront investments might be required, operationalizing the notion of the importance of image advertising as a sunk cost, as Sutton (1992) discusses.

Consistent with the notion of saturation advertising, image advertising campaigns frequently have very wide coverage. Moreover, discussions with media practitioners suggest that firms are willing to pay a premium to assure that image ads are coordinated and reach large groups of consumers simultaneously. Thus, firms are sometimes willing to pay high upfront rates for the advance purchase of television air time or print media space to assure that slots for image ads are locked in, even though rates for spot advertising based on current availability are significantly lower.

Saturation aspects of image advertising are also evident in the projection of images far beyond immediate buyers of a good. One well-publicized example is the controversial *Old Joe* campaign for Camel cigarettes launched in 1988, which critics claimed was aimed at youths (see Pierce et al. 1991). In 1990, about 26 per cent of the U.S. population over age 18 smoked, about 12 per cent of youths ages 12 to 18 did so (United States 1992b). Among smokers, Camel's market share historically had been modest – less than 5 per cent of smoking adults in 1986 and 8.1 per cent of teenage smokers in a 1989 survey (United States 1990, 1992a). Yet a 1991 survey of high school students in selected states indicated that more than 97 per cent had seen *Old Joe* and 93 per cent knew the Camel brand; similar results for adults were 72 per cent and 57 per cent, respectively (DiFranza et al. 1991). Thus, although a minority of the population smoked at all and only a tiny fraction of the population smoked Camels, the *Old Joe* campaign reached virtually all of the youths surveyed and a majority of adults.

We ignored the possibility of fraudulent signalling in our basic model. But, for a host of situations, it is clear that large gains could be realized by counterfeiting. The well-dressed confidence man who seeks to project an image of success and prosperity for predatory purposes is an archetype; so, too, is the modestly dressed millionaire (or billionaire) seeking to camouflage herself from potential predators. One well-known solution to the problem of fraud is to adopt signals that are costly to fake. In our own analysis, this has a number of implications that might be interesting to explore in future research, perhaps the most obvious of which is possible interactions between the innate characteristics of goods and their use as signals. Suppose the good that is most attractive to a particular group of individuals is also readily acceptable to those lacking that group's characteristic; then its consumption will have little cost for counterfeiters. Suppose a second good exists that is equally acceptable to the group but is substantially less attractive to potential counterfeiters; clearly, this good will be preferred as a signal. By extension, affective advertising might be employed to endow goods with attributes that assist in the sorting process. Thus, if the image projected for a particular brand of beer or cigarette is appealing to the target group but not to potential counterfeiters, it might serve to raise the implicit costs of fraud. Hence, there might be synergy between the affective and signalling dimensions of image advertising.

NOTE

1  This paper is a revised version of a 1992 Simon Fraser University discussion paper (Eaton and White 1992), which was submitted to the *Journal of Political Economy* in the fall of 1992, but rejected. Subsequently, it morphed into two

papers, one (Eaton and White 2002) that focuses on aspects of image advertising, and another (Arifovic and Eaton 1998) that uses a genetic algorithm to explore the process by which the coordination problem at the heart of this paper might be solved in the absence of image advertising. On rereading the original discussion paper and the papers that grew out it, it became clear that the overall vision and many of the insights in the original paper were simply lost. So it seemed to be worthwhile to publish the original discussion paper in this volume.

## REFERENCES

Arifovic, J., and B.C. Eaton. 1998. 'The Evolution of Communication in a Sender/Receiver Game of Common Interest with Cheap Talk.' *Journal of Economic Dynamics and Control* 22 (8-9): 187–207.

Cafferata, P., and A.M. Tybout, eds. 1989. *Cognitive and Affective Responses to Advertising* Lexington, MA: D.C. Heath.

Carr, J.L., and J.T. Landa. 1983. 'The Economics of Symbols, Clan Names, and Religion.' *Journal of Legal Studies* 12 (1): 135–54.

DiFranza, J.R., et al. 1991. 'RJR Nabisco's Cartoon Camel Promotes Camel Cigarettes to Children.' *Journal of the American Medical Association* 266 (22): 3149–53.

Eaton, B.C., and W.D. White. 1992. 'Image Building.' Discussion Paper 92-17, Department of Economics, Simon Fraser University.

– 2002. 'Image Advertising.' In *Applied Microeconomic Theory: Selected Essays of B. Curtis Eaton*, edited by B.C. Eaton. Cheltenham, UK: Edward Elgar.

Frank, R.H. 1988. *Passions within Reason: The Strategic Role of Emotions.* New York: W.W. Norton.

Jones, S.R.G. 1984. *The Economics of Conformism.* Oxford: Basil Blackwell.

Kihlstrom, R.E., and M.H. Riordan. 1984. 'Advertising as a Signal.' *Journal of Political Economy* 92 (3): 427–50.

Klein, B., and K. Leffler. 1981. 'The Role of Market Forces in Assuring Contractual Performance.' *Journal of Political Economy* 89 (4): 615–41.

Nelson, P. 1974. 'Advertising as Information.' *Journal of Political Economy* 82 (4): 729–54.

Pierce, J.P., et al. 1991. 'Does Tobacco Advertising Target Young People to Start Smoking?' *Journal of the American Medical Association* 266 (22): 3154–8.

Spence, M.A. 1974. *Market Signaling: Informational Transfer in Hiring and Related Screening Processes.* Cambridge, MA: Harvard University Press.

Sutton, J. 1992. *Sunk Costs and Market Structure.* Cambridge, MA: MIT Press.

United States. 1990. Centers for Disease Control. 'Cigarette Brand Use among Adult Smokers – United States, 1986.' *Morbidity and Mortality Weekly Report* 39 (38): 665, 671–3.

– 1992a. Centers for Disease Control. 'Comparison of the Cigarette Brand Preferences of Adult and Teenaged Smokers – United States, 1989, and 10 U.S. Communities, 1988 and 1990.' *Morbidity and Mortality Weekly Report* 41 (10): 169–73.

– 1992b. Department of Health and Human Services. National Center for Health Statistics. *Health United States, 1991*. Public Health Service Publication PHS 92-1232. Washington, DC.

Wintrobe, R. 1983. 'Taxing Altruism.' *Economic Inquiry* 21 (2): 255–70.

# 10 Worker Participation and Adverse Selection[1]

GREGORY K. DOW

Worker participation in the management of firms comes in many shades and hues, from quality circles and autonomous work teams to joint consultative committees, works councils, co-determination, and fully worker-controlled firms. It is convenient, however, to imagine a simple continuum running from strongly hierarchical firms at one extreme to strongly participatory firms at the other. In a hierarchical firm, front-line workers have narrowly defined tasks, do what they are told, and receive pay unrelated to the financial performance of the firm as a whole. Full knowledge of the firm's technology and market environment is confined to upper echelons of management. In a participatory firm, by contrast, front-line workers have broader responsibilities, some influence over managerial decisions, and a stake in the firm's financial results. Workers in such firms are typically better informed about the technological and market challenges facing the firm.

Many economists and industrial relations experts believe that worker participation in decision-making raises productivity. Such claims lead to obvious questions. If worker participation is always a good thing, why is it not universal? If more worker participation is always better, why are firms not fully managed by their employees? If participation is sometimes not a good thing, what determines the optimal amount of it in a given firm or industry? Could market failure lead to a suboptimal level of worker participation?

A large body of empirical research does suggest a positive correlation between productivity and worker participation in decision-making. Such results have been found using data sets for many countries and industries, with many different ways of defining and measuring the key variables, many different controls, and many different estimation techniques (see Doucouliagos 1995). The benefits from worker involvement in decision-making appear to be enhanced when accompanied by financial participation (see Ben-Ner, Han, and Jones 1996; Ben-Ner et al. 2000). However, different forms of participation have different effects on productivity, both directly and when interacted with firm characteristics (see Pérotin and Robinson 2000; Robinson and Wilson 2006).

This empirical literature raises econometric issues about causality, simultaneity, omitted variables, and selection bias that cannot be addressed here. However, one point requires emphasis. Even if there is a positive correlation between firm-level productivity and participation, it does not follow that productivity can be increased by extending worker participation to firms that do not currently use it. To see why, suppose that some firms use simple technologies while others use complex technologies. The gains from participation are arguably larger when firm technology is more complex, and there is evidence that employees do in fact have a larger voice in decision-making within firms that use more complex technologies (Ben-Ner et al. 2000). An empirical researcher who was unable to observe technological complexity would find a significant correlation between participation and productivity, and might be perplexed by the apparent failure of some entrepreneurs or managers to grasp the benefits of worker participation. But, by assumption, firms with simple technologies would gain nothing by introducing it. The same argument applies to any unobserved firm characteristic that influences the productivity gains from participation (Robinson and Wilson 2006).

In this paper, I take a different approach to the relationship between participation and productivity. I argue that workers can participate in managerial decisions only if they understand the firm's technology. The disclosure of technological knowledge to the workforce, accompanied by a policy of worker participation, always raises productivity. However, this comes at a cost to the entrepreneur, because revealing technological details to workers gives them bargaining power and entails a loss of entrepreneurial rent.

Whether it makes sense for an entrepreneur to disclose the technology to workers depends on informational asymmetries about its value. When most new projects are good and adverse selection problems are correspondingly small, workers might be ready to pay a substantial amount up front in order to gain access to the entrepreneur's technology. The entrepreneur can use these *ex ante* side payments to undo most of the redistributive effect from *ex post* worker bargaining. An entrepreneur with a good project then will create a firm with substantial worker participation. When most projects are bad, workers will not offer much for the entrepreneur's technological knowledge. An entrepreneur with a good project then will conceal information and create a hierarchical firm.

The model unfolds in three stages. At the *organizational* stage, the entrepreneur decides on a level of worker participation and solicits membership fees from uninformed workers in exchange for disclosure of a new production technology. At the *bargaining* stage, workers who understand the firm's technology divide the entrepreneurial rent. Finally, at the *production* stage, the informed workers receive signals about the state of the world, choose actions, and produce output.

It will be most convenient to work backwards from the end of this process to the beginning. Accordingly, the discussion begins with the production stage and then proceeds to the bargaining stage. I then move back to the organizational stage and present the main results. I show that a separating equilibrium always exists and always yields a hierarchical firm. A pooling equilibrium, on the other hand, might support some worker participation, but this depends on the severity of adverse selection. If most projects are bad, pooling also yields hierarchy. As the average quality of projects improves, other pooling equilibria emerge in which technical knowledge is disseminated more widely, more workers share in profit, and decisions are made in a more participatory way. But even when almost all projects are good, there are still pooling equilibria with no (or limited) participation and no (or limited) productivity gains. The actual level of worker participation depends on the nature of worker beliefs, which could be fragile.

These conclusions are in the same spirit as Curt Eaton's point that organizational and cultural interactions typically involve complex signalling problems with many equilibria, and that these equilibria can often be Pareto-ranked (see, for example, Eaton and White in this volume; and Arifovic and Eaton 1995, 1998). By contrast with these papers, however, I depart from the assumption that the players have common interests, and focus instead on the incentives for bad entrepreneurs to masquerade as good ones.

In the next-to-last section, I develop empirical implications of the model and conclude by applying it to an episode in the history of plywood cooperatives.

**The Production Stage**

An entrepreneur faces a horizontal demand curve at a price of $p$ per unit up to a maximum total demand of $N$ units (see Figure 10.1). In one interpretation, the entrepreneur provides a new good for which there are $N$ potential consumers, each with the reservation price $p$. Alternatively, the entrepreneur could have a better technique for producing an existing good, which is currently produced by many firms at an average cost equal to $p$.

Figure 10.1: Demand and Cost

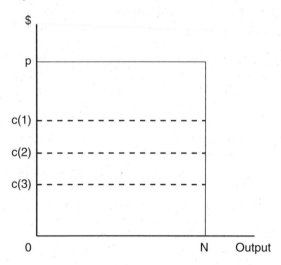

A unit of output requires one unit of labour plus materials. Each unit of labour is supplied by a distinct worker who is paid the competitive wage $w$. The expected cost of the materials needed to produce one unit of output is $k(n)$, where $n$ is the number of workers who understand the firm's technology. The basis for this function is discussed below. Unit cost $c(n) = w + k(n)$ is always below $p$, so the entrepreneur always hires $N$ workers. I index the degree of worker participation by $n \in \{1 \, .. \, N\}$ and label workers so that $i = 1 \, .. \, n$ understand the technology while $i = n + 1 \, .. \, N$ do not. The reduction in average cost resulting from increased worker participation is indicated in Figure 10.1.

The central issue for later analysis is the way in which profit depends on the number of informed workers. Let expected profit be

$$\pi(n) = [p - c(n)]N, \tag{1}$$

where $c(n) \equiv w + k(n)$. The function $\pi(n)$ is assumed to have two key features:

$A1$   $0 < \pi(n) < \pi(n + 1)$ for all $n = 1 \, .. \, N - 1$, and

$A2$   $\pi(n)/n > \pi(n + 1)/(n + 1)$ for all $n = 1 \, .. \, N - 1$.

A1 holds as long as $k(n)$ is decreasing in $n$. A2 holds under conditions explained below, and its significance is discussed in a later section.

Production activities can be modelled in a number of different ways that yield A1 and A2, and it will not matter how this is done. Here I present just one way of reaching these results. Assume the amount of material needed to produce one unit of output is affected by a random state of the world $x \in [0, 1]$ common to all workers and an action $a_i \in [0, 1]$ taken by worker $i$ who produces the particular unit in question. The state $x$ is distributed uniformly on $[0, 1]$ and the expected cost of the materials used by worker $i$ is $E(x - a_i)$.[2] Workers are indifferent among actions.

When there are $n$ workers who understand the firm's production technology, each informed worker monitors an equal subinterval of the space $[0, 1]$: thus worker 1 watches $[0, 1/n]$, worker 2 watches $[1/n, 2/n]$, and so on, up to worker $n$, who watches $[(n-1)/n, 1]$. Each worker can see whether or not the state of the world $x$ is in her subinterval, although not the precise value of $x$ (I ignore boundary cases, which have zero probability). Once a worker announces that $x$ is in her subinterval, all workers minimize the expected material cost $E(x - a_i)^2$ conditional on this information. Bayesian reasoning shows that the cost-minimizing choice is $a_i = (i - 1/2)/n$ when $x$ is in the subinterval monitored by worker $i$. Suppose also that uninformed workers are instructed to take the same action and do so. This yields the material cost $k(n) = E(x - a_i)^2 = 1/12n^2$ for every unit, regardless of which subinterval contains the true value of $x$. Clearly, A1 holds because $k(n)$ is decreasing in $n$ (we need $p - w > 1/12$ to get $\pi(1) > 0$). It can be shown that A2 holds when $p - w > 7/4$.

One could replace this framework with a more complicated information structure in which the informed workers receive noisy signals about the true state of the world and aggregate this information to choose production activities (for an example, see sections 6 and 7 of Dow 1988). In any reasonable system of this kind, expected profit should be an increasing function of the number of signals so that A1 holds, and at least eventually the marginal gain from another signal should fall so that A2 holds over some range.

**The Bargaining Stage**

Now suppose there are $n$ informed workers who bargain over the distribution of the rent $\pi(n)$ before production occurs. At this stage, the entrepreneur is included in the set of informed workers. I assume that bargaining gives each informed worker an equal payoff $\pi(n)/n$. This conclusion can again be reached in various ways, and the details are not crucial. However, I briefly sketch the issues involved (related bargaining models are examined in Dow 1988, 1989).

At the bargaining stage, the informed workers know they will receive signals about the state of the world later, and they know that expected profit is $\pi(n)$ if all of these signals are disclosed. There is no incentive to conceal or distort signals after they arrive as long as each worker's payoff is a nondecreasing function of *ex post* profit, because revealing the true signal is costless and workers are indifferent among actions at the production stage.

I ignore any bargaining activity that might occur after signals arrive but before they are disclosed. A worker who knows that her private information is very important – in other words, that it is likely to alter the actions of the firm at the production stage – might threaten to withhold this information unless the other workers provide side payments. However, any worker can claim to have such information. Because the workers are symmetric, there is no reason why *ex post* bargaining would alter the results from *ex ante* bargaining.

Due to the *ex ante* symmetry of the informed workers, it is natural to suppose that they will get equal shares in $\pi(n)$. However, this might not be true if the entrepreneur can make commitments that have lasting consequences for relative bargaining power before the production technology is disclosed to other workers. I ignore this complication here, but pursue it at length in Dow (1989).

For reasons to be discussed later, I do not want to assume that agents can contract on the *ex post* profit of the firm. Instead, I assume that one worker is singled out as the 'residual claimant' and that this person has ownership of all firm output, as well as the obligation to pay wages and *ex post* material costs. The residual claimant can make side payments to the other informed workers at the bargaining stage. If all agents are risk neutral, the utility possibility set is the same no matter who is chosen for this role. In particular, it makes no difference whether an agent receives the side payment $\pi(n)/n$ from the residual claimant or whether the agent is the residual claimant and receives expected profit $\pi(n)$ minus $n - 1$ side payments, each worth $\pi(n)/n$.

The only remaining question is whether the full rent $\pi(n)$ is exposed to bargaining or whether individual workers can guarantee themselves payoffs above zero through unilateral actions. In short, one needs to say why the disagreement point at the bargaining stage is the origin $(0, 0 .. 0)$. One rationale is to suppose that each informed worker can commit to disclose the firm's proprietary technology publicly unless her demands are met. Disclosure would destroy the rent $\pi(n)$ by allowing free entry. If only one worker made such a commitment, this worker would gain a bargaining advantage; however, the other informed workers could counter with similar commitments. If all workers are committed to destroying the rent in case of disagreement, the disagreement point becomes the origin.

The outcome would be the same if informed workers threatened to establish rival firms in case of disagreement, because price competition among firms could then destroy the rent. This scenario is slightly subtler than the standard Bertrand equilibrium because here each firm has increasing returns to scale. This follows from the fact that, as output increases, the number of workers employed by the firm increases. If all of these workers understand the production technology, average cost falls due to the increasing number of signals about the state of the world available within the firm. But one can still fall back on contestability: although total demand may be satisfied by one firm in equilibrium, this firm must set price equal to average cost, otherwise entry would occur.

A third way to model the bargaining stage is to introduce a dynamic framework in which the rent vanishes with positive probability in each period, perhaps because another entrepreneur independently replicates the new technology. If no rent can be appropriated until an agreement is reached, a standard limiting argument shows that the outcome is the symmetric Nash bargaining solution with the origin as the disagreement point (Binmore, Rubinstein, and Wolinsky 1986).

To highlight the idea that all workers who understand the firm's technology are on an equal footing with the entrepreneur in their ability to appropriate rent at the bargaining stage, in the rest of the paper I refer to these workers as 'members' of the firm.

**The Organizational Stage**

We are now ready to consider the first stage of the model, where an entrepreneur decides how to organize the firm. The entrepreneur (E), who becomes one of the workers in the firm, has an idea for a new production technology. If the idea is a good one, E faces the profit function $\pi(n)$ and chooses $n \in \{1 .. N\}$. The analysis then goes through as in the previous two sections. If the idea is bad, average cost cannot be reduced below the price $p$ shown in Figure 10.1 and profit is zero regardless of $n$. E knows whether the idea is good or bad, but uninformed workers cannot observe this *ex ante*.

An entrepreneur with a good idea would like to capture the increased profit from worker participation. However, sharing proprietary information gives the other workers bargaining power. If E chooses $n \geq 2$, at the bargaining stage E's payoff is only $\pi(n)/n$ rather than $\pi(n)$. The entrepreneur thus gets a smaller share of a larger pie. From A2 above, $\pi(n)/n$ is decreasing in $n$, so the bargaining effect dominates the productivity effect. (If $\pi(n)/n$ is increasing in $n$, the entrepreneur always prefers more participation. This case is uninteresting, however, and I ignore it below.)

Because $\pi(1) > \pi(n)/n$ for all $n \geq 2$, it might seem that an entrepreneur with a good idea will always create a hierarchical firm in which she obtains signals about the state of the world, tells other workers what to do, and collects the resulting profit. In principle, though, E could capture the gains from worker participation by charging a fee for access to the proprietary technology. This would enable E to undo the *ex post* bargaining power of the informed workers by forcing them to compete *ex ante* for membership in the firm. Indeed, if everyone knew with certainty that E had a good idea, E could choose $n = N$ and appropriate the maximum profit $\pi(N)$ by selling membership rights up front. However, whether this mechanism can provide a sufficient incentive to create a participatory firm depends on the severity of the adverse selection problem (for a related model in which two-sided adverse selection undermines membership markets, see Dow forthcoming).

To formalize these ideas, consider the following sequence of events.

(a) Nature decides whether the new technology is good or bad. A good technology occurs with probability $\theta$. The true quality is revealed only to E.

(b) E chooses a number of agents $n \in \{1 .. N\}$ to become members of the firm. This always includes E and might include another $n - 1$ agents as well. If $n = 1$, the game moves to step (e) with E as the residual claimant. Otherwise, it moves to step (c).

(c) After observing E's choice of $n$, many uninformed workers bid for membership in the firm. E discloses the new technology to the $n - 1$ workers who offer the largest membership fees, with randomization in case of ties. After paying their fees, these workers find out whether the technology is good or bad. If the technology is bad, the game ends and all agents receive zero payoffs apart from the fees already paid to E, which are now sunk. If the technology is good, the game moves to step (d).

(d) Bargaining occurs as described earlier. A residual claimant is chosen who gives each of the other $n - 1$ informed workers a side payment equal to $\pi(n)/n$.

(e) Production occurs as described earlier and the residual claimant gets the profit $\pi(n)$.

I assume it is impossible to write contracts under which agents settle up after the true value of the production technology is revealed. If such contracts could be arranged, entrepreneurs with good projects would set $n = N$ and promise to refund membership fees in the event that the technology turned out to be bad, knowing that no refund would have to be paid. This would remove the effect of the parameter $\theta$ on the structure of the firm. Commitments to refund membership fees are taken to be infeasible either because the courts cannot verify project quality or because fly-by-night entrepreneurs can disappear after pocketing the fees (an example of the latter type is discussed in the last section).

Let $\mu(n)$ be the probability that uninformed workers assign at step (c) to the event that E's technology is good. Competition among uninformed agents implies that workers who become firm members receive zero surplus, so each pays E the membership fee

$$m(n) = \mu(n)\pi(n)/n. \tag{2}$$

When E chooses to have $n$ members, E's total revenue from these fees is

$$M(n) = (n-1)m(n) = \mu(n)(n-1)\pi(n)/n. \tag{3}$$

Let $E_g$ denote an entrepreneur with a good technology and $E_b$ an entrepreneur with a bad technology. The payoffs of these two agent types are

$$U_g(n) = \pi(n)/n + M(n) \tag{4}$$

and

$$U_b(n) = M(n).$$

Two kinds of equilibria can arise: separating equilibrium (SE) and pooling equilibrium (PE). Let $n_g$ be the number of members chosen by $E_g$ and $n_b$ the number chosen by $E_b$. SE has $n_g \neq n_b$ while PE has $n_g = n_b$. Proofs of all propositions and lemmas are in the appendix.

*Proposition 1.* A separating equilibrium always exists. Every SE has $n_g = 1$ and $n_b \geq 2$. This outcome can be supported by beliefs $\mu(1) = 1$ and $\mu(n) = 0$ for $n \geq 2$. The resulting payoffs are $U_g(n_g) = \pi(1)$ and $U_b(n_b) = 0$.

This proposition shows that there is always an equilibrium in which entrepreneurs with good projects create hierarchical firms. Those with bad projects try to sell membership rights but the equilibrium fee is zero. A separating equilibrium thus eliminates the bad projects, but the benefits from worker participation in good projects are lost.

The analysis of pooling equilibrium is more complex. Let $n_g = n_b = n_p$ where Bayes's rule requires $\mu(n_p) = \theta$.

*Lemma 1:* (a) If a deviation $n' < n_p$ is profitable for $E_b$, then it is also profitable for $E_g$.

(b) If a deviation $n' > n_p$ is profitable for $E_g$, then it is also profitable for $E_b$.

Because a downward deviation is never profitable for $E_b$ unless it is also profitable for $E_g$, the uninformed workers should not interpret such deviations as a reason to assign higher probability to $E_b$. Similarly, an upward deviation should never result in the assignment of higher probability to $E_g$. This motivates the following restriction on beliefs.

*A3*    (a)    $\mu(n) \geq \theta$ for all $n < n_p$;
         (b)    $\mu(n) \leq \theta$ for all $n > n_p$.

Now define the function,

$$\phi(n,\theta) \equiv \theta\pi(n) + (1 - \theta)\pi(n)/n. \tag{5}$$

*Proposition 2.* The choice $n_p$ can be supported by a pooling equilibrium consistent with A3 if and only if $\phi(n,\theta) \leq \phi(n_p,\theta)$ for all $n \leq n_p$. This can be done using the beliefs $\mu(n) = \theta$ for all $n \leq n_p$ and $\mu(n) = 0$ for all $n > n_p$. The resulting payoffs are $U_g(n_p) = \phi(n_p,\theta)$ and $U_b(n_p) = \theta(n_p - 1)\pi(n_p)/n_p$.

The intuition behind this proposition is straightforward. We can always use $\mu(n) = 0$ for $n > n_p$ to deter upward deviations because this ensures that such deviations generate zero membership revenue. This deters $E_b$ because this type cares only about membership fees, and from Lemma 1(b) it also deters $E_g$. Now consider a downward deviation. If $E_g$ can be deterred from such a deviation, then from Lemma 1(a), $E_b$ is also deterred. The beliefs $\mu(n) = \theta$ are the most pessimistic permitted by A3 and yield the minimum membership revenue to a deviator. Subject to this constraint, $E_g$ can be deterred from a downward deviation if and only if $\phi(n,\theta) \leq \phi(n_p,\theta)$ for all $n \leq n_p$.

Existence of a PE follows because $n_p = 1$ satisfies the condition in Proposition 2. From an economic standpoint, this is identical to SE because, in each case, entrepreneurs with good technologies create hierarchical firms while those with bad technologies have zero payoffs. However, Proposition 2 also opens up the possibility that positive levels of worker participation ($n_p \geq$ 2) could occur.

Write $\phi^*(\theta) \equiv \max \{\phi(n,\theta)$ for $n = 1 \ldots N\}$ and let $n^*(\theta)$ be the largest n such that $\phi(n,\theta) = \phi^*(\theta)$. No choice $n_p > n^*(\theta)$ can satisfy the condition in Proposition 2, but $n^*(\theta)$ does satisfy this condition and some $n_p < n^*(\theta)$ may also satisfy it (in addition to $n_p = 1$).

*Lemma 2*. If $n_p{}^0$ and $n_p{}^1$ both satisfy the condition in Proposition 2 with $n_p{}^0$ $< n_p{}^1$, then a PE involving $n_p{}^1$ is Pareto-superior to a PE involving $n_p{}^0$.

Pooling equilibria can be Pareto-ranked because (i) uninformed workers receive zero *ex ante* surplus in any PE; (ii) good entrepreneurs do at least as well with increased worker participation by the condition in Proposition 2; and (iii) bad entrepreneurs strictly prefer increased worker participation due to the additional membership revenue it generates.

Each value of $\theta$ is therefore associated with a pooling equilibrium that supports the (constrained) Pareto-efficient participation level $n^*(\theta)$. Next, let us study the effect of varying the information parameter $\theta$ on the efficient outcome $n^*(\theta)$.

*Proposition 3*. There are finitely many points $\{\theta_a, \theta_b, \ldots \theta_z\}$ with $0 < \theta_a < \theta_b < \ldots < \theta_z < 1$ such that
(i)  $n^*(\theta) = 1$ for $\theta < \theta_a$ and $n^*(\theta) = N$ for $\theta \geq \theta_z$;
(ii) $n^*(\theta)$ is constant on each of the half-open intervals $[\theta_a,\theta_b), [\theta_b,\theta_c) \ldots$
     $[\theta_y,\theta_z)$; and
(iii) $n^*(\theta)$ is larger on intervals with higher values of $\theta$.

The equilibrium payoffs for $E_g$ and $E_b$ in the efficient equilibrium $n^*(\theta)$ are

$$V_g(\theta) = \phi^*(\theta) \equiv \max \{\phi(n,\theta) \text{ for } n = 1 \ldots N\};$$
$$V_b(\theta) = \theta[n^*(\theta) - 1]\pi[n^*(\theta)]/n^*(\theta).$$

$V_g(\theta)$ is positive, continuous, nondecreasing, and convex on $0 \leq \theta \leq 1$. $V_b(\theta)$ is strictly increasing in $\theta$.

The shape of $V_g(\theta)$ for the case $N = 3$ is shown in Figure 10.2. This function is the upper envelope of the lines $\phi(n,\theta)$ for each fixed value of $n$, where the increasing slope of $V_g(\theta)$ reflects upward jumps in $n^*(\theta)$ at $\theta_a$ and $\theta_b$.

Figure 10.2: The Payoff Function $V_g(\theta)$ for a Pooling Equilibrium ($N = 3$)

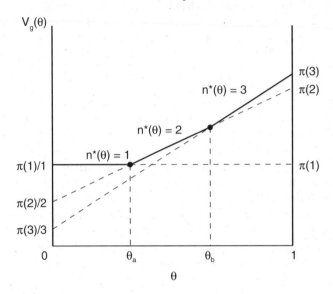

Proposition 3 shows that when the average quality of projects is sufficiently low, a good entrepreneur always establishes a hierarchical firm. It is not worthwhile to introduce worker participation because the entrepreneur will have to share rents with the workforce *ex post*, and cannot extract enough *ex ante* compensation due to the adverse selection problem. As the average quality of projects rises, a good entrepreneur is increasingly willing to share proprietary knowledge with the workforce (assuming selection of the constrained efficient PE) because workers are willing to pay more for a claim on profit. The entrepreneur thus captures a larger fraction of the gain from worker participation and offers membership to a larger number of workers. When the probability of a good project is close enough to unity, the entrepreneur informs the entire workforce about the firm's technology and the firm becomes fully participatory (again, assuming selection of the efficient PE).

The key results of the analysis can now be summarized. A separating equilibrium always leads to hierarchy: an entrepreneur with a good project hoards information, tells workers what to do, and appropriates all of the firm's profits. The productivity gains from participation are lost. The same result can occur in a pooling equilibrium (hierarchy is always an equilibrium outcome), but there might be other equilibria in which participation is viable. When Pareto-efficient equilibria are selected, participation (both in decision-making and in financial returns) becomes more extensive as adverse selection becomes less severe. But high-participation outcomes might be fragile because, typically, there are also numerous inefficient pooling equilibria supported by more pessimistic worker beliefs.

**Empirical Implications**

The model is broadly consistent with the empirical evidence discussed in the first section. There is a direct causal channel from participation to productivity, so the existence of a positive correlation between the two is unsurprising. However, firms can have different levels of worker participation due to (a) multiple equilibria for a given degree of adverse selection and (b) the variable extent of adverse selection across firms and industries.

The analysis above shows that firms with zero or low worker participation need not have unobserved characteristics that make participation especially unproductive or costly. It might instead be true that participation would be highly valuable if it could be implemented, but firms and workers are stuck in a bad equilibrium. Participation does not occur because workers do not trust assurances from entrepreneurs or managers that profit shares will be valuable. This lack of trust makes workers unwilling to provide sufficient compensation to the entrepreneurs or managers for the reduction in the latter's own profit shares, and these entrepreneurs or managers therefore find participation unattractive.

In the model in this paper, imposing full worker participation in all firms would enhance total surplus. This would reduce cost in firms with good projects and do no harm in firms with bad projects. Such a policy intervention is not feasible, however, because entrepreneurs with good ideas cannot be forced to disclose their ideas to others. Thus, there is no easy solution to the multiple equilibrium problem, although fraudulent claims about the value of membership can sometimes be punished.

The empirical relevance of the model is limited to cases where participation gives workers substantial bargaining power at the expense of entrepreneurs or managers, and where the bargaining effect dominates the productivity effect so that A2 applies. Some forms of worker participation clearly do not satisfy these conditions. Suggestion boxes, for example, do not give workers any bargaining power.

Even when workers do gain more bargaining power, the productivity effect might dominate over some range. This can lead entrepreneurs or managers to introduce some degree of participation – such as employee representation on committees or employee access to credible accounting data – even when they do not receive any compensation from workers.

The model seems best suited to cases where participation entails large gains in workers' bargaining power and the associated productivity benefits display diminishing returns. This might be true for workers' representation on boards of directors, employee buyouts of conventional firms, or the creation of labour-managed firms.

A number of empirical predictions flow from the model. First, participatory firms are more likely to be created if other entrants into the same industry have succeeded and there have been few visible failures. Such a track record would show that the average quality of new projects in the industry is high, and it would encourage workers to pay for profit shares. This is not equivalent to the trivial prediction that participatory firms are likely to enter industries in which *participatory* firms have already succeeded. A history of this kind naturally indicates that the benefits of participation are large. Rather, the prediction here is that later entrants are more likely to adopt participation *whether or not* the earlier successes involved participation.

Another implication involves the life cycles of firms. Suppose the average quality of new projects is low, so entrepreneurs with good technologies create hierarchical firms. Over time it might become clear to workers that these firms have solid foundations, that their product niches are profitable, and that the entrepreneurs are not of the fly-by-night variety. If so, employees should gradually become more inclined to acquire profit shares and entrepreneurs should become more willing to disseminate technological knowledge.

Movement toward a participatory structure need not occur rapidly. Considerable time might have to elapse before a particular project can confidently be judged a success or failure. A run of good or bad luck might mask the true merits of a project for years, or a project might require investments that pay off (if at all) only over decades. Accordingly, participatory practices should be less extensive and should be introduced more slowly in industries where projects have high variance or long time horizons.

Furthermore, the fact that past projects have succeeded is no guarantee that future projects will succeed. Sophisticated employees should recognize that adverse selection problems can recur with each new round of innovation and that the firm's entrepreneurs, owners, or managers might take the money and run if they have a bad project in the current round. This difficulty might be mitigated by reputational factors or the repeated nature of the relationships within the firm, but it is unlikely to vanish entirely. Thus, participation should be less extensive in industries where project qualities are uncorrelated over time.

The model can be extended by assuming that both capital and labour are required for production. An entrepreneur who has a good project but lacks the personal wealth to finance it must now obtain capital as well as labour from uninformed agents. Depending on whether or not outside investors gain knowledge of the technology, one might want to think of them as contributing either equity or debt. Given physical asset specificity and the possibility of bankruptcy, for some parameter values a good entrepreneur cannot get financing of either type. However, an entrepreneur with sufficient personal wealth can avoid outside financing and will only need to transact with workers. The analysis then reduces to the situation analysed in earlier sections.

This framework links two related ideas. First, when adverse selection is severe, capital suppliers usually will be the organizers of firms, because only they can overcome the financial obstacles involved. Second, firms that arise under severe adverse selection will have a hierarchical structure in which technical knowledge is closely guarded and workers are compensated through fixed wages rather than profit shares. For further discussion of the obstacles to worker-controlled firms, see Dow (2003).

### An Application to Plywood Cooperatives

The limiting case of worker participation occurs in labour-managed firms, where workers can hire and fire top managers. The plywood cooperatives of the U.S. Pacific Northwest have been among the most intensively studied firms of this kind (see Pencavel 2001; and Dow 2003: 50–7, for historical accounts and references). These firms have gradually disappeared as the plywood industry has declined across the region. However, the plywood co-ops competed successfully with conventional firms for several decades and compared favourably on standard productivity measures.

I close with an anecdote from the history of these cooperatives. Roughly 20 plywood cooperatives were formed in the 1940s and early 1950s. Although a few had been created decades earlier, the entry of these new co-ops occurred during a postwar boom in housing construction and was encouraged by rapid capital gains on membership shares. The new cooperatives were often organized by outside promoters who knew little about the industry and had no intention of working in a mill. Two such efforts resulted in criminal trials for securities fraud and mail fraud, at which the promoters were sentenced to jail terms of seven and twelve years. This brought the formation of new plywood cooperatives to an abrupt halt. There is no evidence that any cooperatives entered after this point, although conventional plywood mills continued to enter for many years.

This story is consistent with the earlier analysis. Once it became known that some entrepreneurs had bad or fraudulent projects, workers revised their beliefs in a way that made the creation of more cooperatives impossible, because entrepreneurs were no longer able to convince workers to pay in advance for membership rights. In short, a pooling equilibrium that had supported the entry of co-ops collapsed and was replaced by an equilibrium in which all firms were organized hierarchically. This occurred despite the highly visible presence of existing co-ops that competed effectively with conventional firms. Indeed, members of established co-ops often became quite wealthy by selling their shares to outside investors. The formation of worker-controlled firms thus was sensitive to information conditions, while the formation of conventional firms was not.

## Appendix

### Proof of Proposition 1

Suppose $n_g \neq n_b$ with $n_g \geq 2$. Bayes's rule gives $\mu(n_g) = 1$, and it follows from equation (3) that $M(n_g) > 0$. Bayes's rule also gives $\mu(n_b) = 0$, so $M(n_b) = 0$. Since $E_b$ can deviate to $n_g$ and obtain $M(n_g) > 0$, from equation (4) this cannot be an equilibrium. Therefore, $n_g = 1$ and $n_b \geq 2$ must hold in every SE. Now let $n_g = 1$ and consider any $n_b \geq 2$, where $\mu(n) = 0$ for all $n \geq 2$. It is unprofitable for $E_g$ to deviate to any $n' \geq 2$ because $M(n') = 0$ and thus $U_g(n') = \pi(n')/n' < \pi(1) = U_g(1)$ using equations (3), (4), and A2. It is unprofitable for $E_b$ to deviate to any $n' \neq n_b$ because $U_b(n_b) = U_b(n') = 0$ from equations (3) and (4). This shows that $n_g = 1$, $n_b \geq 2$, $\mu(1) = 1$, and $\mu(n) = 0$ for $n \geq 2$ is an SE. The payoffs follow from equations (3) and (4).

### Proof of Lemma 1

(a) Consider any $n' < n_p$. If $E_b$ prefers $n'$ to $n_p$ then $M(n') > M(n_p)$ by equation (4). This result, A2, and $n' < n_p$ imply that $\pi(n')/n' + M(n') > \pi(n_p)/n_p + M(n_p)$. Hence, $E_g$ prefers $n'$ to $n_p$ by equation (4).
(b) Consider any $n' > n_p$. If $E_g$ prefers $n'$ to $n_p$, then $\pi(n')/n' + M(n') > \pi(n_p)/n_p + M(n_p)$ by equation (4). This result, A2, and $n' > n_p$ imply that $M(n') > M(n_p)$. Hence, $E_b$ prefers $n'$ to $n_p$ by equation (4).

### Proof of Proposition 2

*Sufficiency.* Suppose $\phi(n,\theta) \leq \phi(n_p,\theta)$ for all $n \leq n_p$. Set $\mu(n) = \theta$ for $n \leq n_p$ and $\mu(n) = 0$ for $n > n_p$. First, consider some upward deviation, $n' > n_p$. For any $n'$

$> n_p$, we have $M(n') = 0$ due to equation (3). However, $M(n_p) \geq 0$, so no upward deviation can be profitable for $E_b$ due to equation (4). Lemma 1(b) then implies that no upward deviation is profitable for $E_g$ either. Next, consider some downward deviation, $n' < n_p$. If no such deviation is profitable for $E_g$, then from Lemma 1(a) no such deviation is profitable for $E_b$ either. For any $n' < n_p$, $E_g$ has the payoff $\phi(n',\theta)$ due to equations (3), (4), and $\mu(n') = \theta$. But, at $n_p$, this agent has the payoff $\phi(n_p,\theta)$, where $\phi(n',\theta) \leq \phi(n_p,\theta)$, so no downward deviation can be profitable for $E_g$. Thus, $n_p$ can be supported by a pooling equilibrium. The payoffs are derived from equations (3) and (4).

*Necessity.* Suppose $\phi(n',\theta) > \phi(n_p,\theta)$ for some $n' < n_p$. $E_g$'s payoff from $n_p$ is $\phi(n_p,\theta)$. $E_g$'s payoff from $n'$ is $\pi(n')/n' + M(n') \geq \phi(n',\theta) > \phi(n_p,\theta)$, where the first inequality follows from equations (3), (4), and A3. Because a deviation to $n'$ is profitable for $E_g$, the choice $n_p$ cannot be supported by a pooling equilibrium consistent with A3.

## Proof of Lemma 2

From equation (4), the equilibrium payoffs of $E_b$ are $M(n_p^0)$ and $M(n_p^1)$. Using equation (3), A1, A2, and the Bayesian requirement $\mu(n_p^0) = \mu(n_p^1) = \theta$, we have $M(n_p^0) < M(n_p^1)$ whenever $n_p^0 < n_p^1$. The equilibrium payoffs of $E_g$ are $\phi(n_p^0,\theta)$ and $\phi(n_p^1,\theta)$. Because $n_p^1$ is supported by a PE, it satisfies the condition in Proposition 2, and hence $n_p^0 < n_p^1$ implies that $\phi(n_p^0,\theta) \leq \phi(n_p^1,\theta)$. Uninformed agents are indifferent between PE with $n_p^0$ and $n_p^1$ because they receive zero expected surplus in both cases.

## Proof of Proposition 3

Consider $\phi(n,\theta) \equiv \theta\pi(n) + (1 - \theta)\pi(n)/n$ as a function of $\theta$ for a fixed value of $n$. The resulting line $L_n$ has a left intercept $\pi(n)/n$ at $\theta = 0$, a right intercept $\pi(n)$ at $\theta = 1$, and the slope $\pi(n)(1 - 1/n)$. There are $N$ such lines corresponding to $n = 1 .. N$. Due to A1 and A2, lines with larger values of $n$ have steeper slopes (see Figure 10.2 for the case $N = 3$).

Since $L_1$ has the largest left intercept among all $L_n$, there is an interval $[0, \theta_a)$ on which $L_1$ lies above all $L_n$ with $n \geq 2$, where

$$\theta_a \equiv \text{the smallest } \theta \text{ such that } \phi(1,\theta) = \phi(n,\theta) \text{ for some } n \geq 2.$$

Whenever $N \geq 2$, we have $0 < \theta_a < 1$ because the right intercept of $L_N$ exceeds the right intercept of $L_1$ so that $L_1$ and $L_N$ intersect at an interior point $\theta \in (0, 1)$. By definition, $n^*(\theta) = 1$ is the unique maximizer of $\phi(n,\theta)$ with respect to $n$ at any $\theta \in [0, \theta_a)$. Moreover, $n^*(\theta) = 1$ is a maximizer (although not unique) at $\theta_a$. Now define

$A \equiv$ the largest $n \geq 2$ such that $\phi(1,\theta_a) = \phi(n,\theta_a)$.

Since the largest maximizer is selected at each $\theta$, it follows that $n^*(\theta_a) = A$.

Because the slopes of the lines $L_n$ are strictly increasing in $n$ and $\phi(n,\theta_a) \leq \phi(A,\theta_a)$ for all $n \leq A$, the lines $L_n$ for $n < A$ all lie strictly below the line $L_A$ on $(\theta_a,1]$. Thus, no $n < A$ is a candidate to maximize $\phi(n,\theta)$ with respect to $n$ at any $\theta \in (\theta_a,1]$. If $A = N$, then $\theta_a = \theta_z$ and this part of the proof is finished. If $A < N$, then observe that $\phi(n,\theta_a) < \phi(A,\theta_a)$ for all $n = A + 1 \,..\, N$. This follows because otherwise we contradict the definition of $\theta_a$ or $A$. Thus, there is an interval $(\theta_a,\theta_b)$ on which $L_A$ lies above all $L_n$ with $n \geq A + 1$, where

$\theta_b \equiv$ the smallest $\theta$ such that $\phi(A,\theta) = \phi(n,\theta)$ for some $n \geq A + 1$.

Whenever $N \geq A + 1$, we have $\theta_a < \theta_b < 1$ because the right intercept of $L_N$ exceeds the right intercept of $L_A$ so that $L_A$ and $L_N$ intersect at an interior point $\theta \in (\theta_a, 1)$. By definition, $n^*(\theta) = A$ is the unique maximizer of $\phi(n,\theta)$ with respect to $n$ at any $\theta \in (\theta_a, \theta_b)$. Moreover, $n^*(\theta) = A$ is a maximizer (although not unique) at $\theta_b$. Now define

$B \equiv$ the largest $n \geq A + 1$ such that $\phi(A,\theta_b) = \phi(n,\theta_b)$.

Since the largest maximizer is selected at each $\theta$, it follows that $n^*(\theta_b) = B$.

This procedure can be repeated as many times as necessary for $n = C, D \ldots$ At most there are $N - 1$ points of the form $\theta_a, \theta_b \,..\, \theta_z$ at which two or more $n$ are indifferent. Hence, at most there are $N$ intervals of the form $[0,\theta_a), [\theta_a,\theta_b), \,..\, [\theta_z,1]$. These have the property that $n^*(\theta) = 1$ is chosen on $[0,\theta_a)$, $n^*(\theta) = A$ is chosen on $[\theta_a,\theta_b)$, and so on, with $n^*(\theta) = N$ chosen on $[\theta_z,1]$. The structure of the proof ensures that $1 < A < B < C \,..\, < N$. The maximizer is unique in the interior of each interval and at the endpoints $\theta = 0$ and $\theta = 1$.

The function $V_g(\theta)$ is positive for all $\theta \in [0,1]$ due to A1; it is continuous because it is the maximum of continuous functions; it is nondecreasing because $\pi(n) \geq \pi(n)/n$ for all $n$; and it is convex because $\phi(n,\theta)$ is linear in $\theta$ when $n$ is held constant, but optimal adjustments in $n$ might yield a larger payoff as $\theta$ varies. The payoff for $E_g$ follows from equation (4), the fact that $E_g$ receives $\phi(n_p,\theta)$ in any PE, and the fact that $n_p = n^*(\theta)$ is set for each $\theta \in [0, 1]$. The payoff for $E_b$ is obtained by substituting $n^*(\theta)$ and $\mu(n^*(\theta)) = \theta$ in equation (4). This payoff is increasing due to A1, A2, and the fact that $n^*(\theta)$ is nondecreasing.

## NOTE

1  Comments on previous drafts were provided by Saul Estrin and members of the Association for Comparative Economic Studies, the International Association for Employee Participation, and the Alberta Industrial Organization Workshop. The Social Sciences and Humanities Research Council of Canada provided financial support.

## REFERENCES

Arifovic, Jasmina, and B. Curtis Eaton. 1995. 'Coordination via Genetic Learning.' *Computational Economics* 8 (3): 181–203.
–  1998. 'The Evolution of Communication in a Sender/Receiver Game of Common Interest with Cheap Talk.' *Journal of Economic Dynamics and Control* 22 (8-9): 1187–207.
Ben-Ner, Avner, W. Allen Burns, Gregory Dow, and Louis Putterman. 2000. 'Employee Ownership: An Empirical Exploration.' In *The New Relationship: Human Capital in the American Corporation*, edited by Margaret M. Blair and Thomas A. Kochan. Washington, DC: Brookings Institution.
Ben-Ner, Avner, Tzu-Shian Han, and Derek C. Jones. 1996. 'The Productivity Effects of Employee Participation in Control and in Economic Returns: A Review of Empirical Evidence.' In *Democracy and Efficiency in the Economic Enterprise*, edited by Ugo Pagano and Robert Rowthorn. New York: Routledge.
Binmore, Ken, Ariel Rubinstein, and Asher Wolinsky. 1996. 'The Nash Bargaining Solution in Economic Modeling.' *RAND Journal of Economics* 17 (2): 176–88.
Doucouliagos, Chris. 1995. 'Worker Participation and Productivity in Labor-Managed Firms and Participatory Capitalist Firms: A Meta-Analysis.' *Industrial and Labor Relations Review* 49 (1): 58–77.
Dow, Gregory K. 1988. 'Information, Production Decisions, and Intra-firm Bargaining.' *International Economic Review* 29 (1): 57–79.
–  1989. 'Knowledge Is Power: Informational Precommitment in the Capitalist Firm.' *European Journal of Political Economy* 5 (2/3): 161–76.
–  2003. *Governing the Firm: Workers' Control in Theory and Practice*. New York: Cambridge University Press.

– Forthcoming. 'Partnership Markets with Adverse Selection.' *Review of Economic Design.*

Pencavel, John. 2001. *Worker Participation: Lessons from the Worker Co-ops of the Pacific Northwest.* New York: Russell Sage Foundation.

Pérotin, Virginie, and Andrew Robinson. 2000. 'Employee Participation and Equal Opportunities Practices: Productivity Effect and Potential Complementarities.' *British Journal of Industrial Relations* 38 (4): 557–83.

Robinson, Andrew M., and Nicholas Wilson. 2006. 'Employee Financial Participation and Productivity: An Empirical Reappraisal.' *British Journal of Industrial Relations* 44 (1): 31–50.

# 11 Signalling Risk Tolerance: Nuclear Arsenals and Alliance Formation in the Cold War[1]

CLIFF T. BEKAR, GREGORY K. DOW, CLYDE G. REED, AND JOSHUA STINE

According to deterrence theory, the most important function of nuclear arsenals is to ensure that they are never used.[2] To achieve deterrence, a state must possess a deterrent arsenal and the credibility to launch it. There is no deterrent value in the accumulation of additional warheads once a state has: (a) threatened the utter destruction of any potential enemy via a nuclear strike; (b) achieved a desirable force mix (in terms of the types and deployment of warheads); and (c) achieved a guaranteed redundant strike capability. Explaining the size of nuclear arsenals would seem to be a straightforward application of deterrence theory.

During the Cold War, both the United States and the former Soviet Union held arsenals far in excess of that predicted by deterrence theory. The launch of even a fraction of either arsenal represented a wholly unacceptable cost to any nation that might initiate a nuclear exchange.[3] At their peaks, the arsenals of both countries represented enough destructive capacity to threaten the future of the planet many times over. It appears that both superpowers overinvested in nuclear arsenals, in the sense that the return on the marginal warhead was negative (and large).[4] Each nation's arsenal exceeded that of a deterrent by an order of magnitude. This was no small mistake.[5]

How is it that, in the high-stakes game of the Cold War, both superpowers reached such a poor allocation of their scarce defence resources? Since such large overinvestment is difficult to reconcile with rational decision-making, most explanations attribute some form of irrationality to superpower states.[6] This is not our approach. One theme of Curtis Eaton's early work with Richard Lipsey (Eaton and Lipsey 1979) focused on the rational overinvestment in capital by firms – relative to their profit-maximizing level of capital – in order to barricade markets credibly. Our analysis builds on this insight, modelling a superpower's incentive to overinvest in nuclear arsenals. We propose a model in which superpowers use nuclear arsenals to signal their willingness to play risky brinkmanship games on the behalf of themselves and their client states. In this framework, an overinvestment in nuclear arsenals is the equilibrium outcome of rational play.

Throughout the Cold War, both superpowers, as potential hegemons, sought to expand their spheres of influence around the globe. One way to achieve this objective was to establish alliance systems made up of explicit military agreements (NATO, the Warsaw Pact), as well as political and economic commitments. An important challenge facing the superpowers was how to convince allies to sublimate their short-run interests to those of the alliance in exchange for the promise of a nonbinding security arrangement (see Morrow 1994): when a threat emerges, it might be in a superpower's short-term interest simply to renege on the security arrangement (see Kydd 2005, chap 2). Knowing this, the minor power would be reluctant to join, and the alliance would become fragile or fail to form altogether. In this environment, the major power would value the ability to signal credibly its willingness to intervene. Investment in redundantly large nuclear stockpiles served as such a signalling device.

### Nuclear Arsenals during the Cold War

During the late 1940s, the United States held an arsenal that was fewer than a thousand warheads. The Soviets probably held fewer than a thousand warheads until the early to mid-1960s. Both arsenals grew dramatically during the height of the Cold War (see Figure 11.1).

Using an estimate of around 400 warheads for a deterrent arsenal (see the assumption below), both sides persistently overinvested in scarce defence resources for decades. Even using an extreme upper-bound estimate (about 1,000 warheads), the United States overinvested starting in the late 1950s, the Soviets starting in the late 1960s. The arsenals were so large (relative to deterrent requirements) for so long that, as McKinzie et al. conclude, 'The unconstrained U.S.-Soviet nuclear arms race that actually occurred did not derive from any analysis of the size of an arsenal needed for deterrence' (2001, 22). The scope of the arsenals was such that, by any calculation, both superpowers held arsenals far larger than predicted by classical deterrence theory (see Gay and Pearson 1987).

### Deterrence Arsenals: When Is Enough, Enough?

For conventional arsenals, deterrence is best viewed in relative terms: the ratio of one's own forces to those of the enemy. Broadly speaking, states with dramatic numerical superiority in conventional armaments are better able to

Figure 11.1: U.S. and Soviet Strategic Warheads, 1945–2001

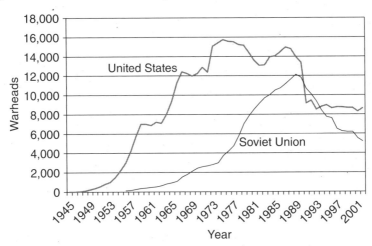

Source: Figure 11.1 is derived from estimates presented by McKinzie et al. (2001) (work done at the Natural Resources Defense Council). These estimates include strategic warheads (excluding tactical theatre-based warheads) based in silos, submarines, and bombers.

deter attack than those without, but this is not the case with nuclear weapons. Jervis (1979-80, 618) notes: 'it does not matter which side has more nuclear weapons. In the past, having a larger army than one's neighbor allowed one to conquer it and protect one's own population. Having a larger nuclear stockpile yields no such gains. *Deterrence comes from having enough weapons to destroy the other's cities; this capability is an absolute, not a relative one'* (emphasis added) (see also Jervis 1984; Brodie 1946, 1978).

Former U.S. defense secretary Robert McNamara argued that deterrence was achieved when the United States could credibly threaten 25 per cent of the Soviet population. This goal could have been met with remarkably few warheads: '400 one megaton warheads delivered on Soviet cities, so as to maximize fatalities, would destroy 40 per cent of the urban population and nearly 30 per cent of the population of the entire nation ... If the number of delivered warheads were doubled to 800, the proportion of the total population destroyed would be increased by only three percentage points' (McNamara, quoted in Schwartz 1998, 115).

As the quote suggests, the theoretical idea of an efficient deterrent arsenal has an engineering counterpart. Past some point, delivered megatonnage suffers from severe diminishing returns in producing effective megatonnage. This is known as 'McNamara's knee,' named for the pronounced kink in the curve tracing the destructive capacity of delivered megatonnage.[7] Taking

McNamara's deterrence objective as their benchmark, McKinzie et al. (2001), in a detailed study employing new simulation techniques and geographic information system software, find that 51 warheads would deter Russia, 368 would deter China, 300 would deter all of the NATO member countries, 124 the United States,[8] and 11 Canada. Adding up the total of all the countries in the sample (14 countries plus NATO), it would take 1,000 warheads to 'deter the world.'

Perhaps the goal was not just deterrence but strategic flexibility. According to this argument, the relative size of a nuclear arsenal might matter if it buys sufficient countervalue attack or escalation dominance (for a rebuttal of this argument, however, see Jervis 1984, chaps 3, 5). But analysis of modern first-strike or countervalue capabilities implies that only a small fraction of the U.S. arsenal was needed to inflict major damage to the Soviet state in any strategic scenario (see especially McKinzie et al. 2001). Nuclear arsenals of more than 12,000 warheads at the height of the Cold War were excessive relative to all strategic possibilities, including a nested series of second- and third-strike options. After a second strike, there would be nothing of strategic value left to bomb.

*The Expense of Arsenals*

The overinvestment by both superpowers was also excessive in terms of budget expenditures. Nuclear arsenals have very high fixed (development) costs and are also subject to high variable costs, especially with the introduction of the nuclear triad (warheads in silos, on continuously deployed submarines, and on continuously deployed bombers). Estimates of the initial costs to the United States of developing a nuclear capability range from US$3 billion to US$5 billion (in 1996 dollars). Estimates of the costs of upkeep and maintenance from 1940 to 1996 put the total cost at US$5.4 trillion. In comparison, the total expenditure over the same period for Medicare was US$2.3 trillion, and for transportation and transportation infrastructure US$1.7 trillion. Over the period 1940 to 1996, expenditures on nuclear arsenals were the U.S. government's third-largest budget item, behind only broader measures of national defence and social security.

**Existing Explanations**

Given the importance of the issue, the theoretical literature explicitly concerned with modelling the size of nuclear arsenals is surprisingly small. Here, we review some standard explanations for excessive arsenals.

*Natural Arms Race Dynamics*

Some analysts believe that arsenal size really needs no explanation. They view overinvestment as the natural by-product of a spiralling arms race with positive feedback effects. Theoretically, however, such explanations are on shaky ground. To the extent that positive feedback models are designed to capture increasing returns to arsenal size, they are fundamentally at odds with the nature of nuclear war (and 'McNamara's knee'). The standard spiral model does not explain where the positive feedback originates, nor does it predict stopping points. In the presence of positive feedback over the relevant range, arsenals produced by a spiralling arms race should grow without limit. Generating a stopping point requires some form of braking effect, typically modelled as a state's decreased ability to support spending as arsenal sizes grow as a fraction of gross domestic product (GDP). In the first model, arsenals grow without limit; in the second, they grow at the rate of GDP growth.

Explanations that invoke an unconstrained spiral of arms spending need to account for the empirical fact that, in fact, Cold War arsenals did not grow without limit – that the arsenals of both superpowers displayed a high degree of stability. Further, if arsenals were purely a function of Cold War arms race dynamics, it is difficult to explain why there has not been a more significant decline in the destructive capacity of current arsenals. Lastly, this type of explanation fails to explain why the United States held a larger arsenal than did the Soviets and why other key actors in the Cold War failed to overinvest to the same extent as did the superpowers.

*Irrational Actors*

Were the nuclear superpowers irrational? Jervis (1984) attributes the tendency of military analysts to think about deterrent arsenals in relative terms to a category error that conflates nuclear and conventional arsenals (see also Cimbala 1998). Other potential sources of 'irrationality' include the possibility that an enemy might be willing to sacrifice people at a faster rate, that it might seek status rather than deterrence (the 'peacock theory' of excessive arsenals), or that a state suffers a specific error in perception concerning either its own capabilities or those of others (see, for example, Erickson 1982).

These types of explanations are problematic for at least two reasons. First, they do not constitute an explanation in the sense of producing well-defined predictions about the relative size of nuclear arsenals. Irrational decision-making is theoretically consistent with almost any level of arsenal and is thus extremely hard to test. While it may be true that problematic modes of analysis have contributed to the conception of U.S. and Soviet nuclear policy, it is a large step to argue that a systematic form of irrationality permeated the entire decision-making apparatus of both countries, especially when the particular form of irrationality is (allegedly) easy to diagnose. The nuclear arsenals of both sides represented, by a large margin, their single-largest military budget item. The disposition and management of these nuclear arsenals absorbed an enormous amount of human capital and has been the subject of much scrutiny by the military, policymakers, and academics. In view of all this, it is difficult to imagine that extreme forms of resource misallocation would have gone unnoticed.

Second, even when a specific form of irrationality is modelled and, therefore, specific predictions made, such theories have difficulty explaining the facts. One would need to believe that the United States and the Soviet Union were relatively more susceptible to irrational tendencies than the other nuclear powers. Or, on the other hand, that they suffered sustained mistakes in decision-making due to their position as superpowers. Some have argued, for example, that the United States displayed an irrational need to maintain its reputation of hawkishness. But it seems more likely that states with smaller arsenals would be most concerned with being credibly hawkish.

*Rational Actors Facing Uncertainty*

The arms race was beset with technological uncertainty. One could misjudge the rate of an enemy's technological advance, how many warheads might survive a first strike, which countries might be involved in an exchange, or how the various elements of the nuclear delivery system would perform in an actual exchange.

A specific example of uncertainty in the efficacy of the delivery system is the possibility that significant numbers of military personnel might find it psychologically impossible to launch missiles that might destroy the world. Thus, very large numbers of warheads/launchers would be needed to guarantee nuclear credibility. Evidence of this concern is reflected in the highly publicized slogan 'better dead than red' during the 1950s, after the Soviets were known to have nuclear capabilities. However, the fact that arsenal inventories were unaffected by a series of innovations surrounding automated launching mechanisms argues against this explanation. Further, it is again hard to see why the superpowers were uniquely susceptible to this problem.

Undoubtedly, portions of both superpowers' arsenals can be explained by the need to hedge against uncertainties of all types. Risk considerations also imply that increases in the predicted rates of warhead survivability should be associated with reductions in the size of arsenals (relative to prior periods). Thus, the advent of the U.S., and then Soviet, nuclear triads should have decreased the size of both arsenals. Further, the Soviets should have held a larger arsenal relative to the United States since they relied more on relatively vulnerable land-based warheads. The evidence contradicts these predictions.

*Insurance*

The seemingly large mistake of overinvesting actually might have been small if nuclear arsenals constituted a form of cheap insurance, with 'cheapness' resulting from potential economies of scale in the holding of nuclear arsenals, the perceived 'bang for the buck' of nuclear weapons, or the perceived uncertainties of the arms race – for example, some argue that, since the United States and its NATO allies persistently lagged behind the Warsaw Pact in terms of conventional arsenals, they substituted into nuclear arsenals.[9] But nuclear arsenals did not provide cheap insurance.

First, up to a point it may well be rational to substitute out of conventional arms into nuclear arms,[10] but redundant warheads are poor substitutes for scarce conventional arms. The idea that large arsenals are able to provide insurance is based on the argument that the relative size of nuclear arsenals matters. To use Jervis's construction, as long as one's 'cities are hostage,' an insurance arsenal is an absolute concept (1984; see also Brodie 1946).

Second, nuclear weapons were expensive. Schwartz (1998) estimates that '[s]ince the government first began work on the atomic bomb in 1940, the U.S. nuclear arsenal has cost about [US]$4 trillion in 1995 dollars – or approximately three times more...than was spent on procurement for all of World War II.' At least one dollar in four of defence spending went toward nuclear weaponry.

*Bankrupting the Soviet Union*

Scholars of the Cold War argue that, in their attempt to keep pace with the United States on the nuclear front, the Soviets' spending ultimately contributed to their collapse. Perhaps the United States deliberately overspent in order to bankrupt the Soviets. Today, some Russian policy-makers argue that their economy cannot afford to maintain a strategic triad (land-, air-, and water-based warheads). Given the expense of water- and air-based warheads, Russia ultimately might move to a strategic dyad. Others note that Russia cannot even afford to maintain the land-based missiles bargained for under the START III agreement. In fact, Russia currently has difficulty securing its existing arsenal from plunder.

A major problem with this explanation is that it is difficult to understand why the Soviets would choose to play the 'deep pockets' game when it was clear they would lose. We can motivate such a decision in a signalling framework through their need to maintain and expand their sphere of influence through signalling efforts. In this view, bankrupting the Soviet Union is seen not as a strategic cause for excessive nuclear arsenals, but as a by-product of alliance formation.

### Rent Seeking by the Military-Industrial Complex

Another class of explanations concerns rent-seeking behaviour. The hypothesis is simply that those who stood to gain the most from spending on nuclear weapons captured their governments' decision-making apparatus and overinvested as a way to transfer resources to themselves. This explanation has the desired characteristic of rendering the size of nuclear arsenals beyond the logic of deterrence. It might also explain the relative size of the arsenals. Given relatively similar problems with rent seeking, the United States, with its larger economy than that of the Soviet Union, would produce a larger arsenal.

As an explanation of overinvestment, however, rent seeking faces a major theoretical challenge. It does not explain how the various actors coordinated to control and corrupt nuclear budgets. Moreover, there were far more efficient ways to transfer rents. For example, it is unclear why rent seeking would manifest as an inflation of highly visible warhead counts as opposed to hidden markups, redundant reinforcement of silos, or other military expenditures. Moreover, rent seeking cannot explain adequately why the superpowers would be so reluctant to give up existing missiles. Given the costs of deconstruction, there presumably was as much money to be made by the replacement of existing warheads. Finally, rent seeking fails to explain why the superpowers were uniquely plagued with this specific form of rent seeking while secondary nuclear powers were not. Were the United Kingdom and France somehow more resistant to 'nuclear corruption'?

### Our Explanation

Our story starts with the desire of both superpowers during the Cold War to build military/political/economic alliances. We assert that such alliances had a high payoff to members in the form of military security; diplomatic benefits (such as votes in the United Nations and other international bodies); access to powerful punishment/reward mechanisms via trade, diplomacy, and limited military action; and the economic advantages of being part of a large trading network.

But were these payoffs high enough to compensate for the enormous expense of excessive arsenals? Consider the costs both superpowers were willing to endure in order to protect and subsidize relatively minor states within their sphere of influence. The United States fought two very costly wars in Asia (Korea, Vietnam) on the theory that marginal states have a very large value (the domino theory); on the same basis, the Soviet Union fought an extremely costly war in Afghanistan. Both superpowers expended vast resources on (almost constant) proxy wars and other 'low-intensity' conflicts in order to preserve their spheres of influence. Further, consider the cost to a superpower of not leading an alliance. In our view, the Soviet Union persisted in indulging huge expenditures on its nuclear arsenal even after it had to have been aware that such expenditures were not sustainable in the long run. Why? We suspect it was because the cost of being isolated militarily, politically, and economically was so large that its existence as an independent state was compromised.

For client states to enter into such alliances (or, in the case of the involuntary aspects of the Soviet empire, to cooperate fully in the alliance), they had to give up some freedom over a range of political, economic, and military decisions. They were willing to do this in return for a promise of intervention in the future on behalf of the client state. The most obvious source of intervention was a brinkmanship response to demands from the other superpower.

Given this context, we focus on two problems for superpowers. The first was how to eliminate competition from nonsuperpowers in alliance formation. Excessive nuclear arsenals solved this problem because they were so expensive that only superpowers could afford them. The second problem was how to make their promise of future brinkmanship intervention credible. Here we see a signalling role for excessive nuclear arsenals. Large arsenals are dangerous because of the possibility of accidental launch, or purposeful launch by a 'Dr. Strangelove' type. The history of the Cold War contains a number of instances of close calls to full nuclear exchange or some lesser nuclear incident (see, for example, Little 1998; Lloyd 2002; Bevins 2004). We argue that this aspect of excessive arsenals demonstrated a willingness to tolerate risk that, in turn, signalled a willingness to engage in risky brinkmanship. Put another way, since a large buildup of nuclear weapons also increases the probability of total nuclear war, brinkmanship types can credibly signal with excessive arsenals that they are less likely to back down in situations when a conflict (nuclear or otherwise) is a possibility.[11]

Reputation through repeated play is another potential mechanism for establishing such a commitment. We do not pursue this alternative, however, for several reasons. Morgan (1985, 131) notes, 'the fact is that where nuclear weapons might have to be involved in upholding a commitment, *there are no intrinsic interests of sufficient value to make that commitment inherently credible*...States may be quite capable of fighting nuclear wars... but one cannot learn from the past behavior of these states just when they will' (emphasis in original). Moreover, for a reputation to produce credibility, all players in the game must agree on a common interpretation of a given history (see Nalebuff 1988; Morrow 1994).

The hypothesis that excessive nuclear arsenals were a signal of high risk tolerance implies that the signal was both sent and received. It is revealing in this regard that, while most aspects of each superpower's military capabilities were closely guarded secrets, the size of the nuclear arsenal was not.[12] Indeed, each superpower shared knowledge about the number of warheads with its adversary. They further undertook to maintain agreements that made the size of their arsenals public knowledge. However, they were not so forthcoming with the qualitative characteristics of their arsenals (survivability, quality of targeting, and so on). In addition, both powers actively sought talks over their arsenals. These negotiations were very effective in revealing the minimum number of warheads each superpower held without achieving the stated goal of reducing those warheads. In our view, the talks can be interpreted as a mechanism to broadcast the 'excessive nuclear arsenal' signal.

Finally, the nuclear arsenals were not characterized exclusively by sunk costs. Maintaining a triad delivery system was a major part of the cost. We hypothesize that one purpose of both NORAD and NATO was to signal credibly to alliance members that the United States was continuing to incur these expenses.

## A Formal Model of the Deterrence Game

Here, we consider a game involving three players: an entrepreneurial state (E), a rival hegemon (R), and an unaligned state (U). As explained above, E would benefit by having U join an alliance. U would do so if it were convinced that joining the alliance would not trigger an attack by R. Both U and R have incomplete information about E's preferences, which might be either hard line (more willing to take risks) or soft line (less willing).

## Figure 11.2: Game Tree

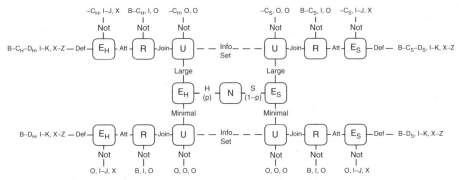

Note: all payoff vectors in the game tree have the form (E, U, R).

**Entrepreneur:**
$B$ = benefit of an alliance with U;
$C_H$ = cost of large arsenal to the hard liner;
$C_S$ = cost of large arsenal to the soft liner;
$D_H$ = cost of conflict to the hard liner; and
$D_S$ = cost of conflict to the soft liner;
    where $B - D_S < 0 < B - D_H$.

**Unaligned:**
$I$ = benefit of an alliance with E;
$J$ = cost of an attack from R when undefended by E; and
$K$ = cost of an attack from R when defended by E;
    where $I - J, I - K < 0 < I$.

**Rival:**
$X$ = benefit of an attack on U; and
$Z$ = cost of an attack when U is defended by E;
    where $X - Z < 0 < X$.

The game unfolds in two stages: a *signalling* stage and a *conflict* stage (see Figure 11.2). The signalling stage begins with a move by nature (N), which makes the entrepreneurial state hard line with probability $p$ and soft line with probability $1 - p$. E knows its own preferences once they are determined by nature, but the other players do not. U and R do, however, know the prior probability $p$ (or have a common belief about it). After E's type is determined, E builds a nuclear arsenal, which might be either large (more than is needed to deter a direct attack by R) or minimal (just enough to deter a direct attack). Everyone observes the resulting arsenal size.

The game then moves to the conflict stage. U must now choose whether or not to join E's alliance. If U does not join, the game ends and all three players receive their appropriate payoffs (this might involve incorporation of U into R's sphere of influence). If U does join, R decides whether or not to attack U. If R does not attack, again the game is over and payoffs are received. Finally, if R attacks, E decides whether or not to defend U. In each case, the players receive their associated payoffs.

The conflict stage plays out starting from whichever of the four possible branches arose during the signalling stage. Although U and R do not observe directly which branch occurred, they might draw inferences about E's type from E's arsenal size. In turn, these inferences might affect their beliefs about what E will do if faced with a decision about whether or not to defend U later in the game.

We make the following payoff assumptions about the conflict stage:

- $E_H$ (the hard type) will defend U in the event of an attack by R;
- $E_S$ (the soft type) will not defend U in the event of an attack by R;
- R will attack if E will not defend U;
- R will not attack if E will defend U;
- U will join E's alliance if joining leads to no attack by R; and
- U will not join E's alliance if joining leads to an attack by R (whether or not E subsequently defends U).

Thus, if R believes that E is hard line for sure, R will not attack; but if R believes that E is soft line for sure, R will attack. Let $\pi$ be the probability that R assigns to a hard-line E at the point where R makes a decision. It follows from our payoff assumptions that there is a threshold probability of a hard-line E (call it $\pi^*$) such that, if $\pi < \pi^*$, then R will attack, but if $\pi > \pi^*$, then R will not attack. The numerical value of $\pi^*$ depends on R's payoffs but, under our assumptions, $0 < \pi^* < 1$ must hold. For simplicity, we ignore boundary cases where the players are indifferent between actions (as when $\pi = \pi^*$).

U and R have identical beliefs at the conflict stage because they have the same prior probability ($p$) of a hard-line E, and they make the same observations about E's arsenal size. Let $\pi(L)$ be the probability that U and R assign to a hard-line E if they observe a large arsenal, and let $\pi(M)$ be the probability that they assign to a hard-line E if they see a minimal arsenal. In equilibrium, these beliefs must be consistent with E's actual behaviour. For example, if a hard-line E chooses $L$ at the node $E_H$ and a soft-line E chooses $M$ at the node $E_S$, then, at the conflict stage, U and R must set $\pi(L) = 1$ and $\pi(M) = 0$.

Next, we move back to the signalling stage and consider E's choice of an arsenal size. It is convenient to treat the hard-line and soft-line versions of E as separate players, so call them $E_H$ and $E_S$ (these players move at the respective nodes shown in Figure 11.2). Let $C_H$ be the cost to $E_H$ of the additional risk of accidental nuclear war from a large stockpile and let $C_S$ be the corresponding cost to $E_S$. We assume that E types that are more willing to intervene on behalf of an ally are also more willing to tolerate the risk of an accidental nuclear exchange ($C_H < C_S$).

Recall that we are interpreting $M$ to be the minimal stockpile that deters a direct nuclear attack by R. We assume that both $E_H$ and $E_S$ want at least this large an arsenal, and both are willing to tolerate the associated risk of accidental war. Therefore, all that matters in the model is the added risk in going from $M$ to $L$. We ignore purely financial costs of building an arsenal larger than the minimum because willingness to incur such costs does not signal anything about whether E would intervene to save U from R.

Let $B$ be the benefit to E from having U join an alliance. We assume this is the same regardless of E's type (hard line or soft line). In general, there could be many U nations, and $B$ would then be the aggregate value of having all of these nations join, rather than none. The model is uninteresting if $B < C_H < C_S$ because then neither type of E would choose $L$, since the benefit from an alliance would be too small relative to the cost of using $L$ as a signal, even for a hard liner. We assume $C_H < B$ in what follows.

There are two possible kinds of equilibria for the game: *separating equilibrium* (SE), where $E_H$ and $E_S$ choose different arsenal sizes, and *pooling equilibrium* (PE), where $E_H$ and $E_S$ choose the same arsenal size. We consider only pure-strategy equilibria (we discuss mixed-strategy equilibria briefly at the end of this section).

*Separation*

The intuitive kind of SE is where $E_H$ chooses $L$ (the large arsenal) and $E_S$ chooses $M$ (the minimal arsenal). In this case, $\pi(M) = 0 < \pi^* < 1 = \pi(L)$, where $\pi^*$ is the deterrence threshold described earlier. This implies that $E_H$ gets the benefit $B$ at the cost $C_H$ (U joins the alliance if a large arsenal is observed), while $E_S$ does not enjoy $B$ but also incurs no cost (U does not join if a minimal arsenal is observed).

This is an equilibrium if and only if (a) $E_H$ does not want to deviate by switching to a minimal arsenal and (b) $E_S$ does not want to deviate by switching to a large arsenal. First consider (a). If $E_H$ imitates $E_S$ by choosing $M$, $E_H$ will forego the alliance benefit $B$ because R and U will believe (incorrectly) that $E_H$ is soft. Therefore, R is no longer deterred and U will not join. Since $C_H < B$ by assumption, this cannot be profitable for $E_H$. Next consider (b). If $E_S$ imitates $E_H$ by choosing $L$, $E_S$ gains the benefit $B$ because R and U will believe (incorrectly) that $E_S$ is hard. Therefore, R is now deterred and U joins. But the cost of this to $E_S$ is $C_S$. Such a SE exists if and only if $B < C_S$.

For completeness, we need to consider the possibility of a counterintuitive SE in which the hard-line E chooses the minimal arsenal and the soft-line E chooses the large arsenal. It is easy to show that this cannot be an equilibrium. In this case, we would need to have $\pi(M) = 1$ because, in equilibrium, the hard liner is choosing $M$ and the beliefs of U and R must be consistent with E's equilibrium behaviour. But then $E_S$ could imitate $E_H$ by switching to the minimal arsenal, which deters R, induces U to join, and lowers the risk of accidental war. Such a deviation is clearly profitable for the soft-line type.

*Pooling*

There are two candidates for PE: one where both types choose the large arsenal and another where both types choose the minimal arsenal. In each case, U and R gain no information about E's true type by observing its arsenal, but must rely on their prior beliefs (hence, $\pi = p$ whenever the equilibrium arsenal size is observed). We need to consider two possibilities: (a) $p < \pi^*$, so that the prior probability of a hard-line type is not high enough to deter R from attacking U; and (b) $p > \pi^*$, so that the prior probability of a hard-line type is high enough to deter such an attack.

First, we show that, in case (a), no PE can exist. Suppose both $E_H$ and $E_S$ choose $L$. Because $p < \pi^*$, R is not deterred and U does not join, so neither E type gets the alliance benefit $B$. Either $E_H$ or $E_S$ (or both) could deviate to $M$. The resulting benefit cannot be lower (U might or might not join if arsenal size $M$ is observed), but E avoids the cost of a large stockpile. Thus, the deviation is profitable, and this is not an equilibrium.

Now, suppose both $E_H$ and $E_S$ choose $M$. Again, R is not deterred and U does not join, so neither E type gets $B$. However, the hard-line $E_H$ can deviate to a large arsenal $L$. Under the quite reasonable assumption that this disequilibrium behaviour induces U and R to hold the belief $\pi(L) = 1$ (that E is hard line for sure), this deters R. Therefore, $E_H$ gets the benefit $B$ at a cost $C_H$. Since we earlier assumed $C_H < B$, this is profitable, and we do not have an equilibrium.

Therefore, a PE exists only in case (b), where $p > \pi^*$. Now R is deterred and U joins. If both $E_S$ and $E_H$ choose $M$, this provides E with the alliance benefit $B$ at no cost beyond that of the minimal arsenal. This is an equilibrium because neither type can gain by deviating to $L$, which has costs but provides no additional benefit.

If both $E_H$ and $E_S$ choose $L$ in equilibrium, it is reasonable to assume that, in a disequilibrium situation where U and R observe the minimal arsenal $M$, these players hold the belief $\pi(M) = 0$. That is, if both types are expected to build large arsenals but E unexpectedly builds a small one, other nations infer that E is soft line. Under this assumption about disequilibrium beliefs, $E_H$ will not deviate to $M$ because this will fail to deter R and U will no longer join the alliance. $E_H$ thus loses $B$ and saves only the cost $C_H < B$. Such a deviation cannot be profitable. $E_S$ finds it profitable to switch to $M$ if and only if $B < C_S$ (the benefit from the alliance is less than the cost of a large arsenal). A PE with large arsenals, therefore, exists in case (b) if and only if $C_S < B$.

*Equilibrium Outcomes*

Table 11.1 summarizes our results, showing the equilibria that can arise for each combination of parameter values (bearing in mind that we assume $C_H < C_S$ throughout, and that we exclude the case $B < C_H$ because it can never lead to large arsenals).

The 'no equilibrium' result in the lower left cell of Table 11.1 arises because SE can occur only in the top row, where $C_H < B < C_S$, while PE can occur only in the right column, where $p > \pi^*$. Together, SE and PE exhaust all of the possibilities for an equilibrium involving pure strategies. Therefore, any equilibrium in the lower left cell must involve the use of mixed strategies. We do not pursue this issue further here.

An important implication of the model is that excessive nuclear arsenals are possible whenever a pure-strategy equilibrium exists. This investment can take different forms depending on the payoffs and the prior beliefs of the players. In the top row, a large arsenal can occur only via a separating equilibrium where the hard liner builds a large arsenal but the soft liner does not. In the top left cell, such separation must occur (the equilibrium is unique), while in the top right cell, it is one of two possibilities (the other being deterrence through the creation of minimal arsenals by both types). In the lower right cell, there are again two equilibria, but now both involve pooling. When overinvestment occurs (the PEL outcome), both types pursue this strategy.

Another important implication of the model is that equilibrium can be inefficient. Consider the lower right cell. Here, both kinds of PE exist. In one case, both hard liners and soft liners build small arsenals (PEM); in the

Table 11.1
Pure-Strategy Equilibria for the Deterrence Game

|  |  | Prior Beliefs | |
| --- | --- | --- | --- |
|  |  | $p < \pi^*$ | $p > \pi^*$ |
| Payoffs | $C_H < B < C_S$ | SE | SE or PEM |
|  | $C_S < B$ | no equilibrium | PEM or PEL |

SE =   separating equilibrium, where the hard liner builds a large
        arsenal and the soft liner builds a minimal arsenal.
PEM =  pooling equilibrium, where both types build minimal arsenals.
PEL =  pooling equilibrium, where both types build large arsenals.

other case, both build large arsenals (PEL). In each situation, deterrence is achieved and U joins the alliance, so the payoffs to R and U are identical in the two equilibria. Moreover, in both equilibria, E benefits from having U join the alliance. But PEL involves a higher risk of accidental nuclear war than PEM because E's stockpile is larger in the former case.

Despite this unnecessary risk, it is possible for the players to get stuck in the bad PEL equilibrium. Starting from this situation, if E were to deviate to a lower stockpile, both U and R would infer that E must be soft. As a result, deterrence would collapse. U would conclude correctly that joining the alliance would lead to an attack by R, and therefore it would not join. E thus would have to weigh the loss of an alliance with U against the reduced risk of accidental nuclear war. If the benefits to E from an alliance with U were large enough (consider the case where there are many similar unaligned nations), even a genuinely soft-line E would not want to appear soft. Instead, a soft liner would emulate the risky policies of a hard liner.

**Concluding Remarks**

Models that focus on deterrence dramatically underpredict the size of U.S. and Soviet arsenals during the Cold War. The degree of the two countries' overinvestment in nuclear warheads was vast and persistent. We argued that existing explanations fail to explain adequately the historical evolution of U.S. and Soviet arsenals, and we proposed an explanation that focuses on excessive arsenals as a signal to client states in a collective security alliance. Our model offers a consistent explanation for some of the most important stylized facts concerning nuclear arsenals during the Cold War (and beyond).

Specifically, the model predicts that only potential hegemons (superpowers) will hold excess arsenals since they have a unique incentive (and ability) to establish and maintain political, economic, and military alliances. The model also helps to explain why arsenals grew so large, but did not grow without bound. The model sheds light on why the superpowers were uniquely eager to share data regarding the size of their arsenals – in contrast, Israel has yet to confirm its possession of nuclear warheads – but simultaneously kept secret most of the qualitative characteristics of those arsenals. The model also suggests why the United States held a larger arsenal than the Soviet Union. As a representative democracy, it might have had more difficulty persuading both friends and foes that it was committed to intervening on behalf of its allies. In order to compensate, the U.S. political leadership needed to send a more convincing nuclear signal about its willingness to take military risks.

Currently, China holds a deterrent-sized nuclear arsenal. With its rise as a potential hegemon challenging the United States, we expect China to increase the size of its nuclear arsenal dramatically in an effort to increase its sphere of influence and to avoid diplomatic and economic isolation.

## NOTES

1 We thank Curt Eaton, Eban Goodstein, Richard Lipsey, Bob Mandel, and all of the conference participants. We also thank Lewis and Clark College for support in the form of a faculty/student research grant. We accept responsibility for all shortcomings.

2 The classic reference for this position is Brodie (1946): 'Thus far the chief purpose of our military establishment has been to win wars. From now on its chief purpose must be to avert them. It can have almost no other useful purpose' (76).

3 According to McKinzie et al. (2001, x), 'in excess of 50 million casualties could be inflicted upon Russia in a "limited" countervalue attack. That attack [would use] less than three percent of the current U.S. nuclear forces, which includes over 7,000 strategic nuclear warheads.'

4 See, for example, Bundy (1969); Jervis (1979-80); Jervis, Lebow, and Stein (1985); Jervis et al. (1990); Schwartz (1998); and McKinzie et al. (2001).

5 See Schwartz (1998) for a thorough summary of this literature; see also Bundy (1978). Schwartz (1995, 3) calculates that the construction, maintenance, and deconstruction of the U.S. nuclear arsenal represented the third-largest government expenditure from 1946 to 1998, exceeding all other government programs except other defence spending and social security.

6  According to McKinzie et al. (2001, 1), '[w]hat is less clear is...whether the nuclear war planning process is rational, or is actually a hall of mirrors, creating extravagant requirements, yet blind to what would happen if they were used.'

7  The estimated relationship between effective megatonnage ($E$) and delivered megatonnage ($D$) is $E = D^{2/3}$.

8  Soviet scholars made similar arguments about deterring the United States; see Miasnikov (1996).

9  Cimbala (1998, 19) notes that large arsenals might have provided flexibility in the face of possible cheating by the other party or unforeseen technological advances. They also might have increased survivability, deterred regional powers, and provided more flexibility in counterforce measures. Related to the idea of deterring regional powers, James (2000) argues that the size of an arsenal matters if deterrence is to be extended over multiple dyads.

10  Assuming a deterrent arsenal of $D$, and a loss rate of $F$ per cent when suffering a first strike, a nation would need to hold an arsenal of size $D/(1 - F)$. Suppose $D = 400$ and $F = 90$ per cent; then, a nation would need to hold an arsenal of only 4,000 warheads to be 'safe.'

11  Lang (1965, 187) notes that 'governments that are accustomed to [U.S.] protection...fear that arms control might lead to the withdrawal of that protection.'

12  Only recently has the United States sought to classify such information. A *Washington Post* article notes that the Bush administration sought to classify the size of the U.S. arsenal – information 'the government long provided even to its enemy the former Soviet Union.' The article notes that, '[d]uring the Cold War, the United States devoted substantial manpower and money to counting Soviet missiles....At the same time, U.S. officials sometimes were quite open about the number of American missiles, using the data to illustrate the deterrent power of the U.S. nuclear arsenal and to make the case for more defense spending. Indeed, such numbers were routinely disclosed in annual reports to Capitol Hill by secretaries of defense dating to at least the 1960s' (Lee 2006).

## REFERENCES

Bevins, M. 2004. 'Armageddon almost not averted.' *Moscow Times*, 27 May.
Brodie, B., ed. 1946. *The Absolute Weapon*. New York: Harcourt Brace.
–  1978. 'The Development of Nuclear Strategy.' *International Security* 2 (4): 65–83.
Bundy, M. 1969. 'To Cap the Volcano.' *Foreign Affairs* 48 (1): 1–20.
–  1978. 'Maintaining Stable Deterrence.' *International Security* 3 (3): 5–16.

Cimbala, S. 1998. *The Past and Future of Nuclear Deterrence*. Westport, CT: Praeger.

Eaton, B.C., and R.G. Lipsey. 1979. 'The Theory of Market Pre-emption: The Persistence of Excess Capacity and Monopoly in Growing Spatial Markets.' *Economica* 46 (182): 149–58.

Erickson, J. 1982. 'The Soviet View of Deterrence: A General Survey.' *Survival* 24 (6): 242–51.

Gay, W., and M. Pearson. 1987. *The Nuclear Arms Race*. Chicago: American Library Association.

James, C. 2000. 'Nuclear Arsenal Games: Size Does Make a Difference.' Paper presented at the 41st Annual Convention of the International Studies Association, Los Angeles, 14–18 March.

Jervis, R. 1979-80. 'Why Nuclear Superiority Doesn't Matter.' *Political Science Quarterly* 94 (4): 617–33.

– 1984. *The Illogic of American Nuclear Strategy*. Ithaca, NY: Cornell University Press.

Jervis, R., N. Lebow, and J. Stein, eds. 1985. *Psychology and Deterrence*. Baltimore: Johns Hopkins University Press.

Jervis, R., P.C. Stern, C. Tilly, and P.E. Tetlock, eds. 1990. *Behavior, Society, and Nuclear War*. New York: Oxford University Press.

Kydd, A. 2005. *Trust and Mistrust in International Relations*. Princeton, NJ: Princeton University Press.

Lang, D. 1965. *An Inquiry into Enoughness: Of Bombs, and Men, and Staying Alive*. New York: McGraw-Hill.

Lee, C. 2006. 'Cold war missiles target of blackout.' *Washington Post*, 21 August.

Little, A. 1998. 'How I stopped nuclear war.' *BBC News*, 21 October.

Lloyd, M. 2002. 'Soviets close to using A-bomb in 1962 crisis.' *Boston Globe*, 13 October, p. A20.

McKinzie, M., T. Cochran, R. Norris, and W. Arkin. 2001. *The U.S. Nuclear War Plan: A Time for Change*. New York: Natural Resource Defense Council.

Miasnikov, E. 1996. *The Future of Russia's Strategic Nuclear Forces: Discussions and Arguments*. Moscow: Center for Arms Control, Energy and Environmental Studies.

Morgan, P. 1985. 'Saving Face for the Sake of Deterrence.' In *Psychology and Deterrence*, edited by R. Jervis, N. Lebow, and J. Stein. Baltimore: Johns Hopkins University Press.

Morrow, J. 1994. 'Alliances, Credibility, and Peacetime Costs.' *Journal of Conflict Resolution* 38 (2): 270–97.

Nalebuff, B. 1988. 'Minimal Nuclear Deterrence.' *Journal of Conflict Resolution* 32 (3): 411–25.

Schwartz, S. 1995. 'Four Trillion Dollars and Counting.' *Bulletin of the Atomic Scientists* 51 (6): 32–52.

– ed. 1998. *Atomic Audit: The Costs and Consequences of U.S. Nuclear Weapons since 1940*. Washington, DC: Brookings Institution Press.

# 12 Social Learning in a Model of Adverse Selection[1]

JASMINA ARIFOVIC AND ALEXANDER KARAIVANOV

It is well known from the mechanism design literature that the optimal contracts that arise in environments with asymmetric information can take complicated forms due to the need to satisfy various, typically nonlinear, constraints – such as participation, incentive compatibility, and/or self-selection. Further, these optimal contracts crucially depend on the participating agents' preferences, the properties of the endowment process or production technology, and various elements of the institutional environment – such as the degree of contractibility, contract enforcement, and agents' ability to commit. Usually, this literature solves for the best possible contract assuming that certain actions, states, or types are unobservable to the contract designer – typically, the principal in a principal-agent setting. At the same time, however, it assumes that this designer has perfect knowledge of objects that are likely much harder to know or observe, such as the agent's preferences or decision-making process in general.

In this paper, we explicitly model the principal's learning process about what contracts to offer based only on observable information such as the principal's profits. Our main objective is to investigate whether and under what conditions this learning process converges to the optimal mechanism design contract. If the learning process does converge, we are also interested in how quickly convergence occurs. On the other hand, if the learning process does not converge to the theoretically optimal contract, we are interested in what the (suboptimal) contracts might look like.

In our previous related work (Arifovic and Karaivanov 2009), we study and compare the relative performance of two major learning paradigms from the literature, social and individual learning – that is, 'learning from others' versus 'learning by doing' – in the context of a principal-agent model of output sharing under moral hazard. The principal tries to learn the optimal agency contract without knowing the agent's preferences and the production technology. We find that learning is hard in this type of environment due both to its stochastic nature and to the discontinuity of the payoff space in the neighbourhood of the optimal contract.[2] In this difficult learning environment, we find that 'learning from others' (social learning) is much more successful in reaching the optimal contract.

It is worth noting that Curtis Eaton and Jasmina Arifovic have studied social learning in a context of a sender/receiver game of common interest with cheap talk in which players use messages to communicate their type (Arifovic and Eaton 1995, 1998). The 'order' of an equilibrium in the game is given by the number of player types that is successfully communicated. In addition, there are multiple equilibria of each order, and equilibria of different orders can be Pareto-ranked. The evolutionary social learning process results in interesting dynamics in which a population of genetic algorithm players climbs an equilibrium payoff ladder, moving from equilibrium of one order to equilibrium of the next-highest order. Eventually, this process results in convergence to the Pareto-optimal equilibrium of the highest order.

In this paper, we further examine the social learning process in an environment of adverse selection and monopolistic screening (see Maskin and Riley 1984). Specifically, we study the problem of a principal who needs to learn how to design an optimal wage contract, based only on observable information, when facing two types of agents who differ in effort costs. Agents' effort and output are observable but their type is unknown to and unobserved by the principal, which results in an adverse selection problem. We model the principal's learning process using the 'social evolutionary learning' (SEL) algorithm – see Arifovic (2000) for a discussion of the social learning paradigm – in which players (a set of principals) update their strategies based on imitating strategies of those players who have performed better in the past and occasionally experiment with new strategies.

The optimal contract (wage-effort pair) in our theoretical setting is (for any cost parameters) always a separating contract. Thus, a fully rational profit-maximizing principal who is aware of the preferences of both agent types – but does not know who is who – optimally will offer two types of contracts that the agents optimally will self-select. Naturally, we find that such a separating outcome – that is, when the two types accept different wage-effort pairs – is one possible result of the learning process. However, we also find that it is possible that the principal is unable to learn the optimal separating contract and instead ends up offering contracts such that one of the types (the high cost) is excluded – that is, that both contract offers violate her participation constraint. It can also happen that the learning process converges to a 'pooling' outcome, whereby both agent types take one of the two contracts offered.

We find that, although learning the optimal separating contract in the screening environment is very hard, even when using social learning, the learning process and outcomes are rich and interesting. Our results show that the SEL algorithm we implement always converges to one of three outcomes: separating, pooling, or excluding. That is, our principals might need to learn three different types of contracts. Our main finding is that, conditional on the type of contract reached in the final simulation period, the principals achieve payoffs that are quite close to the maximum possible payoff within that contract class. That is, if the principals were somehow able to restrict agents' choices so to stay within a given class, their learning process would lead very closely to the best possible contract in the class. Such a restriction is, of course, not optimal for the agents who 'shop' for the best contract offered, which might result in any of the three outcomes depending on the particular offers. Because of this, if we look at the average deviation to the maximum possible payoff[3] achieved across all runs (and, hence, across the three outcome types), it is quite high, indicating poor performance of the learning algorithm, although, at the same time, convergence within each outcome type is much better.

The main impediment to the learning process is not one of local stability – indeed, if we introduce a principal who offers the optimal separating contract in the initial population, all principals converge to the optimal contract in 99 per cent of the runs. Rather, the main impediment is one of global stability – that is, getting into the 'right' region of the contract space to ensure that adaptation is to the separating contract, not to one of the two alternative outcomes. The pooling and excluding cases do not maximize profits in the global sense (that is, among all feasible contracts) but can be locally optimal and stable within certain regions of the contract space.

More specifically, over all simulations with our baseline SEL specification,[4] our principals learn or converge with the highest frequency to an excluding contract (63 per cent), followed by a separating contract (25 per cent), and, finally, a pooling contract (12 per cent). The outcome types to which the learning algorithm converges critically depend on the agents' effort cost parameters and on the learning algorithm parameters, including the random seed. In each case, the convergence is not necessarily to the optimal (profit-maximizing) contract within that class. We find that the profit-maximizing excluding and pooling contracts are much easier to learn (where the profits achieved are close to the theoretical maximums within the corresponding class of contracts) than the optimal separating contract (where the profits achieved are, on average, a smaller fraction of the theoretical optimum). We investigate the factors that affect the adaptation process and the types of contracts to which social learning leads, and we discuss the intuition behind the observed outcomes. We also perform a wide range of additional simulations to analyze the robustness of our findings.

. The rest of the paper is organized as follows. In the next section, we describe the theoretical model, solve for the optimal separating contract, and derive the profit-maximizing wage-effort pairs within the classes of excluding and pooling contracts. We then describe our implementation of the social learning algorithm, and report the results from the baseline simulations and a range of robustness checks. Finally, we discuss the theoretical and computational issues relevant for the learning process performance in our environment, and offer some concluding comments.

## The Model

Consider a model of monopolistic screening with hidden information (second-degree price discrimination). Suppose that there are types of agents who differ in their costs of supplying a given level of labour effort, $x$, that is used to produce output, $y$, using the constant returns to scale technology, $y = x$. Specifically, for simplicity, let there be two agents[5] and let $c_i(x)$ be the cost of agent $i = L, H$ supplying effort level $x$. Each agent knows her effort costs.

*Assumption A1*: The cost function $c$ is increasing and strictly convex with $c_H(0) = c_L(0) = 0$ and satisfies the single-crossing property – that is, $c'_H(x) > c'_L(x)$ for all $x > 0$.

A risk-neutral principal wants to design an optimal wage contract that maximizes his profits by employing one or both agents. A wage contract specifies an amount of output (or, equivalently, effort/work to be done by the agent), $x$, and a wage, $w$. Output is perfectly observable and contractible but the worker's type is not – that is, the principal does not know the preferences of the agent he employs but is aware that there are only two types of agents and knows perfectly their preferences and fractions in the population; he just cannot tell who is who. This asymmetric information creates an adverse selection problem in the spirit of Akerlof (1970) or Stiglitz and Weiss (1981): the contracts the principal offers affect which agent(s) apply for the job and the total profits the principal receives as a result. The principal has full commitment – that is, he cannot renege on or modify *ex post* a contract once an agent has accepted it.

Let $(w, x)$ be a contract – a wage/effort pair the principal offers. As is standard in such settings, the principal optimally will offer two such contracts to 'screen' the two types. Assume the agents' utility is equal to the wage, $w_i$, minus the cost of effort, $c_i(x_i)$, $i = L, H$. The outside option of each agent is normalized to 0. There is no capacity constraint – that is each offered contract might be accepted by neither agent, a single agent, or both agents. The employer's problem is

$$\max_{w_L, x_L, w_H, x_H} x_L - w_L + x_H - w_H, \tag{1}$$

subject to

$$w_L - c_L(x_L) \geq 0, \tag{pcL}$$
$$w_H - c_H(x_H) \geq 0, \tag{pcH}$$
$$w_L - c_L(x_L) \geq w_H - c_L(x_H), \tag{ssL}$$
$$w_H - c_H(x_H) \geq w_L - c_H(x_L). \tag{ssH}$$

The first two constraints, (pcL) and (pcH), are the participation constraints stating that the agent must obtain at least her reservation utility from a contract she takes. The latter two constraints, (ssL) and (ssH), are the self-selection constraints ensuring that agent type $i = L, H$ is screened correctly and takes her intended contract $(x_i, w_i)$.

*The Optimal Contract*

Applying the revelation principle and standard arguments, Assumption A1 implies that, in the optimal separating contract,

- the participation constraint for the low-marginal-cost type (agent L), (pcL) is not binding;
- the self-selection constraint for the high-marginal-cost type (agent H), (ssH) is not binding; and
- the participation constraint for the high-cost type (pcH) and the self-selection constraint for the low-cost type (ssL) are binding.

Therefore, the optimal contract extracts all surplus from the high-cost type and gives the low-cost type just enough surplus to discourage her from pretending that she is a high-cost type. Plugging in the binding constraints (pcH) and (ssL), the first-order conditions for the principal's problem are

$$1 - c_L'(x_L) = 0, \tag{2}$$

$$1 + c'_L(x_H) - 2c'_H(x_H) = 0, \tag{3}$$

which, together with the binding constraints (pcH) and (ssL), can be solved for the optimal separating contract $(x^*_H, w^*_H, x^*_L, w^*_L)$. Denote by $\pi^*$ the principal's profits from offering this contract. By assumption A1, equations (2) and (3) imply that $x^*_L > x^*_H$ and $w^*_L > w^*_H$ – the low-cost agent is assigned higher output and receives a higher wage. This implies that the principal would never optimally offer a pooling contract – that is, a contract with $x_H = x_L$ and $w_L = w_H$, despite the fact that such a contract satisfies the self-selection constraints.

Note that, in the optimal contract, the low-cost agent obtains utility strictly higher than her reservation value (an information rent). That is, the monopolist cannot extract all the surplus from the contractual relationship and, hence, his profits from the low-cost type are lower than those the employer could achieve if the high-cost agent were not present. If this reduction in profits needed to satisfy the self-selection constraint (ssL) is large enough, it might instead pay off for the employer to exclude the high-cost agent[6] by offering a contract that violates (pcH) and maximizes the principal's profits from agent L. Clearly, it is not optimal to exclude agent L instead, since she works more than agent H at any wage level. The optimal contract excluding agent H solves

$$\max_{w_L, x_L} x_L - w_L, \tag{4}$$

subject to

$$w_L - c_L(x_L) \geq 0,$$
$$w_L - c_H(x_L) < 0.$$

It is easy to see that the first constraint must bind at optimum and, then, by assumption A1, it is clear that the second constraint is satisfied. Thus, the profit-maximizing excluding contract, $(x^e_L, w^*_L)$ solves

$$1 - c'_L(x_L) = 0 \text{ and } w_L = c_L(x_L).$$

Note that $x^e_L$ takes the same value as in the optimal separating contract, $x^*_L$, but the corresponding wage is lower – that is, $x^e_L < w^*_L$. Call the employer's profits associated with this contract $\pi^e$.

## A Computable Example

Assume a quadratic effort cost function, $c_i(x_i) = a_i \frac{x_i^2}{2}$ for $i = L, H$, with $a_H > a_L > 0$. Clearly, assumption A1 is satisfied. The first-order conditions, equation (2) – (3) become

$$1 - a_L x_L = 0,$$

$$1 + a_L x_H - 2a_H x_H = 0.$$

Solving those, together with the binding constraints, gives the optimal separating contract

$$x_L^* = \frac{1}{a_L}, \; x_H^* = \frac{1}{2a_H - a_L},$$

and

$$w_H^* = c_H(x_H^*) = \frac{a_H}{2(2a_H - a_L)^2},$$

$$w_L^* = c_L(x_L^*) + w_H^* - c_L(x_H^*) = \frac{1}{2a_L} + \frac{a_H - a_L}{2(2a_H - a_L)^2}.$$

Further, the contract that maximizes profits from agent L if agent H is excluded solves problem (4) above,[7] which, in our example, yields

$$x_L^e = \frac{1}{a_L} \text{ and } w_L^e = \frac{1}{2a_L}$$

with profits $\pi^e = \frac{1}{2a_L}$. It is easy to verify that, for any $a_H > a_L > 0$, the firm makes larger profits by keeping both agents contracted – that is, $\pi^* > \pi^e$ – so, with our quadratic cost function, it is never optimal to exclude the high-cost agent. In the simulation runs, we always assume that the principal offers two contracts (wage-effort pairs), but in the exclusion scenario, both contracts fail to satisfy agent H's participation constraint.

Our main objective is to examine whether social learning via a genetic algorithm can be used to learn the optimal contract. That is, we study how hard or easy it is for boundedly rational players to learn what the optimal contract looks like. As a first pass, we assume one-sided learning – that workers are perfectly rational, know their preferences, and optimally pick the better of the two contracts offered. In contrast, employers know only that they must offer effectively four numbers: two wages and two output levels $(w_L, w_H, x_L, x_H)$. They observe the resulting profits from their choices each period and use those to update the offered contracts according to the social learning algorithm (see the next section for details). This implies that, along the learning path, suboptimal contracts inevitably would be offered, and sometimes both agents could pick the same contract (wage-output pair) or a contract might not be picked by any agent. Assume that, if an offered contract, $(w_L, x_L)$ or $(w_H, x_H)$, is not taken by any agent, the principal obtains zero profits from it. Similarly, if both offered contracts violate some agent's participation constraint, this agent obtains a payoff of zero.

We classify the contracts to which the social learning process can converge as three types: separating contracts (when both agents accept an offered wage-output pair and these pairs are not the same); excluding contracts (when agent L accepts a wage-output pair from the two offered but agent H accepts neither); and pooling contracts (when both agents accept the same wage-output pair of the two offered and the other pair is accepted by no one).[8] Indeed, in our simulations, we observe the occurrence of all three outcomes as a result of using the social learning algorithm. This implies that the learning algorithm performance is not perfect since we know from theory that the only optimal contract is the separating one. We investigate how the fraction of runs (for various cost parameters and random seeds) converging to each of the three outcomes depends on the learning algorithm parameters and also how close we get to the optimal contract or to the optimal profit level. We compare both the absolute/overall performance of the learning algorithm (relative to the optimal separating contract) and its relative performance – that is, conditional on converging to an excluding or a pooling contract, how close we get to the best contract within that class.

For the latter exercise, we need to solve for the profit-maximizing pooling contract – that is, when the principal offers the same $x,w$ pair:

$$\max_{w,x} x - w,$$

subject to

$$w - c_H(x) \geq 0.$$

Since for the same $(x,w)$, the (pcH) always binds before (pcL), we do not need to include (pcL). The profit-maximizing pooling contract is then

$$x^p = \frac{1}{a_H} \text{ and } w^p = \frac{1}{2a_H},$$

with profits $\pi^p = \frac{1}{2a_H}$.

## The Social Evolutionary Learning Algorithm

We implement the SEL paradigm to investigate whether and/or how quickly a population of principals that can learn from each other adapts to the optimal screening contract. Specifically, the population of principals learns collectively over time, imitating the strategies (contracts) of more successful principals (those earning higher profits) and occasionally experimenting with new contracts.

A *contract* for principal $i$, $i \in \{1,...,N\}$ at time $t$ is a pair of real numbers, $z^i_t \equiv \{x^i_t, w^i_t\} \in Z \equiv X \times W$. The sets $X$ and $W$ are uniformly spaced grids[9] for outputs and wages of sizes $\#X$ and $\#W$, respectively, defined on the intervals $[0, 1.1\overline{x}]$ and $[0, 1.1\overline{w}]$, where $\overline{x}$ is largest level of $x^*_L$ and $\overline{w}$ is the largest level of $w^*_L$ achieved across all cost parameterizations $\{a_L, a_H\}$ that we consider.[10]

A *strategy* for principal $i$ at time $t$ is a pair of contracts, $s^i_t \equiv (z^i_{1,t}, z^i_{2,t}) \in G \equiv Z \times Z$, where $G$ is the strategy space. Finally, for any $t$, the *strategy set*, $S_t \equiv \{s^1_t,...,s^N_t\}$, where $N$ is the size of the population of principals, consists of all principals' time $t$ strategies. There are $\#X(\#W)$ possible output-wage pairs in $Z$ and, hence, $(\#X)^2(\#W)^2$ feasible strategies for each principal, who chooses to play a single one each period.

Every period, each principal meets two agents (one low cost and one high cost) but does not know who is what type. Each principal, $i = 1,..,N$, then offers the two contracts prescribed by his strategy, $s^i_t$, to both agents, and each agent either accepts a contract or rejects both contracts. An agent cannot accept more than one contract. We assume that both the high-cost and the low-cost agents always respond optimally, by accepting or rejecting the contracts offered by comparing the utilities they would obtain in each contract as well as their reservation utility. Then, the principals compute their profits based on the outcome: total output produced and total wages paid out, according to the selected contracts. In theory, this implies that there are eight possible acceptance-rejection outcomes (four for each contract); in practice, however, some of these outcomes violate agents' self-selection constraints and would never be observed.

The principals are assumed to be boundedly rational and thus unable to solve directly the maximization problem in equation (1) – that is, they do not have the computational ability to set up first-order conditions and maximize. Moreover, they do not have any information about the preferences of each type of agent. By endowing the principals with strategies that consist of a pair of contracts, we assume only that they know that they face two different types of agents. The principals also lack information on the cost function and parameters that are part of the solution for the optimal contract.

Once the principals' payoffs are computed, updating of the principals' strategies takes place. The first step of the SEL algorithm is *replication*, which allows for potentially better-paying alternatives to replace worse ones. As our baseline replication operator, we use proportionate (biased 'roulette wheel') replication. Specifically, each strategy, $s_t^i$, $i = 1,...,N$, in the current strategy set has the following probability of obtaining a replicate:

$$prob_t^i = \frac{\exp(\lambda \pi_t^i)}{\sum_{j=1}^{N} \exp(\lambda \pi_t^j)}, \tag{5}$$

where $\pi_t^i$ is the profit that principal $i$ earned at time $t$ and $\lambda$ is a parameter governing the relative fitness weight. Replication is thus used to generate (drawing at random with the above probabilities) a population of $N$ replicates, $r_{t+1}^j$, $j = 1,...,N$, of the strategies that were used in the population at period $t$.

The new replicate, $r_{t+1}^j$, however, replaces the strategy $s_t^j$ that was previously implemented only if it yields a higher payoff. If this is not the case, we assume that the principal keeps his previous strategy. More formally, for each principal, $j = 1,...,N$, the payoff of using strategy, $r_{t+1}^j$, $j = 1,...,N$, is compared to the payoff of using the existing strategy, $s_t^j$ – the $j^{th}$ member of the strategy collection at time $t$. That is, the strategy at location $j$ that has a higher payoff between $r_{t+1}^j$ and $s_t^j$ becomes the member of the set $S_{t+1}$ at $t + 1$:

$$S_{t+1}^j = \max\{s_t^j, r_{t+1}^j\} \text{ for } j = 1,...,N. \tag{6}$$

As a robustness check, we also did simulation runs with what we call *simple replication*, whereby each newly selected replicate, $r_{t+1}^j$, *always* replaces the existing strategy, $s_t^j$, independent of whether it yields a higher or lower payoff.

Once the replication stage is complete, *experimentation* takes place. That is, we subject each strategy, $s_{t+1}^i$, in the new strategy pool obtained after replication is completed to random experimentation (mutation) with probability $\mu$. Specifically, if experimentation takes place for some principal, $j$, his strategy, $s_{t+1}^j$, is replaced by a new strategy randomly drawn from the strategy space $G$.[11] Both strategy elements, $z_{1,t+1}^j$ and $z_{2,t+1}^j$, undergo experimentation simultaneously. For each $k = 1, 2$, the new strategy is drawn from a square centred at $z_{k,t+1}^j$ with sides of length $2r_m$. We refer to the parameter $rm$ as the 'experimentation distance,' as it determines the size of the area in the contract space[12] in the neighbourhood of the current strategy within which experimentation can take $z_{k,t+1}^j$. The strategy set, $S_{t+1}$, is thus updated with the new experimental strategies as applicable. The strategy-updating process continues for $T$ periods. After some threshold period, $\tilde{T} < T$, the experimentation rate (constant until then) is subject to decay governed by the parameter $\chi$.[13]

To summarize the learning process in words, in each period a 'biased roulette wheel' is spun for each principal, which yields as an outcome (a replicate) one of the strategies from the current strategy set consisting of all $N$ principals' strategies. Strategies with higher payoffs have higher probabilities to be replicated (copied). This replication step is the heart of the SEL algorithm. Then, for each principal, $i$, we compare the payoff of his replicate strategy with that of his own time $t$ strategy, $s_t^i$, and, if the former payoff is larger than the latter, $s_t^i$ is replaced with the replicate. Finally, after the replication stage, each principal's strategy can be also subject to 'experimentation,' which occurs with probability $\mu$. That is, the strategy that the principal intended to play in period $t + 1$ is replaced (mutates) with another, (locally) randomly drawn strategy from $G$.

The learning process models the interactions in a population of principals that learns 'collectively' through gathering information about the behaviour of others and the imitation of successful strategies. Via the replication process, those strategies that yield above-average payoffs tend to be used by more principals in the following period. The experimentation stage incorporates innovations by principals, done either on purpose or by chance.

## Results

*Computational Implementation of the Learning Algorithm*

In this section, we describe the computational procedure we followed to initialize and implement the SEL algorithm in our theoretical setting.[14] Table 12.1 shows the baseline parameters we use to initialize the learning algorithm.

Table 12.1
Baseline Parameter Values

| Parameter | Values Used |
|---|---|
| Cost parameter for agent L, $a_L$ | 10 uniformly spaced points on [1, 2] |
| Cost parameter for agent H, $a_H$ | 10 uniformly spaced points on [3, 4] |
| Random seeds | 70 random integers on [1, 10,000] |
| Population size, $N$ | 30 |
| Simulation run length, $T$ | 2,400 |
| Experimentation rate, $\mu$ | 0.05 |
| Experimentation distance, $r_m$ | 0.1 |
| Experimentation decay factor, $\chi$ | 0.9998 |
| Weighting factor, $\lambda$ | 1 |
| Number of grid points, $\#X$, $\#W$ | 100 |

The cost parameters are ten uniformly spaced points on the interval [1,2] for the low-cost agent $L$ and ten on [3, 4] for the high-cost agent $H$. For each pair of cost parameters (100 in total), we conduct 70 runs using a different random generator seed. Thus, for a given variant of social learning (baseline or robustness run), we conduct a total of 7,000 runs. We also perform various robustness and comparative statics runs varying the parameters in Table 12.1 (see below).

The contract space from which the contracts $z_{k,t}$ are chosen is composed of all possible output-wage $(x, w)$ pairs such that $x$ belongs to a uniformly spaced linear grid, $X$, of 100 points on the interval [0, 1.1] and $w$ belongs to a uniformly spaced linear grid, $W$, of 100 points on the interval [0,0.594]. Thus, there are $\#X(\#W) = 10,000$ distinct feasible contracts yielding 108 distinct feasible strategies in the strategy space $G$. The grid bounds $1.1x$ ($= 1.1$) and $1.1w$ ($= .594$) are implied by the cost parameters in Table 12.1. To start with, $N$ strategies are randomly chosen from $G$ at $t = 1$ and assigned an initial pay-off of zero. Each run continues for $T = 2,400$ periods. At period $T = 2,000$, the experimentation rate, $\mu$, (constant until then) begins to decay at rate $\chi$.

*Baseline Simulation Results*

As described in the theory section, there are three possible outcomes to which the social learning process might converge. Since the experimentation rate decays to zero by period $T$, all runs converge to a single contract offered by all principals – that is, all $N$ strategies in the time $T$ strategy pool, $S_T$, are the same and correspond to one of three outcome types:

1 If each agent accepts a different contract, then the outcome is classified as a 'separating' outcome.
2 If the low cost agent accepts a contract and the high cost agent rejects both contracts, then the outcome is classified as an 'excluding' outcome.
3 If both agents accept the same contract, then the outcome is classified as a 'pooling' outcome.

The results from the baseline simulation runs show that 24.9 per cent of all runs converge to outcomes falling into the separating category, 63.4 per cent converge to an excluding outcome, and the remaining 11.8 per cent converge to a pooling outcome.

We begin our discussion of the baseline results by looking at the payoff space that the principals face. Figure 12.1 illustrates the various possibilities in terms of wages and effort levels that matter in determining the principal's profits from a given contract (it is hard to illustrate on a two-dimensional figure what happens in terms of total profits as the two offered contracts interact). The principal's iso-profit curves are upward-sloping straight lines with slope 1. Profits increase moving in the east direction.

The '\'-pattern shaded area on the upper-left side of the figure indicates the region that generates negative profits for the principal. If a contract is offered below the participation constraint for the low-cost agent (the horizontal-line-pattern area on the right), profits from that contract are zero; note that zero is also the principal's outside option, so profits can never be nonpositive at optimum. All other areas on Figure 12.1 generate positive profits. The crescent-shaped shaded area at the bottom left between the zero profits iso-profit line (the 45-degree line through the origin) and the PC constraint for agent H indicates the set of contracts that the high-cost agent would accept and that, at the same time, generate positive profits for the principal. Points $S_L$ and $S_H$ indicate the output-wage pairs corresponding to the optimal separating contract ($S_L$ for agent L and $S_H$ for agent H). By theory, points $S_L$ and $S_H$ lie on the same indifference curve of agent L. Finally, point $E$ denotes the profit-maximizing excluding contract (which occurs at the tangency point between the line labelled $pcL$ and an iso-profit line), and point $P$ denotes the profit-maximizing pooling contract, as derived in the theory section.

Figure 12.2 plots the frequencies of the three possible outcomes (separating, excluding, and pooling) that the learning process results in as functions of the $a_L$ and $a_H$ cost values we consider. We can see from the figure

Figure 12.1: Principal's Payoff Space

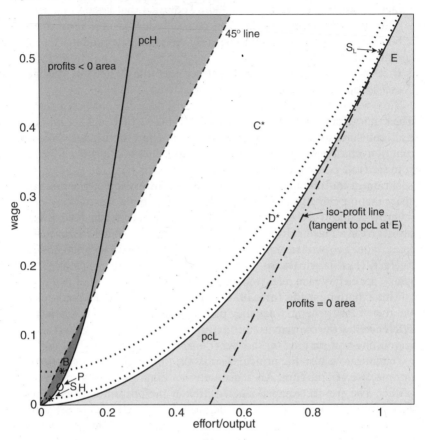

that the excluding outcome is by far the most frequent. However, an interesting observation is that the different outcomes achieve their highest frequencies for distinct regions of the cost parameter space. Specifically, the pooling outcomes' highest frequencies are observed in the area where there is the smallest difference between $a_L$ and $a_H$. This is also exactly the area where the frequency of 'excluding' outcomes is the lowest. The intuition for this is that, for relatively low $a_H$ and relatively high $a_L$, the cost functions of both agents are most similar and the chances that agent H will accept a contract are the highest. A question that remains at this point is why such pooling outcomes occur at all – that is, why the principal does not move one of the offered contracts below pcL and also move the contract for agent L toward the optimal excluding contract that lies on that agent's participation constraint, which would result in higher profits. A possible reason is that, as we move in an easterly direction, the principal's profits can drop locally. Similarly, why is the separating contract so hard to learn so that, as a result, most of the runs converge to an excluding outcome? These issues are further illustrated and discussed in detail below.

Next, we report results on the rate of convergence in our baseline simulation runs as defined by the parameters in Table 12.1. We define and examine the behaviour of several measures that reflect both qualitative and quantitative aspects of the learning dynamics. These measures refer both to the overall performance of the learning process relative to the optimal (separating) contract and to its performance within each of the three possible outcome classes (separating, excluding, and pooling).

One measure is the time paths of the fractions of all runs with average payoffs within a given 'distance' from the profit-maximizing contract. Each point on the plotted line equals the average fraction over all strategies over the 7,000 runs. Three distance criteria are considered: 0 per cent, 5 per cent, and 10 per cent, which refer to the percentage deviations from the theoretically maximum profits (overall or conditional on the outcome class). Another measure is the frequency distribution over all simulations of the differences between simulated and profit-maximizing[15] payoffs of all strategies in the final period.

The four panels of Figure 12.3 display the time paths of the fractions of all runs with offered contracts that result in average principals' total profits (at each $t$ we take the average over $N$) within a given percentage deviation of the theoretically maximal profits overall (the top panel) and conditional on each of the three outcome classes. The top panel represents the fractions over time of all runs attaining average profits within 0, 5, and 10 per cent of the maximum profits. These fractions remain quite low over the entire 2,400 periods, indicating that overall convergence to the optimal separating contract does not occur in the majority of cases. The lower three panels help clarify the reason for the low overall convergence rates – namely, because the 7,000 runs are actually split among the three possible convergence outcomes (separating, excluding, and pooling). Thus, even if convergence turns out to be quite good within each outcome class, the overall performance, as measured relative to the optimal separating contract, is quite unsatisfactory.

To address the latter point further, let us look more closely at the algorithm performance within each outcome class. The second panel of Figure 12.3 shows the time paths of the fraction of runs that fall into the

## Figure 12.2: Frequencies of the Three Possible Outcomes

Baseline: frequency of convergence to a separating contract as function of agents' costs

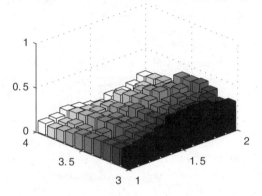

Baseline: frequency of convergence to an excluding contract as function of agents' costs

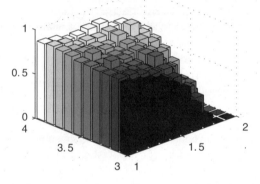

Baseline: frequency of convergence to a pooling contract as function of agents' costs

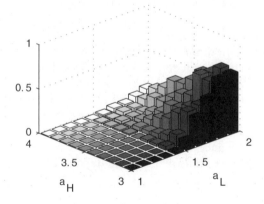

Figure 12.3: Time Paths of the Fractions of Runs with Average Payoffs within x% of the Payoff of the Profit-Maximizing Outcome

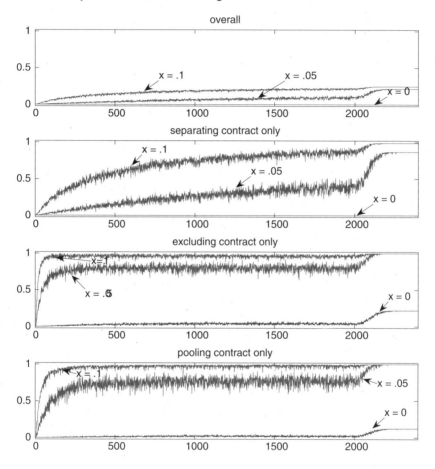

'separating contract' category, based on what type of contract (as defined in the beginning of this section) they converge to at time $T$. The fraction of runs with profits equal to those in the optimal contract remains very close to zero over time. However, the fraction of runs coming within 5 per cent of the optimal separating contract profits increases over time and reaches more than 85 per cent at period 2,400. The fraction within 10 per cent of the theoretically maximum profits increases even more substantially over time and almost reaches the maximum value of 1 at the end.

The remaining two panels show the same graphs for the runs that reach excluding and pooling outcomes at time $T$. The fraction of runs that reach average profits within 0 per cent – that is, that coincide with the best pooling or excluding contracts – naturally increases sharply at the end of the runs as the rate of experimentation goes to zero.[16] Further, in contrast to the separating case, the 'within 5 per cent' and 'within 10 per cent' profits deviation time paths reach the maximum value for both outcomes, indicating that the separating contract is the hardest to learn. As the figure shows, the payoff fractions exhibit some volatility. This is a result of the fact that small changes in the offered contracts could result, because of the rugged payoff landscape, in relatively large fluctuations in payoffs (see more on this below).

The four panels of Figure 12.4 show the distribution (histogram), computed over all 7,000 runs, of the distance between the average realized profit and the profit-maximizing outcomes in the last period. The first panel illustrates the distribution of the distance in terms of profits from the optimal separating contract over all 7,000 runs – that is, these are the overall profit 'errors' or absolute differences relative to the optimum. The panel illustrates that only a tiny fraction of all runs comes close to the payoffs associated with the optimal separating contract. This reflects two facts. First, a minority (about 25 per cent) of all runs converges to a separating outcome. All other runs converge to other outcomes that have strictly lower profits. Second, even among the runs that converge to a separating outcome, only a small percentage gets close to the optimal separating contract. This latter point is evident in the second panel of Figure 12.4, which displays the distribution of profit distances from the optimal separating contract profit only within runs with separating learning outcomes. Still, cumulatively, more than 60 per cent of these runs achieve payoffs within 5 per cent of the optimal contract's payoff.

Finally, panel 3 of Figure 12.4 shows the distribution of percentage differences between the realized and theoretically maximal profits only for runs classified as excluding outcomes based on the values of $(z_{1,T}, z_{2,T})$. Evidently, all simulations that converge toward excluding outcomes reach payoffs equal or very close to the payoff from the profit-maximizing excluding contract. Finally, the last panel of the figure shows the profit errors distribution for runs classified as 'pooling' outcomes. As in the excluding case, a large fraction of these runs reaches the payoff of the profit-maximizing pooling contract, while the rest come within 2.5 per cent of it.

Figure 12.4: Histograms of Last-Period Outcomes (distance from maximum payoff)

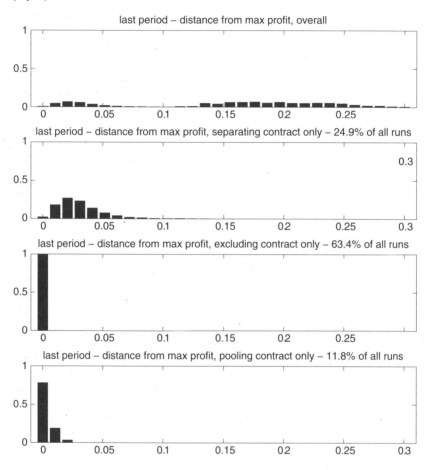

*Robustness Runs*

In addition to the baseline runs defined by the parameters in Table 12.1, we also conducted numerous robustness simulation runs (see Table 12.2). Apart from the baseline run as the benchmark, the table lists numerous variations of the learning algorithm and its parameters that we implemented to test the robustness of our results: 'selective experimentation,'

Table 12.2
Types of Learned Contract Outcomes

|  | Fraction of All Runs Converging to: | | |
|---|---|---|---|
|  | Separating Contract | Excluding Contract | Pooling Contract |
|  | (per cent) | | |
| Baseline | 24.9 | 63.4 | 11.8 |
| Robustness | | | |
| Selective experimentation | 22.8 | 64.7 | 12.5 |
| Normally distributed experimentation | 24.9 | 61.5 | 13.6 |
| Tournament selection | 23.1 | 64.1 | 12.7 |
| SEL weighting factor, $\lambda = 3$ | 25.9 | 62.6 | 11.5 |
| Simple replication | 12.8 | 73.4 | 13.8 |
| Experimentation distance, $r_m = 2$ | 77.8 | 14.7 | 7.5 |
| $N = 100$ | 28.2 | 63.5 | 8.3 |
| Coarse grids ($\#X = \#W = 10$) | 27.5 | 61.6 | 10.9 |
| Optimal contract in initial pool | 99.9 | 0.1 | 0.0 |
| Optimal contract H only in initial pool | 31.8 | 51.8 | 16.4 |

experimentation with normally distributed draws, a 'tournament selection' replication operator, 'simple replication,' a 'large' experimentation distance ($r_m = 2$), an increase in the size of the pool of principals to $N = 100$, and the use of a coarser strategy space. We also conducted runs with both optimal separating contracts $(x_L^*, w_L^*)$ and $(x_H^*, w_H^*)$ or only the high-cost agent's optimal contract $(x_H^*, w_H^*)$ included in the initial strategy pool, $S_0$.

Table 12.2 demonstrates that the excluding contract as an attractor for the largest fraction of learning outcomes remains robust across most of the different variants of our social learning algorithm. The only exceptions are the treatments where we explicitly include the optimal separating contracts for both agents in the initial pool, and when we increase the experimentation radius to 2 so that the area of experimentation covers the whole contract space (global experimentation). In the treatment with the separating contract in the initial strategy pool, virtually all runs (99.9 per cent) converge to separating outcomes. This is reassuring with regard to the local stability of the optimal contract (once in the pool it is not knocked out during the learning process). It also shows, however, how hard it is to learn the optimal screening contract in our setting: if the principals are somehow 'shown' what is optimal, they stick to this strategy; otherwise they seem to struggle to find it and instead adapt to other outcomes (most likely excluding, but sometimes pooling), depending on the cost parameters and random seeds. In contrast, the runs in which we included $(x_H^*, w_H^*)$ but not

$(x_L^*, w_L^*)$ in the initial strategy pool still feature mostly excluding outcomes, although the fraction of runs with separating outcomes is significantly higher relative to the baseline and most other treatments.

The second-highest percentage of separating outcomes (77.8 per cent) occurs in the runs conducted within a large experimentation range parameter, $r_m = 2$, that covers the whole strategy space, $G$ – that is, where experimentation is not local, as in the baseline, but global. Intuitively, this should help break away from the local maximums associated with the best excluding and pooling contracts, and so it does: the fraction of runs converging to a separating outcome more than triples relative to the baseline. Below we also show that the 'separating contract in the pool' runs converge very close to the optimal separating contract. Finally, observe that the lowest fraction of outcomes (16.4 per cent) across all of the treatments are pooling.

Next, we study the SEL algorithm performance in terms relative to the optimal contracts overall and within each outcome class. Table 12.3 shows how close the contracts to which SEL converges are, in terms of principals' profits, to the profit-maximizing contracts, both overall and within the sets of runs classified in each of the separating, excluding, and pooling categories. The first three columns report the fractions of runs with final-period profits within a given distance of the optimal (separating contract) profits – that is, the SEL algorithm's overall performance. We report these fractions for runs with profits within 0, 5, and 10 per cent deviation from the theoretical maximum. As Figure 12.4 also shows, these fractions are quite low for the baseline specification: 0 per cent for the 0 per cent deviation criterion, 21.6 per cent for the 5 per cent deviation criterion, and 24.6 per cent for the 10 per cent deviation criterion. As the rest of Table 12.3 shows, however, the main reason for this bad performance overall is the high incidence of convergence to other (suboptimal) contractual outcomes, pooling or excluding, and not necessarily bad convergence to a separating outcome when such is learned.

Looking at the profit differences with the theoretical maximum within or, conditional on, each outcome type, the percentage of runs with average final-period profits exactly equal to those in the profit-maximizing contract in each category (the $x = 0$ per cent columns in Table 12.3) is fairly low. Based on this 'zero distance' criterion, the baseline runs with excluding outcomes at $T$ yield the highest fraction (22.0 per cent) of runs converging exactly to the profit-maximizing excluding contract, compared with 12.4 per cent for the class of pooling outcomes and only 0.2 per cent within the runs with separating outcomes.

These percentages, however, increase significantly when we allow for a tolerance of within 5 per cent or 10 per cent of the theoretically maximum

Table 12.3
Social Learning Performance

| Run | Percentage of Last-Period Payoffs within x% of Optimal Payoff (overall and per contract type converged to) | | | | | | | | | | | |
|---|---|---|---|---|---|---|---|---|---|---|---|---|
| | Overall | | | Separating Contract Only | | | Excluding Contract Only | | | Pooling Contract Only | | |
| | x = 0 | x = 5 | x = 10 | x = 0 | x = 5 | x = 10 | x = 0 | x = 5 | x = 10 | x = 0 | x = 5 | x = 10 |
| | | | | | | (per cent) | | | | | | |
| Baseline | 0.0 | 21.6 | 24.6 | 0.2 | 86.7 | 98.9 | 22.0 | 100.0 | 100.0 | 12.4 | 100.0 | 100.0 |
| Robustness | | | | | | | | | | | | |
| Selective experimentation | 0.0 | 19.8 | 22.6 | 0.1 | 87.1 | 99.4 | 22.9 | 100.0 | 100.0 | 12.1 | 100.0 | 100.0 |
| Normally distributed experimentation | 0.0 | 20.7 | 24.5 | 0.1 | 83.2 | 98.6 | 23.6 | 100.0 | 100.0 | 11.3 | 100.0 | 100.0 |
| Tournament selection | 0.0 | 20.1 | 22.9 | 0.1 | 86.9 | 99.0 | 22.7 | 100.0 | 100.0 | 12.5 | 100.0 | 100.0 |
| SEL weighting factor, $\lambda = 3$ | 0.1 | 22.5 | 25.7 | 0.2 | 87.0 | 99.3 | 22.3 | 100.0 | 100.0 | 11.3 | 100.0 | 100.0 |
| Simple replication | 0.0 | 1.1 | 3.9 | 0.0 | 8.7 | 30.4 | 0.1 | 33.8 | 62.5 | 0.2 | 23.6 | 49.2 |
| Experimentation distance, $r_m = 2$ | 0.0 | 4.0 | 23.6 | 0.0 | 5.1 | 30.3 | 6.3 | 100.0 | 100.0 | 2.7 | 98.5 | 100.0 |
| $N = 100$ | 0.4 | 27.9 | 28.2 | 1.4 | 99.1 | 100.0 | 23.7 | 100.0 | 100.0 | 9.5 | 100.0 | 100.0 |
| Coarse grid ($\#X = \#W = 10$) | 8.0 | 16.5 | 18.2 | 29.0 | 60.1 | 66.1 | 0.0 | 38.6 | 78.5 | 0.0 | 0.0 | 43.1 |
| Optimal contract in initial pool | 99.2 | 99.8 | 99.9 | 99.2 | 99.9 | 100.0 | 0.0 | 100.0 | 100.0 | 0.0 | 100.0 | 100.0 |
| Optimal contract H only in initial pool | 0.1 | 27.8 | 31.5 | 0.2 | 87.4 | 99.1 | 22.6 | 100.0 | 100.0 | 12.8 | 100.0 | 100.0 |

profits within each outcome category. Overall, the optimal separating contract is the hardest to adapt to, even conditionally, within the runs with separating outcomes, with 86.7 per cent reaching profits within 5 per cent of the maximum payoff in the baseline and 98.9 per cent reaching profits within 10 per cent of the theoretical maximum. In contrast, all of the runs with excluding or pooling outcomes yield profits within 5 per cent of the theoretically maximum profits within their corresponding class – that is, convergence to the profit maximizing contracts in the excluding and pooling cases is much better than in the separating case.

The remaining rows of Table 12.3 report results from various robustness runs in which we vary the parameters of the baseline social learning algorithm or modify the learning operators. The 'selective experimentation,' experimentation drawing from a normal distribution, 'tournament selection,' and the $\lambda = 3$ (where we place a larger weight on the best-performing strategy) treatments all result in numbers that are very close to those in the baseline, demonstrating the robustness of our findings in these dimensions of the SEL algorithm.

In contrast, using 'simple replication' leads to uniformly much lower fractions of runs that yield profits within a given distance of the theoretically maximum profits, both overall and within each class (compare with the baseline row of Table 12.3), as some good strategies can be replaced by worse ones during the learning process.

Interestingly, the 'large experimentation distance' specification also performs quite poorly in terms of its overall adaptation to the optimal contract. While we saw in Table 12.2 that, under this treatment, many more runs than in the baseline converge to a separating outcome, because of the extra volatility introduced by the large experimentation range, these runs on average do not get near the optimal contract, as demonstrated by the low numbers in Table 12.3. For example, for $r_m = 2$, only 5.1 per cent of the runs with separating outcomes are within 5 per cent of the theoretically maximum profits compared with 86.7 per cent in the baseline. That is, while allowing for global experimentation, we can achieve better performance in the qualitative sense – the 'correct' type of contract is learned – but this comes at the expense of worse quantitative performance in terms of getting close to the theoretically optimal profit level.

Increasing the number of strategies/principals, $N$, from 30 to 100 naturally leads to better performance than the baseline but the differences are not large. Using coarser grids ($\#X = \#W = 10$) helps the principals adapt to the optimal contract more often (in 8 per cent of the runs overall), but with only 100 feasible points in total in the strategy space $G$, the chances are simply mechanically quite higher than are the case with 10,000 points, as in the baseline. Nevertheless, the overall percentage of runs within 5 per cent or 10 per cent of the theoretically maximum profit in this treatment is lower than in the baseline.

Finally, the performance results for the treatment in which we include the optimal separating contract in the initial pool are very different. Here, 99.9 per cent of all simulation runs converge to a separating outcome (see Table 12.2) and, furthermore, almost all (99.2 per cent) converge to the optimal separating contract even though we do nothing to 'protect' this strategy from being extinguished by replication or changed by experimentation. On the other hand, the simulations with only one of the elements of the optimal contract $(x_H^*, w_H^*)$ in the initial strategy pool result in performance outcomes and convergence rates quite close to those in the baseline.

**Discussion**

Why do our principals have such a hard time figuring out what the optimal separating contract is? The principals modify and adapt their strategies in response to the payoffs they receive. However, for the problem at hand, the payoff landscape as a function of $x$ and $w$ is extremely rugged and shifts shape over time as a result of the interaction between the principals' actions (the specific contract offers) and the agents' optimal responses. It is important to point out here that, despite the ruggedness of the payoff landscape for the principals, this is not due to the agents' behaviour changing over time – agents are fully rational and always pick the best (for them) of the two contracts offered – but instead is due to the discrete shifts in agents' choices as the offers are varied.

To illustrate this point further, look back at Figure 12.1, which shows why learning the optimal separating contract ($S_L$ and $S_H$) might be quite hard. For example, suppose one of the two wage-effort pairs offered is (by chance or design) at $S_L$. Then, any point such as $B$ would cause agent L to switch to it (the dotted line through $B$ is agent L's indifference curve). In fact, both agents would choose $B$ if B and $S_L$ were offered simultaneously. Clearly, as a result, we would move away from the optimal contract for agent L, $(S_L)$, even if we start quite close to it, and only a point such as $C$ on the graph (and not, for example, $D$ or, in general, any point between the indifference curves through $S_L$ and $B$, no matter how close to $S_L$) might attract agent L away from the 'wrong' area of the wage-effort space near $B$. Thus, in a given run, even if a principal 'discovers' a separating contract, even one near the optimal one, it is relatively easy, due to the randomness in the replication and experimentation process, for this contract to disappear after being replaced by a pooling or excluding outcome that generates higher profits.

In contrast, suppose one of the offered contracts is point $E$ – the optimal excluding contract. Then, the principal would not choose any other points nearby and above the line pcL as that would reduce his profits (since agent L would switch). Even if we explicitly introduce point $S_H$ into the pool, profits would be lower than those at $E$ (as both agents would switch to point $S_H$), and the principal would experience this and go back to offering $E$. Thus, point $E$ can be locally stable and robust to experimentation in terms of profits generated, unless a principal manages to deviate from it in the direction of $S_L$ and simultaneously offer another contract close to $S_H$ (but such that agent L does not take it), which seems quite hard.

Figure 12.5 helps to explain further the difficulties with converging to the optimal contract by illustrating the principal's total profits, plotted as a function of varying one of the offered contracts over the whole wage-output space while fixing the other contract[17] (point $A$ on the figure, chosen between pcH and pcL). Note first the flat area on the bottom right of the figure (bounded by the axes, pcH, and agent L's indifference curve through point $A$). For any contract offered in that area, agent L chooses contract $A$, while agent H chooses not to participate. Note also the two local maximums: one at the bottom left (where agent H chooses such a contract while agent L stays at $A$) and one at the top right (where the maximum profits are achieved by an excluding contract). These local extrema of the joint-profit function might make learning the optimal separating contract quite hard. For example, if the other contract (given $A$ is offered) is in the northeast region of the $(x, w)$ space, it is likely that the principal's strategy pool would converge to an excluding contract. The same is true if we start in the flat area to the right of pcL. Fixing point $A$, it might seem possible that, if the other contract is nearby, the optimal separating contract for agent H (the local peak at the bottom left 'ridge') can be learned, but if we allow point $A$ to move as well (which it does in reality), agent L at some point might switch to that contract, too (see the discussion on Figure 12.1 above), which would reduce the principal's profits.

Finally, as we show in Arifovic and Karaivanov (2009), given that the maximum profits are achieved by contracts located right on the constraints – that is, on the 'cliffs' of the two elevated 'ledges' – profits drop discontinuously for a small mutation to the right, which again creates problems for the learning process.[18]

Figure 12.5: Principal's Total Profits from Fixing One Contract (A) and Varying the Other (B)

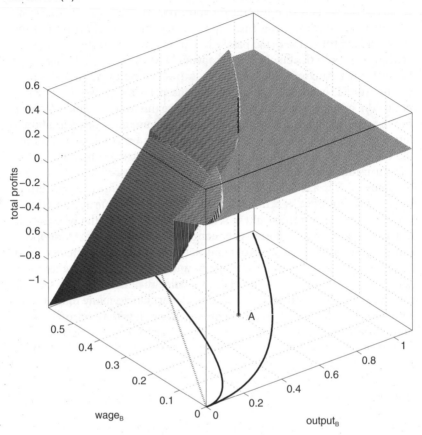

## Concluding Remarks

In this paper, we have investigated the dynamics of social evolutionary learning in the context of a model of optimal monopolistic screening. Principals learn about what wage/work effort contracts to offer based only on observable information – namely, principals' profits. They have no other information about the costs of two types of agents they face or the agents' preferences in general. In addition, the principals do not have the computational ability to solve for the optimal screening contract. Instead, they learn over time through a process of trial and error by imitating the contracts of other principals who have made larger profits in the past and by occasional experimentation with new contracts.

Our results suggest that it is rather hard to learn the optimal separating contract in this environment. Instead, most frequently (63.4 per cent of the 7,000 baseline runs), the principals' adaptation process converges toward a contract that excludes the high-cost agent. Next in terms of frequency is the separating outcome (24.9 per cent). A pooling outcome (where a contract is offered that both types of agents accept) is also possible (11.8 per cent of the baseline runs). Even if a separating outcome is achieved, exact convergence to the optimal contract is rare. In contrast, when the adaptation process leads to a pooling or an excluding outcome, the resulting offered contract gets very close to the profit-maximizing contract.

In terms of possible extensions, it might be interesting to study the performance of our learning algorithm in a competitive screening setting where principals offer contracts that compete for the same agents. In that case, only the two contracts in the strategy pool that yield the best payoffs for the agents would be chosen, in contrast to our current 'local monopoly' setting in which various types of contracts are chosen by some agents at the same time. *Ex-ante* it is not clear how this would affect the learning algorithm performance. An extra layer of strategy reinforcement would be introduced by the competition, but there also would be many more strategies that no agents would take and that would produce zero payoffs, which might 'stall' the learning dynamics, especially given that the optimal contract must also feature zero profits for the principals.

## NOTES

1 We thank Greg Dow, an anonymous referee, and the participants in the 2008 Conference in Honour of B. Curtis Eaton for their extremely helpful comments and suggestions. Nick Kasimatis and Sophie Wang provided excellent research assistance. Both authors acknowledge the support of the Social Sciences and Humanities Research Council of Canada.

2 The theoretically optimal contract satisfies the incentive compatibility and participation constraints with equality, so, for a very small perturbation to the contract that violates the constraints, the principal's payoff drops discontinuously.

3 That is, the payoff achieved by the optimal separating contract.

4 In total, there were 7,000 runs, with different cost parameters and random seeds. The random seeds determined the random number draws that were used in the probabilistic operators of the social learning algorithm.

5  This is not essential. As long as the principal knows the fractions of each type in the population, our results generalize easily, assuming that the principal maximizes (population-weighted) total expected profits.

6  Comparing the profits in each case, it is easy to verify that such exclusion would pay off if $c_L(x_H^*) - 2c_H(x_H^*) + x_H^* < 0$, where $x_H^*$ solves $c_H'(x_H) = 1$. This inequality would hold if the profit from agent H, $x_H^* - c_H(x_H^*)$ is not high enough to compensate for the cost differential, $c_L(x_H^*) - c_H(x_H^*)$.

7  The constraint $w_L - c_H(x_L) < 0$ is implied by $w_L - c_L(x_L) = 0$ and thus is omitted.

8  Clearly, it is impossible to offer a contract that excludes only agent L. Excluding both agents yields a zero payoff and never occurs as an outcome of the learning process (each of the three other outcomes has a positive payoff).

9  In principle, we can use continuous sets in the numerical implementation of the algorithm. However, learning is likely to be even harder in that setting.

10  Note that, by the results from the second section, all other contracts of interest, $(x_H^*, w_H^*)$, $(x^P, w^P)$, and $(x^e, w^e)$, feature lower $x$ and $w$ compared with $(x_H^*, w_H^*)$ and so always lie strictly within the space $X \times W$.

11  Our baseline simulation uses uniformly distributed draws. As a robustness check, we also implement experimentation with normally distributed draws.

12  We conducted sets of simulations using both 'small' experimentation distance ($r_m = .1$) and 'large' distance ($r_m = 2$). The latter covers the entire strategy space $G$. If the drawn contract falls outside the edges of the strategy space, it is replaced by the nearest element on the edge. In addition, we conducted sets of simulations with 'selective experimentation,' where the new randomly drawn experimental strategy replaces the existing one only if it yields a higher payoff, similarly to that the replication operator.

13  That is, the experimentation rate at time $t$ follows: $\mu_t = \mu_{t-1} \chi^{t-\bar{T}}$ for all periods, $t \in [T,T]$.

14  The MATLAB code for all simulations is available from the authors upon request.

15  Profit maximizing refers to the respective of the three contract outcomes.

16  This indicates that, in those cases, it is the continued experimentation that prevents earlier convergence and, if we start decreasing the experimentation rate earlier, adaptation would obtain even sooner.

17  It is impossible to illustrate on a single figure the total profits when varying both offered contracts simultaneously.

18  A possible extension that could alleviate this problem is to allow the agent's participation decision to be probabilistic – that is, to have the principal's payoff go down continuously near the constraint. This would be the case, for example, if the agent needed to learn about her optimal action and the location of the participation constraint.

REFERENCES

Akerlof, G. 1970. 'The Market for 'Lemons': Quality Uncertainty and the Market Mechanism.' *Quarterly Journal of Economics* 84 (3): 488–500.

Arifovic, J. 2000. 'Evolutionary Algorithms in Macroeconomic Modeling: A Survey.' *Macroeconomic Dynamics* 4 (3): 373–414.

Arifovic, J., and B.C. Eaton. 1995. 'Coordination via Genetic Learning.' *Computational Economics* 8 (3): 181–203.

– 1998. 'Evolution of Communication in a Sender/Receiver Game of Common Interest with Cheap Talk.' *Journal of Economic Dynamics and Control* 22 (8-9): 1187–1207.

Arifovic, J., and A. Karaivanov. 2009. 'Learning by Doing vs. Learning from Others in a Principal-Agent Model.' Working paper, Simon Fraser University.

Maskin, E., and J. Riley. 1984. 'Monopoly with Incomplete Information.' *RAND Journal of Economics* 15 (2): 171–96.

Stiglitz, J., and A. Weiss. 1981. 'Credit Rationing in Markets with Imperfect Information.' *American Economic Review* 71 (3): 393–410.

# 13 Intertemporal Discounting with Veblen Preferences: Theory and Evidence[1]

MUKESH ESWARAN AND ROB OXOBY

In his classic work, *The Theory of the Leisure Class*, written more than a century ago, Thorstein Veblen (1899) argued that a considerable part of consumption is motivated by the desire to demonstrate one's social position. Consumers undertake conspicuous consumption, as he called it, to set themselves apart from others – that is, the goal is not enjoyment of the goods per se but the status their consumption confers. Veblen's ideas have attracted renewed interest in recent decades. They form the basis of a theory of savings of Duesenberry (1949) and the distinction between ordinary goods and status goods underlying much of the work of Frank (1985, 1999). More recently, status concerns and their implications for resource allocation have been modelled quite formally.[2]

This paper deals with the intertemporal effects of conspicuous consumption. The topic is very appropriate for this volume in honour of Curtis Eaton because Veblen effects have been a major preoccupation of his in recent years. We examine this issue with a simple two-period model and a laboratory experiment. We theoretically demonstrate that Veblen effects bias consumption toward the first period, thereby seriously magnifying the effect of discounting. We show that increases in the marginal worth of conspicuous consumption and in productivity improvements increase the disparity between first- and second-period consumptions. These findings suggest that, if we infer the discount rate from observed patterns of intertemporal consumption without accounting for Veblen effects, we impute too high a discount rate: status concerns exaggerate the emphasis on the present and lead to an intertemporal misallocation of resources. Even a mild pure time preference can seriously distort choices in the presence of Veblen's consumption externality.

To test these ideas, we conduct a laboratory experiment in which we elicit discount rates from participants using a menu procedure akin to those used by Coller and Williams (1999); Harrison, Lau, and Williams (2002); and McLeish and Oxoby (2009). The results of our experiments reveal that, in the absence of information on relative earnings, discount rates are the same for participants with high and low earnings. When they do have information on their relative earnings, however, we observe that participants with relatively high earnings display higher discount rates than those with low earnings. This is our predicted Veblen effect, but in our experiments it is manifest only through hyperbolic and quasi hyperbolic discounting (see Laibson 1997; O'Donoghue and Rabin 1999, 2001).

Recently, Veblen effects have started receiving considerable prominence in the work on 'happiness research.'[3] The essential findings for our purposes are easy to summarize: in the developed countries, aggregate measures of happiness do not show any upward trend, although at a given point in time cross-sectional studies show that those with higher income register higher levels of happiness. This almost invites an explanation along the lines of Veblen's conspicuous consumption: if well-being is gauged in relative terms, equal absolute improvements in the standard of living of all people will not register as higher levels of happiness.[4] Using the 1987–88 and 1992–93 waves of the National Survey of Families and Households in the United States, Luttmer (2005) finds that, after controlling for own income and a host of other variables, an increase in the average earnings in their neighbourhood makes individuals register lower levels of happiness. In fact, the effects of equal increases in own and average neighbourhood incomes roughly cancel out. This is strong evidence in favour of Veblen's hypothesis.

The findings we report here add one possible dimension to the manner in which Veblen effects undermine well-being: by an intertemporal misallocation of resources. In fact, Veblen effects might well magnify the effects of pure time preference, thereby leading to higher measured discount rates. Our simple two-period model suggests that Veblen effects bias (conspicuous) consumption toward the present. Furthermore, this intertemporal bias increases with the marginal utility of conspicuous consumption and with the productivity of labour. The latter result underscores the point that affluent societies are more prone to discounting the future heavily, all else constant. This is ominous if true, for it suggests that the very thing capable of improving our standard of living (productivity increases) also might be equally capable of dissipating those gains through Veblen effects. The intertemporal inconsistency we observe in our experiments seems to confirm that there might be important efficiency losses resulting from Veblen effects.

If, indeed, Veblen effects increase discount rates *de facto*, then they have serious consequences for the depletion of natural resources. To the extent that Veblen goods are intensive in the use of natural resources, we would expect too rapid a rate of depletion. If, further, conspicuous consumption increases the demand for commonly owned resources, the effects clearly will be even worse. Gowdy (1996) cites examples of how the demand for conspicuous consumption of coral reef fish from wealthy Hong Kong consumers has devastated the coral reefs in the Indian and Pacific Oceans. Similarly, Japanese consumers' demand for the fat of the Atlantic bluefin tuna has had dire effects on the stock of that fish. Our finding that greater productivity (affluence) skews the pattern of consumption toward the present does not bode well for future generations. Nor does it bode well for the present generations of poor countries – for they will see commonly owned resources exploited beyond the point of no return by people living in rich countries.

In the next section, we present a simple model with intertemporal choice in the presence of Veblen effects. We then present our experiment and the accompanying results, and offer some concluding thoughts.

### Veblen Effects in Intertemporal Choice

To see how Veblen effects might impinge on intertemporal choice, consider the simplest model of how an individual allocates a given amount of resources over two periods. Consider a society with identical agents who choose quantities of a consumption good $C$ that is consumed in both periods. We assume preferences are additively separable. We denote by $u(c)$ the direct utility derived in any period from consuming an amount $c$ of the good. This measures the utility due to the intrinsic worth of the good. We assume that marginal utility increases at a diminishing rate, $u' > 0$ and $u'' < 0$. We assume that the component of utility derived from conspicuous consumption of the Veblen kind depends on the *difference* between an individual's own consumption and the average consumption of others. We denote this utility by $v(c - \bar{c})$, where $\bar{c}$ is the per capital level of consumption prevailing in the society in that period. We assume that $v(0) = 0$, and $v' > 0$. We assume that the one-period utility function is $u(c) + v(c - \bar{c})$. If we further assume that $v'' < 0$, the effect of an increase in the average consumption on the marginal utility of consumption of an individual, given by $-v''(c - \bar{c})$, will be positive, implying that the marginal utility from own consumption is higher when others consume more, an effect dubbed 'keeping up with the Joneses' (see Dupor and Liu 2003).

Suppose every person in the society is endowed with an amount $z$ that can be allocated over two periods. For simplicity, we assume that what is saved in period 1 earns zero returns. We write the two-period utility from consumption, $U(c_1,c_2)$, in the additively separable form

$$U(c_1,c_2) = u(c_1) + v(c_1 - \overline{c}_1) + \delta[u(c_2) + v(c_2 - \overline{c}_2)],\qquad(1)$$

where the parameter $\delta$ (with $0 \leq \delta \leq 1$) denotes the discount rate, common to all individuals, and $\overline{c}_1$, and $\overline{c}_2$ are the respective per capita consumptions in periods 1 and 2.

The problem confronting an individual is to maximize equation (1) subject to the constraint $c_1 - c_2 \leq z$. We assume that each consumer takes the period averages for consumption as given and beyond her control. Eliminating the budget constraint by substituting $c_2 = z - c_1$ in the objective function and taking the derivative with respect to $c_1$, we obtain the first order condition:

$$u'(c_1) + v'(c_1 - \overline{c}_1) = \delta[u'(z - c_1) + v'(z - c_1 - \overline{c}_2).\qquad(2)$$

In writing this condition down, we assume that an individual takes the economy's average consumption as exogenous to her. Since all individuals are identical, however, in equilibrium they will make identical choices. Invoking symmetry – that is, setting $\overline{c}_1 = c_1$ and $\overline{c}_2 = z - c_1$ – the above first-order condition evaluated at the equilibrium reduces to

$$u'(c_1) = \delta u'(z - c_1) - (1 - \delta)s,\qquad(3)$$

where $s \equiv v'(0) > 0$ is the marginal utility of conspicuous consumption at the average consumption level. The magnitude of $s$ measures the perceived status conferred by a marginal deviation from the mean consumption, and we refer to it as the 'status parameter.' Denote the solution to equation (3) by $\{c_1^*(z,s), c_2^*(z,s)\}$.

We note from equation (3) that, when $\delta = 1$ or when $s = 0$, the allocation of the resource across the two periods is dictated by

$$u'(c_1) = \delta u'(z - c_1).\qquad(4)$$

That is, the discounted marginal utility of consumption is the same across two periods, as in standard models without Veblen effects. When $\delta < 1$ and $s > 0$, we see from equation (3) that, at the equilibrium, the allocation yields a marginal utility in period 1 that is less than the discounted marginal utility in period 2 – that is, consumption is tilted toward the present. Even though the aggregate consumption is the same as before (equal to the endowment, $z$), this leads to a *decline* in each consumer's discounted utility compared with what would have obtained had the choice been dictated by equation (4), because the transfer induces a deviation from the optimal allocation without adding anything to the Veblen component in equilibrium. The self-defeating nature of the externality embodied in Veblen effects is well known by now in static contexts.[5] But the misallocation here is an intertemporal one leading to a present period bias, and this despite the fact that Veblen effects operate in all periods.

We can easily identify the effect of an increase in the importance of conspicuous consumption, $s$. Totally differentiating equation (3) with respect to $s$ yields

$$[u''(c_1) + \delta u''(z - c_1)]\frac{dc_1^*}{ds} = -(1 - \delta). \tag{5}$$

*Proposition 1*: When the endowment is fixed and $\delta < 1$, an increase in the marginal utility of conspicuous consumption at average consumption increases the first-period consumption.

Thus, if we infer discount rates from people's intertemporal consumption patterns without accounting for Veblen effects, we will attribute *too high* a discount rate. In other words, the allocation attributable to Veblen effects will be erroneously attributed to intertemporal time preference. This might partly explain why the discount rates that have been found experimentally tend to be considerably higher than market interest rates (see Frederick, Lowenstein, and O'Donoghue 2002). To press the point, suppose we examine intertemporal allocation of a resource and seek to infer the discount rate from it by fitting the data to the utility function, $u(c_1) + \beta u(c_2)$, where $\beta$ is the *imputed* discounted factor. Using the first-order condition, we can write the imputed discount factor as

$$\beta = \frac{u'(c_1^*(z,s))}{u'(c_1^*(z,s))}. \tag{6}$$

This tells us the imputed discount factor when the data contain Veblen effects, but our theory does not. Naturally, this value of $\beta$ also depends on the true discount factor, $\delta$, in addition to $z$ and the status parameter, $s$. The following result obtains an immediate consequence of the above proposition:

*Corollary 1*: The imputed discount factor declines when the marginal utility of conspicuous consumption at average consumption increases.

The greater the value of $s$, the more consumption will be tilted toward the present for a given value of the true discount factor, $\delta$, because of Veblen effects and the lower will be the imputed discount factor, $\beta$. It is as if the desire for status magnifies the extent of intertemporal discounting.

Figure 13.1 displays the comparative statics with respect to $s$ when $u(c)$ is logarithm – that is, $u(c) = \ln(c)$. In panel A, we plot the consumption levels in period 1 (top curve) and in period 2 (bottom curve) as the status parameter increases. The endowment in this exercise is assumed to be $z = 1$ and the true discount factor is $\delta = 0.8$. As the importance of status, $s$, increases, consumption is reallocated toward period 1. As status consciousness increases (in both periods), Veblen effects put increasing weight on the first-period consumption because of discounting. From panel B, we see that the imputed discount factor, $\beta$, declines sharply with $s$.

In order to isolate the intertemporal misallocation, we consider a model with only one good (the Veblen good). Suppose, for a moment, we had introduced another good – a standard consumption good, say $X$, with no Veblen characteristics. Denote the period 1 and period 2 consumptions of this good by $x_1$ and $x_2$. An increase in the marginal utility of conspicuous consumption in such a model would induce an intertemporal reallocation to toward $c_1$, as above, as well as an allocation away from $X$ toward the Veblen good in period 1 and possibly in period 2 also.

We should mention that the theoretical prediction of Veblen effects depends on how the comparison with others is modelled. We model the utility from conspicuous consumption as depending on the *difference* between own and average consumption. One might also consider modelling this utility as depending on the *ratio* of own to average consumption according to some function, $w(c/\bar{c})$, with $w' > 0$.[6] If we model it in this manner and redefine the marginal utility of conspicuous consumption at average consumption as $w'(1)$, Proposition 1 holds true if $c_2^*(z,s) > \delta c_1^*(z,s)$, an unhelpful condition because it is couched in terms of endogenous entities.[7] This unfortunate dependence on functional form, however, is not a peculiarity only of our analysis. The many papers examining Veblen effects in a growth context invariably assume specialized functional forms for the utility function.[8] The recent review by Clark, Frijters, and Shields (2008) briefly outlines the nature of the intricacies on which the results obtained from such models depend. We caution that the simple models we present here with an eye to motivating our experimental finding to follow cannot claim generality. Nevertheless, perhaps they do offer a transparent view of one theoretical issue related to conspicuous consumption – namely, that it can skew intertemporal consumption and thereby bias measured discount rates.

Figure 13.1: Conspicuous Consumption when $u(c) = \ln(c)$

A. The top (bottom) curve is the consumption in period 1 (2) as a function of status concern.

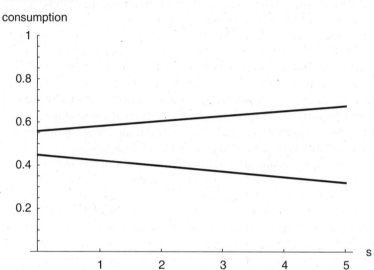

B. How the imputed discount factor varies with status concern.

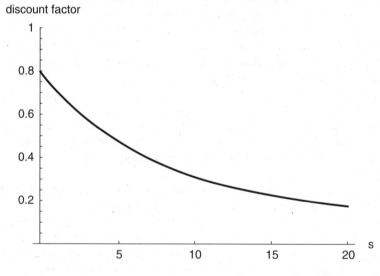

*The Effect of Unequal Endowments*

Above, we assumed that all people were identical. We now briefly inquire how aggregate behaviour changes when there is inequality of endowments. A person with endowment $z$ solves the problem stated in equation (1). The relevant first order condition for this individual is

$$u'(c_1) + v'(c_1 - \overline{c_1}) - \delta[u'(z - c_1) + v'(z - c_1 - \overline{c_2}) = 0.$$

The argument of the function $v'(.)$ does not necessarily vanish when evaluated at the equilibrium now because not everyone consumes the same amount. If we assume that the marginal utility of conspicuous consumption is constant at value $s$ – that is, derivative $v'(.) = s$ is constant – an individual's period 1 consumption is obtained as the solution to

$$u'(c_1) = \delta u'(z - c_1) - (1 - \delta)s, \tag{7}$$

which is the same as equation (4). We denote the solution to equation (7) by $\{\hat{c}_1(s,z), \hat{c}_2(s,z)\}$.

The assumption that $v'(.)$ is constant makes the above first-order condition independent of the distribution of endowments in the economy. One scenario in which this assumption is obviously reasonable is when income distribution is approximately egalitarian. An alternative scenario in which this might be reasonable is where people compare themselves not with everybody in the population but only with people who fall in a similar income bracket. This presumption of *localization* in Veblen comparisons fits in well with casual observations of the circumscribed nature of self-interest. Academics, for example, are likely to compare themselves not so much with the general population or with other academics in different universities or even in the same university but with others in their own department. Although the above first-order condition is independent of the endowment distribution, it does depend on an individual's own endowment, and so aggregate behaviour in this economy will depend on the distribution.

Figure 13.2 displays the behaviour of this model as a function of the worth of conspicuous consumption when the endowment can take on two possible values, $z_1$ and $z_2$, equally weighted in the population. As before, we assume $u(.)$ is the logarithm function. Panel A shows the aggregate consumption in period 1 when $z_1 = z_2 = 1$ (bottom curve) and for the mean-preserving spread, $z_1 = 1.5$, and $z_2 = 0.5$ (top curve). We see that aggregate consumption is tilted toward period 1 when the endowment is asymmetrically distributed. Panel B shows the mirror image of this for period 2. In panel C, we show the imputed discount factor in the egalitarian society (middle curve), and for the rich (bottom curve) and the poor (top curve) in the inegalitarian society. All else constant, the rich have a lower imputed discount factor than do the poor: the intrinsic marginal utility from consumption declines while the marginal utility from conspicuous consumption (being measured from the average consumption) does not. So the rich dissipate a greater proportion of their endowment in the futile search for status. This result suggests that a Benthamite welfare function that employs the true discount factor would deem the inegalitarian economy inferior to an egalitarian one because greater inefficiency is induced in the former.[9]

*A Model with Leisure*

Here, we consider a two-period model in which the endowment is not fixed but is determined by a tradeoff between labour and leisure in period 1. Period 2 is deemed to be one of retirement, and so there is no effort applied. We denote by the increasing and strictly concave function $R(l)$ the utility derived in period 1 from an amount of rest or leisure, $l$. To keep the model tractable, however, we revert to the scenario where all people are identical. we assume each individual is endowed with one unit of time in both periods, and in period 1 each chooses how much of this he devotes to working. We also assume the productivity of labour to be constant at $A$ for all individuals. A typical individual solves the problem as

$$\max_{c_1, c_2, l} \quad u(c_1) + v(c_1 - \bar{c}_1) + R(l) +$$

$$\delta[u(c_2) + v(c_2 - \bar{c}_2)] \quad s.t. \quad c_1 + c_2 = A(1 - l). \tag{8}$$

Substituting $c_2 = A(1 - l) - c_1$ from the budget constraint into the objective function, writing down the first-order conditions for $c_1$ and $l$, and then evaluating these at the point of symmetry in equilibrium, we obtain the respective equations:

$$c_1: \ u'(c_1) + s - \delta[u'(A(1 - l) - c_1) + s] = 0, \tag{9}$$

$$l: \ R'(l) - \delta A[u'(A(1 - l) - c_1) + s] = 0, \tag{10}$$

Figure 13.2: How Concern for Status Affects Conspicuous Consumption

A. How aggregate consumption in period 1 varies with status concern when
the wealth distribution is egalitarian (bottom) and inegalitarian (top).

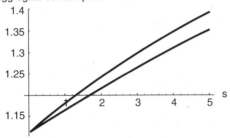

B. How aggregate consumption in period 2 varies with status concern when
the wealth distribution is egalitarian (top) and inegalitarian (bottom).

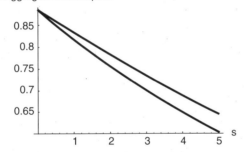

C. How the imputed discount factor varies with status concern when the
wealth distribution is egalitarian (middle) and inegalitarian (top for poor,
bottom for rich).

where, as before, $s \equiv v'(0)$ is a measure of the marginal utility of conspicuous consumption at the average income. We can solve the previous two equations for $c_1$ and $l$ and then obtain $c_2$ from the budget constraint. Denote the solution to an individual's problem by the triplet $\{c_1^\dagger(s,A), c_2^\dagger(s,A), l^\dagger(s,A)\}$. This formulation yields the following comparative static results:[10]

*Proposition 2*: An increase in the marginal utility of conspicuous consumption at average consumption (a) increases the consumption in the first period if $\delta < 1$, and (b) decreases leisure in period 1 for any $\delta$.

Part (a) of the proposition indicates that, as before, if there is any intrinsic discounting, its presence shifts consumption to the first period, when conspicuous consumption becomes more relevant. However, part (b) informs us that leisure declines whether or not there is any discounting – conspicuous consumption induces people to work harder. Previous studies show that Veblen effects result in reductions in leisure.[11]

It is instructive to assume the following special functional forms for the rest of this subsection: $u(c) = \ln c$ and $R(l) = \ln l$. The above first-order conditions then reduce, respectively, to

$$\frac{1}{c_1} = \frac{\delta}{A(1-l)-c_1} - (1-\delta)s, \tag{11}$$

$$\frac{1}{l} = \frac{\delta A}{A(1-l)-c_1} + \delta sA. \tag{12}$$

Before proceeding to examine this solution, we note that, when Veblen effects are absent (that is, when $s = 0$), we readily obtain a closed form solution:

$$c_1^\dagger(0,A) = A/(2+\delta); \quad c_2^\dagger(0,A) = A\delta/(2+\delta); \quad l^\dagger(0,A) = 1/(2+\delta). \tag{13}$$

In this special case, leisure is independent of the productivity of labour and the two consumption levels increase linearly in $A$. In fact, the ratio $c_2^\dagger(0,A)/c_1^\dagger(0,A)$ is equal to $\delta$, the discount factor. So these functional forms for the utility of consumption of the good and leisure are convenient ones to adopt because, for them, in the absence of Veblen effects, we can *correctly infer* the discount rate simply by taking the ratio of the observed consumption in period 2 to that in period 1.

In the presence of Veblen effects (when $s > 0$), the solution to an individual's optimization problem in the symmetric equilibrium is given by $\{c_1^\dagger(s,A), c_2^\dagger(s,A), l^\dagger(s,A)\}$. A researcher who ignores Veblen effects (that is, who assumes $s = 0$) and seeks to estimate an individual's discount factor from her actual consumption pattern that does embody conspicuous consumption will impute the discount factor given by $\beta = c_2^\dagger(s,A)/c_1^\dagger(s,A)$. In general, this imputed discounted factor will differ from the true discount factor, $\delta$, and will depend on the labour productivity and the magnitude of the status parameter.

In Figure 13.3, we assume that the true discount factor is $\delta = 0.8$. In panel A, labour productivity is fixed at $A = 2$. We see that, as the status parameter increases, consumption in period 1 increases, while, in period 2, it initially increases but then declines. Aggregate consumption increases because individuals consume less leisure. Panel B shows that leisure declines monotonically with greater status concern, while panel A brings out the effects of intertemporal allocation of the consumption that foregone leisure brings about. Panel C displays the behaviour of the imputed discount factor (bottom curve) relative to its true value (flat line). The error entailed in ignoring Veblen effects in inferring intertemporal preferences is apparent from this figure.

In Figure 13.4, we display the interesting effects of increases in labour productivity, $A$, when the status parameter is fixed at $s = 2$. In panel A, both the period 1 consumption (highest curve) and the period 2 consumption (lowest curve) increase with productivity, but the former increases relatively faster. The two other curves that are in-between show the period 1 and period 2 consumptions when there are no Veblen effects (that is, when $s = 0$). As we have seen, when $s = 0$, these increase linearly in $A$. In the presence of Veblen effects, an increase in labour productivity results in a 'fanning out' of the consumption levels in the two periods. In panel B, we see that leisure declines with productivity (bottom curve) relative to when status effects are absent (top curve), as in earlier static models (see Eaton and Eswaran 2009). Veblen effects induce people to work harder when productivity is higher and then dissipate the salutary effects of the productivity improvement.

Figure 13.4, panel C, shows how the imputed discount factor (bottom curve) changes relative to its true value (flat line) when labour productivity increases. All else constant, then, more affluent societies appear to have lower discount factors if these are imputed from intertemporal consumption patterns. In their review of time discounting, Frederick, Lowenstein, and O'Donoghue (2002) catalogue the numerous studies that have sought to infer the discount factor. As they point out, most of the attempts simply take the intertemporal choices and figure out the discount factor that will rationalize them. One of the regularities they note is that, in most studies, high

Figure 13.3: Conspicuous Consumption When the True Discount Factor Is
$\delta = 0.8$

A. Consumption in period 1 (top) and 2 (bottom) as status concern increases
in a model with leisure.

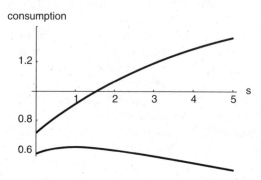

B. Consumption of leisure as status concern increases.

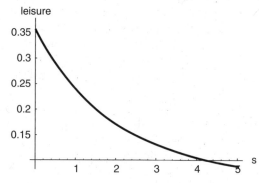

C. Imputed discount factor (bottom) and true discount factor (top) as status
concern increases.

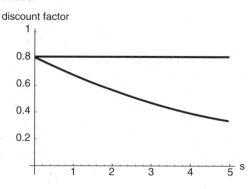

Figure 13.4: Conspicuous Consumption under Increases in Labour Productivity

A. Consumption in period 1 (top) and 2 (bottom) as a function of labour productivity in the presence of Veblen effects; curves in-between are the corresponding consumption levels in the absence of Veblen effects.

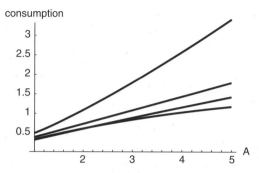

B. Leisure as a function of labour productivity in the presence (bottom) and absence (top) of Veblen effects.

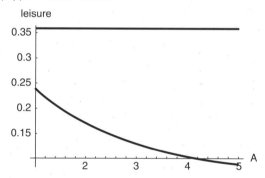

C. Imputed discount factor (bottom) and true discount factor (top) as labour productivity increases.

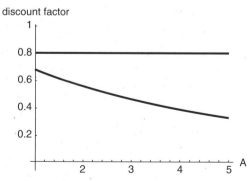

discounting seems to prevail. They argue that, to understand intertemporal choices correctly, we need to incorporate many factors that impinge on them in addition to pure time preference. We suggest that the presence of Veblen effects might be one such factor, and an important one at that.

## An Intertemporal Experiment

To assess our model, we conducted a simple economic experiment in intertemporal decision-making along the lines of those by Coller and Williams (1999), Harrison, Lau, and Williams (2002), and McLeish and Oxoby (2007). These experiments use an incentive-compatible elicitation mechanism to determine individuals' rates of impatience. Among their findings are that, while discount rates are stable, men's rates are higher than women's (Wilson and Daly 2006; McLeish and Oxoby 2007); and that rates are reduced significantly when individuals have information on the rate of return on riskless bonds (Coller and Williams 1999).

In our experiment, we elicited two dependent measures of individuals' discount rates using the same protocol. Individuals were asked, in two series of intertemporal questions, to indicate their preference between a sum of money in the near future and a larger sum of money in the more distant future (see Tables 13.1 and 13.2). Specifically, one set of questions asked participants their preferences between $40 in one week and $40 + y, $y \in \{1,2,\dots 10\}$ in four weeks. The second set of questions asked participants their preferences between $40 in three weeks and $40 + y, $y \in \{1,2,\dots 10\}$ in six weeks. The tables present amounts more distant in the future, with three-week interest rates ranging from 2.5 per cent to 25 per cent in increments of 2.5 per cent. To ensure incentive compatibility between the two intertemporal choice questions, participants were informed that one of the twenty questions would be randomly selected and that they would be paid in accord with their response to the question. Participants were given postdated cheques, payable only upon the appropriate date (depending on their answer and the date of the experiment). After completing these questions, participants answered a series of demographic questions.

Thus, in each table, the respondent indicates her preference between an amount of money sooner and a larger amount of money later. To proxy an individual's discount rate, we use the point at which respondents cease choosing the sooner option and begin choosing the larger, more distant sum of money (Coller and Williams 1999). We refer to this measure from Table 13.1 as the dependent variable *Arate*; we refer to the same measure from Table 13.2 as *Brate*.

Our experimental manipulation aimed at exploring the role of Veblen effects took the following form. Participants were randomly assigned to

Table 13.1
Discount Rate Elicitation,
First Series of Questions

| Option | Amount in 1 Week | Amount in 4 Weeks |
|--------|--------|--------|
| | ($) | |
| 1 | 40 | 41 |
| 2 | 40 | 42 |
| 3 | 40 | 43 |
| 4 | 40 | 44 |
| 5 | 40 | 45 |
| 6 | 40 | 46 |
| 7 | 40 | 47 |
| 8 | 40 | 48 |
| 9 | 40 | 49 |
| 10 | 40 | 50 |

Table 13.2
Discount Rate Elicitation,
Second Series of Questions

| Option | Amount in 3 Weeks | Amount in 6 Weeks |
|--------|--------|--------|
| | ($) | |
| 1 | 40 | 41 |
| 2 | 40 | 42 |
| 3 | 40 | 43 |
| 4 | 40 | 44 |
| 5 | 40 | 45 |
| 6 | 40 | 46 |
| 7 | 40 | 47 |
| 8 | 40 | 48 |
| 9 | 40 | 49 |
| 10 | 40 | 50 |

groups of four, then asked to complete a 12-question quiz culled from the Graduate Record Exam (GRE), with a payoff to be received based on the number of correctly answered questions: fewer than 6 correct, $10 with a 75 per cent probability and $20 with a 25 per cent probability; 6 or more correct, $20 with a 75 per cent probability and $10 with a 25 per cent probability. In contrast to the payment for answering intertemporal choice questions, these payments would be made in cash at the end of the experimental session. Our desire to have participants 'earn' this money was based on previous literature and experiments on mental accounting and found-money effects,[12] which have shown that individuals treat money they have earned as more salient than money allocated by the experimenter. As we based the source of our Veblen effects on these endowments, we had participants earn funds so that their endowments were salient in their intertemporal decision-making.[13]

Our treatment variable (independent measure) was whether or not individuals knew their relative earnings from this quiz. In the baseline conditions, individuals were informed of their score and their earnings before answering the intertemporal choice questions. In our relative wealth treatment, participants were informed of their score and earnings and those of the three other individuals in their group. Our intent was that this would make salient in participants' minds their relative earnings and hence produce a Veblen effect. Importantly, this manipulation was not directly referenced in the instructions. Rather, information on scores, earnings, and the earnings of others was displayed on-screen for 30 seconds before the experiment continued with Tables 13.1 and 13.2.

From our experiment, we have two hypotheses regarding responses to the two tables and the role of relative wealth.

*Hypothesis 1*: Individuals' discount rates should be consistent across time – that is, for each respondent $i$, $Arate = Brate$.

This hypothesis follows research on exponential discounting in which individuals' discounting is consistent across all time periods. A rejection of this hypothesis would indicate that participants display discounting behaviour akin to that found in models of hyperbolic and quasi-hyperbolic discounting (see Strotz 1956; Laibson 1997; O'Donoghue and Rabin 1999, 2001). Our second hypothesis concerns our manipulation and Veblen effects:

*Hypothesis 2*: Individuals' discount rates should be independent of their relative wealth.

This hypothesis, too, is based on the standard model of intertemporal choice. It implies that our manipulations should have no effect on individuals' intertemporal preferences. A rejection of this hypothesis would be evidence of a Veblen effect regarding intertemporal choice in which knowing individuals' relative wealth alters the manner in which they make intertemporal choices.

*Results*

Our experiment involved a total of 82 participants, all of whom were recruited from the undergraduate population at the University of Calgary. The experiments were conducted in the University's Behavioural and Experimental Economics Laboratory using the software z-Tree (see Fischbacher 2007).

Table 13.3 presents the summary statistics of our experiments. Our measure of consistency is calculated as the difference, $Arate - Brate$. Recall that these numbers represent the point at which an individual ceased choosing the sooner, smaller option in favour of the later, larger option; as such, they are indices of an individual's impatience with higher numbers, reflecting the individual's need of a larger, more distant payment to entice her to choose to defer receiving money. That is, the elicited numbers move in the opposite direction as the discount factor $\delta$ (more in the same direction as the subjective rate of impatience).

To analyse the data, we focus on the results of nonparametric Kolmgorov-Smirnov tests on the distributions of responses. This gives us the most general approach to the analysis, avoiding the violations of normality and issues

Table 13.3
Summary Statistics, Discount Rate Experiment
(standard deviations in parentheses)

| Treatment | Participant's Earnings | Arate | Brate | Consistency |
|---|---|---|---|---|
| Baseline | $10 ($n$ = 20) | 7.00 (4.25) | 7.00 (4.25) | 0.00 (0.79) |
| Baseline | $20 ($n$ = 15) | 4.46 (4.09) | 5.23 (4.69) | −0.77 (2.00) |
| Relative wealth | $10 ($n$ = 26) | 7.54 (2.95) | 8.88 (2.98) | −1.35 (2.41) |
| Relative wealth | $20 ($n$ = 23) | 7.30 (3.89) | 7.30 (2.87) | −0.04 (4.96) |

with sample size inherent in the analysis of experimental data.[14] To begin, we find support for Hypothesis 1 in that none of our measures of consistency is significantly different from zero (KS $p$ > 0.20). However, it is interesting to note that participants who earned $10 in the relative wealth treatment appear to display less consistency than others. Within a given level of earnings (between all those earning $10 and all those earning $20), there were no differences in intertemporal choices: the distributions of responses measured by *Arate*, *Brate* and consistency do not differ in any significant manner. While these results support Hypothesis 1, we do find evidence of an interesting Veblen effect when we consider the decisions made by those earning different wealth levels in the relative wealth treatment.

Specifically, we test for Veblen effects by asking if the distribution of the *Arate* (*Brate*) is different between people who know only their own earnings and those who also know the earnings of the others in their group. We find no difference in the distribution of *Arate*, but a significant difference in the distribution of *Brate*. The Kolmogorov-Smirnov test reveals that the *Brate* for those who know only their own earnings is *less than* that of those who know also their relative earnings (KS $p$ = 0.081), which rejects Hypothesis 2, about the absence of Veblen effects. In other words, our experiments provide some evidence (at the 8 per cent or higher level of significance) that Veblen effects increase the discount rate, as our theory predicts.

The absence of discernible effects in the *Arate* but its presence in the *Brate* in our results suggest that Veblen effects in intertemporal decision-making are manifest in the form of quasi-hyperbolic discounting, where and individual's utility is given by

$$U(c_0,\ldots,c_T) = u(c_o) + \gamma \sum_{t=1}^{T} \delta^t u(c_t),$$
(14)

where $c_t$ is period $t$ consumption, $\delta$ is the traditional discount factor, and $\gamma < 1$ is an individual's 'present-day bias' resulting in an increased desire for immediate rewards (see O'Donoghue and Rabin 1999, 2001). Note that an individual with these preferences discounts consistently between periods $t$ and $t + s$, but an inconsistency arises in that the discounting between period 0 and any other period is increased by a factor of $1/\gamma$. The increasing impatience of these individuals (as demonstrated by their intertemporal inconsistency relative to other participants) is consistent the quasi-hyperbolic discounting identified experimentally by McLeish and Oxoby (2007). In that study, participants completed tables similar to our Table 13.1 and 13.2 and displayed an inconsistency wherein the term $\gamma$ in equation 14 fell between five and seven weeks in the future; our results suggest this term falls between three and six weeks in the future.

What do our findings imply? Although individuals are consistent in their intertemporal decision-making, we observe a Veblen effect in which richer individuals are more impatient about sums of money to be received in the (relatively) distant future. That is, richer individuals require additional compensation to defer consumption when their high relative wealth is salient in their decision-making. While this result is consistent with our earlier model, which predicted that Veblen effects make wealthier individuals more impatient, it is apparently inconsistent with Shapiro (2005), who associates increased impatience among U.S. food stamp recipients with a 15 per cent decline in caloric intake over the distribution month. Similarly, Eckel, Johnson, and Montmarquette (2005) find greater impatience among the poor with respect to relatively short-term decisions over monetary amounts. More broadly, Kelso (1994) and Squires (2006) argue that biases in intertemporal decision-making have a detrimental effect on the decision-making of the poor, who are more likely to engage in highly expensive short-term financing (such as payday loans) and to eschew savings opportunities. How do we square these findings with ours? Our theory assumed that the pure rate of time preference was identical for all individuals. In reality, this is unlikely to be the case. We believe that the pure time preference hardwired in humans for evolutionary reasons triggers different discount rates when they are in abundance than when they are near subsistence. Our results are picking up this difference in time preferences between rich and poor. Our experiment attempts to isolate the Veblen effect with relatively small differences in earnings, keeping all else constant.

### Conclusions

In this paper, with the aid of fairly simple models, we have considered the effect of conspicuous consumption on the intertemporal allocation of consumption and effort. We demonstrated that Veblen comparisons can magnify the effects of intrinsic discounting. Consumption is tilted toward the present, and the higher the productivity of labour, the greater is this present bias. An increase in the marginal utility of conspicuous consumption has the same effect: in an inegalitarian economy, the proportional front loading of consumption of the rich skews the aggregate consumption of the economy toward the present. We show that, if discount rates are inferred from consumption patterns without taking Veblen effects into account, the discount rate will be biased upward, possibly seriously, although our experimental results admittedly provide only weak evidence for our claim.

We skirted the issue of whether people desire to be conspicuous in their consumption of goods or in their consumption of leisure. Veblen, after all, spoke of the leisure class, and one might well argue that it is the consumption leisure, not goods, that is meant to be ostentatious. This, of course, is an empirical issue. But, as Frijters and Leigh (2005) point out, there is empirical evidence from the United States that, since goods are more visible than leisure activities, they are preferred only in neighbourhoods with low rates of turnover, where one's leisure activities would be better known to others. In our model, incorporating a choice between conspicuous consumption and conspicuous leisure likely would reinforce the bias toward consumption of goods in the present but leisure in the future. This is because, by staggering the choices, a reduction in present leisure can finance not only conspicuous consumption now but also conspicuous leisure later; the reverse is not possible. So, one likely would see an excessive application of effort when one is young and an excessive consumption of leisure when one is older. If we incorporated conspicuous consumption only into leisure, however, our two-period model, in which people necessarily retire in the second period, would generate no intertemporal inefficiency in consumption. It would merely predict that people consume too much leisure relative to when this externality is absent.

## Appendix

*Instructions*[15]

This is an experiment in the economics of decision-making. During this session you will make a number of decisions. These decisions will result in a payoff, which will be paid in cash.

At the start of the experiment, the computer will randomly put you into groups of four participants. The experiment will then begin with a short quiz. You will have 10 minutes to answer 12 questions. You will receive a payment based on the number of questions you answer correctly. Specifically, if you answer fewer than 6 questions correctly, you will receive $10 with a 75 per cent probability and $20 with a 25 per cent probability. If you correctly answer 6 or more questions, you will receive $20 with a 75 per cent probability and $10 with a 25 per cent probability. These payments will be made in cash at the end of today's session.

After the quiz, you will be informed of your score and your payment for today's portion of the experiment. The computer will choose a random number, which will be used to determine your payoff based on your score and the probabilities mentioned above.

After this, a number of choices will be presented to you where you are to indicate your preference over a sum of money in one week or a different sum of money in four weeks. For each choice, indicate which payment option you prefer. After making these choices, please click the continue button. You will then be asked a similar set of questions regarding your preference between a sum on money in three weeks and a different sum of money in six weeks. Your payment for participating in this experiment will be based on these choices: one of your choices will be randomly selected by the computer and you will receive the amount of money you chose at the time you chose (in what week or in what month). These payments will be made by postdated cheque and you will receive these cheques at the end of the experiment.

After completing the series of questions, you will be asked to provide us with some demographic information. This information is confidential and is used in our analysis of the data.

Once everyone has had an opportunity to ask any final questions, we will begin the session.

NOTES

1  We thank Ralph Winter for comments on an earlier draft.
2  See, for example, Brekke, Howarth, and Nyborg (2003); Oxoby (2003, 2004); Hopkins and Kornienko (2004); and Eaton and Eswaran (2009).
3  This research, which started with the seminal work of Easterlin (1974), has been reviewed more recently by Frey and Stutzer (2002); Layard (2005); and Clark, Frijters, and Shields (2008).

4  See, for example, Eaton and Eswaran (2003) for an evolutionary explanation for preferences of the Veblen type.
5  See, for example, Brekke, Howarth, and Nyborg (2003); Oxoby (2003, 2004); Hopkins and Kornienko (2004); and Eaton and Eswaran (2009).
6  See Eaton and Eswaran (2009) for a one-period model that incorporates both these forms of Veblen preferences.
7  Harbaugh (1996) uses an analogous model to show that savings can increase when income is *rising* in an economy.
8  See, for example, Ljungqvist and Uhlig (2000); Cooper, Garcia-Penalosa, and Funk (2001); Dupor and Liu (2003); Van Long and Shimomura (2004); and Pham (2005).
9  These observations would need to be modified if the poor do not compare themselves with others who are poor but, rather, seek to emulate the rich. Then it is conceivable that the poor would display lower discount factors than the rich.
10 Total differentiation with respect to $s$ yields the two equations:

$$u''(c_1^\dagger) + \delta u''(c_2^\dagger)]dc_1 + \delta A u''(c_2^\dagger)]dl^\dagger = (1 - \delta)ds,$$

$$\delta A u''(c_2^\dagger)]dc_1 + [\delta A^2 u''(c_2^\dagger) + R''(l^\dagger)]dl^\dagger = \delta A ds.$$

Applying Cramer's rule and invoking the assumption that the second-order sufficient conditions hold, we obtain the two comparative static results stated in the proposition.
11 See, for example, Neumark and Postlewaite (1998); Brekke, Howarth, and Nyborg (2003); Bowles and Park (2005); and Eaton and Eswaran (2009).
12 Similar means for having participants earn their endowments have been used by Cherry, Frykblom, and Shogren (2002) and Oxoby and Spraggon (2008).
13 The instructions are presented in the appendix. Copies of the quiz and the z-Tree treatment files are available from the authors.
14 Our results are robust to alternate pairwise nonparamteric tests (Wilcoxon ANOVA).
15 These instructions were used in both treatments. Copies of the quiz used in the experiment are available from the authors

REFERENCES

Bowles, S., and Y. Park. 2005. 'Emulation, Inequality, and Work Hours: Was Thorstein Veblen Right?' *Economic Journal* 115 (507): F397–F412.

Brekke, K., R. Howarth, and K. Nyborg. 2003. 'Status Seeking and Material Affluence: Evaluating the Hirsch Hypothesis.' *Ecological Economics* 45 (1): 29–39.

Cherry, T.L., P. Frykblom, and J.F. Shogren. 2002. 'Hardnose the Dictator.'
*American Economic Review* 92 (4): 1218–21.

Clark, A.E., P. Frijters, and M.A. Shields. 2008. 'Relative Income Happiness, and
Utility: An Explanation for the Easterlin Paradox and Other Puzzles.' *Journal
of Economic Literature* 46 (1): 95–144.

Coller, M., and M.B. Williams. 1999. 'Eliciting Individual Discount Rates.' *Experimental Economics* 2 (2): 107–27.

Cooper, B., C. Garcia-Penalosa, and P. Funk. 2001. 'Status Effects and Negative
Utility Growth.' *Economic Journal* 111 (473): 642–65.

Duesenberry, J.S. 1949. *Income, Saving and the Theory of Consumer Behavior.*
Cambridge, MA: Harvard University Press.

Dupor, B., and W.-F. Liu. 2003. 'Jealousy and Equilibrium Overconsumption.'
*American Economic Review* 93 (1): 423–8.

Easterlin, R. 1974. 'Does Economic Growth Improve the Human Lot?' In *Nations
and Households in Economic Growth: Essays in Honour of Moses Abramovitz,*
edited by P.A. David and M.W. Reder. New York: Academic Press.

Eaton, B.C., and M. Eswaran. 2003. 'The Evolution of Preferences and Competition: A Rationalization of Veblen's Theory of Invidious Comparisons.' *Canadian Journal of Economics* 36 (4): 832–59.

– 2009. 'Well-Being and Affluence in the Presence of a Veblen Good.' *Economic
Journal* 119 (539): 1088–1104.

Eckel, C., K. Johnson, and C. Montmarquette. 2005. 'Saving Decisions of the
Working Poor: Short- and Long-Term Horizons.' In *Field Experiments in Eco-
nomics: Research in Experimental Economics,* vol. 10, edited by J. Carpenter,
G.W. Harrison, and J.A. List. Greenwich, CT: JAI Press.

Fischbacher, U. 2007. 'Toolbox for Readymade Economic Experiments.' *Experimental Economics* 10 (2): 171–8.

Frank, R.H. 1985. 'The Demand for Unobservable and Other Nonpositional
Goods.' *American Economic Review* 75 (1): 101–16.

– 1999. *Luxury Fever: Why Money Fails to Satisfy in an Era of Excess.* New York:
The Free Press.

Frederick, S., G. Lowenstein, and T. O'Donoghue. 2002. 'Time Discounting and
Time Preference: A Critical Review.' *Journal of Economic Literature* 40 (2):
351–401.

Frey, B.S., and A. Stutzer. 2002. 'What Can Economists Learn from Happiness
Research?' *Journal of Economic Literature* 40 (2): 402–35.

Frijters, P., and A. Leigh, A. 2005. 'Materialism on the March: From Conspicuous Leisure to Conspicuous Consumption?' Discussion Paper 495. Australian
National University, Centre for Economic Policy Research.

Gowdy, J.M. 1996. 'Discounting, Hierarchies, and the Social Aspects of Biodiversity Protection.' *International Journal of Social Economics* 23 (4-6): 49–63.

Harbaugh, R. 1996. 'Falling Behind the Joneses: Relative Consumption and the Growth-Savings Paradox.' *Economics Letters* 53 (3): 297–304.

Harrison, G.W., M.I. Lau, and M.B. Williams. 2002. 'Estimating Individual Discount Rates in Denmark: A Field Experiment.' *American Economic Review* 92 (5): 1606–17.

Hopkins, E., and T. Kornienko. 2004. 'Running to Keep in the Same Place: Consumer Choice as a Game of Status.' *American Economic Review* 94 (4): 1085–1107.

Kelso, W. 1994. *Poverty and the Underclass.* New York: New York University Press.

Laibson, D. 1997. 'Hyperbolic Discounting and Golden Eggs.' *Quarterly Journal of Economics* 112 (2): 443–77.

Layard, R. 2005. *Happiness: Lessons from a New Science.* New York: Penguin Press.

Ljungqvist, L., and H. Uhlig. 2000. 'Tax Policy and Aggregate Demand Management under Catching Up with the Joneses.' *American Economic Review* 90 (3): 356–66.

Luttmer, E.F.P. 2005. 'Neighbors as Negatives: Relative Earnings and Well-Being.' *Quarterly Journal of Economics* 120 (3): 963–1002.

McLeish, K.N., and R.J. Oxoby. 2007. 'Gender, Affect and Intertemporal Consistency: An Experimental Approach.' IZA Discussion Papers 2663. Bonn, Germany: Institute for the Study of Labor.

– 2009. 'Stereotypes in Intertemporal Choice,' *Journal of Economic Behavior and Organization* 70 (1): 135–41.

Neumark, D., and A. Postlewaite. 1998. 'Relative Income Concerns and the Rise in Married Women's Employment.' *Journal of Public Economics* 70 (1): 157–83.

O'Donoghue, T., and M. Rabin. 1999. 'Doing It Now or Doing It Later.' *American Economic Review* 89 (1): 103–24.

– 2001. 'Choice and Procrastination.' *Quarterly Journal of Economics* 116 (1): 121–60.

Oxoby, R.J. 2003. 'Attitudes and Allocations: Status, Cognitive Dissonance, and the Manipulation of Attitudes.' *Journal of Economic Behavior and Organization* 52 (3): 365–85.

– 2004. 'Cognitive Dissonance, Status and Growth of the Underclass.' *Economic Journal* 114 (498): 727–49.

Oxoby, R.J., and J.M. Spraggon. 2008. 'Mine and Yours: Property Rights in Dictator Games.' *Journal of Economic Behavior and Organization* 65 (3-4): 703–13.

Pham, T. 2005. 'Economic Growth and Status Seeking through Personal Wealth.' *European Journal of Political Economy* 21 (2): 407–27.

Shapiro, J.M. 2005. 'Is There a Daily Discount Rate? Evidence from the Food Stamp Nutrition Cycle.' *Journal of Public Economics* 89 (2-3): 303–25.

Squires, G.D. 2006. *Why the Poor Pay More*. Westport, CT: Praeger.

Strotz, R.H. 1956. 'Myopia and Inconsistency in Dynamic Utility Maximization.' *Review of Economic Studies* 23 (3): 165–80.

Van Long, N., and K. Shimomura. 2004. 'Relative Wealth, Status-Seeking, and Catching-Up.' *Journal of Economic Behavior and Organization* 53 (4): 529–42.

Veblen, T. 1899. *The Theory of the Leisure Class: An Economic Study of Institutions*. New York: Macmillan Company.

Wilson, M., and M. Daly. 2003. 'Do Pretty Women Inspire Men to Discount the Future?' *Biology Letters* 271 (S4): 177–9.

# Contributors

**Simon P. Anderson** is the Commonwealth Professor of Economics at the University of Virginia. He received his Ph.D. from Queen's University in 1985. He wrote his thesis on address models of value theory, inspired by the joint work of Eaton and Lipsey on product differentiation. Industrial organization is Anderson's main field of research.

**Jasmina Arifovic** has been a faculty member at Simon Fraser University since 1993. Arifovic received a Ph.D. in Economics from the University of Chicago in 1991. Her main research interests are adaptation and learning in economic environments and experimental economics. Arifovic and Eaton were departmental colleagues at Simon Fraser University from 1993 to 1999. During that time, they collaborated and published work on evolution of communication in sender/receiver games.

**Richard Arnott** received his Ph.D. from Yale University in 1975. He is currently a Distinguished Professor at the University of California, Riverside, and he has visited many universities around the world. His primary research interest is in urban economic theory. Arnott has been a 'fellow traveller' of Curtis Eaton's – sharing Curtis's general approach to theory and many of his research interests – and a long-time admirer of his work.

**Cliff T. Bekar** is an Associate Professor of Economics at Lewis and Clark College, where he started teaching in 1998. Bekar received a Ph.D. in Economics from Simon Fraser University in 1999. His main research interests include medieval English agriculture, the Industrial Revolution, and the economics of technology and innovation. Bekar was a student of B. Curtis Eaton's at Simon Fraser University.

**Harry Bloch** has been Professor of Economics at Curtin University of Technology in Perth, Australia, since 1997, and is currently Director of the university's Centre for Research in Applied Economics (CRAE). He received his Ph.D. in Economics from the University of Chicago in 1971. His main research interests have been industrial pricing, international trade, economic development, productivity analysis and dynamic competition. He has been working with Curtis recently on developing a model of cost-reducing technological change in oligopolies, but their association goes back to the early 1970s when they were on the faculty together at the University of British Columbia.

**Gregory K. Dow** has been Professor of Economics at Simon Fraser University since 1995. He was previously a faculty member at the University of Alberta and Yale University. Dow received a Ph.D. in Economics from the University of Michigan in 1981. His main research interests are in economic prehistory and the theory of firm organization. Dow and Eaton were departmental colleagues at Simon Fraser University from 1995 to 1999.

**B. Curtis Eaton** has been a Professor of Economics at the University of Calgary since 1999, and a University Professor at the University of Calgary since 2002. He was previously a member of the Economics Departments at the University of British Columbia, the University of Toronto, and Simon Fraser University. Eaton received his Ph.D. in Economics from the University of Colorado in 1969. His research interests include applied microeconomics, social interaction, applied game theory, industrial organization, and public policy.

**Andrew Eckert** received his Ph.D. in Economics from the University of British Columbia in 1999, and is currently an Associate Professor of Economics at the University of Alberta. His research interests include industrial organization and competition policy. B. Curtis Eaton was the external examiner for Eckert's Ph.D. thesis.

**Mukesh Eswaran** is a Professor of Economics at the University of British Columbia, from which he received his Ph.D. in 1981. His research fields include economic development, gender in economic issues, and applied microeconomic theory. Eswaran and Eaton have co-authored and published a number of papers since 1984.

**Richard G. Harris** is the Telus Professor of Economics at Simon Fraser University. His major research interests are international trade and finance, and Canadian economic policy. He was a colleague of Curt Eaton's at Simon Fraser University during the 1990s, and was a graduate student at the University of British Columbia when Curtis first taught there in the early 1970s.

**Alexander Karaivanov** has been a faculty member at the Department of Economics of Simon Fraser University since 2003, when he received a Ph.D. in Economics from the University of Chicago. His main research interests are in development economics and applied contract theory.

**Richard G. Lipsey** is Professor Emeritus at Simon Fraser University. He is a former president of both the Canadian Economics Association and the International Atlantic Economic Society. He received his Ph.D. from the London School of Economics in 1957. His research interests include modelling economic growth, growth-inducing technological change, and coping with climate change. He began co-authoring papers with Curt Eaton in the 1970s, and they were colleagues together at Simon Fraser University.

**Robert Oxoby** is an Associate Professor at the University of Calgary and Director of the University of Calgary Behavioural and Experimental Economics Laboratory. He received his Ph.D. from the University of California, Davis, in 2000. His research interests include behavioural economics and economic psychology, microeconomics and applied game theory, and political economy and social theory. Oxoby and Eaton are colleagues at the University of Calgary.

**Clyde G. Reed** is Professor of Economics at Simon Fraser University, where he joined the faculty in 1972. Reed's research interests include economic prehistory, medieval English agriculture, and the economics of culture. Reed and Eaton were departmental colleagues at Simon Fraser University from 1987 to 1999.

**Peter E. Robertson** is an Associate Professor in Economics at the University of New South Wales, Sydney, Australia. He was educated at the University of Otago, New Zealand, and the University of New England, Australia, and completed his Ph.D. at Simon Fraser University, where he studied graduate microeconomics with Curtis Eaton. His research interests include economic growth and development, international trade, and environmental economics.

**Nicolas Schmitt** is Professor of Economics at Simon Fraser University. He has had regular appointments at Laval University, the University of Western Ontario, and the University of Geneva. His main field of research is international trade. Curtis Eaton supervised his Ph.D. thesis at the University of Toronto, from which he received his Ph.D. in 1986.

**Joshua Stine** is a researcher at the Hudson Institute. He received his degree in International Affairs at Lewis and Clark College in 2005. Stine's research interests include international organizations and arms control.

**Yundong Tu** is currently a graduate student in the Department of Economics at the University of California, Riverside. He received his B.A. in Mathematics (2004) and M.A. in Economics (2006) from Wuhan University, China. His research is in productivity analysis, economic modelling, macroeconomic forecasting, semi-/nonparametrics, and panel data econometrics.

**Douglas S. West** is a Professor of Economics at the University of Alberta. He received his Ph.D. in Economics from the University of British Columbia in 1979. His research interests include spatial competition analysis, competition policy, and industrial organization. Curtis Eaton was West's Ph.D. thesis supervisor.

**William D. White** is a Professor of Policy Analysis and Management at Cornell University and Director of the Sloan Program in Health Administration at Cornell. He received a Ph.D. in Economics from Harvard University in 1975 and a B.A. in History from Haverford College in 1967. His research interests are microeconomics and health economics and the organization of health care markets. He and Curtis Eaton first met when both were visiting at Yale in 1979–80.

**Ralph A. Winter** is Professor of Economics in the Sauder School of Business at the University of British Columbia. He also holds the Canada Research Chair in Business Economics and Public Policy at UBC. Winter received his Ph.D. in Economics from the University of California, Berkeley, in 1979. His research interests include competition policy, industrial organization, and applied microeconomics. Winter and Eaton were colleagues at the University of Toronto from 1981 to 1988.